W9-DBC-736

THE BOOK OF DISCIPLINE
OF
THE UNITED METHODIST CHURCH

THE
BOOK OF DISCIPLINE
OF THE
UNITED METHODIST CHURCH
1968

The Methodist Episcopal Church
The Methodist Episcopal Church, South
The Methodist Protestant Church
The Methodist Church
The Evangelical United Brethren Church

The Methodist Publishing House
Nashville, Tennessee

"An Editorial Committee shall be charged with the duty of editing, and in the exercise of their judgment shall have wide authority to make such changes in text and phraseology as may be necessary to harmonize the proposed legislation without changing its intent or substance. The Editorial Committee shall be the book editors of the two denominations and the executive secretaries of the two Commissions on Church Union."

—*Journal of the General Conference, 1968*

Emory Stevens Bucke
Book Editor of The Methodist Church

Curtis A. Chambers
Book Editor of The Evangelical United Brethren Church

Charles C. Parlin
Executive Secretary of The Methodist Committee on Church Union

Paul A. Washburn
Executive Secretary of The Evangelical United Brethren Commission on Church Union

Lovick Pierce
Publisher of The Methodist Church

Donald A. Theuer
Publisher of The Evangelical United Brethren Church

Copyright © 1968 The Methodist Publishing House. All rights reserved.

PRINTED IN THE UNITED STATES OF AMERICA

EPISCOPAL GREETINGS

"Change in all around we see" is both lyric and fact. To any careful observer of the life of The United Methodist Church, this axiom is also the prudent estimate of our condition.

The churches forming The United Methodist Church—The Evangelical United Brethren Church and The Methodist Church—bear the marks of change. We trust it has been change with a purpose, that the prophetic voice of the Holy Spirit has been heard and obeyed. That our obedience has not always been forthright and straight-line we acknowledge with deep regret.

Through their histories both churches have dealt with the world as they found it, ministering to the immediate human condition. The huddled seaboard cities and the loneliness of the frontier, the inland towns and the wide agrarian expanses, provided our early arena of service. Agriculture and industry, slave and field labor, the workman in the shop and the mill, the captain in finance and development, immigration and assimilation, the subduing of an invitingly wild and beautiful continent—these have been some of the items on our agenda of service. These conditions and circumstances have dictated successive and continuing emphases and expeditions demanding imagination and dedication in education, missionary expansion, social and economic justice, international peace, ecumenical experiment, interracial relations, and the use and misuse of vast and growing national power. Our response to all these situations, given our commitment to Christ as Lord, has been reflected in our successive Disciplines.

Throughout this galaxy of unpredictable change the generations have tried to maintain the warm heart, the trained mind, and the dedicated hand at work doing his will.

At the beginning, when our structures were as uncomplicated as the society in which the Church lived and labored, the Discipline was small and simple, vest-pocket size. Over the past decades, almost unnoticed, our structures tended toward more rigorous conformity. This present Discipline, more complex and bulky than many would desire, attempts to aid the United Methodist community in serving its Lord in these revolutionary times, as did its forerunners. Its substance bears witness to our nature as a "connectional church," each local church organically related to the whole, the whole dependent upon each branch.

This volume is sent forth trusting it will be used as a tempered instrument, flexible to serve the immediate demands of humanity in this time and location. This book is designed to open new doors of choice and action into the larger room of life for the local congregation.

We launch this Discipline in the fervent hope that even as the bonds of this marriage unite, so also they free us to the vast enterprise of exploring the meaning and reality of a life dedicated to Christian love.

The Book of Discipline is the first written instrument uniting us in The United Methodist Church. We trust it shall be a vehicle aiding us in exploring the land of God's love more courageously.

The Council of Bishops
Lloyd C. Wicke
Reuben H. Mueller

CONTENTS

Note: The basic unit in the Book of Discipline is the paragraph (¶) rather than page, chapter, section, etc. The paragraphs are numbered consecutively within each chapter, but many numbers are skipped between parts and chapters in order to allow for future enactments and to fit with the following plan:

PART I
THE CONSTITUTION
¶¶ 1-66

PART II
DOCTRINAL STATEMENTS AND THE GENERAL RULES
¶¶ 91-95

CONTENTS

PART III
SOCIAL PRINCIPLES
¶¶ 96-97

PART IV
ORGANIZATION AND ADMINISTRATION
¶¶ 101-1760

Chapter One
THE LOCAL CHURCH

Chapter Two
THE MINISTRY

CONTENTS

Chapter Three
THE LAY WORKER
¶¶ 501-508

Chapter Four
THE CONFERENCES

Chapter Five
ADMINISTRATIVE ORDER

CONTENTS

Chapter Six
CHURCH PROPERTY

Chapter Seven
JUDICIAL ADMINISTRATION

United Methodist Bishops

A List Compiled for
The Book of Discipline
by the Council of Bishops

NAME	CONSECRATED
Francis Asbury	1784
Thomas Coke	1784
Martin Boehm	1800
Philip William Otterbein	1800
Richard Whatcoat	1800
Jacob Albright	1807
William McKendree	1808
Christian Newcomer	1813
Enoch George	1816
Robert R. Roberts	1816
Andrew Zeller	1817
Joseph Hoffman	1821
Elijah Hedding	1824
Joshua Soule	1824
Henry Kumler, Sr.	1825
James O. Andrew	1832
John Emory	1832
William Brown	1833
Samuel Hiestand	1833
Thomas A. Morris	1836
Beverly Waugh	1836
Jacob Erb	1837

NAME	CONSECRATED
John Seybert	1839
John Coons	1841
Henry Kumler, Jr.	1841
Joseph Long	1843
Leonidus L. Hamline	1844
Edmund S. Janes	1844
Jacob Glossbrenner	1845
William Hanby	1845
John Russel	1845
William Capers	1846
Robert Paine	1846
David Edwards	1849
Henry B. Bascom	1850
Edward R. Ames	1852
Osmon C. Baker	1852
Levi Scott	1852
Matthew Simpson	1852
Lewis Davis	1853
John Early	1854
Hubbard R. Kavanaugh	1854
George F. Pierce	1854
Francis Burns	1858

NAME	CONSECRATED	NAME	CONSECRATED
William Orwig	1859	Alpheus W. Wilson	1882
Jacob Markwood	1861	Charles H. Fowler	1884
Daniel Shuck	1861	Willard F. Mallalieu	1884
John Esher	1863	William X. Ninde	1884
Davis W. Clark	1864	William Taylor	1884
Calvin Kingsley	1864	John M. Walden	1884
Edward Thomson	1864	Daniel Flickinger	1885
Jonathan Weaver	1865	William W. Duncan	1886
David S. Doggett	1866	Charles B. Galloway	1886
Enoch M. Marvin	1866	Eugene R. Hendrix	1886
Holland N. McTyeire	1866	Joseph S. Key	1886
John W. Roberts	1866	James N. FitzGerald	1888
William M. Wightman	1866	Daniel A. Goodsell	1888
John Dickson	1869	Isaac W. Joyce	1888
John C. Keener	1870	John P. Newman	1888
Reuben Yeakel	1871	James M. Thoburn	1888
Edward G. Andrews	1872	John H. Vincent	1888
Thomas Bowman	1872	James Hott	1889
Randolph S. Foster	1872	Oscar P. Fitzgerald	1890
William L. Harris	1872	Atticus G. Haygood	1890
Gilbert Haven	1872	Sylvanus Breyfogel	1891
Stephen M. Merrill	1872	William Horn	1891
Jesse T. Peck	1872	Job Mills	1893
Isaac W. Wiley	1872	Wesley Stanford	1894
Thomas Bowman	1875	Earl Cranston	1896
Rudolph Dubs	1875	Joseph C. Hartzell	1896
Nicholas Castle	1877	Charles C. McCabe	1896
Milton Wright	1877	Warren A. Candler	1898
Cyrus D. Foss	1880	Henry C. Morrison	1898
Erastus O. Haven	1880	John W. Hamilton	1900
John F. Hurst	1880	David H. Moore	1900
Henry W. Warren	1880	Edwin W. Parker	1900
Ezekiel Kephart	1881	Frank W. Warne	1900
John C. Granbery	1882	Henry Hartzler	1902
Robert K. Hargrove	1882	William Heil	1902
Linus Parker	1882	E. Embree Hoss	1902

2

UNITED METHODIST BISHOPS

NAME	CONSECRATED
George Mathews	1902
A. Coke Smith	1902
James W. Bashford	1904
Joseph F. Berry	1904
William Burt	1904
Merriman C. Harris	1904
William F. McDowell	1904
Thomas B. Neely	1904
William F. Oldham	1904
John E. Robinson	1904
Isaiah B. Scott	1904
Henry Spellmeyer	1904
Luther B. Wilson	1904
William Bell	1905
Thomas Carter	1905
William Weekley	1905
James Atkins	1906
John J. Tigert	1906
Seth Ward	1906
Samuel Spreng	1907
William F. Anderson	1908
Frank M. Bristol	1908
Edwin H. Hughes	1908
Wilson S. Lewis	1908
Robert McIntyre	1908
John L. Nuelson	1908
William A. Quayle	1908
Charles W. Smith	1908
Collins Denny	1910
William Fouke	1910
John C. Kilgo	1910
Walter R. Lambuth	1910
James H. McCoy	1910
Edwin D. Mouzon	1910
William B. Murrah	1910
Uriah Swengel	1910

NAME	CONSECRATED
Richard G. Waterhouse	1910
Richard J. Cooke	1912
William P. Eveland	1912
Theodore S. Henderson	1912
Frederick D. Leete	1912
Naphtali Luccock	1912
Francis J. McConnell	1912
John W. Robinson	1912
William O. Shepard	1912
Homer C. Stuntz	1912
Wilbur P. Thirkield	1912
Henry H. Fout	1913
Alfred T. Howard	1913
Cyrus J. Kephart	1913
Gottlieb Heinmiller	1915
Lawrence Seager	1915
Alexander P. Camphor	1916
Franklin Hamilton	1916
Matthew S. Hughes	1916
Eben S. Johnson	1916
Adna W. Leonard	1916
Charles B. Mitchell	1916
Thomas Nicholson	1916
Herbert Welch	1916
William Washinger	1917
William N. Ainsworth	1918
James Cannon, Jr.	1918
Urban V. W. Darlington	1918
Horace M. Du Bose	1918
Matthew Maze	1918
William F. McMurry	1918
John M. Moore	1918
Anton Bast	1920
George H. Bickley	1920
Lauress J. Birney	1920
Edgar Blake	1920

3

NAME	CONSECRATED	NAME	CONSECRATED
Charles W. Burns	1920	Jashwant R. Chitamber	1931
Matthew W. Clair	1920	Ralph S. Cushman	1932
Frederick B. Fisher	1920	Juan E. Gattinoni	1932
Robert E. Jones	1920	J. Ralph Magee	1932
Frederick T. Keeney	1920	Elmer W. Praetorius	1934
Charles E. Locke	1920	Charles H. Stauffacher	1934
Charles L. Mead	1920	Roberto Elphick	1936
Ernest G. Richardson	1920	Charles W. Flint	1936
H. Lester Smith	1920	Wilbur E. Hammaker	1936
Ernest L. Waldorf	1920	F. H. Otto Melle	1936
Arthur Clippinger	1921	G. Bromley Oxnam	1936
William B. Beauchamp	1922	J. Waskom Pickett	1936
Hiram A. Boaz	1922	Alexander P. Shaw	1936
James E. Dickey	1922	John M. Springer	1936
Hoyt M. Dobbs	1922	Ralph A. Ward	1937
John F. Dunlap	1922	John L. Decell	1938
Sam R. Hay	1922	Ivan Lee Holt	1938
Brenton T. Badley	1924	William C. Martin	1938
Wallace E. Brown	1924	William W. Peele	1938
George R. Grose	1924	Clare Purcell	1938
Titus Lowe	1924	Charles C. Selecman	1938
George A. Miller	1924	William T. Watkins	1938
Arthur Statton	1925	Victor O. Weidler	1938
John S. Stamm	1926	John C. Broomfield	1939
S. J. Umbreit	1926	James H. Straughn	1939
James C. Baker	1928	Bruce R. Baxter	1940
Edwin F. Lee	1928	William A. C. Hughes	1940
Raymond J. Wade	1928	Lorenzo H. King	1940
Grant D. Batdorf	1929	Enrique C. Balloch	1941
Ira D. Warner	1929	W. Y. Chen	1941
George Edward Epp	1930	Fred L. Dennis	1941
John Gowdy	1930	Z. T. Kaung	1941
Paul B. Kern	1930	Carleton Lacy	1941
Arthur J. Moore	1930	Shot K. Mondol	1941
A. Frank Smith	1930	Clement D. Rockey	1941
Chih P'ing Wang	1930	Newell S. Booth	1944

4

NAME	CONSECRATED	NAME	CONSECRATED
Charles W. Brashares	1944	Matthew W. Clair, Jr.	1952
Robert N. Brooks	1944	D. Stanley Coors	1952
Fred P. Corson	1944	F. Gerald Ensley	1952
Paul N. Garber	1944	A. Raymond Grant	1952
Schuyler E. Garth	1944	Edgar A. Love	1952
Costen J. Harrell	1944	Frederick B. Newell	1952
Lewis O. Hartman	1944	Julio B. Sabanes	1952
Edward W. Kelly	1944	Edwin E. Voigt	1952
Willis J. King	1944	H. Bascom Watts	1952
W. Earl Ledden	1944	Odd Hagen	1953
Paul E. Martin	1944	Friedrich Wunderlich	1953
W. Angie Smith	1944	L. L. Baughman	1954
Arthur F. Wesley	1944	H. R. Heininger	1954
J. Balmer Showers	1945	Reuben H. Mueller	1954
John A. Subhan	1945	Ferdinand Sigg	1954
Dionisio D. Alejandro	1946	Hobart B. Amstutz	1956
Theodor Arvidson	1946	Ralph E. Dodge	1956
J. W. E. Sommer	1946	Eugene M. Frank	1956
J. W. E. Bowen	1948	Nolan B. Harmon	1956
Dana Dawson	1948	Bachman G. Hodge	1956
Marvin A. Franklin	1948	Mangal Singh	1956
Gerald H. Kennedy	1948	Gabriel Sundaram	1956
John W. Lord	1948	Prince A. Taylor, Jr.	1956
H. Clifford Northcott	1948	J. Gordon Howard	1957
Glenn R. Phillips	1948	Paul E. V. Shannon	1957
Richard C. Raines	1948	Paul M. Herrick	1958
Marshall R. Reed	1948	H. W. Kaebnick	1958
Roy H. Short	1948	W. Maynard Sparks	1958
Donald H. Tippett	1948	Ralph T. Alton	1960
Jose L. Valencia	1948	Kenneth W. Copeland	1960
Hazen G. Werner	1948	Paul V. Galloway	1960
Lloyd C. Wicke	1948	Edwin R. Garrison	1960
Sante Uberto Barbieri	1949	Charles F. Golden	1960
Raymond L. Archer	1950	Walter C. Gum	1960
D. T. Gregory	1950	Paul Hardin, Jr.	1960
John W. Branscomb	1952	Marquis L. Harris	1960

5

UNITED METHODIST BISHOPS

NAME	CONSECRATED	NAME	CONSECRATED
James W. Henley	1960	Edward J. Pendergrass	1964
Fred G. Holloway	1960	Thomas M. Pryor	1964
James K. Mathews	1960	John Wesley Shungu	1964
W. Vernon Middleton	1960	W. McFerrin Stowe	1964
Paul W. Milhouse	1960	R. Marvin Stuart	1964
Noah W. Moore, Jr.	1960	James S. Thomas	1964
T. Otto Nall	1960	Lance Webb	1964
Everett W. Palmer	1960	Escrivao A. Zunguze	1964
William K. Pope	1960	Stephen T. Nagbe	1965
O. Eugene Slater	1960	A. J. Shaw	1965
John O. Smith	1960	Franz Schafer	1966
B. Foster Stockwell	1960	L. Scott Allen	1967
Aubrey G. Walton	1960	Benjamin Guansing	1967
W. Ralph Ward	1960	Arthur J. Armstrong	1968
Pedro Zottele	1962	William R. Cannon	1968
Harry P. Andreassen	1964	Alsie H. Carleton	1968
H. Ellis Finger, Jr.	1964	Abel T. Muzorewa	1968
W. Kenneth Goodson	1964	Roy C. Nichols	1968
Earl G. Hunt, Jr.	1964	John V. Samuel	1968
Francis E. Kearns	1964	Carl E. Sommers	1968
Dwight H. Loder	1964	Paul A. Washburn	1968
Robert F. Lundy	1964	D. Frederick Wertz	1968

HISTORICAL STATEMENT

The Plan of Union proposes to bring together The Methodist Church and the Evangelical United Brethren Church, two churches that share a common historical and spiritual heritage. They hold the same fundamental doctrines of faith. Ecclesiastical organization is similar. They are Protestant churches, whose streams of spiritual life and thought come out of the Protestant Reformation of the sixteenth century.

Since their beginnings they have lived and worked side by side in friendly fellowship. Had it not been for the difference in language— the Methodists working among English-speaking people and the Evangelical and United Brethren working among those speaking German —they might, from the beginning, have been one church. Today the language barrier is gone and the uniting of forces for our common task and calling seems appropriate and timely. Brief historical sketches of the two churches, taken from their respective Disciplines, follow.

The Methodist Church

The Methodist Church is a church of Christ in which "the pure Word of God is preached, and the Sacraments duly administered." This church is a great Protestant body, though it did not come directly out of the Reformation but had its origin within the Church of England. Its founder was John Wesley, a clergyman of that church, as was his father before him. His mother, Susanna Wesley, was a woman of zeal, devotion, and strength of character who was perhaps the greatest single human influence in Wesley's life.

Nurtured in this devout home, educated at Oxford University, the young John Wesley, like a second Paul, sought in vain for religious

7

satisfaction by the strict observance of the rules of religion and the ordinances of the church. The turning point in his life came when, at a prayer meeting in Aldersgate Street, London, on May 24, 1738, he learned what Paul had discovered, that it is not by rules and laws, nor by our own efforts at self-perfection, but by faith in God's mercy as it comes to us in Christ, that man may enter upon life and peace.

The gospel which Wesley thus found for himself he began to proclaim to others, first to companions who sought his counsel, including his brother Charles, then in widening circles that took him throughout the British Isles. His message had a double emphasis, which has remained with Methodism to this day. First was the gospel of God's grace, offered to all men and equal to every human need. Second was the moral ideal which this gospel presents to men. The Bible, he declared, knows no salvation which is not salvation from sin. He called men to holiness of life, and this holiness, he insisted, is "social holiness," the love and service of their fellowmen. Methodism meant "Christianity in earnest." The General Rules which are still found in the Discipline are the directions which Wesley gave to his followers to enable them to test the sincerity of their purpose and to guide them in this life.

Wesley did not plan to found a new church. In his work he simply followed, like Paul, the clear call of God, first to preach the gospel to the needy who were not being reached by the Established Church and its clergy, second to take care of those who were won to the Christian life. Step by step he was led on until Methodism became a great and transforming movement in the life of England. He gathered his people in groups, in classes and societies. He appointed leaders. He found men who were ready to carry the gospel to the masses, speaking on the streets, in the open fields, and in private homes. These men were not ordained ministers but lay preachers, or "local preachers," as they were called. He appointed these men, assigned them to various fields of labor, and supervised their work. Once a year he called them together for a conference, just as Methodist preachers meet in their Annual Conference sessions today.

Wesley thus united in extraordinary fashion three notable activities, in all of which he excelled. One was evangelism; "The world is my parish," he declared. His preachers went to the people; they did not wait for the people to come to them, and he himself knew the highways and byways of England as did no other man of his day. The second was organization and administration, by which he conserved the fruits of this preaching and extended its influence. The third was his appreciation of education and his use of the printed page. He made the press a servant of the Church and was the father of the mass circu-- lation of inexpensive books, pamphlets, and periodicals.

From England, Methodism spread to Ireland and then to America. In 1766 Philip Embury, a lay preacher from Ireland, began to preach in the city of New York. At about the same time Robert Strawbridge, another lay preacher from Ireland, settled in Frederick County, Maryland, and began the work there. In 1769 Wesley sent Richard Boardman and Joseph Pilmoor to America, and two years later Francis Asbury, who became the great leader of American Methodism.

Methodism was especially adapted to American life. These itinerant preachers served the people under conditions where a settled ministry was not feasible. They sought out the scattered homes, followed the tide of migration as it moved west, preached the gospel, organized societies, established "preaching places," and formed these into "circuits." Thus by the close of the American Revolution the Methodists numbered some fifteen thousand members and eighty preachers.

In the beginning Wesley had thought of his fellows not as constituting a church but simply as forming so many societies. The preachers were not ordained, and the members were supposed to receive the Sacraments in the Anglican Church. But the Anglican clergy in America were few and far between. The Revolution had severed America from England, and Methodism to all intents and purposes had become an independent church. Wesley responded to appeals for help from America by asking the Bishop of London to ordain some of his preachers. Failing in this, he himself ordained two men and set aside Dr. Thomas Coke, who was a presbyter of the Church of England, to be a superintendent, "to preside over the flock of Christ" in America. Coke was directed to ordain Francis Asbury as a second superintendent.

At the Christmas Conference, which met in Baltimore December 24, 1784, some sixty preachers, with Dr. Coke and his companions, organized the Methodist Episcopal Church in America. Wesley had sent over *The Sunday Service,* a simplified form of the English Book of Common Prayer, with the Articles of Religion reduced in number. This book they adopted, adding to the articles one which recognized the independence of the new nation.

Our present Articles of Religion come from this book and unite us with the historic faith of Christendom. Our Ritual, too, though it has been modified, has this as its source. However, the forms for public worship taken from the Book of Common Prayer were not adapted to the freer religious life of American Methodism and never entered into common use. Instead, Methodism created a book of its own, its Discipline. This contains today the Articles of Religion, Wesley's General Rules, the Ritual and other forms of worship, and a large section which deals with the ministry, the various church organizations, and the rules governing the life and work of the Church.

In the history of Methodism two notable divisions occurred. In 1828 a group of earnest and godly persons, largely moved by an insistence on lay representation, separated and became The Methodist Protestant Church. In 1844 there was another division, the cause being construed by some as the question of slavery, by others as a constitutional issue over the powers of the General Conference versus the episcopacy. After years of negotiation a Plan of Union was agreed upon; and on May 10, 1939, The Methodist Episcopal Church, The Methodist Episcopal Church, South, and The Methodist Protestant Church united to form The Methodist Church.

The Methodist Church believes today, as Methodism has from the first, that the only infallible proof of a true church of Christ is its ability to seek and to save the lost, to disseminate the Pentecostal spirit and life, to spread scriptural holiness, and to transform all peoples and nations through the gospel of Christ. The sole object of the rules, regulations, and usages of The Methodist Church is to aid the Church in fulfilling its divine commission. United Methodism thanks God for the new life and strength which have come with reunion, while realizing the new obligations which this brings. At the same time it rejoices in the fact that it is a part of the one Church of our Lord and share in a common task. Its spirit is still expressed in Wesley's words: "I desire to have a league, offensive and defensive, with every soldier of Christ.

We have not only one faith, one hope, one Lord, but are directly engaged in one warfare."

The Evangelical United Brethren Church

The Evangelical United Brethren Church had its roots in the spiritual quickening which emerged in the United States in the late eighteenth and early nineteenth centuries. This movement not only challenged religious indifference, but also the contemporary tendency to substitute "religion" for a vital and experiential relationship with God. In its present form the Evangelical United Brethren Church represents the union, consummated in 1946, of the Church of the United Brethren in Christ and The Evangelical Church.

I. CHURCH OF THE UNITED BRETHREN IN CHRIST

The eighteenth century witnessed the eruption of revolutionary ideas and programs in science, industry, and politics. In this agitated world there were marked evidences of religious revitalization. In the English-speaking world it was associated with, though not confined to, Wesleyanism; in the German-speaking world it was associated with pietism. In some places and in some persons, these two movements impinged upon each other.

Philip William Otterbein, an ordained minister of the German Reformed Church, who served congregations in Pennsylvania and Maryland, and Martin Boehm, a Pennsylvanian of Mennonite parentage, were among those who sensed a call to preach the Good News of God's redeeming mercy and love as demonstrated in Jesus Christ, especially among neglected German-speaking settlers of the Middle Colonies. In obedience to this call, they invited men to accept salvation. To be saved, they held, meant both awareness, as real as any sensory awareness, of God's acceptance and personal commitment to Christ. Their labors were blessed, and thriving societies were established which were conceived not so much as alternatives or rivals to established churches, as centers for renewal in those churches. This work expanded, and helpers were sought to devote themselves to this evan-

11

gelistic effort. As persons responded, they were received as fellow laborers.

The gracious work of renewal and reformation spread through Pennsylvania, Maryland, and Virginia. Otterbein's leadership was increasingly acknowledged. In the larger "big meetings" and in more intimate circles, he emphasized the necessity to persuade men to accept the divine invitation to salvation and to lead a new kind of life. To share experiences in this ministry and to seek greater effectiveness in this mission, it was resolved that preachers' meetings be held. One such meeting was held in Baltimore, Maryland, in 1789; another in Paradise Township, York County, Pennsylvania, in 1791.

Beginning with the meeting, September 25, 1800, in Frederick County, Maryland, these ministers' meetings were held annually. They agreed each of them should have liberty as to the mode of baptism, each administering it according to his own conviction. They agreed that Otterbein and Boehm should be their leaders as superintendents or bishops. About this time the name United Brethren in Christ came into use. The work soon extended across the Appalachian Mountains into Ohio, and this prompted the decision to organize a Conference in Ohio in 1810.

Martin Boehm died in 1812; Philip William Otterbein was incapacitated by ill health. Accordingly, in 1813 Christian Newcomer was elected bishop to superintend the concerns of the growing church. Up to this time there was no book of discipline, so it was determined that a General Conference should be called to provide such a book. The first General Conference of this church convened June 6, 1815, near Mt. Pleasant, Pennsylvania. After deliberation, the conference recommended a book of Discipline containing the doctrines and rules of the church with the exhortation that these together with the Word of God should be strictly observed, and admonished the members that "God is a God of order, but where there is no order and no church discipline, the spirit of love and charity will be lost."

The book of Discipline, together with a Constitution which was adopted in 1841, provided regulations under which the Church of the United Brethren in Christ expanded in numbers and mission in the nineteenth and twentieth centuries. The Constitution, with several other factors, was the ground for a division in the denomination in

1889 as the majority, authorized by a referendum in the church, made changes in the Constitution.

II. The Evangelical Church

Jacob Albright, an unordained Pennsylvania tilemaker-farmer, began preaching that religion was a personal, conscious experiential relationship with God. About 1800, small groups of people living in three separated communities, impressed by Albright's ideas, covenanted themselves to seek God's grace which would enable them to live holily. Following his experience of salvation in 1791, Albright began to witness in the German language to God's saving grace. He and those associated with him agreed to measures of self-discipline and Christian witness. The number of those inclined to participate in this endeavor increased, and this in turn promoted the enlistment of helpers.

The transition from movement to ecclesiastical organization was marked by the first council of those acknowledging Albright as leader on November 3, 1803. Beginning in 1807, with a meeting at Kleinfeltersville, Lebanon County, Pennsylvania, the preachers gathered in annual meetings. In 1809 a book of Discipline was adopted and printed. In 1816, at the first General Conference of the body, the name, The Evangelical Association, was adopted. For the courageous ministry of this church, conversion was the central theme and purpose, a word which signified the gracious, conscious vitalization of the life of a man by an act of God.

During the nineteenth century the operations of this church enlarged in evangelism, education, and publications. In the latter part of the century differences arose in The Evangelical Association which in 1891 culminated in a division. A considerable number of ministers and laymen withdrew and took the name, The United Evangelical Church, which held its first General Conference in 1894. Both churches continued their activities, side by side, both endeavoring to carry on the work of the Lord with zeal and devotion. Both churches grew in numbers and in missionary enterprise. By 1910 the growing conviction that the two churches should be reunited found articulate expression,

13

and in 1922 The Evangelical Association and The United Evangelical Church were united under the name The Evangelical Church.

III. UNION IN 1946

Negotiations, beginning in 1933, were consummated in 1946 when the Church of the United Brethren in Christ and The Evangelical Church became The Evangelical United Brethren Church. This church has sought to serve its Lord faithfully in the proclamation that salvation is available to any upon the free, personal acceptance of God's offer. Conversion, while personal, is not a private matter and finds its consummation in holy living and in serving as an instrument of God for the redemption of the whole world. In this task, it views itself as one fold, in the one flock, whose Shepherd is our Lord.

The United Methodist Church

The United Methodist Church brings together two streams of spiritual life with similar emphases which had their beginnings in the evangelistic concerns and passion of John Wesley, Francis Asbury, Philip William Otterbein, Jacob Albright, Martin Boehm, and others who labored with them. These men were dedicated to the task of preaching the gospel to their fellow countrymen.

Since they were men who were deeply moved by a common faith and zeal and held a like emphasis upon personal spiritual experience of salvation, it is no surprise to find instances of fraternity and cooperation among them. They often conferred with each other and sometimes traveled together on their preaching missions. In many communities they shared the same building, with the Methodist preachers conducting services in English at one hour and the Evangelical or United Brethren preachers conducting a German service at another hour. There are many references to the Asbury groups as "English Methodists" and the Otterbein-Boehm-Albright groups as "German Methodists" or "Dutch Methodists."

The firm conviction that Christian faith and experience ought to be expressed in holy living led these early leaders to adopt similar

14

patterns of ecclesiastical organization and discipline to assist Christians in spiritual growth and Christian witness.

When Asbury was ordained and consecrated as bishop in 1784, Otterbein participated with the laying on of hands. When Otterbein ordained Christian Newcomer in 1813, he requested that a Methodist minister participate. William Ryland responded and joined Otterbein in the act of ordination.

There is evidence that Asbury conferred with Otterbein when he was working on the book of Discipline for the Methodists. When this Discipline was later translated into German, it became the basis for the Discipline of the *Evangelische Gemeinschaft* (later known as The Evangelical Church) and—to a lesser degree—the *Vereinigten Bruder* (later known as the United Brethren in Christ).

Over the years there have been many conversations concerning union. Bishop Newcomer's journal records such a conversation as early as April 1, 1803. In 1871 The Evangelical Association voted by a narrow margin of one to join the Methodists, but union was never consummated. During the past several years these conversations, under the instruction and authorization of the respective General Conferences, led to a plan and basis of union that united The Evangelical United Brethren Church and The Methodist Church into The United Methodist Church. This union embodies the history and traditions of the following churches which are Methodist in name or tradition:

The Methodist Episcopal Church
The Methodist Episcopal Church, South
The Methodist Protestant Church
The Methodist Church (merged into the Protestant Methodist Church in 1877)

United Brethren in Christ
The Evangelical Association
The United Evangelical Church
The Evangelical Church
The Methodist Church
The Evangelical United Brethren Church

Part I

THE CONSTITUTION

PREAMBLE

The Church is a community of all true believers under the Lord-ship of Christ. It is the redeemed and redeeming fellowship in which the Word of God is preached by men divinely called, and the Sacraments are duly administered according to Christ's own appointment. Under the discipline of the Holy Spirit the Church seeks to provide for the maintenance of worship, the edification of believers, and the redemption of the world.

The Church of Jesus Christ exists in and for the world, and its very dividedness is a hindrance to its mission in that world.

The prayers and intentions of The Methodist Church and The Evangelical United Brethren Church have been and are for obedience to the will of our Lord that His people be one, in humility for the present brokenness of the Church and in gratitude that opportunities for reunion have been given. In harmony with these prayers and intentions these churches do now propose to unite, in the confident assurance that this act is an expression of the oneness of Christ's people.

Conversations concerning union between the two churches and their constituent members have taken place over a long period of years, and the churches have a long and impressive history of fellowship and cooperation.

Therefore, we, the Commissions on Church Union of The Methodist Church, and of The Evangelical United Brethren Church, holding that these churches are essentially one in origin, in belief, in spirit, and in purpose, and desiring that this essential unity be made actual in organization and administration in the United States of America and throughout the world, do hereby propose and transmit to our respective General Conferences the following Plan of Union and recommend to the two churches its adoption by the processes which they respectively require.[1]

DIVISION ONE

¶ 1. *Article I. Declaration of Union.*—The Evangelical United Brethren Church and The Methodist Church shall be united in one Church. The united Church, as thus constituted, is, and shall be, the ecclesiastical and legal successor of the two uniting churches.

¶ 2. *Article II. Name.*—The name of the Church shall be The United Methodist Church. The name of the Church may be translated freely into languages other than English as the General Conference may determine.

¶ 3. *Article III. Articles of Religion and the Confession of Faith.* —The Articles of Religion and the Confession of Faith shall be those currently held by The Methodist Church and The Evangelical United Brethren Church respectively.

¶ 4. *Article IV. Inclusiveness of the Church.*—The United Methodist Church is a part of the Church Universal which is one Body in Christ. Therefore all persons, without regard to race, color, national origin, or economic condition, shall be eligible to attend its worship services, to participate in its programs, and, when they take the appropriate vows, to be admitted into its membership in any local church in the connection. In The United Methodist Church no conference or other organizational unit of the Church shall be structured so as to exclude any member or any constituent body of the Church because of race, color, national origin, or economic condition.

¶ 5. *Article V. Ecumenical Relations.*—As part of the Church Universal, The United Methodist Church believes that the Lord of the

---

[1] The Constitution was adopted in Chicago, Illinois, on Nov. 11, 1966, by the General Conferences of The Evangelical United Brethren Church and The Methodist Church and thereafter by the requisite vote in the Annual Conferences of the two churches. The Plan of Union was made effective by the Uniting Conference in Dallas, Texas, on April 23, 1968.

Church is calling Christians everywhere to strive toward unity, and therefore it will seek, and work for, unity at all levels of church life: through world relationships with other Methodist churches and united churches related to The Methodist Church or The Evangelical United Brethren Church, through councils of churches, and through plans of union with churches of Methodist or other denominational traditions.

¶ 6. *Article VI. Title to Properties.*—Titles to properties in The Evangelical United Brethren Church and The Methodist Church shall, upon consummation of the union, automatically vest in The United Methodist Church. Nothing in the Plan of Union at any time after the union is to be construed so as to require any local church or any other property owner of the former The Evangelical United Brethren Church or the former The Methodist Church to alienate or in any way to change the title to property contained in its deed or deeds at the time of union, and lapse of time or usage shall not affect said title or control.

DIVISION TWO—ORGANIZATION

Section I. Conferences.

¶ 7. *Article I.*—There shall be a General Conference for the entire Church with such powers, duties, and privileges as are hereinafter set forth.

¶ 8. *Article II.*—There shall be Jurisdictional Conferences for the Church in the United States of America and Canada, with such powers, duties, and privileges as are hereinafter set forth; *provided* that in The United Methodist Church there shall be no jurisdictional or central conference based on any ground other than geographical and regional division.

¶ 9. *Article III.*—There shall be Central Conferences for the Church outside the United States of America and Canada and, if necessary, Provisional Central Conferences, all with such powers, duties, and privileges as are hereinafter set forth.

¶ 10. *Article IV.*—There shall be Annual Conferences as the fundamental bodies of the Church and, if necessary, Provisional Annual

Conferences, with such powers, duties, and privileges as are hereinafter set forth.

¶ 11. *Article V.*—There shall be a Charge Conference for each church or charge with such powers, duties, and privileges as are hereinafter set forth.

Section II. General Conference.

¶ 12. *Article I.*—The General Conference shall be composed of not less than 600 nor more than 1,000 delegates, one half of whom shall be ministers and one half lay members, to be elected by the Annual Conferences.

¶ 13. *Article II.*—The General Conference shall meet in the month of April or May once in four years at such time and in such place as shall be determined by the General Conference or by its duly authorized committees.

A special session of General Conference, possessing the authority and exercising all the powers of the General Conference, may be called by the Council of Bishops, or in such other manner as the General Conference may from time to time prescribe, to meet at such time and in such place as may be stated in the call. Such special session of the General Conference shall be composed of the delegates to the preceding General Conference or their lawful successors, except that when a particular Annual Conference shall prefer to have a new election it may do so. The purpose of such special session shall be stated in the call, and only such business shall be transacted as is in harmony with the purpose stated in such call unless the General Conference by a two-thirds vote shall determine that other business may be transacted.

¶ 14. *Article III.*—The General Conference shall fix the ratio of representation in the General, Jurisdictional, and Central Conferences from the Annual Conferences and the Provisional Annual Conferences, computed on a two-factor basis: (1) the number of ministerial members of the Annual Conference and (2) the number of church members in the Annual Conference; *provided* that each Annual Conference or Provisional Annual Conference, except for the Provisional Annual Conferences of a Central Conference or a Provisional Central Conference, shall be entitled to at least one ministerial and one lay delegate in the General Conference and also in the Jurisdictional or Central Conference.

¶ **15.** *Article IV.*—The General Conference shall have full legislative power over all matters distinctively connectional, and in the exercise of this power shall have authority as follows:

1. To define and fix the conditions, privileges, and duties of church membership which shall in every case be without reference to race or status.

2. To define and fix the powers and duties of elders, deacons, supply preachers, local preachers, exhorters, and deaconesses.

3. To define and fix the powers and duties of Annual Conferences, Provisional Annual Conferences, Missionary Conferences and Missions, and of Central Conferences, District Conferences, Charge Conferences, and Congregational Meetings.

4. To provide for the organization, promotion, and administration of the work of the Church outside the United States of America and Canada.

5. To define and fix the powers, duties, and privileges of the episcopacy, to adopt a plan for the support of the bishops, to provide a uniform rule for their retirement, and to provide for the discontinuance of a bishop because of inefficiency or unacceptability.

6. To provide and revise the Hymnal and Ritual of the Church and to regulate all matters relating to the form and mode of worship, subject to the limitations of the first and second Restrictive Rules.

7. To provide a judicial system and a method of judicial procedure for the Church, except as herein otherwise prescribed.

8. To initiate and to direct all connectional enterprises of the Church and to provide boards for their promotion and administration.

9. To determine and provide for raising and distributing funds necessary to carry on the work of the Church.

10. To fix a uniform basis upon which bishops shall be elected by the Jurisdictional Conferences and to determine the number of bishops that may be elected by Central Conferences.

11. To select its presiding officers from the bishops, through a committee; *provided* that the bishops shall select from their own number the presiding officer of the opening session.

12. To change the number and the boundaries of Jurisdictional Conferences upon the consent of a majority of the Annual Conferences in each Jurisdictional Conference involved.

13. To establish such commissions for the general work of the Church as may be deemed advisable.

14. To secure the rights and privileges of membership in all agencies, programs, and institutions in The United Methodist Church regardless of race or status.

15. To enact such other legislation as may be necessary, subject to the limitations and restrictions of the Constitution of the Church.

Section III.   Restrictive Rules.

¶ **16.** *Article I.*—The General Conference shall not revoke, alter, or change our Articles of Religion or establish any new standards or rules of doctrine contrary to our present existing and established standards of doctrine.

Article II.—The General Conference shall not revoke, alter, or change our Confession of Faith.

¶ **17.** *Article III.*—The General Conference shall not change or alter any part or rule of our government so as to do away with episcopacy or destroy the plan of our itinerant general superintendency.

¶ **18.** *Article IV.*—The General Conference shall not do away with the privileges of our ministers of right to trial by a committee and of an appeal; neither shall it do away with the privileges of our members of right to trial before the church, or by a committee, and of an appeal.

¶ **19.** *Article V.*—The General Conference shall not revoke or change the General Rules of Our United Societies.

¶ **20.** *Article VI.*—The General Conference shall not appropriate the net income of the publishing houses, the book concerns, or the Chartered Fund to any purpose other than for the benefit of retired or disabled preachers, their wives, widows, and children or other beneficiaries of the ministerial pension systems.

¶ **21.** Article VII.—The General Conference shall not do away with the following rights, which are hereby defined: In order that The

Evangelical United Brethren Church shall be assured of effective representation in The United Methodist Church it is agreed that at the level of the General Conference, Jurisdictional Conferences, and Central Conferences and on all boards and agencies at the Annual Conference, Central Conference, Jurisdictional Conference, and General Conference levels, in every instance there shall be chosen, during the first three quadrenniums following union, at least twice the number of representatives coming from The Evangelical United Brethren Church membership as the relative numerical membership in said particular conference would indicate in relationship to the number of representatives coming from The Methodist Church, and further agreed that during such period every General Conference and Jurisdictional Conference, and if practical every Central Conference and Annual Conference, board, or agency, regardless of size, shall have at least one such representative; *provided* that this provision shall not be applied so as to give to representatives coming from The Evangelical United Brethren Church a majority position which, except for this provision, they would not have; and further *provided* that in the Germany Central Conference during the first three quadrenniums following union the relative number of representatives coming from the former Methodist Church and the former *Evangelische Gemeinschaft* shall be equal. The relative numerical membership shall be computed by taking the membership of The Evangelical United Brethren Church as reported immediately prior to union and the total membership of the particular conference immediately after union. The General Conference may adopt legislative rules designed to carry out the intent and spirit of this provision. At the termination of the first three quadrenniums following union, this Article VII shall be automatically deleted from the Constitution.

Section IV.   Jurisdictional Conferences.

¶ **22.** *Article I.*—The Jurisdictional Conferences shall be composed of as many representatives from the Annual Conferences as shall be determined by a uniform basis established by the General Conference.

¶ **23.** *Article II.*—All Jurisdictional Conferences shall have the same status and the same privileges of action within the limits fixed by the Constitution. The ratio of representation of the Annual Conferences in the General Conference shall be the same for all Jurisdictional Conferences.

¶ **24.** *Article III.*—The General Conferences shall fix the basis of representation in the Jurisdictional Conferences; *provided* that the Jurisdictional Conferences shall be composed of an equal number of ministerial and lay delegates to be elected by the Annual Conferences and the Provisional Annual Conferences.

¶ **25.** *Article IV.*—Each Jurisdictional Conference shall meet at the time determined by the Council of Bishops or its delegated committee, each Jurisdictional Conference convening on the same date as the others and at a place selected by the Jurisdictional Committee on Entertainment, appointed by its College of Bishops unless such a committee has been appointed by the preceding Jurisdictional Conference.

¶ **26.** *Article V.*—The Jurisdictional Conferences shall have the following powers and duties and such others as may be conferred by the General Conferences:

1. To promote the evangelistic, educational, missionary, and benevolent interests of the Church, and to provide for interests and institutions within their boundaries.

2. To elect bishops and to cooperate in carrying out such plans for their support as may be determined by the General Conference.

3. To establish and constitute Jurisdictional Conference boards as auxiliary to the general boards of the Church as the need may appear and to choose their representatives on the general boards in such manner as the General Conference may determine.

4. To determine the boundaries of their Annual Conferences; *provided* that there shall be no Annual Conference with a membership of fewer than fifty ministers in full connection, except by the consent of the General Conference; and *provided* further that this provision shall not apply to Annual Conferences of the former The Evangelical United Brethren Church during the first three quadrenniums after union.

5. To make rules and regulations for the administration of the

work of the Church within the jurisdiction, subject to such powers as have been or shall be vested in the General Conference.

6. To appoint a Committee on Appeals to hear and determine the appeal of a traveling preacher of that jurisdiction from the decision of a trial committee.

Section V. Central Conferences.

¶ 27. *Article I.*—There shall be Central Conferences for the work of the Church outside the United States of America and Canada with such duties, powers, and privileges as are hereinafter set forth. The number and boundaries of the Central Conferences shall be determined by the Uniting Conference. Subsequently the General Conference shall have authority to change the number and boundaries of Central Conferences. The Central Conferences shall have the duties, powers, and privileges hereinafter set forth.

¶ 28. *Article II.*—The Central Conferences shall be composed of as many delegates as shall be determined by a basis established by the General Conference. The delegates shall be ministerial and lay in equal numbers.

¶ 29. *Article III.*—The Central Conferences shall meet within the year succeeding the meeting of the General Conference at such times and places as shall have been determined by the preceding respective Central Conferences or by commissions appointed by them or by the General Conference. The date and place of the first meeting succeeding the Uniting Conference shall be fixed by the bishops of the respective Central Conferences, or in such manner as shall be determined by the General Conference.

¶ 30. *Article IV.*—The Central Conferences shall have the following powers and duties and such others as may be conferred by the General Conference:

1. To promote the evangelistic, educational, missionary, social-concern, and benevolent interests and institutions of the Church within their own boundaries.

2. To elect the bishops for the respective Central Conferences in number as may be determined from time to time, upon a basis fixed

by the General Conference, and to cooperate in carrying out such plans for the support of their bishops as may be determined by the General Conference.

3. To establish and constitute such Central Conference boards as may be required and to elect their administrative officers.

4. To determine the boundaries of the Annual Conferences within their respective areas.

5. To make such rules and regulations for the administration of the work within their boundaries including such changes and adaptations of the General Discipline as the conditions in the respective areas may require, subject to the powers that have been or shall be vested in the General Conference.

6. To appoint a Judicial Court to determine legal questions arising on the rules, regulations, and such revised, adapted, or new sections of the Central Conference Discipline enacted by the Central Conference.

7. To appoint a Committee on Appeals to hear and determine the appeal of a traveling preacher of that Central Conference from the decision of a Committee on Trial.

Section VI. Episcopal Administration in Central Conferences.

¶ **31.** *Article I.*—The bishops of the Central Conferences shall be elected by their respective Central Conferences and inducted into office in the historic manner.

¶ **32.** *Article II.*—The bishops of the Central Conferences shall have membership in the Council of Bishops with vote.

¶ **33.** *Article III.*—The bishops of the Central Conferences shall preside in the sessions of their respective Central Conferences.

¶ **34.** *Article IV.*—The bishops of each Central Conference shall arrange the plan of episcopal visitation within their Central Conference.

¶ **35.** *Article V.*—The Council of Bishops may assign one of their number to visit each Central Conference. When so assigned, the bishop shall be recognized as the accredited representative of the general Church and when requested by a majority of the bishops resident in that conference may exercise therein the functions of the episcopacy.

Section VII. Annual Conferences.

¶ **36.** *Article I.*—The Annual Conference shall be composed of ministerial members as defined by the General Conference, together with a lay member elected by each charge, the conference president of the Women's Society of Christian Service, the conference president of United Methodist Men, and the conference lay leader. Each charge served by more than one minister shall be entitled to as many lay members as there are ministerial members. The lay members shall be at least twenty-one (21) years of age and shall have been for the four years next preceding their election members of one of the constituent churches forming this union or of The United Methodist Church.

¶ **37.** *Article II.*—The Annual Conference is the basic body in the Church and as such shall have reserved to it the right to vote on all constitutional amendments, on the election of ministerial and lay delegates to the General and the Jurisdictional or Central Conferences, on all matters relating to the character and conference relations of its ministerial members, and on the ordination of ministers and such other rights as have not been delegated to the General Conference under the Constitution, with the exception that the lay members may not vote on matters of ordination, character, and conference relations of ministers. It shall discharge such duties and exercise such powers as the General Conference under the Constitution may determine.

¶ **38.** *Article III.*—The Annual Conference shall elect ministerial and lay delegates to the General Conference and to its Jurisdictional or Central Conference in the manner provided in this section, Articles IV and V. The persons first elected up to the number determined by the ratio for representation in the General Conference shall be representatives in that body. Additional delegates shall be elected to complete the number determined by the ratio for representation in the Jurisdictional or Central Conference, who, together with those first elected as above, shall be delegates in the Jurisdictional or Central Conference. The additional delegates to the Jurisdictional or Central Conference shall in the order of their election be the reserve delegates to the General Conference. The Annual Conference shall also elect reserve ministerial and lay delegates to the Jurisdictional or Central Conference as it may deem desirable.

¶39. *Article IV.*—The ministerial delegates to the General Conference and to the Jurisdictional or Central Conference shall be elected by the ministerial members in full connection with the Annual Conference or Provisional Annual Conference; *provided* that such delegates shall have been traveling preachers in the constituent churches forming this union or in The United Methodist Church for at least four years next preceding their election and are in full connection with the Annual Conference or Provisional Annual Conference electing them when elected and at the time of holding the General and Jurisdictional or Central Conferences.

¶ 40. *Article V.*—The lay delegates to the General Conference and to the Jurisdictional or Central Conferences shall be elected by the lay members of the Annual Conference or Provisional Annual Conference; *provided* that such delegates be at least twenty-one (21) years of age and shall have been members of one of the constituent churches forming this union or of The United Methodist Church for at least four years next preceding their election, and are members thereof within the Annual Conference electing them at the time of holding the General and Jurisdictional or Central Conferences.

¶ 41. *Article VI.*—For a period of twelve years following union, Annual Conferences shall not have their names or boundaries changed without their consent; and during such period Annual Conferences formerly of The Evangelical United Brethren Church may in electing delegates to General, Jurisdictional, and Central Conferences and their superintendents of districts continue their time-honored methods, the provisions of Division Two, Section VII, Arts. IV and V; Division Two, Section VIII, Art. IV; and Division Three, Art. IX, notwithstanding; but nothing herein shall be construed as preventing the elimination of Annual Conferences based on race.

Section VIII. Boundaries.

¶42. *Article I.*—The United Methodist Church shall have Jurisdictional Conferences made up as follows:

Northeastern—Maine, New Hampshire, Vermont, Massachusetts, Rhode Island, New York, Connecticut, Pennsylvania, New Jersey,

Maryland, West Virginia, Delaware, District of Columbia, Puerto Rico, Province of Ontario.

Southeastern—Virginia, North Carolina, South Carolina, Georgia, Florida, Alabama, Tennessee, Kentucky, Mississippi.

North Central—Ohio, Indiana, Illinois, Michigan, Wisconsin, Minnesota, Iowa, North Dakota, South Dakota.

South Central—Missouri, Arkansas, Louisiana, Nebraska, Kansas, Oklahoma, Texas, New Mexico.

Western—Washington, Idaho, Oregon, California, Nevada, Utah, Arizona, Montana, Wyoming, Colorado, Alaska, Hawaii, Provinces of Manitoba, Saskatchewan, Alberta, and British Columbia.

¶ 43. *Article II.*—The work of the Church outside the United States of America and Canada may be formed into Central Conferences, the number and boundaries of which shall be determined by the Uniting Conference, the General Conference having authority subsequently to make changes in the number and boundaries.

¶ 44. *Article III.*—Changes in the number, names, and boundaries of the Jurisdictional Conferences may be effected by the General Conference upon the consent of a majority of the Annual Conferences of each of the Jurisdictional Conferences involved.

¶ 45. *Article IV.*—Changes in the number, names, and boundaries of the Annual Conferences may be effected by the Jurisdictional Conferences in the United States of America and Canada and by the Central Conferences outside the United States of America and Canada according to the provisions under the respective powers of the Jurisdictional and the Central Conferences.

¶ 46. *Article V. Transfer of Local Churches.*—1. A local church may be transferred from one Annual Conference to another in which it is geographically located upon approval by a two-thirds vote of those present and voting in each of the following:

　　a) The Charge Conference

　　b) The Congregational Meeting of the local church

　　c) Each of the two Annual Conferences involved

The vote shall be certified by the secretaries of the specified conferences or meeting to the bishops having supervision of the Annual

Conferences involved, and upon their announcement of the required majorities the transfer shall immediately be effective.

2. The vote on approval of transfer shall be taken by each Annual Conference at its first session after the matter is submitted to it.

3. Transfers under the provisions of this article shall not be governed or restricted by other provisions of this Constitution relating to changes of boundaries of conferences.

Section IX. District Conferences.

¶ **47.** *Article I.*—There may be organized in an Annual Conference, District Conferences composed of such persons and invested with such powers as the General Conference may determine.

Section X. Charge Conferences.

¶ **48.** *Article I.*—There shall be organized in each charge a Charge Conference composed of such persons and invested with such powers as the General Conference shall provide.

¶ **49.** *Article II. Election of Church Officers.*—Unless the General Conference shall order otherwise, the officers of the church or churches constituting a charge shall be elected by the Charge Conference or by the members of said church or churches at a meeting called for that purpose, as may be arranged by the Charge Conference, unless the election is otherwise required by local church charters or state or provincial laws.

DIVISION THREE—EPISCOPAL SUPERVISION

¶ **50.** *Article I.*—There shall be a continuance of an episcopacy in The United Methodist Church of like plan, powers, privileges, and duties as now exist in The Methodist Church and in The Evangelical United Brethren Church in all those matters in which they agree and may be considered identical; and the differences between these historic episcopacies are deemed to be reconciled and harmonized by and in this Plan of Union and Constitution of The United Methodist Church and actions taken pursuant thereto so that a unified superintendency and episcopacy is hereby created and established of, in, and by those who now are and shall be bishops of The United Methodist Church; and the said episcopacy shall further have such powers, privileges, and duties as are herein set forth.

¶ 51. *Article II.*—The bishops shall be elected by the respective Jurisdictional and Central Conferences and consecrated in the historic manner at such time and place as may be fixed by the General Conference for those elected by the jurisdictions and by each Central Conference for those elected by such Central Conference.

¶ 52. *Article III.*—There shall be a Council of Bishops composed of all the bishops of The United Methodist Church. The council shall meet at least once a year and plan for the general oversight and promotion of the temporal and spiritual interests of the entire Church and for carrying into effect the rules, regulations, and responsibilities prescribed and enjoined by the General Conference and in accord with the provisions set forth in this Plan of Union.

¶ 53. *Article IV.*—The bishops of each Jurisdictional and Central Conference shall constitute a College of Bishops and such College of Bishops shall arrange the plan of episcopal supervision of the Annual Conferences, Mission Conferences, and Missions within their respective territories.

¶ 54. *Article V.*—The bishops shall have residential and presidential supervision in the Jurisdictional Conferences in which they are elected or to which they are transferred. Bishops may be transferred from one jurisdiction to another jurisdiction for presidential and residential supervision under the following conditions: (1) The transfer of bishops may be on either of two bases: (*a*) a jurisdiction which receives a bishop by transfer from another jurisdiction may transfer to that jurisdiction or to a third jurisdiction one of its own bishops eligible for transfer, so that the number transferred in by each jurisdiction shall be balanced by the number transferred out, or (*b*) a jurisdiction may receive a bishop from another jurisdiction and not transfer out a member of its own College of Bishops. (2) No bishop shall be transferred unless he shall have given his specific consent. (3) No bishop shall be eligible for transfer unless he shall have served one quadrennium in the jurisdiction which elected him to the episcopacy. (4) All such transfers shall require the approval by a majority vote of the members, present and voting, of the Jurisdictional Conferences which are involved after consideration by the Committees on Episcopacy. After the above procedures have been followed, the transferring bishop shall become a member of the receiving College of Bishops and shall be subject to residential assignment by that Jurisdictional Conference.

A bishop may be assigned by the Council of Bishops for presidential service or other temporary service in another jurisdiction than that which elected him, provided request is made by a majority of the bishops in the jurisdiction of the proposed service.

In the case of an emergency in any jurisdiction or Central Conference through the death or disability of a bishop or other cause, the Council of Bishops may assign a bishop from another jurisdiction or Central Conference to the work of the said jurisdiction or Central Conference with the consent of a majority of the bishops of that jurisdiction or Central Conference.

¶ 55. *Article VI.*—The bishops, both active and retired, of The Evangelical United Brethren Church and of The Methodist Church at the time union is consummated, shall be bishops of The United Methodist Church.

The bishops of The Methodist Church elected by the jurisdictions, the active bishops of The Evangelical United Brethren Church at the time of union, and bishops elected by the jurisdictions of The United Methodist Church shall have life tenure. Each bishop elected by a Central Conference of The Methodist Church shall have such tenure as the Central Conference electing him shall have determined.

The Jurisdictional Conference shall elect a standing Committee on Episcopacy, to consist of one ministerial and one lay delegate from each Annual Conference, on nomination of the Annual Conference delegation. The committee shall review the work of the bishops, pass on their character and official administration, and report to the Jurisdictional Conference its findings for such action as the conference may deem appropriate within its constitutional warrant of power. The committee shall recommend the assignments of the bishops to their respective residences, for final action by the Jurisdictional Conference.

¶ 56. *Article VII.*—A bishop presiding over an Annual, Central, or Jurisdictional Conference shall decide all questions of law coming

31

before him in the regular business of a session; *provided* that such questions be presented in writing and that his decisions be recorded in the journal of the conference.

Such an episcopal decision shall not be authoritative except for the pending case until it shall have been passed upon by the Judicial Council. Each bishop shall report in writing annually all his decisions of law, with a syllabus of the same, to the Judicial Council, which shall affirm, modify, or reverse them.

¶ **57.** *Article VIII.*—The bishops of the several Jurisdictional and Central Conferences shall preside in the sessions of their respective conferences.

¶ **58.** *Article IX.*—In each Annual Conference there shall be one or more district superintendents who shall assist the bishop in the administration of the Annual Conference and shall have such responsibilities and term of office as the General Conference may determine.

¶ **59.** *Article X.*—The bishops shall appoint, after consultation with the district superintendents, ministers to the charges, and they shall have such responsibilities and authorities as the General Conference shall prescribe.

DIVISION FOUR—THE JUDICIARY

¶ **60.** *Article I.*—There shall be a Judicial Council. The General Conference shall determine the number and qualifications of its members, their terms of office, and the method of election and the filling of vacancies.

¶ **61.** *Article II.*—The Judicial Council shall have authority:

1. To determine the constitutionality of any act of the General Conference upon an appeal of a majority of the Council of Bishops or one fifth of the members of the General Conference, and to determine the constitutionality of any act of a Jurisdictional or Central Conference upon an appeal of a majority of the bishops of that Jurisdictional or Central Conference or upon the appeal of one fifth of the members of that Jurisdictional or Central Conference.

2. To hear and determine any appeal from a bishop's decision on

a question of law made in the Annual Conference when said appeal has been made by one fifth of that conference present and voting.

3. To pass upon decisions of law made by bishops in Annual Conferences.

4. To hear and determine the legality of any action taken therein by any General Conference board or Jurisdictional or Central Conference board or body, upon appeal by one third of the members thereof, or upon request of the Council of Bishops or a majority of the bishops of a Jurisdictional or a Central Conference.

5. To have such other duties and powers as may be conferred upon it by the General Conference.

6. To provide its own methods of organization and procedure.

¶ 62. *Article III.*—All decisions of the Judicial Council shall be final. When the Judicial Council shall declare unconstitutional any act of the General Conference then in session, that decision shall be reported back to that General Conference immediately.

¶ 63. *Article IV.*—The General Conference shall establish for the Church a judicial system which shall guarantee to our ministers a right to trial by a committee and an appeal and to our members a right to trial before the church, or by a committee, and an appeal.

DIVISION FIVE—AMENDMENTS

¶ 64. *Article I.*—Amendments to the Constitution shall be made upon a two-thirds majority of the General Conference present and voting and a two-thirds affirmative vote of the aggregate number of members of the several Annual Conferences present and voting, except in the case of the first, second, and seventh Restrictive Rules which shall require a three-fourths majority of all the members of the Annual Conferences present and voting. The vote, after being completed, shall be canvassed by the Council of Bishops, and the amendment voted upon shall become effective upon their announcement of its having received the required majority.

¶ 65. *Article II.*—Amendments to the Constitution may originate in either the General Conference or the Annual Conferences.

¶ **66. *Article III.***—A Jurisdictional Conference may by a majority vote propose changes in the Constitution of the Church, and such proposed changes shall be submitted to the next General Conference. If the General Conference adopts the measure by a two-thirds vote, it shall be submitted to the Annual Conferences according to the provision for amendments.

Part II
DOCTRINAL STATEMENTS AND
THE GENERAL RULES

PREFACE

The doctrinal traditions of both The Methodist Church and The Evangelical United Brethren Church stem from the Evangelical Revival of the eighteenth century and have been conserved and developed through the generations until now. In this Plan of Union it is proposed that this vital heritage be cherished and its authentic development insured.

In their original Constitution (1808), the American Methodists placed a restrictive rule designed to inhibit irresponsible doctrinal changes, "contrary to our present existing and established standards of doctrine." This rule has remained in force and unamended through subsequent schisms and reunion. It was renewed by the Uniting Conference of 1939 and is once again repeated in this Plan of Union (¶ 16).

The phrase, "our present existing and established standards of doctrine," has never been formally defined. In its original reference, however, it included as a minimum John Wesley's forty-four *Sermons on Several Occasions* and his *Explanatory Notes Upon the New Testament*. Their function as "standards" had already been defined by the "Large Minutes" of 1763, which in turn had been approved by the American Methodists in 1773 and 1785. To these *Sermons* and *Notes* the Conference of 1808 added *The Articles of Religion*—an abridgment of the XXXIX Articles of the Church of England prepared by

35

Mr. Wesley in his revised version of *The Book of Common Prayer* (*The Sunday Service*).

In 1962, after sixteen years of union under two confessions of faith, The Evangelical United Brethren Church adopted a *Confession of Faith* based upon the doctrinal traditions of the former Church of the United Brethren in Christ and The Evangelical Church and intended as a convenient summary of the basic beliefs of evangelical Christianity. In the present Plan of Union, this *Confession* is placed alongside *The Articles of Religion* and becomes a stipulated reference in the Restrictive Rules. The *Confession, The Articles of Religion,* and the Wesleyan "standards" are thus deemed congruent if not identical in their doctrinal perspectives and not in conflict.

The purpose of such "standards" is certainly not to displace the direct and primary authority of the Bible nor to stultify the responsible freedom of thoughtful Christians in the development of Christian doctrine. In all matters of faith and morals, the authority of Holy Scripture stands supreme (cf. Art. V. in *The Articles of Religion* and Art. IV in the *Confession*). Moreover, in the ongoing enterprise of theological reflection, the Wesleyan "standards" have been rightly construed as the **negative limits of public teaching** in the Church rather than the positive prescription of an inflexible system of doctrine. This principle was clearly stated in the *Deed of Union of the British Methodist Church* (1932):

> The *Notes on the New Testament* and the *Forty-Four Sermons* are not intended to impose a system of formal or speculative theology on Methodist Preachers, but to set up standards of preaching and belief which should insure loyalty to the fundamental truths of the Gospel of Redemption and insure the continued witness of the Church to the realities of the Christian experience of salvation.

Our concern is that these Wesleyan doctrinal traditions shall continue as a fruitful source of theological understanding. They make no pretension to infallibility in and of themselves. Mr. Wesley constantly appealed to Scripture as the primary locus of divine revelation and to the historic creeds and "the catholic spirit" as the larger context in which the Scriptures are to be interpreted. In like manner, the Wesleyan "standards of doctrine" are designed to serve those who preach and teach in The United Methodist Church as sound guides to valid doctrine.

¶ 91. THE ARTICLES OF RELIGION OF THE METHODIST CHURCH

Article I.—Of Faith in the Holy Trinity

There is but one living and true God, everlasting, without body or parts, of infinite power, wisdom, and goodness; the maker and preserver of all things, visible and invisible. And in unity of this Godhead there are three persons, of one substance, power, and eternity—the Father, the Son, and the Holy Ghost.

Article II.—Of the Word, or Son of God, Who Was Made Very Man

The Son, who is the Word of the Father, the very eternal God, of one substance with the Father, took man's nature in the womb of the blessed Virgin; so that two whole and perfect natures, that is to say, the Godhead and Manhood, were joined together in one person, never to be divided; whereof is one Christ, very God and very Man, who truly suffered, was crucified, dead, and buried, to reconcile his Father to us, and to be a sacrifice, not only for original guilt, but also for the actual sins of man.

Article III.—Of the Resurrection of Christ

Christ did truly rise again from the dead, and took again his body, with all things appertaining to the perfection of man's nature, wherewith he ascended into heaven, and there sitteth until he return to judge all men at the last day.

Article IV.—Of the Holy Ghost

The Holy Ghost, proceeding from the Father and the Son, is of one substance, majesty, and glory with the Father and the Son, very and eternal God.

37

Article V.—Of the Sufficiency of the Holy Scriptures for Salvation

The Holy Scriptures contain all things necessary to salvation; so that whatsoever is not read therein, nor may be proved thereby, is not to be required of any man that it should be believed as an article of faith, or be thought requisite or necessary to salvation. In the name of the Holy Scriptures we do understand those canonical books of the Old and New Testament of whose authority was never any doubt in the Church. The names of the canonical books are:

Genesis, Exodus, Leviticus, Numbers, Deuteronomy, Joshua, Judges, Ruth, The First Book of Samuel, The Second Book of Samuel, The First Book of Kings, The Second Book of Kings, The First Book of Chronicles, The Second Book of Chronicles, The Book of Ezra, The Book of Nehemiah, The Book of Esther, The Book of Job, The Psalms, The Proverbs, Ecclesiastes or the Preacher, Cantica or Song of Solomon, Four Prophets the Greater, Twelve Prophets the Less.

All the books of the New Testament, as they are commonly received, we do receive and account canonical.

Article VI.—Of the Old Testament

The Old Testament is not contrary to the New; for both in the Old and New Testament everlasting life is offered to mankind by Christ, who is the only Mediator between God and man, being both God and Man. Wherefore they are not to be heard who feign that the old fathers did look only for transitory promises. Although the law given from God by Moses as touching ceremonies and rites doth not bind Christians, nor ought the civil precepts thereof of necessity be received in any commonwealth; yet notwithstanding, no Christian whatsoever is free from the obedience of the commandments which are called moral.

Article VII.—Of Original or Birth Sin

Original sin standeth not in the following of Adam (as the Pelagians do vainly talk), but it is the corruption of the nature of every man, that naturally is engendered of the offspring of Adam, whereby man is very far gone from original righteousness, and of his own nature inclined to evil, and that continually.

Article VIII.—Of Free Will

The condition of man after the fall of Adam is such that he cannot turn and prepare himself, by his own natural strength and works, to faith, and calling upon God; wherefore we have no power to do good works, pleasant and acceptable to God, without the grace of God by Christ preventing us, that we may have a good will, and working with us, when we have that good will.

Article IX.—Of the Justification of Man

We are accounted righteous before God only for the merit of our Lord and Saviour Jesus Christ, by faith, and not for our own works or deservings. Wherefore, that we are justified by faith only is a most wholesome doctrine, and very full of comfort.

Article X.—Of Good Works

Although good works, which are the fruits of faith, and follow after justification, cannot put away our sins, and endure the severity of God's judgment; yet are they pleasing and acceptable to God in Christ, and spring out of a true and lively faith, insomuch that by them a lively faith may be as evidently known as a tree is discerned by its fruit.

Article XI.—Of Works of Supererogation

Voluntary works—besides, over and above God's commandments —which are called works of supererogation, cannot be taught without arrogancy and impiety. For by them men do declare that they do not only render unto God as much as they are bound to do, but that they do more for his sake than of bounden duty is required; whereas Christ saith plainly: When ye have done all that is commanded of you, say, We are unprofitable servants.

Article XII.—Of Sin After Justification

Not every sin willingly committed after justification is the sin against the Holy Spirit, and unpardonable. Wherefore, the grant of repentance is not to be denied to such as fall into sin after justification:

after we have received the Holy Spirit, we may depart from grace given, and fall into sin, and, by the grace of God, rise again and amend our lives. And therefore they are to be condemned who say they can no more sin as long as they live here; or deny the place of forgiveness to such as truly repent.

Article XIII.—Of the Church

The visible Church of Christ is a congregation of faithful men in which the pure Word of God is preached, and the Sacraments duly administered according to Christ's ordinance, in all those things that of necessity are requisite to the same.

Article XIV.—Of Purgatory

The Romish doctrine concerning purgatory, pardon, worshiping, and adoration as well of images as of relics, and also invocation of saints, is a fond thing, vainly invented, and grounded upon no warrant of Scripture, but repugnant to the Word of God.

Article XV.—Of Speaking in the Congregation in Such a Tongue as the People Understand

It is a thing plainly repugnant to the Word of God, and the custom of the primitive Church, to have public prayer in the church, or to administer the Sacraments, in a tongue not understood by the people.

Article XVI.—Of the Sacraments

Sacraments ordained of Christ are not only badges or tokens of Christian men's profession, but rather they are certain signs of grace, and God's good will toward us, by which he doth work invisibly in us, and doth not only quicken, but also strengthen and confirm, our faith in him.

There are two Sacraments ordained of Christ our Lord in the Gospel; that is to say, Baptism and the Supper of the Lord.

Those five commonly called sacraments, that is to say, confirmation, penance, orders, matrimony, and extreme unction, are not to be counted for Sacraments of the Gospel; being such as have partly grown out of the *corrupt* following of the apostles, and partly are states of life allowed in the Scriptures, but yet have not the like nature of Baptism and the Lord's Supper, because they have not any visible sign or ceremony ordained of God.

The Sacraments were not ordained of Christ to be gazed upon, or to be carried about; but that we should duly use them. And in such only as worthily receive the same they have a wholesome effect or operation; but they that receive them unworthily, purchase to themselves condemnation, as St. Paul saith, I Cor. 11:29.

Article XVII.—Of Baptism

Baptism is not only a sign of profession and mark of difference whereby Christians are distinguished from others that are not baptized; but it is also a sign of regeneration or the new birth. The baptism of young children is to be retained in the church.[2]

Article XVIII.—Of the Lord's Supper

The Supper of the Lord is not only a sign of the love that Christians ought to have among themselves one to another, but rather is a sacrament of our redemption by Christ's death; insomuch that, to such as rightly, worthily, and with faith receive the same, the bread which we break is a partaking of the body of Christ; and likewise the cup of blessing is a partaking of the blood of Christ.

Transubstantiation, or the change of the substance of bread and wine in the Supper of our Lord, cannot be proved by Holy Writ, but is repugnant to the plain words of Scripture, overthroweth the nature of a sacrament, and hath given occasion to many superstitions.

The body of Christ is given, taken, and eaten in the Supper, only after a heavenly and spiritual manner. And the means whereby the body of Christ is received and eaten in the Supper is faith.

The Sacrament of the Lord's Supper was not by Christ's ordinance reserved, carried about, lifted up, or worshiped.

---

[2] *See* Judicial Council Decision 142.

41

Article XIX.—Of Both Kinds

The cup of the Lord is not to be denied to the lay people; for both the parts of the Lord's Supper, by Christ's ordinance and commandment, ought to be administered to all Christians alike.

Article XX.—Of the One Oblation of Christ, Finished upon the Cross

The offering of Christ, once made, is that perfect redemption, propitiation, and satisfaction for all the sins of the whole world, both original and actual; and there is none other satisfaction for sin but that alone. Wherefore the sacrifice of masses, in the which it is commonly said that the priest doth offer Christ for the quick and the dead, to have remission of pain or guilt, is a blasphemous fable and dangerous deceit.

Article XXI.—Of the Marriage of Ministers

The ministers of Christ are not commanded by God's law either to vow the estate of single life, or to abstain from marriage; therefore it is lawful for them, as for all other Christians, to marry at their own discretion, as they shall judge the same to serve best to godliness.

Article XXII.—Of the Rites and Ceremonies of Churches

It is not necessary that rites and ceremonies should in all places be the same, or exactly alike; for they have been always different, and may be changed according to the diversity of countries, times, and men's manners, so that nothing be ordained against God's Word. Whosoever, through his private judgment, willingly and purposely doth openly break the rites and ceremonies of the church to which he belongeth, which are not repugnant to the Word of God, and are ordained and approved by common authority, ought to be rebuked openly (that others may fear to do the like), as one that offendeth against the common order of the church, and woundeth the consciences of weak brethren.

Every particular church may ordain, change, or abolish rites and ceremonies, so that all things may be done to edification.

Article XXIII.—Of the Rulers of the United States of America

The President, the Congress, the general assemblies, the governors, and the councils of state *as the delegates of the people,* are the rulers of the United States of America, according to the division of power made to them by the Constitution of the United States and by the constitutions of their respective states. And the said states are a sovereign and independent nation, and ought not to be subject to any foreign jurisdiction.

Article XXIV.—Of Christian Men's Goods

The riches and goods of Christians, are not common, as touching the right, title, and possession of the same, as some do falsely boast. Notwithstanding, every man ought, of such things as he possesseth, liberally to give alms to the poor, according to his ability.

Article XXV.—Of a Christian Man's Oath

As we confess that vain and rash swearing is forbidden Christian men by our Lord Jesus Christ and James his apostle, so we judge that the Christian religion doth not prohibit, but that a man may swear when the magistrate requireth, in a cause of faith and charity, so it be done according to the prophet's teaching, in justice, judgment, and truth.

The following Article from the Methodist Protestant Discipline is placed here by the United Conference. It was not one of the Articles of Religion voted upon by the three churches.

¶ 92.   Of Sanctification

Sanctification is that renewal of our fallen nature by the Holy Ghost, received through faith in Jesus Christ, whose blood of atonement cleanseth from all sin; whereby we are not only delivered from the guilt of sin, but are washed from its pollution, saved from its power, and are enabled, through grace, to love God with all our hearts and to walk in his holy commandments blameless.

The following provision was adopted by the Uniting Conference. This statement seeks to interpret to our churches in foreign lands Article XXIII of the Articles of Religion. It is a legislative enactment but is not a part of the Constitution. (*See* Judicial Council Decisions 41, 176.)

¶ 93. Of the Duty of Christians to the Civil Authority

It is the duty of all Christians, and especially of all Christian ministers, to observe and obey the laws and commands of the governing or supreme authority of the country of which they are citizens or subjects or in which they reside, and to use all laudable means to encourage and enjoin obedience to the powers that be.

¶ 94. THE CONFESSION OF FAITH OF THE EVANGELICAL UNITED BRETHREN CHURCH

Article I.—God

We believe in the one true, holy and living God, Eternal Spirit, who is Creator, Sovereign and Preserver of all things visible and invisible. He is infinite in power, wisdom, justice, goodness and love, and rules with gracious regard for the well-being and salvation of men, to the glory of his name. We believe the one God reveals himself as the Trinity: Father, Son and Holy Spirit, distinct but inseparable, eternally one in essence and power.

Article II.—Jesus Christ

We believe in Jesus Christ, truly God and truly man, in whom the divine and human natures are perfectly and inseparably united. He is the eternal Word made flesh, the only begotten Son of the Father, born of the Virgin Mary by the power of the Holy Spirit. As ministering Servant he lived, suffered and died on the cross. He was buried, rose from the dead and ascended into heaven to be with the Father, from whence he shall return. He is eternal Savior and Mediator, who intercedes for us, and by him all men will be judged.

Article III.—The Holy Spirit

We believe in the Holy Spirit who proceeds from and is one in being with the Father and the Son. He convinces the world of sin, of righteousness and of judgment. He leads men through faithful response to the gospel into the fellowship of the Church. He comforts, sustains and empowers the faithful and guides them into all truth.

Article IV.—The Holy Bible

We believe the Holy Bible, Old and New Testaments, reveals the Word of God so far as it is necessary for our salvation. It is to be received through the Holy Spirit as the true rule and guide for faith and practice. Whatever is not revealed in or established by the Holy Scriptures is not to be made an article of faith nor is it to be taught as essential to salvation.

Article V.—The Church

We believe the Christian Church is the community of all true believers under the Lordship of Christ. We believe it is one, holy, apostolic and catholic. It is the redemptive fellowship in which the Word of God is preached by men divinely called, and the sacraments are duly administered according to Christ's own appointment. Under the discipline of the Holy Spirit the Church exists for the maintenance of worship, the edification of believers and the redemption of the world.

Article VI.—The Sacraments

We believe the sacraments, ordained by Christ, are symbols and pledges of the Christian's profession and of God's love toward us. They are means of grace by which God works invisibly in us, quickening, strengthening and confirming our faith in him. Two sacraments are ordained by Christ our Lord, namely, Baptism and the Lord's Supper.

We believe Baptism signifies entrance into the household of faith, and is a symbol of repentance and inner cleansing from sin, a representation of the new birth in Christ Jesus and a mark of Christian discipleship.

We believe children are under the atonement of Christ and as heirs of the Kingdom of God are acceptable subjects for Christian baptism. Children of believing parents through baptism become the special responsibility of the Church. They should be nurtured and led to personal acceptance of Christ, and by profession of faith confirm their baptism.

We believe the Lord's Supper is a representation of our redemption, a memorial of the sufferings and death of Christ, and a token of love and union which Christians have with Christ and with one another. Those who rightly, worthily and in faith eat the broken bread and drink the blessed cup partake of the body and blood of Christ in a spiritual manner until he comes.

Article VII.—Sin and Free Will

We believe man is fallen from righteousness and, apart from the grace of our Lord Jesus Christ, is destitute of holiness and inclined to evil. Except a man be born again, he cannot see the Kingdom of God. In his own strength, without divine grace, man cannot do good works pleasing and acceptable to God. We believe, however, man influenced and empowered by the Holy Spirit is responsible in freedom to exercise his will for good.

Article VIII.—Reconciliation Through Christ

We believe God was in Christ reconciling the world to himself. The offering Christ freely made on the cross is the perfect and sufficient sacrifice for the sins of the whole world, redeeming man from all sin, so that no other satisfaction is required.

Article IX.—Justification and Regeneration

We believe we are never accounted righteous before God through our works or merit, but that penitent sinners are justified or accounted righteous before God only by faith in our Lord Jesus Christ.

We believe regeneration is the renewal of man in righteousness through Jesus Christ, by the power of the Holy Spirit, whereby we are made partakers of the divine nature and experience newness of life. By this new birth the believer becomes reconciled to God and is enabled to serve him with the will and the affections.

We believe, although we have experienced regeneration, it is possible to depart from grace and fall into sin; and we may even then, by the grace of God, be renewed in righteousness.

Article X.—Good Works

We believe good works are the necessary fruits of faith and follow regeneration but they do not have the virtue to remove our sins or to avert divine judgment. We believe good works, pleasing and acceptable to God in Christ, spring from a true and living faith, for through and by them faith is made evident.

Article XI.—Sanctification and Christian Perfection

We believe sanctification is the work of God's grace through the Word and the Spirit, by which those who have been born again are cleansed from sin in their thoughts, words and acts, and are enabled to live in accordance with God's will, and to strive for holiness without which no one will see the Lord.

Entire sanctification is a state of perfect love, righteousness and true holiness which every regenerate believer may obtain by being delivered from the power of sin, by loving God with all the heart, soul, mind and strength, and by loving one's neighbor as one's self. Through faith in Jesus Christ this gracious gift may be received in this life both gradually and instantaneously, and should be sought earnestly by every child of God.

We believe this experience does not deliver us from the infirmities, ignorance and mistakes common to man, nor from the possibilities of further sin. The Christian must continue on guard against spiritual pride and seek to gain victory over every temptation to sin. He must respond wholly to the will of God so that sin will lose its power over him; and the world, the flesh and the devil are put under his feet. Thus he rules over these enemies with watchfulness through the power of the Holy Spirit.

Article XII.—The Judgment and the Future State

We believe all men stand under the righteous judgment of Jesus Christ, both now and in the last day. We believe in the resurrection of the dead; the righteous to life eternal and the wicked to endless condemnation.

Article XIII.—Public Worship

We believe divine worship is the duty and privilege of man who, in the presence of God, bows in adoration, humility and dedication. We believe divine worship is essential to the life of the Church, and that the assembling of the people of God for such worship is necessary to Christian fellowship and spiritual growth.

We believe the order of public worship need not be the same in all places but may be modified by the Church according to circumstances and the needs of men. It should be in a language and form understood by the people, consistent with the Holy Scriptures to the edification of all, and in accordance with the order and DISCIPLINE of the Church.

Article XIV.—The Lord's Day

We believe the Lord's Day is divinely ordained for private and public worship, for rest from unnecessary work, and should be devoted to spiritual improvement, Christian fellowship and service. It is commemorative of our Lord's resurrection and is an emblem of our eternal rest. It is essential to the permanence and growth of the Christian Church, and important to the welfare of the civil community.

Article XV.—The Christian and Property

We believe God is the owner of all things and that the individual holding of property is lawful and is a sacred trust under God. Private property is to be used for the manifestation of Christian love and liberality, and to support the Church's mission in the world. All forms of property, whether private, corporate or public, are to be held in solemn trust and used responsibly for human good under the sovereignty of God.

Article XVI.—Civil Government

We believe civil government derives its just powers from the sovereign God. As Christians we recognize the governments under whose protection we reside and believe such governments should be based on, and be responsible for, the recognition of human rights under God. We believe war and bloodshed are contrary to the gospel and spirit of Christ. We believe it is the duty of Christian citizens to give moral strength and purpose to their respective governments through sober, righteous and godly living.

¶ 95.   **THE GENERAL RULES
OF THE METHODIST CHURCH**

The Nature, Design, and General Rules of Our United Societies

In the latter end of the year 1739 eight or ten persons who appeared to be deeply convicted of sin, and earnestly groaning for redemption, came to Mr. Wesley in London. They desired, as did two or three more the next day, that he would spend some time with them in prayer, and advise them how to flee from the wrath to come, which they saw continually hanging over their heads. That he might have more time for this great work, he appointed a day when they might all come together, which from thenceforward they did every week, namely, on Thursday in the evening. To these, and as many more as desired to join with them (for their number increased daily), he gave those advices from time to time which he judged most needful for them, and they always concluded their meeting with prayer suited to their several necessities.

This was the rise of the **United Society,** first in Europe, and then in America. Such a society is no other than *"a company of men having the form and seeking the power of godliness, united in order to pray together, to receive the word of exhortation, and to watch over one another in love, that they may help each other to work out their salvation."*

That it may the more easily be discerned whether they are indeed working out their own salvation, each society is divided into smaller companies, called **classes,** according to their respective places of abode. There are about twelve persons in a class, one of whom is styled the **leader.** It is his duty,

1. To see each person in his class once a week at least, in order: (1) to inquire how his soul prospers; (2) to advise, reprove, comfort, or exhort, as occasion may require; (3) to receive what he is willing to give toward the relief of the preachers, church, and poor.

2. To meet the ministers and the stewards of the society once a week, in order: (1) to inform the minister of any that are sick, or of any that walk disorderly and will not be reproved; (2) to pay the stewards what he has received of his class in the week preceding.

There is only one condition previously required of those who desire admission into these societies—"a desire to flee from the wrath to come, and to be saved from their sins." But wherever this is really fixed in the soul it will be shown by its fruits.

It is therefore expected of all who continue therein that they shall continue to evidence their desire of salvation,

First: By doing no harm, by avoiding evil of every kind, especially that which is most generally practiced, such as:

The taking of the name of God in vain.

The profaning the day of the Lord, either by doing ordinary work therein or by buying or selling.

Drunkenness, buying or selling spirituous liquors, or drinking them, unless in cases of extreme necessity.

Slaveholding; buying or selling slaves.

Fighting, quarreling, brawling, brother going to law with brother; returning evil for evil, or railing for railing; the using of many words in buying or selling.

The buying or selling goods that have not paid the duty.

The giving or taking of things on usury—that is, unlawful interest.

Uncharitable or unprofitable conversation; particularly speaking evil of magistrates or ministers.

Doing to others as we would not they should do unto us.

Doing what we know is not for the glory of God, as:

The putting on of gold and costly apparel.

The taking of such diversions as cannot be used in the name of the Lord Jesus.

The singing those songs, or reading those books, which do not tend to the knowledge or love of God.

Softness and needless self-indulgence.

Laying up treasure upon earth.

Borrowing without a probability of paying; or taking up goods without a probability of paying for them.

It is expected of all who continue in these societies that they shall continue to evidence their desire of salvation.

Second: By doing good; by being in every kind merciful after their power; as they have opportunity, doing good of every possible sort, and, as far as possible, to all men:

To their bodies, of the ability which God giveth, by giving food to the hungry, by clothing the naked, by visiting or helping them that are sick or in prison;

To their souls, by instructing, reproving, or exhorting all we have any intercourse with; trampling under foot that enthusiastic doctrine, that "we are not to do good unless *our hearts be free to it.*"

By doing good, especially to them that are of the household of faith or groaning so to be; employing them preferably to others; buying one of another; helping each other in business; and so much the more because the world will love its own and them *only.*

By all possible diligence and frugality, that the gospel be not blamed.

By running with patience the race which is set before them, denying themselves, and taking up their cross daily; submitting to bear the reproach of Christ, to be as the filth and offscouring of the world; and looking that men should say all manner of evil of them *falsely,* for the Lord's sake.

It is expected of all who desire to continue in these societies that they shall continue to evidence their desire of salvation,

Third: By attending upon all the ordinances of God; such are:

The public worship of God.

The ministry of the Word, either read or expounded.

The Supper of the Lord.

Family and private prayer.

Searching the Scriptures.

Fasting or abstinence.

These are the General Rules of our societies; all of which we are taught of God to observe, even in his written Word, which is the only rule, and the sufficient rule, both of our faith and practice. And all these we know his Spirit writes on truly awakened hearts. If there be any among us who observes them not, who habitually breaks any of them, let it be known unto them who watch over that soul as they who must give an account. We will admonish him of the error of his ways. We will bear with him for a season. But, if then he repent not, he hath no more place among us. We have delivered our own souls.

Part III

SOCIAL PRINCIPLES

PREFACE

The Methodist Church and The Evangelical United Brethren Church, parties to the Plan of Union, have demonstrated a concern for social justice and have taken forthright positions on controversial issues involving Christian principles. John Wesley's opposition to the slave trade and to smuggling was an early expression of work for social justice. Involvement in the struggle for social justice has become an increasingly important part of the Wesleyan tradition.

The Methodist Social Creed and the Evangelical United Brethren Basic Beliefs Regarding Issues and Moral Standards are in agreement basically. The differences are largely in phraseology or emphasis.

The Methodist Social Creed was adopted in 1908 by the General Conference of The Methodist Episcopal Church (North) meeting in Baltimore. It was a prophetic landmark in the enunciation of Christian conviction on economic issues. That same year the newly formed Federal Council of Churches voted to accept a statement, The Social Ideals of the Churches, based upon it. In 1914 The Methodist Episcopal Church, South, and in 1916 The Methodist Protestant Church adopted social creeds. The Uniting Conference of these three branches in 1939 adopted a social creed.

The United Conference of the Church of the United Brethren in Christ and The Evangelical Church in 1946 endorsed a statement on social beliefs based on the position of the two uniting churches on social issues, patterned after the statements of the Federal Council of Churches.

Social statements of both The Methodist Church and The Evangelical United Brethren Church have been reviewed and revised by

52

successive General Conferences to take into account new and changing social conditions. Both churches have been responding to social changes and complexities by increasing involvement in research, education, and modes of action.

The Methodist Social Creed and the Evangelical United Brethren Basic Beliefs Regarding Social Issues and Moral Standards are important historical documents. The Plan of Union takes this into account by recording the text of each.

¶ 96.   THE METHODIST SOCIAL CREED

"We instruct those in charge of publishing the Discipline to include the Social Creed, with such revisions as may be adopted from time to time, in all future editions unless other directions are received from the General Conference." —Discipline, 1940.

I. OUR HERITAGE.—The interest of The Methodist Church in social welfare springs from the gospel, and from the labors of John Wesley, who ministered to the physical, intellectual, and social needs of the people to whom he preached the gospel of personal redemption.

In our historic position we have sought to follow Christ in bringing the whole of life, with its activities, possessions, and relationships, into conformity with the will of God.

As Methodists we have an obligation to affirm our position on social and economic questions.

II. OUR THEOLOGICAL BASIS.—The Methodist Church must view the perplexing times and problems which we face today in the light of the life and teachings of Jesus. Jesus taught us to love our neighbors and seek justice for them as well as for ourselves. To be silent in the face of need, injustice, and exploitation is to deny him.

We believe that God is Father of all peoples and races, that Jesus Christ is his Son, that all men are brothers, and that each person is of infinite worth as a child of God.

We believe that "the earth is the Lord's and the fulness thereof." Our own capacities and all we possess are gifts of the Creator, and should be held and used in stewardship to him.

We believe that God in Christ is seeking to redeem all men and also society. This redemption is a continuing necessity.

We believe that the grace of God in Christ is available for redemption from individual and social sin as we seek in penitence and obedience to do his holy will.

We believe that all persons have supreme value in the sight of God, and ought to be so regarded by us. We test all institutions and practices by their effect upon persons. Since Jesus died for the redemption of all men, we believe we should live to help save man from sin and from every influence which would harm or destroy him.

III. OUR DECLARATION OF SOCIAL CONCERN.—Applying the foregoing principles, The Methodist Church declares itself as follows:

A. *The Family.*—We seek equal rights and justice for all persons; protection of the individual and the family by high standards of morality; Christian education for marriage, parenthood, and the home; adequate housing; improved marriage and divorce laws.

We believe that the Church must be vitally concerned with the health and welfare needs of all people, first within the family, and, where necessary, through institutional care with high standards of scientific service and Christian dedication.

We believe that planned parenthood, practiced with respect for human life, fulfills rather than violates the will of God. It is the duty of each married couple prayerfully and responsibly to seek parenthood, avert it, or defer it, in accordance with the best expression of their Christian love. Families in all parts of the world should have available to them necessary information and medical assistance for birth control through public and private programs. This issue must be seen in reference to the pressing population problem now before the whole world.

We believe it is the plain responsibility of the family, as it is also the deep concern of the community, that the welfare of children whose mothers are employed outside the home be safeguarded. This responsibility includes provision for the protection, education, spiritual nurture, and wholesome recreation of every child, and for religious and educational programs which will secure these ends.

B. *Economic Life.*—1. *Christianity and the Economic Order.*—With full acknowledgment of stewardship under God and accountability to him, we stand for the acquisition of property by moral processes and the right to private ownership thereof. We refuse to identify Christianity with any economic system. We are under obligation to test each aspect of every economic order by the commands of Christ and judge its practices by the Christian gospel. We believe that it is our duty not only to bring Christ to the individual, but also to bring the increasingly technological society within which we live more nearly into conformity with the teachings of Christ. We believe that a free democratic way of life, influenced by Christian principles, can bring to mankind a society in which liberty is preserved, justice established, and brotherhood achieved.

We believe in the use of such opportunities for political action as are consistent with Christian principles. We urge Christians to view political responsibilities as an opportunity for Christian witness and service.

2. *Responsible Use of Power.*—The Christian point of view demands that concentrations of power in government, labor, business, and religious organizations be used responsibly. The task of the Church in this regard is to help people in positions of power and the organizations which they serve to achieve and exercise a high level of social responsibility.

3. *Poverty and Unemployment.*—We believe that the economic development which makes possible material plenty for all imposes upon us great moral responsibility, in that the physical and spiritual development of millions of persons throughout the world is hindered by poverty. We therefore stand for the eradication of poverty everywhere.

We believe it is our Christian duty to provide opportunities for education and training for people to earn a living for themselves and their dependents, so that they may take advantage of new technology.

Lack of significant employment tends to destroy human self-respect. We believe that employable workers must be safeguarded from enforced unemployment.

4. *Wealth.*—We recognize the perils of prosperity. Our Lord has told us that we cannot serve God and mammon. As Christians we must examine earnestly before God our personal and business practices, lest we adopt the standards and assumptions of a materialistic society. Churches and their institutions as well as individuals own property, invest funds, and employ labor. In these areas practices and relationships must conform to the highest Christian standards.

5. *Working Conditions.*—We oppose all forms of social, economic, and moral waste. We urge the protection of the worker from dangerous and unsanitary working conditions, and from occupational diseases.

We stand for reasonable hours of labor, for just wages, for a fair day's work for a fair day's wages, for just working conditions, for periods of leisure, and for an equitable division of the product of industry.

We believe special protection should be provided for women and children, as well as migrant workers and others especially vulnerable to exploitation.

6. *Social Benefits for Workers.*—We stand for public and private programs of economic security for old age, for adequate insurance covering sickness and injury to the worker, and for increased protection against those preventable conditions which produce want.

7. *The Right to Organize for Collective Bargaining.*—We stand for the right of employees and employers alike to organize for collective bargaining, protection of both in the exercise of their right, the responsibility of both to bargain in good faith, and the obligation of both to work for the public good.

8. *Town and Country Life.*—We recognize the basic significance of town and country areas in relation to population supply, natural resources, community life, and Christian culture. We believe farmers, other agriculture workers, and those displaced by mechanization should have opportunity to earn a fair income.

Methodism, because of its large town and country membership and worldwide impact, must lead in developing an adequate Christian program in rural areas everywhere. This should pertain to people in their relationship to God, to the stewardship of the soil and the conservation of all natural resources, and to family, church, and community welfare.

9. *Urban Life.*—We believe in the inner city to be a mission field crying out for bold new creative ways of witness. Here is emerging a pagan generation committed to values that run counter to those of the Christ. Therefore we call our urban congregations to a deeper involvement in neighborhood life. We call the Church to come into the city for Christ's sake, there to touch all forgotten persons with his compassion.

10. *Christian Vocation.*—We believe that every employable person so far as possible should be engaged in some vocation productive of common good. Every such vocation should be viewed as a Christian calling by those who pursue it as well as by those who receive its benefits, and our daily work should be regarded as a sphere of service to God. The creative use of leisure is also a major responsibility for the Christian.

C. *The Church and General Welfare.*—The Church is called to be a redeeming community of discerning Christian love—a fellowship of those who confess their sin, who rejoice in the love of God freely given, and who commit themselves continually to spiritual excellence in every facet of life.

1. *Alcohol Problems.*—We believe that the Christian principle of love for God and neighbor calls us to abstain from the use of alcoholic beverages and to minister to those victimized by their use. The use of beverage alcohol imperils the abundant life to which Christ calls us. This is especially true in an organized and mechanized society. Individuals and families are destroyed by its use. We join with men of good conscience who seek to overcome the social, economic, and moral waste which this indulgence has created. The Church must become a healing and redemptive fellowship for those who suffer because of beverage alcohol.

2. *Crime and Rehabilitation.*—We stand for the application of the redemptive principle in treating law offenders and for study and action directed toward the improvement of laws, correctional facilities and services, and court procedures in order to facilitate rehabilitation. For this reason we deplore capital punishment.

We do not believe an individual should be excused from his personal responsibility to society; but we recognize that crime, and in particular juvenile delinquency leading to crime, is often a result of family failure and bad social conditions. Christian citizens and churches have a special opportunity and responsibility for creating those conditions of family life and social surroundings, wholesome recreation, vocational training, personal counseling, and social adjustment by which crime may be reduced, and offenders rehabilitated and redeemed by God's grace.

3. *Gambling.*—We stand for the achievement of community and

personal standards which make unnecessary the resort to petty or commercial gambling as a recreation, escape, or producer of public or charitable revenue. As an act of faith and love, Christians should abstain from all gambling, and should participate in efforts to minister to those victimized by the practice, including compulsive gamblers.

4. *Mental Health and Medical Care.*—We stand for the provision of adequate medical care for all people, with special attention being given the aging, the young, and minority and low income groups. We strongly favor the healing ministries of the Church and other private groups. We support our government, individuals, and foundations in required research in public health; and we support legislation to meet these needs.

We believe that adequate facilities with professionally trained staff must be made available for the emotionally ill and the mentally retarded of every community. We also believe that churches may become spiritual centers of healing through worship, pastoral concern, and volunteer service for the emotionally ill.

5. *Drug Abuse.*—We seek to overcome those social and psychological forces which lead so large a part of our society to unhealthful dependence upon tobacco, alcohol, and drugs. The illicit traffic in drugs cannot be tolerated. Society must provide through public and private facilities for the treatment, rehabilitation, and after-care of narcotic addicts and other victims of drug abuse.

6. *Sex in Christian Life.*—We believe that sexual intercourse within holy matrimony with fidelity and love is a sacred experience and constitutes a needed expression of affection. We also believe that sexual intercourse outside the bonds of matrimony is contrary to the will of God. The outrageous exploitation of the strong forces underlying sexual experience is a destructive element of our culture. It not only distorts the meaning of sex experience but constitutes a blasphemous disregard of God's purpose for men and women. A case in point is the distribution of hard-core pornographic and other sex-exploitive material. We advocate thorough educational efforts in home, church, and school designed to elevate our whole understanding of the meaning of sexual experience.

7. *Social Welfare.*—We believe that meeting human need is both a private and a community responsibility. Adequate public assistance

should be made available to all persons solely on the basis of need. Every individual should provide for his own needs and share responsibility for the needs of others to the full extent of his ability, but we believe that no person in an affluent society should be demoralized because of unmet need.

D. *Human Rights.*—1. *Freedom from Discrimination.*—We stand for equal rights for all racial, cultural, and religious groups, and insist that the principles set forth in this creed apply to all alike. The right to choose a home, enter a school, secure employment, vote, and have access to public accommodations should be guaranteed to all regardless of race, culture, national origin, social class, or religion. Neither should any person be denied equal political, economic, or legal rights or opportunities because of sex.

That the Church should ever refuse access to worship or membership in its fellowship to any person because of race, color, or national origin is contrary to our fundamental Christian convictions.

2. *Civil Liberties and Civil Rights.*—We stand for freedom of speech, assembly, and press and broadcasting. The fundamental responsibility in the use of these freedoms and the justification of their exercise is adherence to the truth.

We stand for the right of all individuals and groups to advocate any peaceful and constitutional method for the solution of the problems that confront society.

E. *Peace and World Order.*—We believe that Christianity cannot be nationalistic; it must be universal in its outlook and appeal. The influence of the Church must always be on the side of every effort seeking to remove those conditions of heart and mind, of social, economic, and international injustice, and of ideological conflict in which wars begin.

We must actively and constantly create the conditions of peace. We stand for the promotion of understanding, reconciliation, and good will; the relief of suffering, the lifting of living standards around the world; concern for the freedom and welfare of dependent and subject persons; the removal of racial tensions; the taking of steps toward disarmament; and the support of patient negotiations.

1. *International Organization.*—We believe that the United Nations is a working center of international cooperation which provides

the most hopeful avenue leading to peace and world order. The United Nations with its related agencies should be strengthened through governmental cooperation and support. This effort deserves the support of all Christians. The Church itself, as a world fellowship, makes an important contribution to the development of world order.

2. *The Christian and Military Service.*—The Methodist Church, true to the principles of the New Testament, teaches respect for properly constituted civil authority. It encourages both love of country and love of all men. Believing that government rests upon the support of its conscientious citizens, it holds within its fellowship those who sincerely differ as to the Christian's duty in regard to military service. We ask and claim exemption by legal processes from all forms of military preparation or service for all religious conscientious objectors, as for those of the historic peace churches. We recognize the right of the individual to answer the call of his government according to the dictates of his Christian conscience. We also recognize that non-violent resistance can be a valid form of Christian witness. In all of these situations members of The Methodist Church have the authority and support of their Church.[3]

IV. OUR MANDATE: READ, STUDY, APPLY.—We recommend that this Social Creed be presented to our congregations orally or in printed form at least once a year, and that frequent references be made to it. Every local church shall encourage the study of the Social Creed and seek to apply its principles.

¶ 97. BASIC BELIEFS REGARDING SOCIAL ISSUES AND MORAL STANDARDS OF THE EVANGELICAL UNITED BRETHREN CHURCH

The Church from its beginning has believed in social welfare and moral reform, and has labored to bring the whole of life with all its activities, possessions and relationships into conformity with the will of God. The Church is persuaded that in Jesus Christ alone are to be found the cure for industrial, economic and social ills, and salvation

---

[3] *See* Judicial Council Decision 25.

from the sins that beset and curse society and block its progress.

The Church, therefore, is convinced that it should minister to the physical, intellectual and social needs of those to whom it preaches the gospel of personal redemption, and should guide them in an intelligent and faithful endeavor to improve human conditions and to Christianize every area of human life. The Church should cooperate with worthy movements in the community, nation and world for physical development, intellectual growth, social betterment and spiritual enrichment.

Church and Economic Life

Economic Order.—The Church advocates equal rights and justice for all men in all stations of life; the protection of the family; the fullest possible development and protection of childhood; pensions for the aged; the conservation of health; the elimination of poverty; the equitable distribution of the products of agriculture and of industry; the abolishment of unemployment; a living wage in every vocation and economic justice to all; release from employment for every person of at least one day in seven; such conditions of labor and relationship between employer and employee as will guarantee common justice and social security, and the full acknowledgement of rights and responsibilities on the part of both employers and employees in terms of human welfare. The Church advocates simple, just, honest, unselfish and spiritual living, and stands not for an aristocracy of wealth, power and position, but for an aristocracy of character, culture and service.

Community Life

Amusements.—All members of the Church are urged to refrain from patronizing any entertainment or place of amusement that is not above reproach, and from any diversion that cannot be practiced in the name of Christ. Strict censorship of motion pictures in order to protect society from evident evils is advocated.

Citizenship.—The Church believes that every Christian is obligated to respect, support and obey properly constituted civil authority, and faithfully perform his civic duties, and, through sober, righteous and godly living, give moral strength and purpose to his country. The Church declares its devotion to the nation and pledges its loyalty to the government under whose protection it resides, and offers unceasing prayers for those in rightful authority, that there may be that justice, righteousness, freedom and tranquility which are the people's most precious possessions.

Stewardship of Time.—The Church believes in the proper use of time. The waste and misuse of idle hours, and the exploitation of leisure by selfish and unprincipled interests, obligate every church to provide wholesome activities, and to cooperate with others in presenting opportunities for the wise and constructive use of otherwise unoccupied time through worship, music, reading, study, fellowship, recreation and service activities.

The Lord's Day.—The Lord's Day is ordained of God for rest from labor, spiritual improvement and kingdom extension. The perpetuity of civil liberties and religious institutions demands its proper observance. The Church is concerned with the growing tendency toward the commercialization of Sunday and the growing apathy toward attendance upon the worship services of the Church. Sunday is a hallowed day commemorating our Lord's resurrection. By worship, fellowship and Christian service we glorify our risen Lord. The Church calls for the voluntary closing of all nonessential commercial enterprises on Sunday, refraining from unnecessary labor and worldly pleasures, and urges its members to do good to others and engage in those things which contribute to spiritual growth.

Family Life

Marriage.—Marriage is an institution of divine appointment, upon the proper establishment of which are conditioned human happiness and well-being and the maintenance of the most important factor of civilization—the Christian home. Virtue and morality in society, stability and permanence of free government can be had only as the Christian home is maintained in its integrity.

In view of the gravity of the interests involved in marriage, the Church admonishes all young people as follows:

(1) To cherish only worthy and ennobling thoughts on the subject of courtship and marriage.

(2) To avoid undue haste, and practice intelligent deliberation in every step pertaining to this matter.

(3) To enter into marriage only after a favorable personal acquaintanceship sufficient to insure compatibility and the blessings of a Christian home, and to do so only when it can be "in the Lord" (I Cor. 7:39) and thus avoid being "mismated with unbelievers" (II Cor. 6:14) in life's most intimate relationship.

Divorce.—Since marriage is of divine appointment and the union of one man and one woman entered into mutually, it is sacred and morally binding so long as both shall live and ought not be dissolved at will. When human failure results in placing the marriage in jeopardy, the Church strongly urges the persons involved to seek counsel with their minister in order to effect reconciliation so that the marriage may be preserved. The Church does not sanction nor condone divorce except on the ground of adultery.

Ministers of the Church shall not solemnize any marriage without first counseling earnestly with the couple. Whenever divorced persons seek marriage through the Church, ministers may solemnize such marriages *only* after having ascertained the circumstances through counsel with those persons involved, and after they are satisfied that the divorced persons have sought for and received forgiveness and are seeking a genuine Christian relationship not only in marriage but with God. Ministers may, if it seems desirable, consult with fellow ministers and/or local church officials.

Responsible Parenthood.—The result of a rising birthrate, the decrease of infant mortality, the increase in longevity and improved general health have created the increasing world population. To meet this situation, the Church affirms: (1) that the members uphold the highest standards of love and marriage and urgently teach young people to sanctify marital relationships; (2) that the parents assume the responsibility of planning at long range the family they hope to establish, and plan wisely the spacing of children and provide moral guidance and spiritual nurture for all members of the family; and (3) that the married persons regard as ethically and morally right the proper use of methods and techniques, medically approved, for the purpose of achieving planned and responsible parenthood.

Literature.—The Church views with alarm the widespread circulation and reading of salacious literature giving false and degrading views of life, polluting the mind and undermining character. The Church urges its members to do all in their power to remove such harmful literature from the homes, libraries and newsstands of their communities. Furthermore, the Church urges its members to procure literature that is clean, inspiring and productive of Christian character. Wholesome literature that meets the demand for information, adventure and romance should be furnished. An ample supply of denominational periodicals and books should be found in every home and church.

Moral and Social Conduct

Alcoholic Beverages.—Science and human experience agree in condemning alcoholic beverages as useless, damaging and injurious.

The manufacturing and vending of alcoholic liquors are contrary to the best interests of personal and social morality, economy and welfare. Voluntary total abstinence from all intoxicants is the true ground of personal temperance, and complete legal prohibition of the traffic in alcoholic beverages is the duty of civil government.

The manufacture, sale and use of intoxicating liquors as beverage, the renting and leasing of property to be used for the manufacture or sale of such liquors, the signing of petitions for granting license, or the entering as bondsmen for persons engaged in the traffic in intoxicating liquors, are strictly prohibited.[4]

Narcotics.—The Church is strongly opposed to the illegal use of habit-forming drugs since the use of, or participation in the illegal traffic of habit-forming drugs, unless medically prescribed, is strictly prohibited. Members of the Church are urged to make every effort possible to combat this menace to society.

Tobacco.—The Church believes that the use of tobacco in any

---

[4] This law has been in effect since the earliest days of the Church of the United Brethren in Christ, and of The Evangelical Church.

form is injurious and a needless waste of money which could and should be otherwise applied. All members of the Church are urged to abstain from its use.

Gambling.—Gambling is a menace to society, destructive of good government and deadly to the best interests of moral, social and spiritual life. All members of the Church are expected to abstain from gambling in any form.

Temperance.—Temperance, in its wider meaning, is a Christian virtue, enjoined by the Holy Scriptures, and implies control of all emotions, passions and appetites. It means the proper use of wholesome food and drink, and the entire abstinence from such that are known to be harmful.

Racial and Cultural Relations

Human Relations.—The Church respects human personality which is inherent in every race, nation and creed. We believe that the Bible teaches that there is no basis whatsoever for a belief in the superiority or inferiority of any people. Therefore, the Church protests against all acts and practices of discrimination which are based upon racial, national, creedal or social differences. "He made from one, every nation of men to live on all the face of the earth." (Acts 17:26.)

The Church, following the example of Jesus Christ, upholds the rights and privileges of every individual as clearly defined in the Bible. The Church calls upon all her members to commit their attitudes, their actions and their influences in faithful witness to this fact. The Church opposes segregation which is based upon differences of racial or national origin as a sin against God and man. The Church must continually examine her teachings and practices to be certain that no violations of human rights are being committed within her fellowship or by the Church toward the world. The Church must motivate, inspire and encourage the establishing of fair practices, legislation and law enforcement which are in harmony with the gospel as revealed in Jesus Christ. Christian people, under the leadership of the Church, must work for the establishing of equal opportunities for employment, education, housing, public accommodation and other privileges of citizenship, and must cooperate with other organizations which seek these ends, so that in harmony with the spirit and teachings of Jesus, men may live together in love and fellowship.

Slavery.—The Church regards the traffic in human beings and the institution of slavery as infamous evils, and therefore all slavery, in every sense of the word, is totally prohibited and shall in no way be tolerated by the Church.

World Order

War and Peace.—The Church believes that war and bloodshed are contrary to the Christian conception of human welfare and violate the basic principles of universal brotherhood, and therefore are not compatible with the gospel and spirit of Christ. The Church also believes that a warless world is the ideal toward which all men and all nations should strive; that such an order is possible if men will follow the way of him who is the Prince of Peace; and that it is therefore the duty of every Christian to promote peace and good will, and to foster the spirit of understanding, mutual trust and cooperation among all the peoples and nations of the world. God alone is the Lord of the conscience. Therefore, the Church recognizes the right of the individual member to answer the call of his government according to the dictates of his conscience and his sense of duty. It also recognizes the right of those who for the sake of conscience feel they cannot participate in war in any sense whatsoever.

International Relations.—The Church is convinced that the welfare of the human family is best secured by an honest recognition of the interdependence of the nations and the races of all the world, and that international and interracial cooperation is obligatory upon every nation and people in order that there may be common understanding among all and security for all.

Part IV

ORGANIZATION
AND ADMINISTRATION

Chapter One
THE LOCAL CHURCH

Section I. The Pastoral Charge.

¶ **101. A local church** is a community of true believers under the Lordship of Christ. It is the redemptive fellowship in which the Word of God is preached by men divinely called, and the Sacraments are duly administered according to Christ's own appointment. Under the discipline of the Holy Spirit the Church exists for the maintenance of worship, the edification of believers, and the redemption of the world.

¶ **102.** The Church of Jesus Christ exists in and for the world. It is primarily at the level of the local church that the Church encounters the world. The local church is a strategic base from which Christians move out to the structures of society.

¶ **103.** The local church is a connectional society of persons who have professed their faith in Christ, have been baptized, have assumed the vows of membership in The United Methodist Church, and are associated in fellowship as a local United Methodist church "in order that they may hear the word of God, receive the Sacraments, and carry forward the work which Christ has committed to his Church." Such a society of believers, being within The United Methodist Church and subject to its Discipline, is also an inherent part of the Church Universal, which is composed of all who accept Jesus Christ as Lord and

67

Savior, and which in the Apostles' Creed we declare to be the holy catholic Church.

¶ **104.** In order that each local church may be an effective connectional unit in The United Methodist Church, it shall be the duty of all district superintendents and pastors to organize and administer the charges and churches committed to their care in accordance with the plan hereinafter set forth.

Where size, circumstances, and specific mission responsibilities demand, a local church may in consultation with and approval by the district superintendent modify the organizational plans hereinafter set forth; *provided* that adequate provisions shall be made in such an organizational plan for relating the local church structures to appropriate district, Annual Conference, jurisdictional, and general church agencies and structures.

¶ **105.** Each local church shall have a definite membership and evangelistic responsibility. It shall be responsible for ministering to all its members, wherever they live, and for persons who choose it as their church.

¶ **106.** 1. **A pastoral charge** shall consist of one or more churches which are organized under, and subject to, the Discipline of The United Methodist Church, with a Charge Conference, and to which a minister is or may be duly appointed or appointable as pastor in charge.

2. A pastoral charge of two or more churches may be designated **a circuit.**

3. A **parish** shall be identified as an area of service with the membership and constituency of one or more local churches having a coordinated program and organization to fulfill a ministry directed to all the people of the area. It may include local churches of other denominations.

Section II. Church Membership.

¶ **107.** The United Methodist Church, a fellowship of believers, is a part of the Church Universal. Therefore all persons, without regard to race, color, national origin, or economic condition, shall be eligible to attend its worship services, to participate in its programs, and, when they take the appropriate vows, to be admitted into its membership in any local church in the connection.

¶ 108. The membership of a local United Methodist church shall include all baptized persons who have come into membership by confession of faith or transfer and whose names have not been removed from the membership rolls by reason of death, transfer, withdrawal, or removal for cause. (*See* ¶¶ 129, 131, 135-41.)

¶ 109. A member of any local United Methodist church is a member of the total United Methodist connection.

Section III. The Meaning of Membership.

¶ 110. When persons unite with a local United Methodist church, they profess their faith in God, the Father Almighty, maker of heaven and earth, and in Jesus Christ his only Son, and in the Holy Spirit. They covenant together with God and with the members of the local church to keep the vows which are a part of the order of confirmation and reception into the Church:

1. To confess Jesus Christ as Lord and Savior and pledge their allegiance to his kingdom,

2. To receive and profess the Christian faith as contained in the Scriptures of the Old and New Testaments,

3. To promise according to the grace given them to live a Christian life and always remain faithful members of Christ's holy Church,

4. And to be loyal to The United Methodist Church and uphold it by their prayers, their presence, their gifts, and their service.

¶ 111. Faithful membership in the local church is essential for personal growth and for developing an increasing sensitivity to the will and grace of God. As a member involves himself in private and public prayer, worship, the Sacraments, study, Christian action, systematic giving, and holy discipline, he grows in his appreciation of Christ, his understanding of God at work in history and the natural order, and an understanding of himself.

¶ 112. Faithful participation in the corporate life of the congregation is an obligation of the Christian to his fellow members of the Body of Christ. A member is bound in sacred covenant to shoulder the burdens, share the risks, and celebrate the joys of his fellow members.

He is called to speak the truth in love, always ready to confront conflict in the spirit of forgiveness and reconciliation.

¶ **113.** A member of The United Methodist Church is to be a servant of Christ on mission in the local and worldwide community. This servanthood is performed in his family life, daily work, recreation and social activities, responsible citizenship, the issues of his corporate life, and all his attitudes toward his fellowmen. Participation in disciplined groups is an expected part of his mission involvement. He is called upon to be a witness for Christ in the world, a light and leaven in society, and a reconciler in a culture of conflict. He is to identify himself with the agony and suffering of the world and to radiate and exemplify the Christ of hope. The standards of attitude and conduct set forth in the social principles (¶¶ 96-97) should be considered as an essential resource for guiding each member of the Church in being a servant of Christ on mission.

¶ **114.** Should any member give evidence of a lack of commitment to the faith, it shall be the responsibility of the local church, working through its Council on Ministries, to minister to him to the end that he may reaffirm his faith and his commitment to the Church and its ministry of loving service.

Section IV.   Admission into the Church.

¶ **115. 1.** All persons seeking to be saved from their sins and sincerely desiring to be Christian in faith and practice are proper candidates for full membership in The United Methodist Church. When such persons offer themselves for membership, it shall be the duty of the pastor, or of proper persons appointed by him, to instruct them in the meaning of the Christian faith and the history, organization, and teaching of The United Methodist Church, using materials approved by The United Methodist Church to explain to them the baptismal and membership vows, and to lead them to commit themselves to Jesus Christ as Lord and Savior. When they shall have confessed their faith in Christ and have made known their desire to assume the obligations and become faithful members of The United Methodist Church, after the completion of a reasonable period of training, and after the Sacrament of Baptism has been administered to those who have not been previously baptized, he shall bring them before the congregation, administer the vows, receive them into the fellowship of the Church, and duly enroll them as full members.

2. Membership training is a lifelong process and is carried on through all the activities which may have educational value. The instruction for which the pastor is specifically responsible is confirmation preparation and is a part of the fuller work of membership training. Confirmation preparation focuses attention upon the meaning of full membership and the need for church members to be in mission in all of life's relationships.

3. Preparation for the experience of confirmation shall be provided for all candidates for full membership, including adults, but youth who are completing the sixth grade shall normally be the youngest persons recruited for confirmation preparation and full membership. When younger persons, of their own volition, seek enrollment in confirmation preparation, such preparation shall be at the discretion of the pastor.

4. Persons in preparation for full membership make up the preparatory roll of the church. All baptized children shall be listed on the preparatory membership roll, and other persons who have declared their interest in church membership and have been enrolled in confirmation preparation may be listed as preparatory members pending completion of the confirmation preparation and actual reception into full membership of the Church. (*See also* ¶¶ 122, 131.2.)

¶ 116. A duly authorized minister of The United Methodist Church while serving as chaplain of any organization, institution, or military unit, or as a campus pastor, or while otherwise present where a local church is not available, may receive a person into the membership of The United Methodist Church when such person shall have confessed his faith in Christ and made known his desire to assume the obligations and become a faithful member of the Church. After the vows of membership have been administered, such minister shall issue a statement of membership to the local church of the choice of the person concerned, and the pastor thereof on receiving such statement shall duly enroll him as a member.

¶ 117. When a person in military service or a member of the family of such person is baptized and/or received into the Church by a chaplain and has no local church to which the membership and records may be sent, the chaplain shall send the name, address, and related facts to the General Board of Evangelism for recording on the general roll of military service personnel and families. It is desirable that as soon as possible these persons be transferred to a local United Methodist church of their choice.

¶ **118.** Any candidate for church membership who for good reason is unable to appear before the congregation may, at the discretion of the pastor, be received elsewhere in accordance with the Ritual of The United Methodist Church. In any such case lay members should be present to represent the congregation. Names of such persons shall be placed on the church roll, and announcement of their reception shall be made to the congregation.

¶ **119.** A member in good standing in any Christian denomination who has been baptized and who desires to unite with The United Methodist Church may be received into membership by a proper certificate of transfer from his former church, or by his own declaration of Christian faith, and upon affirming his willingness to be loyal to The United Methodist Church. The pastor will report to the sending church the date of reception of such a member. It is recommended that instruction in the faith and work of the Church be provided for all such persons. Persons received from churches which do not issue certificates of transfer or letters of recommendation shall be listed as "Received from other denominations."

Section V. Children and the Church.

¶ **120.** Because the redeeming love of God, revealed in Jesus Christ, extends to all persons and because Jesus explicitly included the children in his kingdom, the pastor of each charge shall earnestly exhort all Christian parents or guardians to present their children to the Lord in Baptism at an early age. Before Baptism is administered, he shall diligently instruct the parents or guardians regarding the meaning of this Sacrament and the vows which they assume. It is expected of parents or guardians who present their children for Baptism that they shall use all diligence in bringing them up in conformity to the Word of God and in the fellowship of the Church. It is desired that one or both parents or guardians shall be members of a Christian church or that sponsors who are members shall assume the baptismal vows. They shall be admonished of this obligation and be earnestly exhorted to faithfulness therein. At the time of Baptism they shall be informed that the Church, with its church-school program, will aid them in the Christian nurture of their children.

¶ 121. The pastor of the church shall, at the time of administering the Sacrament of Baptism, furnish the parents or guardians of the child who is baptized with a **certificate of Baptism**, which shall also clearly state that the child is now enrolled as a preparatory member in The United Methodist Church. He shall also admonish members of the congregation of their responsibility for the Christian nurture of the child. The pastor shall add the full name of the baptized child to the preparatory membership roll of the church.

¶ 122. The pastor shall keep and transmit to his successor an accurate register of the names of all baptized children in his charge, including both those who have been baptized there and those who have been baptized elsewhere. This register of baptized or dedicated children, along with a list of other preparatory members (¶115.4) shall constitute the preparatory membership roll of the church. It shall give the full name of the child, the date of birth, the date and place of Baptism, and the names of the parents or guardians and their place of residence.

¶ 123. All baptized children under the care of a United Methodist church shall be retained as preparatory members in the church until this status is terminated by: confirmation and reception into full membership after a proper course of training both in the church school and in the pastor's class, transfer with their families to another United Methodist church, transfer with their families to a church of another Christian denomination, death, withdrawal, or transfer to the constituency roll of the church at the age of sixteen. The preparatory membership roll shall be corrected each year by adding and subtracting the names received and removed during the year, using the forms provided for this purpose.

¶ **124.** It shall be the duty of the pastor, the parents or guardians, and the officers and teachers of the church school to provide training for the children of the church throughout their childhood that will lead to an understanding of the Christian faith, to an appreciation of the privileges and obligations of church membership, and to a personal commitment to Jesus Christ as Lord and Savior. The pastor shall, at least annually, building on the preparation which boys and girls have received throughout their childhood, organize into classes for confirmation the youth who, preferably, are completing the sixth grade. He shall base his instruction on materials which the boys and girls have already used and on other resources produced by The United Methodist Church for the purpose of confirmation preparation. Wherever boys and girls so prepared shall give evidence of their own Christian faith and purpose and understanding of the privileges and obligations of church membership, they may be received into full membership.

Section VI. Youth.

¶ **125.** It is strongly recommended that each local church offer for senior high youth who are members of the Church an advanced class of instruction in the meaning of the Christian life and church membership. It is further recommended that this course, taught by the pastor, emphasize the doctrines of The United Methodist Church and the nature and mission of the Church, leading to continued growth in the knowledge, grace, and service of our Lord Jesus Christ.

Section VII. Affiliate and Associate Membership.

¶ **126.** A member of The United Methodist Church, residing for an extended period in a city or community at a distance from his home church, may on his request be enrolled as an **affiliate member** of a United Methodist church located in the vicinity of his temporary residence. His home pastor shall be notified of his affiliate membership. Such membership shall entitle him to the fellowship of that church, to its pastoral care and oversight, and to participation in its activities, including the holding of office, but he shall be counted and reported only as a member of his home church. A member of another denomination may become an **associate member** under the same conditions.

74

Section VIII.   Care of Members.

¶ **127.** The local church shall endeavor to enlist each member in activities for spiritual growth and in participation in the services and ministries of the Church and its organizations. It shall be the duty of the pastor and of the Council on Ministries by regular visitation, care, and spiritual oversight, to provide necessary activities and opportunities for spiritual growth through individual and family worship and individual and group study, and to aid continually the members to keep their vows to uphold the Church by attendance, prayers, gifts, and service. The Church has a moral and spiritual obligation to nurture its nonparticipating and indifferent members and to lead them into a full and active church relationship.

¶ **128.** The pastor in cooperation with the Council on Ministries may arrange the membership in groups—with a leader for each group —designed to involve the membership of the church in its ministry to the community. These groups shall be of such size, usually not larger than eight or ten families, as to be convenient and effective for service. Such groups may be especially helpful in evangelistic outreach by contacting newcomers and unreached persons, by visitation, by holding prayer meetings in the homes, by distributing Christian literature, and by other means. Nonresident members should constitute a special group to be served by correspondence. The groups shall be formed and the leaders appointed by the Council on Ministries upon recommendation of the minister.

¶ **129.** While primary responsibility and initiative rests with each individual member faithfully to perform the vows of membership which he has solemnly assumed, if he should be neglectful of that responsibility, these procedures shall be followed:

1. If a member residing in the community is negligent of his vows, or regularly absents himself from the worship of the church without valid reason, the pastor and the membership secretary shall report his name to the Council on Ministries which shall do all in its power to reenlist him in the active fellowship of the Church. It shall visit him and make clear to him that, while his name is on the roll of his particular local church, he is a member of The United Methodist Church as a whole, and that, since he is not attending the church where his name

is enrolled, he is requested to do one of three things: (*a*) renew his vows and become a regular worshiper in the church where his name is recorded, (*b*) request transfer to another United Methodist church where he will be a regular worshiper, or (*c*) arrange transfer to a particular church of another denomination. If the member does not comply with any of the available alternatives over a period of three years, his name may be removed. (*See* § 4.)

2. If a member whose address is known is residing outside the community and is not participating in the worship or activity of the church, the directives to encourage him to transfer his membership shall be followed each year until he joins another church or requests in writing that his name be removed from the membership roll; *provided,* however, that if after three years the committee has not been able to relate him to the church at his new place of residence, his name may be removed by the procedure of § 4 below.

3. If the address of a member is no longer known to the pastor, the membership secretary and the evangelism work area chairman or the Commission on Evangelism shall make every effort to locate him, including listing his name in the church bulletin, circularizing it throughout the parish, and reading it from the pulpit. If he can be located, the directives of either § 1 or § 2 above shall be followed, but if after three years of such efforts his address is still unknown, his name may be removed from the membership roll by the procedure of § 4 below.

4. If the directives of §§ 1, 2, or 3 above have been followed for the specified number of years without success, the member's name may be removed from the membership roll by vote of the Charge Conference on recommendation of the pastor and the evangelism work area chairman or the Commission on Evangelism, each name being considered individually. On the roll there shall be entered after his name: "Removed by order of the Charge Conference"; and if the action is on the basis of § 3, there shall be added: "Reason: address unknown." The membership of the person shall thereby be terminated, and the record thereof shall be retained.

5. Recognizing that the Church has a continuing moral and spiritual obligation to nurture all persons, even those whose names have been removed from the membership roll, it is recommended that a roll

of persons thus removed shall be maintained. It shall then become the responsibility of the Council on Ministries to provide for the review of this roll at least once a year. (*See also* ¶ 134.) After the review has been made, it is recommended that the pastor and/or the commission contact those whose names appear on this roll, either in person or by other means, in the most effective and practical manner. The names and addresses of those who have moved outside the local church's area should be sent to local churches in their new communities, that those churches may visit and minister to them.

¶ 130. If a local church is discontinued, the district superintendent shall select another United Methodist church and transfer its members thereto, or to such other churches as the members may select.

Section IX.   Membership Records and Reports.

¶ 131. Each local church shall accurately maintain the following membership rolls:

1. **Full Membership Roll** (¶ 108).

2. **Preparatory Membership Roll** (¶ 115.4), containing the names and pertinent information of baptized or dedicated children and youth of the church sixteen years of age and under who are not full members.

3. **Members Removed by Charge Conference Action** (¶ 129.4).

4. **Constituency Roll,** containing the names and addresses of such persons as are not members of the church concerned, including unbaptized children, dedicated children, church school members not yet members of the church, preparatory members who have reached the age of sixteen who have not been received into full membership, and other nonmembers for whom the local church has pastoral responsibility.

5. **Affiliate Membership Roll** (¶ 126).

6. **Associate Membership Roll** (¶ 126).

¶ 132. The pastor shall report to each Charge Conference the names of persons received into the membership of the church or churches of the pastoral charge since the Charge Conference preceding and the names of persons whose membership in the church or churches of the pastoral charge has been terminated during the same period, indicating in the case of each how he was received or how his membership was terminated during the same period, indicating in the case of each how he was received or how his membership was terminated. The Council on Ministries shall appoint a committee to audit the membership rolls, submitting the report annually to the Charge Conference.

¶ **133.** The basic membership records in each local church shall consist of: a permanent church register and a card index or loose-leaf book.

1. The **permanent church register** shall be a bound volume of durable material prepared by The Methodist Publishing House in the form approved by the Council on World Service and Finance. The names shall be recorded chronologically as each person is received into the fellowship of that church, and without reference to alphabetical order. The names shall be numbered in regular numerical order, and the number of each shall appear on the corresponding card or page in the card index or loose-leaf membership roll.

2. The **card index or loose-leaf membership record** shall be kept on a form approved by the Council on World Service and Finance. This record of membership shall be filed in alphabetical order and shall show the number appearing opposite each name on the permanent register. The pastor shall report annually to the Annual Conference the total membership of the charge as shown on the membership records.

¶ **134.** The **membership secretary** shall, under the direction of the pastor, keep accurate records of all membership rolls and report regularly to the Council on Ministries.

Section X. Transfer and Termination of Membership.

¶ **135.** Membership in a local church may be terminated by death, transfer, withdrawal, expulsion, or action of the Charge Conference. It shall be the duty of the pastor of the charge or of the membership secretary to keep an accurate record of all terminations of membership and to report to each Charge Conference the names of all persons whose membership has been terminated since the conference preceding, in each instance indicating the reason for such termination.

¶ **136.** If a member of a United Methodist church shall change his place of residence to another community so far removed from his home church that he cannot participate regularly in its worship and activity, he shall be encouraged to transfer his membership to a United Methodist church in the community of his newly established residence. As soon as his pastor is reliably informed of his change of residence, actual or contemplated, it shall be the pastor's duty and obligation to assist him to establish himself in the fellowship of a church in the community of his future home and to send to a United Methodist pastor in such community, or to the district superintendent, or (if neither is known) to the General Board of Evangelism, a letter of notification, giving the latest known address of the person or persons concerned and requesting local pastoral oversight.

¶ 137. When a pastor discovers a member of The United Methodist Church residing in his community whose membership is in a church so far removed from his place of residence that he cannot participate regularly in its worship and activity, it shall be his duty and obligation to give pastoral oversight to such person and to encourage him to transfer his membership to a United Methodist church in the community where he resides.

¶ 138. When a pastor receives a request for a transfer of membership from the pastor of another United Methodist church, he shall send the proper certificate directly to the pastor of the United Methodist church to which the member is transferring, or if there is no pastor, to the district superintendent. On receipt of such a **certificate of transfer**, the pastor or district superintendent shall enroll the name of the person so transferring after public reception in a regular service of worship, or if circumstances demand, public announcement in such a service. He shall then notify the pastor of the church issuing the certificate whereupon the pastor of the said church shall remove the member from the roll of the church from which he has transferred.

Certificates of transfer shall be accompanied by two blanks, one to be sent to the member by the pastor who transfers his membership, the other to be sent to the former pastor by the pastor who receives the transferred member.

In case the transfer is not made effective, the pastor shall return the certificate to the pastor of the sending church.

¶ 139. A pastor upon receiving a request from a member of his church to transfer to a church of another denomination, or upon receiving such request from a pastor or duly authorized official of another denomination, shall (with the approval of the member) issue a certificate of transfer and, upon receiving confirmation of said member's reception into another congregation, shall properly record the transfer of such person on the membership roll of the local church; and his membership shall thereby be terminated. For the transfer of a member of The United Methodist Church to a church of another denomination, forms shall be used, with the substitution of the name of the other denomination for the words "United Methodist."

¶ 140. If a pastor is informed that a member of his church has without notice united with a church of another denomination, he shall make diligent inquiry, and if the report is confirmed, he shall enter "Withdrawn" after the person's name on the membership roll and shall report the same to the next Charge Conference.

¶ 141. If a member proposes to withdraw from The United Methodist Church, he shall communicate his purpose in writing to the pastor of the local church in which his membership is held. On receiving such notice of withdrawal, the pastor shall properly record the fact of withdrawal on the membership roll. If requested, the pastor shall give a statement of withdrawal to such member.

Section XI. The Method of Organizing a New Local Church.

¶ 142. 1. **A new local church or mission** shall be established only with the consent of the bishop in charge and his Cabinet, and with due consideration of the conference Board of Missions' programs of home missions and church extension. The bishop shall designate the district within whose bounds the church shall be organized, and the district superintendent of that district shall be the agent in charge of the project. He shall recommend to the district Board of Church Location and Building the site for the proposed new congregation. If there is a city or district missionary society, that body shall also be asked to approve this site.

2. The district superintendent shall call the persons interested in the proposed church to meet at an appointed time and place, or he

may by written authorization designate any pastor in his district to call such a meeting.

3. The district superintendent or the pastor holding authority from him shall preside and shall appoint a secretary to keep a record of the meeting. Following a period of worship, opportunity shall be given those in attendance to present themselves for membership by proper certificates of transfer. Pastors issuing such certificates to a church not yet organized shall describe therein the proposed new church to which it is issued, as, for instance, "the proposed new church on Boston Avenue."

4. Persons desiring to become members on profession of their faith in Christ shall also be given opportunity to present themselves for membership. When the presiding minister is satisfied as to the genuineness of their faith and purpose, they shall be received into the membership of the Church.

5. A list shall be made of all the persons received into the membership of the proposed church, by transfer and on profession. Those persons in the membership eighteen years of age and over shall be members of the **Constituting Church Conference,** and each shall be entitled to vote.

6. The Constituting Church Conference shall then be called to order, and it shall proceed to choose the elective stewards of the church on nomination of a committee on nominations. Such committee shall be appointed by the presiding minister or elected on nomination from the floor, as the conference may determine. In either case the presiding minister shall be chairman. When the elective stewards have been chosen in proper number, the presiding minister shall declare the church properly constituted.

7. He shall then adjourn the Constituting Church Conference and call to order the Charge Conference of the pastoral charge. The membership of the Charge Conference shall be those newly elected and any others entitled to membership. The Charge Conference shall then elect such officers of the church as the Discipline requires, including trustees of church property, and shall set up commissions and committees as provided in the Discipline. When such officers have been duly elected and the proper commissions and committees constituted, the church is duly organized, and from this point its work shall proceed as described

in the Discipline; *provided* that when a newly organized church is attached to a circuit, the Charge Conference shall not be held until such time as representatives from all the churches of the charge can be properly assembled for that purpose.

8. The Charge Conference may take action at its discretion, authorizing and directing the newly elected trustees to incorporate the newly organized church in accordance with local laws and the provisions of the Discipline.

Section XII. Protection of Rights of Congregations.

¶ 143. Nothing in the Plan and Basis of Union at any time after the union is to be construed so as to require any local church of the former Church of the United Brethren in Christ, or of the former The Evangelical Church, or of the former The Evangelical United Brethren Church, or of the former The Methodist Church to alienate or in any way to change the title to property contained in its deed or deeds at the time of union; and lapse of time or usage shall not affect said title or control.

Section XIII. The Charge Conference.

¶ 144. *General Provisions.*—1. Within the pastoral charge the **Charge Conference** is the basic unit in the connectional system of The United Methodist Church. The Charge Conference shall therefore be organized from the church or churches in every pastoral charge as set forth in the Constitution (¶ 48). It shall meet annually for the purposes set forth in ¶ 145. It may meet at other times as indicated in § 6 below.

2. The membership of the Charge Conference shall be all members of the Administrative Board (or Administrative Boards, if more than one church is on the pastoral charge) named in ¶ 149 together with retired ministers who elect to hold their membership in said Charge Conference and any others as may be designated in the Discipline.

3. The district superintendent shall fix the time of meetings of the Charge Conference. The Charge Conference shall determine the place of meeting.

4. The district superintendent shall preside at the meetings of the Charge Conference, or he may designate an elder to preside in his place.

5. The members present at any duly announced meeting shall constitute a quorum.

6. Special sessions may be called by the district superintendent after consultation with the pastor of the charge or by the pastor with the written consent of the district superintendent. The purpose of such special session shall be stated in the call, and only such business shall be transacted as is in harmony with the purposes stated in such call.

7. Notice of the time and place of a regular or special session of the Charge Conference shall be given at least ten days in advance.

8. A **Joint Charge Conference** for two or more pastoral charges may be held at the same time and place, as the district superintendent may determine.

¶ 145. *Powers and Duties.*—1. The Charge Conference shall be the connecting link between the local church and the general Church and shall have general oversight of the Administrative Board (s).

2. Its primary responsibility in the annual meeting shall be to evaluate the effectiveness of the program of the charge toward achieving its mission in the community and world, to establish goals for the ensuing year which are in keeping with the objectives of The United Methodist Church, and to develop specific proposals to be implemented by the Administrative Board (s).

3. The Charge Conference shall elect, upon nomination of the Committee on Nominations and Personnel of each local church on the pastoral charge and by vote of each such local church, the following:

a) Lay leader (s), lay member (s) of the Annual Conference, chairman of the Council on Ministries, chairmen of work areas (ecumenical affairs, education, evangelism, missions, social concerns, stewardship, worship), age-level coordinators (family, children, youth, adult), recording secretary, secretary of enlistment, superintendent of study program (optional), district steward (optional), and (if not paid employees of the local church) the church treasurer (s), financial secretary, and membership secretary.

b) Members at large of the Administrative Board as provided in

¶ 146.3, one of whom shall be selected as the Health and Welfare Ministries representative.

c) The Committee on Pastor-Parish Relations and chairman (¶ 161.2).

d) The Committee on Finance (¶ 161.3) and chairman.

e) The Committee on Nominations and Personnel (¶ 161.1).

f) The trustees as provided in ¶¶ 1529, 1531, unless otherwise required by state law.

g) Such other personnel and committees as may elsewhere be ordered by the Discipline.

4. It shall examine and recommend to the district Committee on the Ministry, faithfully adhering to the provisions of ¶ 318.3, candidates for the ministry who have been members in good standing of the local church for at least one year; whose gifts, graces, and call to the ministry clearly establish them as candidates; and who have met the educational requirements.

5. It shall examine and recommend, faithfully adhering to the provisions of ¶ 320, candidates for the renewal of the lay pastor's license.

6. It shall examine and recommend to the responsible church agency and candidates for church-related vocations.

7. It shall affirm the good standing in the congregation of the persons seeking the lay worker relationship in the Annual Conference and transmit this information to the conference Committee on the Lay Worker.

8. It shall recommend to the district Committee on Lay Speaking for certification as lay speakers those persons who have met the standards set forth by the agency to which they are related and shall inquire annually into the gifts, labors, and usefulness of lay speakers. (*See* ¶¶ 1322-25.)

9. It shall in consultation with the district superintendent set the salary and other remuneration of the pastor and other staff appointed by the bishop.

10. It shall determine the amount accepted annually by the Charge Conference for world service and conference benevolences by the following procedure:

As soon as practicable after the session of Annual Conference, each district superintendent shall notify each local church in his district what amounts have been apportioned to it for world service and conference benevolences. It shall be the responsibility of the pastor and the church lay leader to present to a meeting of each Charge Conference a statement of the apportionments for world service and conference benevolences, explaining the causes supported by each of these funds and their place in the total program of the Church. The Charge Conference shall determine annually the amount of its acceptance for world service and conference benevolences. The district superintendent shall also notify each Charge Conference of all other amounts properly apportioned to it. (*See* ¶ 921.)

11. In those instances where there is more than one church on a charge, the Charge Conference may provide for a Charge Administrative Board if deemed advisable. Such a Charge Administrative Board shall operate in accordance with ¶¶ 150-52.

12. In those instances where there is more than one church on a charge, the Charge Conference may elect a charge treasurer (s) to receive and disburse funds and contributions for local expense and benevolence causes for the charge.

13. Where there is more than one church on a charge, there shall be a charge Committee on Nominations and Personnel composed of at least one representative from each Administrative Board Committee on Nominations and Personnel which shall nominate such officers and committees as are necessary for the Charge Conference to carry on its work.

14. Such other duties and responsibilities as the General, Jurisdictional, or Annual Conference may duly commit to it.

¶ **146.** 1. The **lay member(s)** of the Annual Conference and one or more alternates shall be elected annually or quadrennially as the Annual Conference directs. If the charge's lay representative to the Annual Conference shall cease to be a member of the charge or shall for any reason fail to serve, an alternate member in the order of his election shall serve in his place.

Both the lay members and the alternates shall be at least twenty-one years of age, and shall have been members in good standing of The United Methodist Church or one of the churches forming the union for at least four years, and of the local church from which they are elected for at least one year, except in a newly organized church, which shall have the privilege of representation at the Annual Conference session. (*See* ¶ 36.) No lay pastor shall be eligible as a lay member or alternate.

2. The **recording secretary** shall keep an accurate and permanent record of the proceedings and shall be the custodian of all records and reports, and with the presiding officer shall sign the minutes. A copy of the minutes shall be provided for the district superintendent. When there is only one local church on a charge, the secretary of the Administrative Board shall be the secretary of the Charge Conference. When there is more than one church on a charge, one of the secretaries of the Administrative Boards shall be elected to serve as secretary of the Charge Conference.

3. The Charge Conference shall determine the number of **members at large** to serve on the Administrative Board in keeping with the following provisions: Churches of five hundred members or less shall include at least four members at large and may include a total not to exceed thirty-five in number exclusive of ex officio and honorary members. In churches of more than five hundred members there may be elected additional members at large not to exceed the ratio of one for each thirty additional members. The members at large shall include at least two young adults between the ages of eighteen and thirty and at least two youth nominated by the youth coordinator or the Youth Council.

4. The health and welfare representative shall be selected from among the members at large.

5. The **secretary of enlistment** for church-related occupations may be one of the coordinators or work area chairmen of the Council on Ministries.

6. The Charge Conference may establish a limit to the consecutive terms of office for any or all of the elected or appointed officers of the local church except where otherwise mandated. It is recommended that no officer serve more than three consecutive years in office.

7. The Charge Conference may make provision for the recognition of the faithful service of those members of the Administrative Board who have reached the age of seventy-two or who have become physically incapacitated by electing them honorary members. An

honorary member shall be entitled to all the privileges of a member, except the right to vote.

¶ **147.** *The Annual Church Conference.*—To encourage broader participation by members of the Church, the Charge Conference may be convened as the **Annual Church Conference,** extending the vote to all local church members present at such meetings. The Annual Church Conference may be authorized by the district superintendent on request of the Administrative Board. Additional regulations governing the call and conduct of the Charge Conference as set forth in ¶¶ 144-45 shall apply also to the Annual Church Conference. A joint Annual Church Conference for two or more churches may be held at the same time and place, as the district superintendent may determine. (For Church Local Conference see ¶ 1530.)

Section XIV. The Administrative Board.

¶ **148.** In every local church there shall be an administrative body known as the **Administrative Board,** to which the members, organizations, and agencies of the local church are amenable. It functions under and is amenable to the Charge Conference. (*See* ¶¶ 144-47.)

1. *Purpose.*—The purpose of the Administrative Board shall be to initiate planning, receive reports, set goals, authorize action, determine policy, evaluate the church's ministries, and review the state of the church.

2. *Meetings.*—The Administrative Board shall meet at least quarterly. Special meetings may be ordered by the Administrative Board or called by the chairman or the pastor.

3. *Quorum.*—The members present at any duly announced meeting shall constitute a quorum.

¶ **149.** *Membership.*—The membership of the Administrative Board shall consist of the following insofar as the offices and relationships exist within the local church:

The pastor and the associate pastor or pastors; deaconesses appointed to serve therein; the lay leader (s) ; the lay member (s) of the Annual Conference; chairman of the trustees; the church administrator (business manager) ; the chairman of the Committee on Finance; the chairman of the Committee on Pastor-Parish Relations; the secretary of the Committee on Nominations and Personnel; the church treasurer (s) ; the financial secretary, if not a member of the employed staff; the director or the associate of Christian education or the educational assistant; the director or the associate of evangelism; the director or the associate of music or the music assistant; the chairman of the Council on Ministries; the work area chairmen; the age-level and family coordinators; the secretary of enlistment; the superintendent of the study program of the church; the membership secretary, if not a member of the employed staff; the president of the Women's Society of Christian Service; the president of United Methodist Men; members at large; and a health and welfare representative. The employed professional staff who are members of the Administrative Board shall not vote on matters pertaining to their employee relationship.

Members of the Administrative Board shall be persons of genuine Christian character who love the Church, are morally disciplined, are loyal to the ethical standards of The United Methodist Church set forth in ¶¶ 96 and 97, and are competent to administer its affairs. It shall include youth members chosen according to the same standards as adults. All shall be members of the local church, except where Central Conference legislation provides otherwise.

¶ **150.** *Organization.*—The Administrative Board shall be organized annually by the election of a chairman, a vice-chairman, and a recording secretary. These officers shall be lay persons elected by the members of the Administrative Board on the nomination of the Committee on Nominations and Personnel. Additional nominations may be made from the floor.

¶ **151.** *Responsibilities.*—As the executive agency of the Charge Conference, the Administrative Board shall have general oversight of the administration and program of the local church (¶ 148). The pastor shall be the administrative officer and as such shall be an ex officio member of all conferences, boards, councils, commissions, committees, and task groups.

1. The Administrative Board shall be responsible for administering the organization of the local church which shall include: the Council on Ministries (¶ 153), the Committee on Nominations and Personnel (¶ 161.1), the Committee on Pastor-Parish Relations (¶ 161.2), the Committee on Finance (¶ 161.3), and the trustees (¶ 1528).

The Administrative Board may co-opt additional persons from time to time to assist the local church in fulfilling its mission. (*See* ¶¶ 153-60, 161.4.)

2. The Administrative Board may adjust the local church's program year to correspond with the Annual Conference fiscal year. The Administrative Board shall determine the date when all elected personnel shall take office and establish their tenure except when the General Conference or the Annual Conference orders otherwise.

3. The Administrative Board shall annually:

a) Establish the goals for the ministries of the local church.

b) Elect such lay officers and members of the Administrative Board as are authorized by the Discipline. To fulfill this responsibility the Administrative Board shall receive and act upon the reports of the Committee on Nominations and Personnel.

c) Receive reports and review the state of the church. To fulfill this responsibility the Administrative Board shall receive and act upon the reports of all boards and committees amenable to it and the recommendations of the Council on Ministries, and shall provide the necessary personnel and budget to implement the approved program.

d) After consultation with the Committee on Pastor-Parish Relations and the Committee on Finance, recommend to the Charge Conference the salary and other remuneration for the pastor and staff.

e) Establish the budget.

4. The Administrative Board shall cultivate interest in all the benevolent causes authorized by the General, Jurisdictional, Annual, and District Conferences, and encourage the support of world service, conference, and other benevolences, coordinating the same with the activities and study/action groups of the church.

5. It shall make proper and adequate provision for the financial needs of the church, including ministerial support (i.e., for the pastor or pastors, district superintendent, conference claimants, and bishops) ; approved items of local expense; world service, conference, and other benevolences; other items apportioned to the church by the proper authorities; and all obligations assumed by the local church.

6. It shall discharge faithfully any and all duties and responsibilities committed to it by the Charge Conference or by law of the Church.

7. It shall develop in the members of the congregation a concern for and responsibility in the establishment of new churches, new church schools, and other forms of ministry, and when specifically authorized by the district superintendent and the district Board of Church Location and Building, it shall organize and sponsor new churches, church schools, and other forms of ministry needed in the community.

8. It shall foster understanding of the unity of the Church and shall initiate responsibile participation in the ministries of the ecumenical community.

¶ 152. *Lay Officers.*—The membership list of the Administrative Board includes the following lay officers whose roles are not defined elsewhere:

1. The **lay leader** is the person, man or woman, elected by the Charge Conference for the following responsibilities: (*a*) membership in the Charge Conference, the Administrative Board, and the Council on Ministries where, along with the pastor, he shall serve as an interpreter of the actions of the Annual Conference and its boards and agencies; (*b*) continuing involvement in study and training opportunities to develop a growing understanding of the Church's reason for existence and the types of ministry that will most effectively fulfill the Church's mission; (*c*) assisting in the interpretation of the role of the local church in the community; and (*d*) alerting the Administrative Board and its Council on Ministries to the opportunities available for more effective ministry of the Church through its laity. (*See* ¶ 1255.) He shall be expected to take advantage of the opportunities provided for his training by the Annual Conference and shall serve as a member of the district Board of the Laity. (*See* ¶ 1312.) In instances where more than one church is on a charge, the Charge Conference shall elect additional lay leaders so that there will be one lay leader for each church.

2. The **secretary of enlistment** shall coordinate and guide, with the pastor and various interests and agencies of the local church, a program of interpretation and enlistment for church-related occupations and an understanding of vocation in Christian terms. He shall serve as liaison with vocational resources and resource persons beyond the local church, and when desired shall select a representative committee

of persons from age-group and program interests of the congregation in this area and shall serve as its chairman.

3. The Charge Conference may elect a **superintendent of the study program of the church** who shall be responsible, under the guidance of the education work area chairman or commission and the minister or representative of the employed staff, for the supervision of the school of the church. His particular responsibilities shall be those of (*a*) educational consultant to age-group and family coordinators and (*b*) coordinator of study activities involving more than one age group.

4. The **financial secretary** shall recieve the contributions to the local church, keeping records of the contributors and their payments, and transfer them promptly to the treasurer (s) .

5. The **church treasurer(s)** shall disburse all money contributed to causes represented in the local church budget, and such other funds and contributions as the Administrative Board may determine. (*See* ¶ 145.12.) The treasurer (s) shall remit each month to the conference treasurer all world service and conference benevolence funds then on hand. Contributions to benevolences shall not be used for any cause other than that to which they have been given.

6. The **health and welfare representative** shall serve as the chairman of the Committee on Health and Welfare Ministries if it is organized. When no committee is organized, he shall interpret the opportunities for the local church to minister through this area.

Section XV. The Local Church Council on Ministries.

¶ **153.** There shall be a local church **Council on Ministries**, which shall consider, initiate, develop, and coordinate proposals for the church's strategy for mission. It shall receive and, where possible, utilize resources for missions provided by the District, Annual, Jurisdictional, and General Conference Program Councils, boards, and agencies, and shall coordinate these resources with the Church's plan for ministries in the local and other settings. The council shall be amenable to the Administrative Board to which it shall submit its plans for revision and appropriate action. Upon adoption of the program by the

Administrative Board, the council shall implement the plans which are assigned to it.

The Council on Ministries shall make recommendations to the Committee on Finance requesting the financial resources needed to undergird the ministries which it has developed, using local and connectional program suggestions, and which the council recommends to the Administrative Board.

Since local churches vary greatly in needs and size, the structure and organization required will differ. The Council on Ministries with its several elected representatives is the minimum structure for the development and administration of the local church program. The Council on Ministries, in order to implement the Church's mission, may request expansion of the structure to include councils, commissions, task groups, committees, and other groups as needed. Where the committees, councils, task groups, commissions, etc., are not organized, the duties assigned to each become the responsibility of the Council on Ministries.

¶ 154. The basic membership of the local church Council on Ministries shall include: the minister and other staff persons who are engaged in program work; the chairman of the Administrative Board; the lay leader; the president of the Women's Society of Christian Service; the coordinators of age levels: children, youth, and adult; a coordinator of family ministry; the chairman of each work area: ecumenical affairs, education, evangelism, missions, social concerns, stewardship, and worship; and a youth member of the congregation.

The Charge Conference may elect to the Council on Ministries upon nomination of the Committee on Nominations and Personnel: the superintendent of the study program of the church, a representative of United Methodist Men and of the United Methodist Youth Fellowship, and other persons on the basis of their competency in program planning.

The officers of the Council on Ministries shall be a chairman, who shall be a layman or a clergyman who is not a member of the local staff, a vice-chairman, and a secretary. The chairman shall be elected by the Charge Conference upon nomination of the Committee on Nominations and Personnel; the vice-chairman and secretary shall be elected by the council from its own membership.

¶ **155.** *Age-Level and Family Coordinators.*—1. The Charge Conference shall elect annually upon nomination by the Committee on Nominations and Personnel a **coordinator of children's ministries,** a **coordinator of youth ministries,** a **coordinator of adult ministries,** and a **coordinator of family ministries.** Each of the coordinators shall, under the guidance of the minister or a representative from the employed professional staff and the chairman of the Council on Ministries, study the needs of the age group and the goals of the congregation's ministry and coordinate the planning and implementation of a unified and comprehensive ministry with the age group. He shall serve as liaison with organizations, persons, and resources in and beyond the local church which relate to his age level. He shall represent on the Council on Ministries the concerns of age-level organizations when they are not otherwise represented.

2. The coordinator of family ministries shall work with the age-level coordinators and the Council on Ministries to develop a family ministry for the local church, taking into consideration the suggestions of the general church agency and the Annual Conference agency responsible for family life. He shall keep the Council on Ministries aware of resources and activities to be used in planning family activities in the church and home, in the guidance of families in Christian living in the home, in the preparation of youth for marriage, and in helping families find opportunities for service in the community and the world.

¶ **156.** *Age-Level and Family Councils.*—Where the size of the church and the extent of the program indicate the need, the work of the Council on Ministries may be facilitated by one or more **age-level councils** and/or a **family council,** or such other means as fit the needs of the congregation. The age-level councils shall work under the leadership of the age-level coordinators to expedite the work of the Council on Ministries in adapting the program to the age level.

The membership of these councils, except for ex officio members, shall be elected by the Council on Ministries and may include the following:

1. *Children's Council.*—Representative teachers and leaders of children's activities of the church, representative parents, and representatives of work areas (ecumenical affairs, education, evangelism, mis-

sions, social concerns, stewardship, and worship) related to the Church's ministry with children.

2. *Youth Council.*—Representatives of adult leaders and counselors of youth, representative parents, representatives of work areas (ecumenical affairs, education, evangelism, missions, social concerns, stewardship, and worship) related to the Church's ministry with youth, and at least one youth for each adult on the council.

3. *Adult Council.*—Representatives of adult study/action groups; fellowship groups, administrative groups, and service organizations such as the Women's Society of Christian Service, United Methodist Men, and Young Adult Ministry; and representatives of work areas (ecumenical affairs, education, evangelism, missions, social concerns, stewardship, and worship) related to the Church's ministry with adults.

4. *Family Council.*—When the size of the church and the extent of the program indicate the need, the Council on Ministries may designate a group including representatives of the age-group councils to work with the coordinator in planning program suggestions to be submitted to the Council on Ministries.

The minister or a member of the professional staff of the church appointed by the minister shall be an ex officio member of each council. Additional members, such as representatives of community agencies, may be elected to each council on the basis of their interest and competency.

The coordinators shall serve as the chairmen of their respective councils. Each council shall elect a vice-chairman and a secretary annually.

¶ 157. *Work Area Chairmen.*—Major concerns of the Church Universal and local church include ecumenical affairs, education, evangelism, missions, social concerns, stewardship, and worship. Therefore the Charge Conference shall elect annually upon nomination of the Committee on Nominations and Personnel the **chairman of ecumenical affairs**, the **chairman of education**, the **chairman of evangelism**, the **chairman of missions**, the **chairman of social concerns**, the **chairman of stewardship**, and the **chairman of worship**. Where desirable, the Charge Conference may combine coordinators and work area chairmen assignments.

Each work area chairman, under the guidance of the minister or a representative from the employed staff and the chairman of the Council on Ministries, shall contact the program agencies, obtain guidance material, and study the implications for the work area in the total mission of the Church; shall interpret and recommend to the Council on Ministries ways of implementing the mission of the Church represented by the area; shall make specific recommendations of the work area for different age groups; shall serve as liaison within and beyond the local church. When an activity in the area of work is planned by the Council on Ministries to include two or more age levels, the chairman of the work area may serve, when designated by the Council on Ministries, as chairman of a group from the age levels to carry out the activity.

¶ 158. *Work Area Commissions.*—When the size of the church and the extent of the program indicate the need, the Council on Ministries may choose one or more **work area commissions** (ecumenical affairs, education, evangelism, missions, social concerns, stewardship, and worship). The commission shall work under the leadership of the work area chairman to expedite the concerns of the Council on Ministries in the area. The representative of the work area serving on each age-level council shall be a member of the commission. The council may elect other persons to the commission because of unusual interest and competency in the area. The minister or a representative of the employed professional staff appointed by the minister shall serve as an ex officio member of the commission.

1. The **Commission on Education** shall keep the Council on Ministries aware of sound educational procedure, and encourage and facilitate the use of curriculum resources based on curriculum plans developed by the Program-Curriculum Committee and approved by the Board of Education of The United Methodist Church to be used in the achievement of the goals for the Church's educational ministry. The commission shall recommend activities and structure for study and interpretation of the Christian faith and life at each age level. It shall work with the age-group councils to coordinate the study program of the church, particularly when activities involve more than one age group.

The Commission on Education shall recommend to the Council

on Ministries an organization of the study program of the church in keeping with the standards and policies of the General Board of Education, Division of the Local Church, and the Annual Conference Board of Education.

The Commission on Education shall provide locally for the promotion and support of the interests of higher education and campus ministry, in accordance with the Annual Conference and the General Board of Education, Division of Higher Education. It shall plan for the ministry to students related to the local church and shall observe United Methodist Student Day and receive an offering for the support of The United Methodist Scholarships and for The United Methodist Student Loan Fund.

The Commission on Education shall provide locally for the observance of Christian Education Sunday to emphasize the importance of Christian education and to receive an offering for the conference Board of Education for the program of its local church division.

2. The **Commission on Evangelism** shall keep the Council on Ministries aware of the aim and means of evangelism in the goals for the Church's ministry. In keeping with the standards and guidance material supplied by the General Board of Evangelism and the Annual Conference Board of Evangelism, it shall recommend activities and structure to respond to the evangelistic mission of the local church. In cooperation with the pastor and the Council on Ministries it shall develop and implement ministries for membership care. It shall assist the age-group councils to respond to evangelistic opportunities in the community so that every person is included in the responsibility of a local church.

3. The **Commission on Missions** shall keep the Council on Ministries aware of the purpose and needs of programs and institutions supported by the Church in the nation and around the world. In keeping with the standards and guidance material supplied by the General Board of Missions and the Annual Conference Board of Missions, it shall provide resources to be used in the study program of the church. Through the council it shall cooperate with other commissions in surveying the needs of the local community, and recommend to the Council on Ministries plans for local mission and service projects. It shall recommend means of keeping the church informed of the quali-

fications and current needs for personnel to serve through the Church around the world. (*See* ¶ 152.2.) It shall develop a benevolence budget and submit it to the Council on Ministries for their recommendation to the finance committee.

4. The **Commission on Social Concerns** shall keep the Council on Ministries aware of the need for study and action in the areas of peace and world order, human relations, political and economic affairs, and health and general welfare. In keeping with standards and guidance materials supplied by the General Board of Christian Social Concerns and the Annual Conference Board of Christian Social Concerns, it shall recommend to the Council on Ministries study/action projects in the field of social concerns. The commission shall cooperate with other commissions in surveying the needs of the local community and in recommendations for local social-action projects.

5. The **Commission on Stewardship** shall keep the Council on Ministries aware of the meaning of the stewardship of life, time, talent, and material means as one of the evidences of the fruits of the Spirit. In keeping with the standards and guidance material supplied by the General Board of the Laity and the Annual Conference Board of the Laity, it shall recommend to the Council on Ministries or the age-group councils, materials and methods for keeping the people involved in service and mission. In churches where the Commission on Stewardship is organized, the Council on Ministries shall elect representatives of the Committee on Finance to serve on the commission. (*See* ¶ 161.3.)

6. The **Commission on Worship** shall aid the congregation to become increasingly aware of the meaning, purpose, and practice of worship. In keeping with the standards and guidance material supplied by the General Conference Commission on Worship, the commission shall recommend plans for the study by individuals and groups of the art of worship; shall cooperate with the pastor in caring for music, ushering, furnishings, appointments, and sacramental elements for congregational worship; and shall recommend standards for the placement in the church of memorial gifts as aids to worship.

7. The **Commission on Ecumenical Affairs** shall encourage awareness and understanding of ecumenism at all levels (dialogue, councils,

and unions). It shall stimulate studies, plan programs, cooperate in specific ecumenical endeavors, and encourage conversation and fellowship with members of other Christian churches.

¶ **159.** *Program Agencies.*—The ministries of the local church are implemented through the encounter of persons with God's redeeming love for the world and with his action in the world. To achieve this ministry persons are involved in age-level or family groupings. Usually a variety of settings is essential. Some will be formed by the Council on Ministries. Others will emerge with the approval of the Council on Ministries. Another type is historical, expressing itself in organizational structures that are related to counterparts in Annual Conferences and the general Church. These are referred to as **program agencies** and are related to the Council on Ministries through its age-level and family coordinators, work area chairmen, and councils or commissions of the Council on Ministries.

1. *The Church School.*—In each local church there shall be a **church school** for the purpose of accomplishing the church's educational ministry. It provides a variety of settings and resources for all persons—children, youth, and adults—to explore the meanings of the Christian faith in all its dimensions, to discover and appropriate to themselves those meanings which are relevant for their lives and for society, and to assume responsibility for expressing these meanings in all their relationships. The content of the curriculum of the church school will include the meanings and experiences of the Christian faith as found in the Bible, in history, and in man's encounter with the natural world and contemporary society. All the concerns of the Church will be present in the church school's educational ministry: ecumenical affairs, evangelism, missions, social concerns, stewardship, and worship. It will provide opportunity for persons to commit themselves to Christ and encourage them to unite with the Christian community through membership in a local church. The superintendent of the study program of the church, if elected, or the education work area chairman, shall be responsible for relating the educational ministry of the church school to the total ministry of the local church through the Council on Ministries. Leadership and organizational resources for the church school are prepared by the Division of the

Local Church, General Board of Education; curriculum resources are prepared by the Division of Curriculum Resources of the board.

2. *United Methodist Youth Fellowship.*—The youth ministry of The United Methodist Church shall include all persons from the seventh grade through senior high school (approximately twelve through eighteen years of age) who are currently or potentially associated with the Church or any of its activities. This ministry shall take into account all the interests of the Church so that youth may be conscious that together their lives are identified with the total life of the Church. The coordinator of youth ministries and the Youth Council, when organized, shall be responsible for providing guidance and organizing, coordinating, and supporting the varied forms of this ministry in the local church. The comprehensive program of youth work shall be known as the **United Methodist Youth Fellowship.** Resources for the organization and implementation of the youth ministry are available from the General Board of Education, Division of the Local Church.

3. *The Women's Society of Christian Service.*—In every local church there shall be a **Women's Society of Christian Service.** The following is the authorized constitution:

Article 1. Name.—The name of this organization shall be the Women's Society of Christian Service. A **Wesleyan Service Guild**, auxiliary to the Women's Society of Christian Service, composed of employed women, may also be organized in a local church.

Article 2. Relationships.—The Women's Society of Christian Service in the local church is directly related to the district and conference Women's Society of Christian Service and to the General Board of Missions of The United Methodist Church through the Women's Division.

Article 3. Purpose.—The purpose of the Women's Society of Christian Service and Wesleyan Service Guild shall be to help women grow in the knowledge and experience of God as revealed in Jesus Christ, to challenge them to respond to God's redemptive purpose in the world, to unite them in a Christian fellowship to make Christ known throughout the world, and to develop a personal responsibility for the whole task of the Church.

Toward the realization of this purpose, the Women's Society and the Wesleyan Service Guild shall provide opportunities and resources to meet the needs and interests of women; to increase their knowledge of the concerns and responsibilities of the Church in the world; and to share in Christian witness, service, and missionary outreach.

The Women's Society and Guild shall enlist workers and secure funds for the fulfillment of their responsibility in the mission of the Church at home and overseas.

Article 4. Membership.—Any woman may become a member of the society who accepts the purpose and is willing to participate in the work of the society each year through prayer, giving, and service. The pastor may be a member of the society.

Article 5. Officers and Committees.—The local society shall elect a president, a vice-president, a secretary, a treasurer, and a Committee on Nominations. Additional officers and committees shall be elected or appointed as needed, in accordance with the plans of the Women's Division as may be set forth in the bylaws for the local society.

Article 6. Funds.—*a*) All funds from whatsoever source secured by this society belong to this organization and shall be disbursed only in accordance with its constitution and by its order.

b) The total budget to be secured and administered by a Women's Society of Christian Service in the local church shall include pledges and other moneys for the work of the General Board of Missions to be directed through the regular channels of finance of the society and also funds for local church and community activities.

c) All undesignated funds channeled to the Women's Division of the General Board of Missions shall be divided in the office of the treasurer of the division on a basis to be determined by the division. There shall be no division of such funds by the local society.

d) Funds for local church and community activities shall be secured and administered by the Women's Society of Christian Service in the local church.

e) Each society in the local church shall make an annual pledge to the total budget adopted by the district or conference society.

f) Each society in the local church shall include in its budget a definite amount for a cultivation fund.

Article 7. Meetings.—The society shall hold one or more meetings during a month for implementing the purpose (Art. 3) of the Women's Society of Christian Service and for transacting its business.

Article 8. Relationship to the Local Church.—The society as an organization of the local church is responsible through its members for participation in the total life and work of the church.

Designated officers shall represent the society on the various boards, councils, commissions, and committees of the church, as the constitutions and bylaws of such agencies provide.

Article 9. Amendments.—Proposed amendments to this constitution may be sent to the recording secretary of the Women's Division of the Board of Missions at least forty days before the last annual meeting of the division in the quadrennium. Proposed amendments may also be sent directly to the General Conference.

Note: For a description of the Women's Division of the Board of Missions and its subsidiary organizations see ¶¶ 1040-47.

4. *United Methodist Men.*—The ministry of the local church to and through its men shall be concerned with all the men who are a part of its constituency. It shall take into account the search of men for a meaningful faith and the witness of men to that faith in all their relationships. It shall be aware that men's work is achieved in all the groups where men are involved in the life and work of the local church and in special groups and/or organizations of **United Methodist Men.** These groups and/or organizations shall be formed when men in the congregation see the need for them and request their formation or when the Council on Ministries determines that there is need for their formation. Resources for the organization and implementation of men's ministry are available from the General Board of the Laity. (*See* ¶¶ 1269-74.)

¶ 160. **Task groups** may be formed by the Council on Ministries, its councils or commissions, for the purpose of accomplishing specific and particular goals of the Church's mission to the world. These groups shall be oriented to immediate tasks. They shall prepare for their mission by the study of the Scriptures' mandates in the light of the community's immediate needs. They shall meet regularly for study and for planning their strategy in mission. They shall be disciplined to individual and corporate action and shall be amenable to the Council on Ministries and report to it.

Section XVI. **Committees.**

¶ 161. 1. There shall be elected annually by the Charge Conference a **Committee on Nominations and Personnel** composed of not more than nine persons—excluding the pastor, who shall be chairman —which shall nominate to the Charge Conference or Annual Church Conference in its annual session such officers and members of the Administrative Board and Charge Conference and committees as the law of the Church requires or as the conference may determine as necessary to its work; *provided* that to secure experience and stability the membership shall be divided into three classes, one of which shall be elected each year for a three-year term; *provided* further, that to begin the process of rotation on the first year one class be elected for one year, one class for two years, and one for three years; *provided* further, that the members of the Committee on Nominations and Personnel shall be elected from a list of names nominated by the existing Committee on Nominations and Personnel, equal to the number of persons to be elected, and from a like number of additional nominees from the floor. Churches are encouraged to establish a policy that retiring members of the Committee on Nominations and Personnel not succeed themselves. (*See also* ¶ 146.6.)

The Committee on Nominations and Personnel shall serve throughout the year to guide the Administrative Board on personnel matters (other than employed staff) so as to coordinate the leadership and service needs with personnel of the congregation, working in relationship to the Council on Ministries and the committees of the Administrative Board in both its nominations and personnel guidance.

2. There shall be a **Committee on Pastor-Parish Relations** of not fewer than five nor more than nine laymen or laywomen, one of whom shall be a lay member of the Annual Conference. The members, including the chairman, shall be elected annually by the Charge Conference upon nomination by the Committee on Nominations and Personnel. Where there is more than one church on a charge, there shall be a pastor-parish relations committee with at least one representative from each congregation (¶ 145.3c). In those charges where there is a multiple staff, the committee shall relate to the entire staff. It shall elect its own secretary. It shall meet at least twice each year. It shall

meet at the request of the bishop, the district superintendent, the pastor, or the chairman of the committee.

The committee shall meet only with the knowledge of the minister and/or the district superintendent. It may meet with the district superintendent without the minister being present; however, when the minister is not present, he shall be informed prior to such meeting and immediately thereafter be brought into consultation either by the committee or by the district superintendent. In the event that only one congregation on a charge containing more than one church has concerns which it wishes to share, its member (s) in the Committee on Pastor-Parish Relations may meet separately with the minister or the district superintendent or all together as required. It shall be a conferring and counseling committee.

The primary function of the committee is to aid the pastor (staff) in making his ministry effective by being available for counsel, keeping him advised concerning conditions within the congregation as they affect relations between pastor and people, and continually interpreting to the people the nature and function of the pastoral office.

Since a responsibility of the committee is to be at all times sensitive to the relationship between the pastor and people, should it become evident to the committee that the best interests of the charge and pastor will be served by a change of pastors, it shall confer with the pastor and furnish him with this information. It shall cooperate with the pastor, the district superintendent, and the bishop in securing pastoral leadership, and its relationship to the district superintendent and the bishop shall be advisory only.

The committee shall cultivate the pastor-parish relationship, provide opportunities for counseling on matters pertaining to the minister's relationship with the congregation including pulpit supply, proposals for his salary, travel expense, vacation, continuing education, housing, and other matters relating to the effectiveness and well-being of the minister and his family. It may arrange with the Administrative Board for the necessary time and financial assistance for his attendance at such schools or institutions as may serve his intellectual and spiritual growth.

After consultation with the pastor, this committee shall recommend to the Administrative Board personnel for other professional and lay staff positions created by the board but not subject to episcopal appointment. In making recommendations for these positions, consideration shall be given to the training qualifications as set forth by the general church agency to which they may be related. When the size of the local church makes it desirable, there may also be a **Lay Personnel Committee** composed of the pastor-parish relations committee and such additional members as the Charge Conference may designate.

3. There shall be a **Committee on Finance** composed of the pastor; the chairman of the Administrative Board; the chairman of the Council on Ministries; the stewardship work area chairman; a representative of the trustees to be selected by the trustees; the lay leader; the financial secretary, if not a member of the employed staff; the church business manager; the church treasurer (s) ; and such other persons as the Charge Conference may determine. In churches where the Commission on Stewardship is not organized, the stewardship work area chairman shall serve as the chairman of the Committee on Finance. In churches where the Commission on Stewardship is organized, it is recommended that the chairman of the Committee on Finance shall be a member of the Council on Ministries.

All financial askings to be included in the annual budget of the local church shall be submitted to the Committee on Finance. The Committee on Finance shall compile annually a complete budget for the local church and submit it to the Administrative Board for review and adoption. After approval of the budget by the Administrative Board, the Committee on Finance shall be charged with responsibility for developing and implementing plans which will raise sufficient income to meet the budget adopted by the Administrative Board. It shall administer the funds received according to instructions from the Administrative Board.

The committee shall make provision for an annual audit of the records of the financial officers of the local church and all its organizations and shall report to the Charge Conference.

4. The Administrative Board may appoint such other committees as it deems advisable including: **Committee on Public Relations, Committee on Good Literature,** and **Committee on Health and Welfare.**

Section XVII.   Special Days.

¶ **162.** The Uniting Conference designated five special days to be observed with offerings in The United Methodist Church.

1. The special days *with offering* are as follows:

a) One Great Hour of Sharing.—This offering, sponsored cooperatively by the major faiths of the United States, will be observed on or about the fourth Sunday in Lent. The offering shall be channeled through the Annual Conference treasurer to the central treasury. A special One Great Hour of Sharing voucher will be issued. Pastors will report the amount of the offering to the Annual Conference. The treasurer of the Council on World Service and Finance is directed, after deducting the cost of the offering, to make distribution as authorized by the Division of Interpretation.

b) Worldwide Communion Sunday.—The Fellowship of Suffering and Service offering is taken on Worldwide Communion Sunday. Similar communion offerings may be taken each time the Sacrament of the Lord's Supper is observed, and all or a portion of these special offerings will be transmitted through the conference treasurer to the Central Treasury. A special Fellowship of Suffering and Service voucher will be issued. Pastors will report the amount of the offering to the Annual Conference. After the costs of promotion have been deducted, distribution of the offering shall be made by the Central Treasury on the ratio of fifty percent (50%) for the United Methodist Committee on Overseas Relief and fifty percent (50%) for the Commission on Chaplains and Related Ministries.

c) Christian Education Sunday.—This is an annual offering taken in the church school for the Annual Conference Board of Education and goes entirely to the support of that board. This offering may be held any Sunday or as the Annual Conference directs. A special Christian Education Sunday voucher will be issued. Pastors will report the amount of the offering to the Annual Conference.

d) Race Relations Sunday.—This offering, taken on the second Sunday in February, includes an offering for the benefit of the Negro schools related to the United Methodist Board of Education. This offering has become one of major importance to our Negro institutions of higher learning. A special Race Relations Sunday voucher will be issued. Pastors will report the amount of the offering to the Annual Conference.

e) United Methodist Student Day.—This offering, taken annually, preferably on the second Sunday in June, or as designated by the Annual Conference or the Commission on Education of the local church, shall be received for the support of The United Methodist Scholarships and The United Methodist Student Loan Fund. A special United Methodist Student Day voucher will be issued. Pastors will report the amount of the offering to the Annual Conference.

f) Golden Cross Sunday.—This is an annual offering taken for the support of the work of health and welfare ministries for which the Annual Conference has responsibility. This offering shall be held on a Sunday to be determined upon recommendation of the Annual Conference Board of Health and Welfare Ministries. A special Golden Cross Sunday voucher will be issued. Pastors will report the amount of the offering to the Annual Conference.

2. The Division of Interpretation holds responsibility for listing special days without offerings. The following special days *without offering* were approved by the Uniting Conference:

a) Ministry Sunday.—Third Sunday in September.

b) Laymen's Day.—Second Sunday in October.

c) Drug and Alcohol Concerns Sunday.—Second Sunday in November.

d) National Bible Sunday.—Sunday prior to Thanksgiving Day.

Chapter Two

THE MINISTRY

Section I. The Nature of Ministry.

¶ 301. Ministry in the Christian church is derived from the ministry of Christ, the ministry of the Father through the Incarnate Son by the Holy Spirit. It is a ministry bestowed upon and required of the entire Church. All Christians are called to ministry, and theirs is a ministry of the people of God within the community of faith and in the world. Members of The United Methodist Church receive this gift of ministry in company with all Christians and sincerely hope to continue and extend it in the world for which Christ lived, died, and lives again. The United Methodist Church believes that Baptism, confirmation, and responsible membership in the Church are visible signs of acceptance of this ministry.

Section II. The Ordained Ministry.

¶ 302. There are persons within the ministry of the baptized who are called of God and set apart by the Church for the specialized ministry of Word, Sacrament, and Order (¶ 309).

¶ 303. It is the conviction of The United Methodist Church that God calls persons to this ministry and bestows upon them the gifts, graces, and fruits necessary to fulfill this calling.

¶ 304. The ordained ministry of The United Methodist Church cherishes its origins in the Christian tradition and in the Wesleyan tradition, from which it has come. It seeks obedience to the Holy Spirit through cooperative efforts to perfect a ministry for the whole Church. It faces the future eager to share new understandings and forms of the ministry which may be revealed.

¶ 305. In order that The United Methodist Church may be assured that those persons who present themselves as candidates for her ministry are truly called of God to this office, let those who consider recommending such persons for license as ministers in The United Methodist Church prayerfully and earnestly ask themselves these questions:

1. Do they know God as a pardoning God? Have they the love of God abiding in them? Do they desire nothing but God? Are they holy in all manner of conversation?

2. Have they gifts, as well as grace, for the work? Have they a clear, sound understanding; a right judgment in the things of God; a just conception of salvation by faith? Do they speak justly, readily, clearly?

3. Have they fruit? Have any been truly convinced of sin and converted to God, and are believers edified by their preaching?

As long as these marks concur in anyone, we believe he is called of

God to preach. These we receive as sufficient proof that he is moved by the Holy Spirit.[5]

¶ 306. The United Methodist Church seeks assurance in these matters, for only persons of genuine Christian experience and character whose conduct before men is above reproach and who are free from harmful practices that would mar their influence or compromise their witness can receive the approval of The United Methodist Church as ministers of the Word, Sacrament, and Order.

Section III. Classifications.

¶ 307. The ordained ministry of The United Methodist Church consists of **elders** and **deacons**. Where there is need, qualified laymen may be authorized to exercise certain pastoral functions and shall be known as **lay pastors**. These designations are not to be applied so as to deprive any person of any right or privilege permanently granted by either The Methodist Church or The Evangelical United Brethren Church.

1. Elders are ministers who have completed their formal preparation for the ministry of Word, Sacrament, and Order; have been elected itinerant members in full connection with an Annual Conference; and have been ordained elders in accordance with the Order and Discipline of The United Methodist Church. (¶ 313).

2. Deacons are ministers who have progressed sufficiently in their preparation for the ministry to be received by an Annual Conference as either probationary members or associate members and who have been ordained deacons in accordance with the Order and Discipline of The United Methodist Church (¶ 311).

3. Lay pastors are laymen duly licensed to preach who, upon recommendation of the Board of the Ministry, are approved each year by the Annual Conference for appointment as pastors of charges (¶ 338).[6]

---

[5] These questions were first asked by John Wesley at the third conference of Methodist preachers in 1746. They have been retained ever since, in substantially the same words, as the standards by which prospective Methodist preachers have been judged.

[6] "Lay pastor" is the term used here to designate the person formerly known in The Methodist Church as approved supply pastor.

Section IV. General Provisions.

¶ 308. 1. Members of The United Methodist Church authorized to preach shall possess a valid license to preach (¶¶ 318-20).

2. Both men and women are included in all provisions of the Discipline which refer to the ministry.

3. The itinerant system is the accepted method of The United Methodist Church by which ministers are appointed by the bishop to fields of labor (¶¶ 390, 161.2). All ministers shall accept and abide by these appointments.

4. A **ministerial student** in The United Methodist Church, for the purpose of classification, is a person who has formally declared his purpose to enter the Christian ministry, has been officially recognized as such by the Annual Conference, and is in the process of pursuing collegiate or theological education but is not yet a probationary member of the Annual Conference. A person so committed and classified shall immediately seek, with the assistance of his pastor, the guidance of the Board of the Ministry with reference to subsequent procedures and his continuing educational program.

5. The provisions of Chapter II, "The Ministry," shall be administered in such way that until July 1, 1971, any candidate shall be granted the right to proceed to complete the requirements for qualifications under the provisions applying at the time of union. The Department of the Ministry shall be authorized to adjudicate any conflicts which may arise.

Section V. Ordination and Orders.

¶ 309. God in Christ, by the Holy Spirit, has called and still calls his whole Church to minister in his name and under his authority and grace. In exercising this ministry the Church is required to perform certain ministries which the whole Church can perform only through ordained ministers. **Ordination** is the rite of the Church by which some are entrusted with the authority to be ministers of Word, Sacrament, and Order:

1. To be ordained to the ministry of Word is to be authorized to preach and teach the Word of God.

2. To be ordained to the ministry of Sacrament is to be authorized to administer the Sacraments of Baptism and the Lord's Supper.

3. To be ordained to the ministry of Order is to be authorized to equip the laity for ministry, to exercise pastoral oversight, and to administer the Discipline of the Church.

¶ **310.** The act of ordination, by which persons are publicly recognized and authorized as ministers, includes prayers and the laying on of hands. The prayers call upon God to supply the minister with the continuing gifts and grace needful to his responsibility. The laying on of hands symbolizes general authorization from the ordained ministry of the Annual Conference and, through them, the ordained ministry of the whole Church.

1. A deacon shall be ordained by a bishop, employing the Order of Service for the Ordination of Deacons.

2. An elder shall be ordained by a bishop, employing the Order of Service for the Ordination of Elders. The bishop shall be assisted by other elders in the laying on of hands.

¶ **311.** *The Order of Deacon.*—A deacon is a minister who has been received by an Annual Conference either as a probationary member or as an associate member and has been ordained deacon. A deacon has authority to conduct divine worship, to preach the Word, to perform the marriage ceremony where the laws of the state or province permit, and to bury the dead. When invited to do so by an elder, he may assist in the administration of the Sacraments. When serving as a regularly appointed pastor of a charge, he shall be granted authority to administer the Sacraments on the charge to which he is appointed.

¶ **312.** Persons of the following classes are eligble for the order of deacon:

1. Lay pastors who have been received into associate membership after having met the requirements of ¶ 323.

2. Theological students who have been received into probationary membership after having met the requirements of ¶ 327 or 328.

¶ **313.** *The Order of Elder.*—An elder is a minister who has met the requirements of ¶ 314 and therefore has full authority for the ministry of Word, Sacrament, and Order; who has been received as a minister in full connection with an Annual Conference; and who has been ordained elder (¶¶ 331-32).

¶ **314.** Ministers of the following classes are eligible for the order of elder:

1. Deacons who have been probationary members of an Annual Conference, are graduates of theological schools accredited or approved by the University Senate, and have been elected to membership in full connection with an Annual Conference after having met the requirements of ¶ 333.

2. Deacons who have been probationary members of an Annual Conference for at least two years since being received from associate membership and who have been elected to membership in full connection with an Annual Conference after having met the requirements of ¶ 335.

Section VI. Relationship to the Annual Conference.

¶ **315.** The Annual Conference is the basic body of The United Methodist Church. The ministerial membership of an Annual Conference shall consist of members in full connection (¶ 331), probationary members (¶ 325), and associate members (¶ 322). Every minister is amenable to the Annual Conference in the performance of his duties in the position to which he is appointed.

¶ **316.** Every ministerial member who is in good standing in an Annual Conference shall receive an annual appointment by the bishop unless he is granted a sabbatical leave or a disability leave or is in the supernumerary or superannuate relation.

¶ **317.** In addition to the ministerial members, persons who have been granted the license to preach and those who have been approved by vote of the Annual Conference as lay pastors may be appointed as pastors in charge under certain conditions which are hereinafter specified.

¶ **318.** *License to Preach.*—Every candidate for the ministry of The United Methodist Church, upon hearing and heeding the call to preach, shall take the first formal step toward the ministry by qualifying for a license to preach. A license to preach may be issued by the district Committee on the Ministry or the Board of the Ministry after the candidate has met the following conditions. He shall have (1) been a member in good standing of The United Methodist Church, or of one of the churches forming the union, for one year immediately preceding application for license; (2) been graduated from an accredited high school or its equivalent; (3) secured the recommendation of his Charge Conference in the following way: a meeting for the purpose of recommending a candidate for the ministry must be preceded by at least two public announcements and must be held in the presence of the bishop, district superintendent, or an authorized elder, who shall counsel with those present regarding the ability and qualifications of the applicant and make plain the importance of such recommendation to the ministry; to be valid such a recommendation must be voted by written ballot by two thirds of the members of the Charge Conference present at this meeting; (4) applied to the district superintendent in writing; (5) appeared before the district Committee on the Ministry, or the Board of the Ministry where no district committee exists, made himself available for any psychological and aptitude tests it may require and provide, and supplied such other information as it may require for determining his gifts, graces, and fruits; (6) completed one fourth of the work required for the Bachelor of Divinity or equivalent first professional degree in a school of theology accredited or approved by the University Senate or passed the course of study prescribed for a license to preach (¶ 1046.1), including Parts I, II, III, and IV of the Discipline. This course shall be taken under the direction of the Department of the Ministry; (7) agreed for the sake of the mission of Jesus Christ in the world and the most effective witness to the Christian gospel, and in consideration of his influence as a minister, to make a complete dedication of himself to the highest ideals of the Christian life as set forth in ¶¶ 95 (General Rules of The Methodist Church), 96 (the Methodist Social Creed), and 97 (Basic Beliefs Regarding Social Issues and Moral Standards of The Evangelical United Brethren Church), and to this end agreed to exercise responsible self-control by personal habits conducive to bodily health, mental and emotional maturity, social responsibility, and growth in grace and the knowledge and love of God (¶¶ 95-97);[7]

---

[7] In adopting the statements in ¶¶ 318.7 and 326.3*e* on the moral and social responsibility of ministers, the General Conference seeks to elevate the standards by calling for a more thoroughgoing moral commitment by the candidate and for a

(8) prepared a written statement dealing with his age, health, Christian experience with emphasis upon his experience in the Church, call to the ministry, purpose in seeking a license to preach, educational record and plans, which together with the certificate of his recommendation from his Charge Conference shall be presented to the district Committee on the Ministry or the Board of the Ministry; (9) been examined as indicated in ¶ 319.

¶ 319. *Examination for License to Preach.*—The candidate for a license to preach shall be examined by the district Committee on the Ministry or the Board of the Ministry. He shall be asked the following questions:

1. Do you believe yourself to be divinely called to preach the gospel?

2. Have you obtained the pardon of your sins and found peace with God through faith in Jesus Christ, and is the Spirit of God bearing witness with your spirit that you are a child of God?

3. Is it your sincere purpose to seek first the Kingdom of God and his righteousness?

4. Do you understand the doctrines and the Discipline of The United Methodist Church, and will you follow and defend them?

¶ 320. *Renewal of License to Preach.*—A license to preach shall be valid for one year. It may be renewed by the district Committee on the Ministry or the Board of the Ministry on recommendation of the candidate's Charge Conference and on evidence that his gifts, graces, and fruits continue to be satisfactory and that he is making satisfactory progress in the required studies.

---

more careful and thorough examination of candidates by district committees and Boards of the Ministry.

The legislation in no way implies that the use of tobacco is a morally indifferent question. In the light of the developing evidence against the use of tobacco, the burden of proof would be upon any user to show that his use of it is consistent with the highest ideals of the Christian life. Similarly, regarding beverage alcohol, the burden of proof would be upon any user to show that his action is consistent with the ideals of excellence of mind, purity of body, and responsible social behavior.

Therefore, the changes here do not relax the traditional view concerning the use of tobacco and beverage alcohol by ministers in The United Methodist Church. Rather they call for higher standards of self-discipline and habit formation in all personal and social relationships. They call for dimensions of moral commitment that go far beyond any specific practices which might be listed.

1. A person licensed to preach and preparing to become a deacon who is enrolled as a pre-theological or theological student in a school, college, university, or school of theology accredited or approved by the University Senate or by a regional or state accrediting agency shall present annually to the district Committee on the Ministry or the Board of the Ministry a statement of his academic progress from the school he is attending. This statement shall take the place of any formal examination, providing his academic progress and character are satisfactory.

2. A person licensed to preach who is not a student as defined in § 1 above shall pursue the introductory studies and the four-year course of study under the Department of the Ministry. (*See* ¶ 1046.4.) This course must be completed within eight years after the issuance of the first license to preach, except as provided in ¶ 348.2.

3. When a license to preach has lapsed, it may be reinstated only at the discretion of the district Committee on the Ministry or the Board of the Ministry when the candidate has completed satisfactorily the current studies for the license to preach.

¶ **321.** A person licensed to preach shall have authority to preach and to conduct divine worship only in the charge in which his membership is held under the supervision of the pastor in charge or to perform pastoral duties in a charge to which he may be temporarily appointed under the supervision of the district superintendent and the guidance of a duly authorized counseling elder. (*See* ¶¶ 350, 353-54.)

¶ **322.** *Associate Member.*—An **associate member** of an Annual Conference is in the itinerant ministry of the Church and is available on a continuing basis for appointment by the bishop. He offers himself without reserve to be appointed and to serve as his superiors in office shall direct. He shall be amenable to the Annual Conference in the performance of his ministry and shall be granted the same security of appointment as probationary members and members in full connection.

1. An associate member is eligible for ordination as a deacon but may not be ordained elder unless he qualifies through probationary membership for membership in full connection in the Annual Conference (¶ 314.2).

2. An associate member shall have the right to vote in the Annual

Conference on all matters except the following: (*a*) constitutional amendments; (*b*) election of delegates to the General and Jurisdictional or Central Conferences; (*c*) all matters of ordination, character, and conference relations of ministers.

3. An associate member may serve on any board, commission, or committee of an Annual Conference except the Board of the Ministry. He shall not be eligible for election as a delegate to the General or Jurisdictional Conferences.

4. An associate member shall be subject to the provisions governing sabbatical leave, supernumerary relations, location, retirement, minimum salary, and pension.

¶ 323. A candidate may be elected to associate membership by vote of the ministerial members in full connection, upon recommendation of the Board of the Ministry, when he has met the following conditions. He shall have (1) served four years as a full-time lay pastor; (2) completed the four-year ministerial course of study in addition to the license to preach and introductory studies, no more than one year of which may be taken by correspondence; (3) completed a minimum of sixty semester hours toward the Bachelor of Arts or an equivalent degree in a college or university accredited or approved by the University Senate, or in an equivalent curriculum (¶ 1046.1) prescribed by the Department of the Ministry as a supplement to the approved course-of-study school; *provided* that until July 1, 1971, the Annual Conference, upon recommendation of the Board of the Ministry and by a three-fourths vote, may waive the requirement; (4) been recommended by the district Committee on the Ministry and the Board of the Ministry; (5) declared his willingness to accept continuing full-time appointment; and (6) furnished a certificate of good health on the prescribed form from a physician approved by the board. The Annual Conference may require psychological tests to provide additional information on the candidate's fitness for the ministry.

¶ 324. An associate member who exhibits exceptional promise for the ministry may qualify for probationary membership in the Annual Conference under special conditions as set forth hereinafter upon receiving a three-fourths majority vote of the ministerial members of the conference in full connection, present and voting. He shall have (1) reached thirty-five years of age; (2) served as an associate member for a minimum of two full years under full-time appointment; (3) completed a Bachelor of Arts or equivalent degree in a college or university accredited or approved by the University Senate; (4) completed two years of advanced study prescribed by the Department of the Ministry beyond the four-year ministerial courses of study required for admission to associate membership in cooperation with the United Methodist theological schools; (5) been recommended by a three-fourths vote of the Cabinet and a three-fourths vote of the Board of the Ministry, written statements of such recommendations having been read to the conference before the vote is taken, setting forth the particular ways his ministry is exceptional and the special reasons he should be received into probationary membership.

¶ **325.** *Probationary Member.*—A **probationary member** is on trial in preparation for a membership in full connection with his Annual Conference. He is on probation as to his character, preaching, and effectiveness as a pastor. The Annual Conference has jurisdiction over a probationary member. Annually the Board of the Ministry shall review and evaluate his relationship and make recommendation to the Annual Conference regarding his continuance. His continuance as a probationary member shall be equivalent to the renewal of his license to preach. A probationary member may request discontinuance of this relationship or may be discontinued by the Annual Conference, upon recommendation of the Board of the Ministry, without reflection upon his character.

1. A probationary member is eligible for ordination as a deacon but may not be ordained elder until he qualifies for membership in full connection in the Annual Conference.

2. A probationary member shall have the right to vote in the Annual Conference on all matters except the following: (*a*) constitutional amendments; (*b*) election of delegates to the General and Jurisdictional or Central Conferences; (*c*) all matters of ordination, character, and conference relations of ministers.

3. A probationary member may serve on any board, commission, or committee of the Annual Conference except the Board of the Ministry. He shall not be eligible for election as a delegate to the General or Jurisdictional Conferences.

¶ **326.** A candidate may be elected to probationary membership by vote of the ministerial members in full connection on recommendation of its Board of the Ministry after meeting the following conditions:

1. He must have a currently valid license to preach.

2. He must have met the educational requirements (¶¶ 327-29).

3. He must have been examined and approved by the Board of the Ministry with respect to the following questions:

a) Are you convinced that you should enter the ministry of the Church?

b) Are you willing to face any sacrifices that may be involved?

c) Are you in debt so as to interfere with your work, or have you obligations to others which will make it difficult for you to live on the salary you are to receive?

d) If you are married, is your wife or husband in sympathy with your ministerial calling and willing to share in the sacrifices of your vocation?

e) For the sake of the mission of Jesus Christ in the world and the most effective witness to the Christian gospel and in consideration of your influence as a minister, are you willing to make a complete dedication of yourself to the highest ideals of the Christian life as set forth in ¶¶ 95-97; and to this end will you agree to exercise responsible self-control by personal habits conducive to bodily health, mental and emotional maturity, social responsibility, and growth in grace and the knowledge and love of God?

f) Are you willing to relate yourself in ministry to all persons without regard to color or national origin, including receiving them into the membership and fellowship of the Church?

g) Will you keep before you as the one great objective of your life the advancement of God's Kingdom?

4. He must have been recommended in writing on the basis of a three-fourths majority vote of the district Committee on the Ministry.

5. He must present a satisfactory certificate of good health on the prescribed form from a physician approved by the board. The conference may require psychological tests to provide additional information on the candidate's fitness for the ministry.

6. He must file with the board, in duplicate on the prescribed form, satisfactory written answers to such questions as the board may

ask concerning his age, health, family, Christian experience, call to the ministry, educational record, and plans for service in the Church.

7. He must present a written theological statement covering his basic beliefs and at least one written sermon on a specified biblical passage.

¶ **327.** A candidate for probationary membership must (1) have been graduated with a Bachelor of Arts in liberal education or equivalent degree in a college or university accredited or approved by the University Senate, and (2) have completed at least one fourth of the work required for a Bachelor of Divinity or equivalent first professional degree in a school of theology accredited or approved by the University Senate except under the special conditions of ¶ 328.

¶ **328.** Under special conditions an Annual Conference may, by a three-fourths majority vote of the ministerial members in full connection, present and voting, admit to probationary membership a candidate who exhibits exceptional promise for the ministry in the following cases:

1. If he is a graduate with a Bachelor of Arts in liberal education or an equivalent degree from a college not accredited by the University Senate, who has completed one fourth of the work required for the Bachelor of Divinity or equivalent first professional degree in a school of theology accredited or approved by the University Senate.

2. If he has (*a*) reached thirty-five years of age; (*b*) served as an associate member for a minimum of two years under full-time appointment; (*c*) completed a Bachelor of Arts or its equivalent degree in a college or university accredited or approved by the University Senate; (*d*) completed two years of advanced study prescribed by the Department of the Ministry beyond the four-year ministerial courses of study required for admission to associate membership, in cooperation with the United Methodist theological schools; and (*e*) been recommended by a three-fourths vote of the Cabinet and a three-fourths vote of the Board of the Ministry, written statements of such recommendations having been read to the conference before the vote is taken, setting forth the particular ways his ministry is exceptional and the special reasons he should be received into probationary membership.

¶ **329.** To be continued as a probationary member the candidate shall make regular progress in his ministerial studies. In case of failure or delay, the Board of the Ministry shall investigate the circumstances and judge whether to extend the time within the following limits: (1) for completing the theological course for the Bachelor of Divinity or equivalent first professional degree, a total of eight years; (2) for completing the advanced studies in the ministerial course of study, a total of four years. In a case clearly recognized as exceptional the board, by a three-fourths vote, may recommend an extension beyond these limits, which may be approved by a three-fourths vote of the ministerial members in full connection, present and voting; *provided,* however, that no candidate shall be continued on probation beyond the eighth regular conference session following his admission to probationary membership.

¶ **330.** *General Provisions.*—1. An Annual Conference may designate a Bachelor of Divinity or equivalent first professional degree from a school of theology accredited or approved by the University Senate as the minimum educational requirement for probationary membership.

2. The Board of the Ministry shall require a transcript of credits from each applicant before recognizing any of his educational claims. In case of doubt, the board may submit a transcript to the Department of the Ministry for evaluation.

3. When a probationary member finds it necessary to discontinue his theological education, the Board of the Ministry shall review his relation to the Annual Conference. If he desires to continue in the ministry, he shall receive credit in the course of study for his theological work as the Department of the Ministry shall determine.

4. A probationary member who is regularly appointed to a pastoral charge is subject to the provisions of the Discipline in the performance of his pastoral duties.

5. A probationary member in a special appointment shall relate himself to the district superintendent in the area where his work is done. The district superintendent shall give him supervision and report annually to his Board of the Ministry.

6. A probationary member received under the provisions of ¶ 328.2 who is pursuing advanced studies in the course of study shall do so in a school for courses of study; *provided,* however, that in a case of emergency or unusual circumstances, on approval by the Board of

the Ministry, he may be authorized to pursue no more than one year
of the course by correspondence.

7. The educational standards and other requirements for admission and ordination shall be set by the Jurisdictional Conferences for
the bilingual Annual and Provisional Annual Conferences and Indian
Mission within their territories, by the Central and Provisional Central
Conferences for the Annual and Provisional Annual Conferences within their territories, and outside such territories by the Annual or Provisional Annual Conference itself.

¶ 331. *Member in Full Connection.*— A member in full connection with an Annual Conference by virtue of his election and ordination is bound in special covenant with all the ordained ministers of his
Annual Conference. In the keeping of this covenant he performs the
ministerial duties and maintains the ministerial standards established
by those in the covenant. He offers himself without reserve to be appointed and to serve as his superiors in office may direct. He lives with
his fellow ministers in mutual trust and concern and seeks with them
the sanctification of the fellowship. Only those shall be elected to full
membership who are of unquestionable moral character and genuine
piety, sound in the fundamental doctrines of Christianity and faithful
in the discharge of their duties.

¶ 332. Members in full connection shall have the right to vote on
all matters in the Annual Conference except in the election of lay
delegates to the General and Jurisdictional Conferences (¶¶ 601.3,
614.3) and shall have sole responsibility for all matters of ordination,
character, and conference relations of ministers. They shall be eligible
to hold office in the Annual Conference and to be elected delegates to
the General and Jurisdictional Conferences under the provision of the
Constitution (¶ 39, Art. IV). Every effective member in full connection who is in good standing in an Annual Conference shall receive an
annual appointment by the bishop.

¶ 333. A candidate who has been a probationary member for at
least two years may be admitted into membership in full connection in
an Annual Conference by vote of the ministerial members in full connection, on recommendation of the Board of the Ministry, after he
has qualified as follows. He shall have (1) served full-time under
episcopal appointment under the supervision of a district superin-

tendent satisfactorily to the Board of the Ministry in one of the positions specified in ¶ 391.1-.6 for one year following the completion of the educational requirements specified in § 3 below; (2) been previously ordained deacon; *provided* that until July 1, 1971, §§ 1 and 2 above shall not apply to seminary students who have completed one fourth of the work required for the Bachelor of Divinity or the equivalent first professional degree by July 1, 1968; (3) met educational requirements (including a minimum of two semester or quarter hours in each of the fields of United Methodist history, doctrine, and polity; *provided* that a candidate may meet the requirement by undertaking a special course of study and/or examination in these fields provided and administered by the Department of the Ministry; *see* ¶¶ 375.2, 1046.2, 1047, 1053) in either of the following ways: (*a*) graduation with a Bachelor of Divinity or equivalent degree from a school of theology accredited or approved by the University Senate or (*b*) graduation with a Bachelor of Arts or equivalent degree from a college or university approved by the University Senate and completion of two years of advanced study beyond the requirements for probationary membership (¶ 328.2*d*) under the supervision of the Department of the Ministry; (4) satisfied the board regarding his physical, mental, and emotional health; (5) prepared at least one written sermon on a specified biblical passage and given satisfactory answers in a written doctrinal examination administered by the Board of the Ministry. Consideration shall be given to the following questions:

a) What are your reasons for believing in one God, the Father Almighty, Maker and Sustainer of all things visible and invisible?

b) What reasons have you for your belief that the Holy Bible reveals the Word of God so far as it is necessary for salvation?

c) What evidence do you give that man is in need of divine salvation? How do your own experiences verify such need?

d) What do you believe concerning the person of Jesus Christ and the divine atonement through him?

e) What is your conception of the office and work of the Holy Spirit?

f) What is your conception of (1) repentance, (2) faith, (3) justification, (4) regeneration, (5) sanctification?

g) What are the nature and the function of the Church?

h) What is the significance of the two Sacraments, Baptism and the Lord's Supper?

i) What is your conception of man's immortality and future state?

j) What do you understand by "evangelism"?

k) What do you believe to be the place of Christian social action in the program of the Kingdom of God?

l) What is your dominant motive as a Christian minister?

¶ 334. *Examination for Admission into Full Connection.*—The bishop as chief pastor shall engage those seeking to be admitted in serious self-searching and prayer to prepare them for their examination before the conference. At the time of the examination he shall also explain to the conference the historic nature of the following questions and seek to interpret their spirit and intent. The questions are these and any others which may be thought necessary:

1. Have you faith in Christ?

2. Are you going on to perfection?

3. Do you expect to be made perfect in love in this life?

4. Are you earnestly striving after it?

5. Are you resolved to devote yourself wholly to God and his work?

6. Do you know the General Rules of our Church?

7. Will you keep them?

8. Have you studied the doctrines of The United Methodist Church?

9. After full examination do you believe that our doctrines are in harmony with the Holy Scriptures?

10. Will you preach and maintain them?

11. Have you studied our form of church discipline and polity?

12. Do you approve our church government and policy?

13. Will you support and maintain them?

14. Will you diligently instruct the children in every place?

15. Will you visit from house to house?

16. Will you recommend fasting or abstinence, both by precept and example?

17. Are you determined to employ all your time in the work of God?

18. Are you in debt so as to embarrass you in your work?

19. Will you observe the following directions?

a) Be diligent. Never be unemployed. Never be triflingly employed. Never trifle away time; neither spend any more time at any one place than is strictly necessary.

b) Be punctual. Do everything exactly at the time. And do not mend our rules, but keep them; not for wrath, but for conscience' sake.[8]

¶ 335.   Under conditions regarded as exceptional a candidate who was admitted to probationary membership by a three-fourths vote (¶ 328), upon recommendation by the Board of the Ministry when he has completed advanced studies specified by and under the direction of the Department of the Ministry and has met all the other requirements, may be received into full membership by a three-fourths vote of the ministerial members in full connection, present and voting.

¶ 336.   A full member of an Annual Conference shall be eligible for ordination as elder by a bishop and such other elders as the ordaining bishop may determine.

¶ 337.   The bishop and the secretary of the Annual Conference shall provide credentials to each member in full connection, certifying his ministerial standing and his ordination as elder.

¶ 338.   *Lay Pastor.*—A lay pastor is a layman duly licensed to preach who, upon recommendation of the Board of the Ministry, has been approved by the ministerial members in full connection as eligible for appointment as pastor of a charge. He shall have authority within the bounds of the church to which he is appointed to perform the duties of a pastor as specified in ¶¶ 349-50.

¶ 339.   A lay pastor may qualify for probationary membership and follow the specified procedure into full ministerial membership in an Annual Conference. A lay pastor may qualify for associate membership.

¶ 340.   A lay pastor, upon completing each year the educational and other qualifications and upon recommendation of the Board of

---

[8] These are the questions which every Methodist preacher from the beginning has been required to answer upon becoming a full member of an Annual Conference. These questions were formulated by John Wesley and have been little changed throughout the years.

the Ministry, shall be approved each year by the Annual Conference for appointment.

¶ 341. A lay pastor not serving a pastoral charge may assist his pastor in the charge where he resides, as requested by the pastor and under the pastor's supervision, subject to the laws of the Church. He shall be a member of and amenable to the Charge Conference where he resides. When he changes his residence, in order to retain his status he shall procure from his pastor or district superintendent a letter of his official standing and dismissal and shall present it to the pastor of the charge to which he has moved.

¶ 342. A lay pastor, other than a student as defined in ¶ 343, who is appointed to serve under a district superintendent shall procure from his pastor or district superintendent a letter of his dismissal and shall present it to the Charge Conference of the charge to which he is appointed at its next session. His church membership shall be in the charge to which he is appointed, and he shall be a member of the Charge Conference, subject to the authorization of the Annual Conference.

¶ 343. A lay pastor who is serving as student pastor while attending a college or school of theology accredited or approved by the University Senate may retain his membership in his home church and Charge Conference, but in the discharge of his ministerial functions he shall be amenable to the district superintendent under whom he serves.

¶ 344. Whenever a lay pastor severs his relation with The United Methodist Church, he shall surrender his license and credentials to the district superintendent, who shall file them with the secretary of the Annual Conference.

¶ 345. A lay pastor not serving a pastoral charge shall make to the Charge Conference and the district Committee on the Ministry a report of his labors, as follows: (1) number of sermons preached; (2) number of funerals conducted, with the names of the deceased; (3) evangelistic, educational, and missionary work done in cooperation with and under the direction of his pastor; (4) progress made in academic work or in the prescribed course of study; (5) other activities as requested.

¶ 346. 1. A person licensed to preach and desiring to become or to continue as a lay pastor must have his character, fitness, training, and effectiveness approved annually by a three-fourths vote of the district Committee on the Ministry and by the ministerial members in full connection, after reference to and recommendation by its Board of the Ministry.

2. Between conference sessions a person licensed to preach but not on the approved list or a minister of another church may be appointed as pastor of a charge. If he fails to be approved at the following conference session, he cannot thereafter serve as a lay pastor, either in the same or another appointment until he is approved.

¶ 347. On recommendation of the Board of the Ministry, the ministerial members in full connection may approve annually students of other denominations enrolled in a school of theology accredited or approved by the University Senate to serve as lay pastors for the ensuing year under the direction of a district superintendent; *provided* that they shall agree in writing to support and maintain the doctrine and polity of The United Methodist Church while under appointment.

¶ 348. In recommending to the Annual Conference those who have met the requirements to serve as lay pastors for the ensuing year, the Board of the Ministry shall classify them in three categories with educational requirements as hereinafter specified. Every lay pastor shall meet the educational requirements of his category. Any person who fails to meet these requirements shall not be appointed by a district superintendent. The categories shall be as follows:

1. Those eligible to be appointed as full-time lay pastors. A full-time lay pastor is a layman (*a*) who meets the provisions of ¶ 338; (b) who, unless he has completed the course of study, has met the educational requirements by completing in the preceding year a full year's work in the ministerial course of study under the Department of the Ministry in a school for courses of study (¶ 1046.4) ; *provided,* however, that in a case of emergency or unusual circumstances, on approval by the board, he may be authorized to pursue the course for the current year by correspondence, and further *provided* that for candidates beginning the course after the Uniting Conference not more than one year may be taken by correspondence; (*c*) who devotes his entire time to the church in the charge to which he is appointed; and (*d*) whose cash support per annum from all church sources is a sum equivalent to

not less than the minimum salary established by the Annual Conference for full-time lay pastors.

2. Those eligible to be appointed as part-time lay pastors. A part-time lay pastor is a layman (a) who meets the provisions of ¶ 338; (b) who has completed in the preceding year a minimum of one half a year's work in the course of study; *provided* that the entire introductory studies and four-year course shall be completed in a maximum of ten years from the time of first enrollment; (c) who does not devote his entire time to the charge to which he is appointed; and (d) who does not receive in cash support per annum from all church sources a sum equivalent to the minimum salary established by the Annual Conference for full-time lay pastors. A person who has met the qualifications for approval as lay pastor may request to be classified as eligible to be appointed as a part-time lay pastor for the ensuing year.

3. Those eligible to be appointed as student lay pastors. These shall be enrolled as pretheological or theological students under the definitions and requirements of the Discipline.

¶ 349. 1. A lay pastor while serving under appointment as pastor of a charge shall be responsible to perform all the duties of a pastor (¶350) except that he shall not be authorized to administer the Sacraments. In the performance of his pastoral duties he shall be under the supervision of the district superintendent and the guidance of a duly assigned counseling elder.

2. A lay pastor who is in charge of a pastoral appointment shall attend the sessions of the Annual Conference.

3. The lay pastor shall be amenable to the Annual Conference in the performance of his pastoral duties. Continuance in this relation shall be equivalent to renewal of his license to preach. If at any time the conference declines to renew its approval of a lay pastor, the district Committee on the Ministry may renew his license to preach for one year; further renewal shall be subject to the provisions of the Discipline.

4. A lay pastor not under appointment shall be required to make progress in the course of studies under the provisions of ¶ 320.2.

5. On recommendation of the Board of the Ministry and by vote of the Annual Conference, a lay pastor who has served not less than four years as a lay pastor (formerly an approved supply pastor) and

has attained age sixty-five may be recognized as a retired lay pastor and be so listed in answer to the Disciplinary question: "Who are recognized as retired lay pastors?"

Section VII. Pastor.

¶ **350.** *Duties of a Pastor.*—A pastor is responsible for ministering to the needs of the whole community as well as to the needs of the people of his charge, equipping them to fulfill their ministry to each other and to the world to which they are sent as servants under the Lordship of Christ. Among his duties are the following:

1. To read and teach the Holy Scriptures and preach the gospel.

2. To administer the Sacraments of Baptism and the Lord's Supper if he be qualified or to arrange for these sacramental services.

3. To hold or appoint prayer meetings, love feasts, and watch night meetings wherever possible.

4. To administer the provisions of the Discipline and to supervise the work and program of the local church.

a) He shall give an account of his pastoral ministry to the Charge and Annual Conferences, according to the prescribed form. The care of all church records and local church financial obligations shall be included.

b) He shall participate in denominational and conference programs and training opportunities.

c) He shall encourage the distribution and use of United Methodist literature and promotional materials in each local church.

5. To perform the marriage ceremony after due counsel with the parties involved. The decision to perform a ceremony shall be the right and responsibility of the pastor. Qualification for performing marriages shall be in accordance with the laws of the state and The United Methodist Church.

a) He shall hold premarital conferences, using the official manual of the Church. These conferences shall be held as early as possible before the date of the wedding.

b) In view of the seriousness with which the Scriptures and the Church regard divorce, he may solemnize the marriage of a divorced

person only when he has satisfied himself by careful counseling that
(`) the divorced person is sufficiently aware of the factors leading to
th. ilure of the previous marriage, (2) the divorced person is sin-
cerei, preparing to make the proposed marriage truly Christian, and
(3) sufficient time has elapsed between the divorce and the contemplated marriage for adequate preparation and counseling.

c) He shall counsel those who are under the threat of marriage
breakdown in order to explore every possibility for reconciliation.

6. To counsel bereaved families and conduct appropriate memorial services for the dead.

7. To visit in the homes of the parish and community, especially
among the sick, aged, and others in need.

8. To instruct candidates for membership and to receive them
into the Church.

9. To preside over the Charge Conference at the request of the
district superintendent.

10. To search out from among his membership and constituency
young people for the ministry, to help them interpret the meaning of
the call of God, to challenge them with the opportunities of the Christian ministry, to advise and assist them when they commit themselves
thereto, to counsel with them and over them as their pastor through
the course of their preparation, and to keep a careful record of all
such decisions, reporting to the Annual Conference the number of such
students enrolled in schools of theology.

11. To participate in the life and work of the community and in
ecumenical affairs and to lead the congregation to become so involved.

¶ 351. *Special Provisions.*—1. A pastor shall first obtain the written consent of his district superintendent before engaging for an evangelist any person who is not a conference evangelist, a regular member
of an Annual Conference, a lay pastor, or a certified lay speaker in
good standing in The United Methodist Church.

2. No pastor shall discontinue services in a local church between
sessions of the Annual Conference without the consent of the Charge
Conference and the district superintendent.

3. No pastor shall arbitrarily organize a pastoral charge. (*See*
¶ 142 for the method of organizing a local church.)

Section VIII. Special Appointments.

¶ **352.** A conference member may be appointed by his bishop, after consultations with the district superintendents, to a position in a school, college, university, seminary, hospital, home, or agency or to the military or institutional chaplaincy or similar specialized ministry under the following conditions:

1. The institution or agency desiring to employ a conference member shall first, through its appropriate official, consult the member's bishop and secure his approval before completing any agreement to employ the member. If the institution or agency is located in another area, the bishop of that area shall also be consulted.

2. When a bishop appoints a conference member to an institution or agency in another area, he shall notify the resident bishop of the area in which the special appointment is located and shall include any pertinent information about the minister and his work.

3. The bishop in whose area a minister under special appointment resides shall become the minister's pastor and superior to represent him, when necessary, to the bishop who appointed him.

4. A conference member under special appointment is amenable to the Annual Conference of which he is a member and in so far as possible should maintain close working relationships with and effective participation in the work of his Annual Conference, assuming whatever responsibilities he is qualified and requested to assume.

5. A conference member serving under special appointment shall be available and on call to administer the Sacraments of Baptism and the Lord's Supper as requested by the district superintendent of the district in which the special appointment is held.

6. A conference member, on recommendation of the conference Board of Evangelism, confirmed by a two-thirds vote of the Annual Conference, may be appointed a conference evangelist; *provided* that the appointee shall meet the standards set by the General and conference Boards of Evangelism for conference evangelists.

7. A conference member or member on trial may, if he so desires, receive a special appointment to attend any school, college, or theological seminary accredited or approved by the University Senate.

8. All conference secretaries shall submit to the editors of the

General Minutes a list of the special appointments made in their Annual Conferences, and there shall be published in the General Minutes a representative list showing the number of ministers in the Church serving in the major categories under special appointment.

Section IX.　Counseling Elder.

¶ 353.　A **counseling elder** is a member in full connection in an Annual Conference recommended by the Board of the Ministry and assigned by the Cabinet to provide counsel for a lay pastor fulfilling the requirements of the course of study, in the development of his spiritual life and growth, in the administration of the Sacraments, and in all other matters pertaining to the fulfillment of his preaching and pastoral service. He shall work under the direction of and in consultation with the district superintendent and shall make regular reports of his activities to the district superintendent and to the Board of the Ministry.

Section X.　District Superintendent.

¶ 354.　*Duties of a District Superintendent.*—District superintendents are to be chosen and appointed by the bishop. They shall minister to the needs of the pastors and churches in their district by meeting and counseling with pastors and officials. Among the duties of the district superintendent are the following:

1. To travel through his district in order to preach and oversee the spiritual and temporal affairs of the Church.

2. To schedule and preside, or authorize an elder to preside, in each Charge Conference and in the Annual Church Conference.

3. To administer the program of the Church within the bounds of his district in cooperation with the pastors and the Charge Conferences, to encourage adequate salaries for pastors, to promote a concern for continuing education for ministers, and to urge financial support of all conference and denominational causes.

4. To supervise the work of pastors in his district and counsel with them concerning their pastoral responsibilities, continuing educa-

tion, and other matters affecting their ministry and personal life. He shall be available for counsel with each pastor's family.

5. To appraise the needs and opportunities of churches within his district; to evaluate fields of labor; and within an ecumenically responsible perspective to initiate new forms of ministry, mergers, yoked fields, and long-range planning and the establishment and closing of churches.

6. To counsel with pastors and Committees on Pastor-Parish Relations concerning assignments and to consult with the bishop regarding the appointment of persons approved by the Board of the Ministry.

7. To emphasize ministerial recruitment and education and to advise and encourage candidates for the ministry.

8. To issue and renew licenses to preach in accordance with the action of the district Committee on the Ministry or the Board of the Ministry.

9. To cooperate with the district Committee on Church Buildings and Locations and local church Boards of Trustees or building committees in arranging acquisitions, sales, transfers, and mortgages of property and in ensuring that all charters, deeds, and other legal documents conform to the Discipline and to the laws, usages, and forms of the county, state, territory, or country within which such property is situated.

10. To participate with the other district superintendents in submitting a report to the Annual Conference reflecting the state of the conference and setting forth recommendations along with other information pertinent to the operation of the Annual Conference.

11. To see that the provisions of the Discipline are observed and to interpret and decide all questions of church law and discipline raised by the churches in his district, subject to an appeal to the president of the next Annual Conference.

12. To prepare and deliver to his successor: (*a*) a list of all abandoned church properties and cemeteries within the bounds of his district; (*b*) a list of all church properties being permissively used by other religious organizations, with the names of the local trustees thereof; (*c*) a list of all endowments, annuities, trust funds, investments, and unpaid legacies of which he has knowledge belonging to any pastoral charge or organization connected therewith in his district.

Section XI.   Continuing Education.

¶ **355.** The minister shall be encouraged to continue his education throughout his career, including a carefully developed personal program of study augmented periodically by involvement in organized educational activities. In most cases the minister's continuing education program should allow for leaves of absence for study at least one week each year and at least one month during one year of each quadrennium. Such leaves shall not be considered as part of the minister's vacation and shall be planned in consultation with his charge or other agency to which he is appointed as well as his bishop, district superintendent, and Annual Conference continuing education committee.

Section XII.   Sabbatical Leave.

¶ **356.** Any minister who has been in the effective relation in any Annual Conference or Conferences for ten consecutive years from the time of his admission on trial may be granted a **sabbatical leave** by a bishop for one year without losing his relationship as an effective minister. This sabbatical leave is to be allowed for travel, study, rest, or for other justifiable reasons. Sabbatical leave granted by the bishop holding the conference must be upon the vote of the Annual Conference to which the minister belongs after said minister has given notice to his district superintendent and after the district superintendent has given notice to the bishop of his intention to request such sabbatical leave. A sabbatical leave shall not be granted to the same man more frequently than one year in seven.

Section XIII.   Disability Leave.

¶ **357.** 1. When a minister who is an associate member, a probationary member, or a member in full connection in an Annual Conference is forced to give up his ministerial work because of his physical or mental disability, upon joint recommendation of the Board of the Ministry and the conference Board of Pensions and by a majority vote of the ministerial members of the Annual Conference in full connection who are present and voting, he may be granted annual disability leave without losing his relationship to the Annual Conference; *pro-*

vided, however, that such leave may be granted or renewed only after a thorough investigation of the case and examination of medical evidence in accordance with § 3 or § 4 below, up to but not beyond his attainment of the age of voluntary retirement. Each disability leave granted by the Annual Conference shall be recorded in the conference minutes.

2. When a minister is forced to give up his ministerial work between sessions of the Annual Conference on account of his physical or mental disability, with the approval of a majority of the district superintendents, after consultation with the officers of the Board of the Ministry and the executive committee of the conference Board of Pensions, a disability leave may be granted by the bishop for the remainder of the conference year; *provided,* however, that such leave may be granted only after examination of medical evidence in accordance with § 3 or § 4 below. Any such leave granted between sessions of the Annual Conference, with the effective date of such leave, shall be entered in the minutes of the next regular session of the conference.

3. A minister who is a currently participating member of the Ministers Reserve Pension Fund at the time his disability occurs may be granted a disability leave only after medical evidence shall have been secured and reviewed by the General Board of Pensions in accordance with the regulations of the Ministers Reserve Pension Fund pertaining to disability benefits.

4. A minister who is not a currently participating member of the Ministers Reserve Pension Fund at the time his disability occurs may be granted a disability leave only after a medical report shall have been submitted to the Joint Committee on Disability (¶ 665.24) by a medical doctor who has been approved by the joint committee. Such report shall be made on a form approved by the General Board of Pensions.

5. When a minister on disability leave recovers sufficiently to resume ministerial work, with his consent he may receive an appointment from a bishop between sessions of the Annual Conference, thereby terminating the disability leave. Such appointment shall be reported immediately by the Cabinet to the conference Board of Pensions and to the General Board of Pensions. Such termination of leave, together

with the effective date, shall also be recorded in the minutes of the Annual Conference at its next regular session.

Section XIV. Supernumerary Ministers.

¶ **358.** A **supernumerary minister** is one who because of impaired health or other equally sufficient reason is temporarily unable to perform full work. This relation shall not be granted for more than five years in succession except by a two-thirds vote of the conference, upon recommendation of the Board of the Ministry and a statement of the reason for such recommendation. He may receive an appointment or be left without one, according to the judgment of the Annual Conference of which he is a member, and he shall be subject to all limitations of the Discipline in respect to reappointment and continuance in the same charge that apply to effective ministers. He shall report to his Charge Conference and to the pastor all marriages performed and all baptisms administered. Should he reside outside the bounds of his Annual Conference, he shall forward to it annually a certificate similar to that required of a retired minister, and in case of failure to do so the Annual Conference may locate him without his consent. He shall have no claim on the conference funds except by vote of the conference.

Section XV. Superannuated Ministers.

¶ **359.** A **superannuated minister** is one who at his own request or by action of the ministerial members in full connection, on recommendation of the Board of the Ministry, has been placed in the retired relation. (*See* ¶¶ 1374-87 for pension information.)

¶ **360.** The Annual Conference may place any ministerial member thereof in the retired relation with or without his consent and irrespective of his age if such relation is recommended by the Board of the Ministry.

¶ **361.** Every ministerial member of an Annual Conference whose seventy-second birthday precedes the first day of the regular session of his Annual Conference shall automatically be retired from the active ministry at said conference session.

¶ **362.** 1. At his own request and by vote of the Annual Conference, any ministerial member who has attained age sixty-five or has completed forty years of full-time approved service prior to the date of the opening session of the conference may be placed in the retired relation with the privilege of making an annuity claim.

2. Any member of the Annual Conference who has completed twenty years or more of full-time approved service prior to the opening date of the session of the conference may request the Annual Conference to place him in the retired relation with the privilege of receiving his annuity claims for the number of effective years served in the Annual Conference, payment to begin following his sixty-fifth birthday; *provided* that he shall have had his character passed annually since retirement.

¶ 363. 1. If retirement of a minister takes place prior to his attainment of age sixty-five or the completion of forty years of full-time approved service, the right to make an annuity claim from the time of retirement until the minister attains the age of voluntary retirement may be granted only when approved annually by three fourths of those present and voting in the Annual Conference, on joint recommendation of the Board of the Ministry and the conference Board of Pensions.

2. The Annual Conference, at its discretion, upon joint recommendation of the Board of the Ministry and the conference Board of Pensions, may designate any time within the ensuing conference year as the effective date of retirement of a minister who is placed in the retired relation under the provisions of ¶ 362 or who is granted the rights to make an annuity claim under the provisions of § 1 above.

¶ 364. Every retired minister who is not appointed as pastor of a charge shall have a seat in the Charge Conference and all the privileges of membership in the church where he elects to hold such membership except as set forth in the Discipline. He shall report to the Charge Conference and to the pastor all marriages performed and baptisms administered. If he resides outside the bounds of the conference, he shall forward annually to his conference a certificate of his Christian and his ministerial conduct, together with an account of the number and circumstances of his family, signed by the district superintendent or the pastor of the charge within the bounds of which he resides. Without this certificate the conference, after having given thirty days' notice, may locate him without his consent.

Section XVI.　Termination of Annual Conference Membership.

¶ **365.**　Termination of Annual Conference membership, either associate or member in full connection, may be accomplished in the ways indicated in ¶¶ 368-69, 371-73, upon recommendation of the Board of the Ministry.

¶ **366.**　*Voluntary Location.*—An Annual Conference may grant a member a certificate of location at his own request; *provided* that it shall first have examined his character at the conference session when the request is made and found him in good standing, and *provided* further that this relation shall be granted only to one who avowedly intends to discontinue regular ministerial or evangelistic work. Voluntary location shall be certified by the presiding bishop. The minister shall be permitted to exercise ministerial functions under supervision of the pastor in charge only within the bounds of that charge or of the charge to which he may be appointed temporarily. He shall report to the Charge Conference and the pastor all marriages performed, baptisms administered, and funerals conducted and shall be held amenable for his conduct and the continuance of his ordination rights to the Annual Conference within which the Charge Conference membership is held.

¶ **367.**　A minister who has been located may be readmitted by the Annual Conference from which he was located at its discretion upon presentation of his certificate of location and the recommendation of his district Committee on the Ministry and the Board of the Ministry.

¶ **368.**　*Involuntary Location.*—Whenever it is determined by the Board of the Ministry that in their judgment a member of the Annual Conference is unacceptable, inefficient, or indifferent in the work of the ministry or that his conduct is such as to impair seriously his usefulness as a minister or that his engagement in secular business, except as required by the ill health of himself or of his family, disqualifies him for pastoral work, they shall notify him in writing and ask him to request location at the next session of the Annual Conference. If he refuses or neglects to locate as requested, the conference may by count vote, on recommendation of the Board of the Ministry, locate him without his consent. In the case of involuntary location the authority to exercise the ministerial office shall be suspended, and the district superintendent shall require from him his credentials to be deposited with the secretary of the conference.

¶ 369. Whenever it is unanimously determined by the district superintendents that a member of the Annual Conference should be located for any of the reasons cited in ¶ 368, they shall notify him in writing of their judgment at least three months before the next session of the Annual Conference and ask him to request location at such session under the provisions of ¶ 365. If he refuses or neglects to locate as requested, the district superintendent shall certify the fact to the Board of the Ministry, which committee shall proceed to recommend his immediate location without his consent. Upon such action his right to exercise the functions of the ministry shall be suspended, and the district superintendent shall require from him his credentials to be deposited with the secretary of the conference.

¶ 370. If a located person remains a member in good standing of The United Methodist Church until the age of mandatory retirement fixed by the General Conference, he shall thereby retain the right to make an annuity claim, based upon his years of approved service; *provided,* however, that he shall have been readmitted by a two-thirds vote of the Annual Conference which granted him location; if it be nonexistent, then he shall apply for admission to the Annual Conference within the boundaries of which the major part of his service was rendered or its legal successor.

¶ 371. *Surrender of the Ministerial Office.*—Any member of an Annual Conference in good standing who desires to surrender his ministerial office and withdraw from the conference may be allowed to do so by the conference at its session; in which case his credentials shall be filed with the official records of the Annual Conference of which he was a member, and his membership in the Church shall be recorded in the charge where he resides at the time of such surrender.

¶ 372. *Withdrawal.*—When a minister in good standing withdraws to unite with another church, his credentials should be surrendered to the conference, and if he shall desire it, they may be returned to him with the following inscription written plainly across their face:

A. B. has this day been honorably dismissed by the _____
Annual Conference from the ministry of The United Methodist Church.

Dated _____

_____, *President*

_____, *Secretary*

¶ **373.** When in the interval between sessions of an Annual Conference a member thereof shall deposit with a bishop or with his district superintendent a letter of withdrawal from the ministry, or his credentials, or both, the same shall be presented to the Annual Conference at its next session for its action thereon.

Section XVII. Mission Elders.

¶ **374.** **A mission deacon or elder** is one who is a member of a Mission without being a member of an Annual Conference. In the election of mission deacons and elders the Mission shall require of all applicants the conditions and qualifications demanded of deacons and elders by an Annual Conference. The duties, responsibilities, rights, and privileges of mission-traveling deacons and elders shall be the same as those of traveling deacons and elders who are members of an Annual Conference, and such a minister may be transferred to an Annual Conference when he meets the qualifications for membership in the Annual Conference to which he desires to transfer.

Section XVIII. Ministers from Other Churches.

¶ **375.** Ministers coming from other Christian churches, *provided* they present suitable testimonials of good standing through the Board of the Ministry, give assurance of their faith, Christian experience, and other qualifications, give evidence of their agreement with us in doctrine and discipline, present a satisfactory certificate of good health on the prescribed form from a physician approved by the Board of the Ministry, and meet the educational requirements, may be received into our ministry in the following manner:

1. The District Conference or district Committee on the Ministry

may receive them as lay pastors not entitled to administer the Sacraments, pending the recognition of their orders by the Annual Conference.

2. On recommendation of the Board of the Ministry the Annual Conference may recognize their orders and admit them into the membership of the conference; *provided* that their qualifications meet the educational and other requirements of the Discipline, including the requirements in United Methodist history, polity, and doctrine.

3. Ministers from other churches who can meet the educational standards required of United Methodist ministers may apply through the Board of the Ministry to the Annual Conference, which may recognize their credentials and receive them into probationary membership, associate membership, or membership in full connection in the conference.

4. The Annual Conference, on recommendation of the Board of the Ministry, may also receive in equal standing preachers who are on probation in the ministry of another Methodist church, using, however, special care that before they are admitted to membership in full connection, they shall meet all the educational and other requirements.

5. On recommendation of the Board of the Ministry the ministerial members in full connection may approve annually ministers in good standing in other Christian denominations to serve as pastors in charge while retaining their denomination affiliation; *provided* that they shall agree in writing to support and maintain the doctrine and polity of The United Methodist Church while under appointment. Their ordination credentials shall be examined by the Board of the Ministry and upon their recommendation may be recognized as valid in The United Methodist Church while they are under appointment.

¶ 376. The Board of the Ministry of an Annual Conference is required to ascertain from a minister seeking admission into its membership on credentials from another denomination whether or not membership in the effective relation was previously held in an Annual Conference of The United Methodist Church or one of its legal predecessors and if so when and under what circumstances his connection with such Annual Conferences was served.

¶ 377. A minister seeking admission into an Annual Conference on credentials from another denomination who has previously withdrawn from membership in the effective relation in an Annual Conference of The United Methodist Church or one of its legal predecessors shall not be admitted or readmitted without the consent of the Annual Conference from which he withdrew or its legal successor, or the Annual Conference of which the major portion of his former conference is a part.

¶ **378.** Whenever the orders of a minister are recognized according to the foregoing provisions, he shall be furnished with a certificate signed by the bishop.

¶ **379.** When the orders of a minister of another church shall have been duly recognized, his certificate of ordination by said church shall be returned to him with the following inscription written plainly across its face:

Accredited by the _____ Annual Conference of The United Methodist Church, this __ day of _____, 19__, as the basis of new credentials.

_____, *President*

_____, *Secretary*

¶ **380.** With the consent of the bishop in charge, ministers from other Methodist churches may be received by transfer, if they meet United Methodist educational requirements, without going through the process required for ministers coming from other denominations. Similarly, ministers of The United Methodist Church may be transferred by a bishop to other Methodist churches with the consent of the proper authorities in said churches.

Section XIX.　Episcopacy.

¶ **381.** *General Provisions.*—The general plan of episcopal supervision, including the Council of Bishops, is set forth in the Constitution.

¶ **382.** The Jurisdictional and Central Conferences are authorized to fix the percentage of votes necessary to elect a bishop. It is recommended that at least three fifths of those present and voting be necessary to elect.

¶ **383.** The bishop or bishops elected by a Jurisdictional or Central Conference shall be consecrated at the session of the conference at which the election or elections take place, or at an adjourned session thereof, or at a time and place designated by the conference. At the consecration service the other Jurisdictional and Central Conferences and the Church at large may be represented by one or more bishops appointed by the president of the Council of Bishops.

¶ **384.** In the case of an emergency in a Central Conference through the death, expiration of term of service, or any other disability of a bishop, the Council of Bishops may assign one of its members to furnish the necessary episcopal supervision for that field.

¶ **385.** The Council of Bishops may, with the consent of the bishop and with the concurrence of the standing Committee on Episcopacy of the jurisdiction involved, assign one of its members to some specific churchwide responsibility, deemed of sufficient importance to the welfare of the total Church, for a period of a year. In this event he shall be released from the presidential responsibilities within his episcopal area for that term, and another bishop or bishops, active or retired and not necessarily from the same jurisdiction, shall be designated by the Council of Bishops, on recommendation of the College of Bishops of the jurisdiction involved, to assume his presidential responsibilities during the interim. This assignment may be renewed for a second year by a two-thirds action of the Council of Bishops, a majority of the Committee on Episcopacy, and consent of the bishop and the College of Bishops involved. He shall continue to receive his regular stipend.

¶ **386.** A bishop who has served for not less than two quadrenniums may be granted a sabbatical leave for not more than one year for a justifiable reason other than health if he so requests and if the College of Bishops of which he is a member, the Committee on Episcopacy of that jurisdiction, and the Council of Bishops or its executive committee approve. In this event he shall, for the period for which the leave is granted, be released from the presidential responsibilities within his episcopal area, and another bishop or bishops, active or retired and not necessarily from the same jurisdiction, shall be designated by the Council of Bishops, on recommendation of the College of Bishops of the jurisdiction involved, to assume his presidential duties during the interim. He shall continue to receive his housing allowance and one-half salary for the period of the leave.

¶ **387.** The Council of Bishops shall promote the evangelistic activities of the Church and shall furnish such inspirational leadership as the need and opportunity may demand.

¶ **388.** The Council of Bishops, with the cooperation of the Department of the Ministry, may plan for annual regional seminars for the orientation and instruction of ministers newly appointed to the district superintendency.

¶ **389.** There shall be a **Conference of United Methodist Bishops,** composed of all the bishops elected by the General, Jurisdictional, and Central Conferences and bishops of affiliated autonomous Methodist churches, which shall meet in each quadrennium immediately prior to the General Conference on call of the Council of Bishops. In case of an emergency a special meeting of the conference may be called by the Council of Bishops at any time during the quadrennium. The expense shall be charged to the Episcopal Fund. The travel expense of bishops from affiliated autonomous Methodist churches shall be paid on the same basis as that of the bishops of The United Methodist Church.

¶ **390.** *Duties, Powers, and Limitations of Bishops.*—The duties of a bishop are:

1. To oversee the spiritual and temporal affairs of the Church.

2. To preside in the General, Jurisdictional, Central, and Annual Conferences.

3. To form the districts according to his judgment after consultation with the district superintendents and after the number of the same has been determined by vote of the Annual Conference.

4. To fix the appointments of the preachers in the Annual Conferences, Provisional Annual Conferences, and Missions, as the Discipline may direct. He may appoint an associate pastor for a charge when in his judgment such an appointment is necessary.

5. To read the appointments of deaconesses.

6. To fix, either within their own conference or within the conference where they attend school, the Charge Conference membership of all ministers who are appointed to attend school.

7. To transfer, with the consent of the bishop of the receiving

Annual Conference, a ministerial member of one Annual Conference to another, *provided* the ministerial member agrees to said transfer, and to send immediately to the secretaries of both conferences involved, to the registrar of the conference Board of the Ministry in which the member is being received if he is on trial, and to the clearinghouse of the General Board of Pensions, written notices of the transfer of the member and of his standing in the course of study if he is an undergraduate.

8. To organize such Missions as shall have been authorized by the General Conference.

9. To consecrate bishops, to ordain elders and deacons, to consecrate deaconesses, and to see that the names of the persons ordained and consecrated by him be entered on the journals of the conference and that proper credentials be furnished to these persons.

10. To travel through the connection at large. (*See* ¶ 887.)

¶ 391. The following provisions and limitations shall be observed by the bishop when fixing the appointments:

1. He shall appoint preachers to pastoral charges annually after consultation with the district superintendents; *provided* that, before the official declaration of the assignments of the preachers, he shall announce openly to the Cabinet his appointments, and *provided* further that before any announcement of appointments is made, the district superintendents shall consult with the pastors concerning their specific appointments except when the pastors involved have left the seat of the Annual Conference without the permission of the Annual Conference. Bearing in mind the stated goals of an inclusive Church, he shall seek the cooperation of the Cabinet and congregations in the appointment of pastors without regard to race or color.

2. He may make or change the appointments of preachers in the interval between sessions of the Annual Conference as necessity may require, after consultation with the district superintendents.

3. He shall choose and appoint the district superintendents annually, but within the Jurisdictional Conferences of the United States he shall not appoint any minister a district superintendent for more than six years in any consecutive nine years.

4. The years served by a district superintendent in a Methodist Annual Conference or by a conference superintendent in an Evangelical

United Brethren Annual Conference immediately prior to union shall in the first appointment under The United Methodist Church be counted as part of the six-year maximum, except that in the case of a conference superintendent of The Evangelical United Brethren Church no more than a maximum of three years' service prior to his coming to membership in an Annual Conference employing the appointive system shall be counted. (For the rule relating to service on agencies see ¶ 808.4.)

5. On the request in each case of an appropriate United Methodist official, agency, or institution, and after consultation with the district superintendents, he may make appointments annually to positions in or through United Methodist and United Methodist-related agencies.

6. On the request in each case of an appropriate official, agency, or institution, and on the recommendation of the district superintendents, confirmed by a two-thirds vote of the Annual Conference, he may make appointments annually to positions in non–United Methodist agencies; *provided* that in no such case shall The United Methodist Church incur any financial responsibility.

7. On the recommendation of the conference Board of Evangelism, confirmed by a two-thirds vote of the Annual Conference, he may appoint an effective member of the conference as conference evangelist; *provided* that the appointee shall meet the standards set up by the General and conference Boards of Evangelism for conference evangelists.

8. He may appoint a member of an Annual Conference who desires to attend school to any college or school of theology accredited or approved by the University Senate.

9. He shall not appoint any preacher who has been rejected as an applicant or who has been discontinued or located, except at his own request, unless the conference at the time of such rejection, discontinuance, or location shall give such liberty; and he shall not appoint as a supply any preacher who has previously been expelled from the ministry or who has surrendered his credentials to an Annual Conference unless the conference to which he surrendered his credentials or from which he was expelled restores his credentials or recommends it.

10. Every traveling preacher, unless retired, supernumerary, on

sabbatical leave, on disability leave, or under arrest of character, must receive an appointment.

¶ 392. When a bishop judges it necessary, he may divide a circuit, station, or mission into two or more charges and appoint the pastors thereto; and he may unite two or more circuits or stations and appoint one pastor for the united congregations.

¶ 393. Bishops shall discharge such other duties as the Discipline may direct.

¶ 394. *Retired Bishops.*—1. If a bishop cease from traveling at large among the people without the consent of the Jurisdictional Conference, he shall not thereafter exercise in any degree the episcopal office in The United Methodist Church.

2. A bishop may voluntarily resign from the episcopacy at any session of his Jurisdictional Conference. A bishop so resigning shall surrender to the secretary of his Jurisdictional Conference his consecration papers, and he shall be furnished with a certificate of his resignation which shall entitle him to membership as a traveling elder in the Annual Conference of which he was last a member or its successor. When he or his surviving widow and dependent children become conference claimants, the Episcopal Fund shall pay a pension on account of his service as a bishop, and his Annual Conference or Conferences on account of his approved service therein.

3. A bishop who by reason of impaired health is temporarily unable to perform full work may be released by the Jurisdictional Conference from the obligation to travel through the connection at large. He may choose the place of his residence, and the Council of Bishops shall be at liberty to assign him to such work as he may be able to perform. He shall receive his support as provided in the the Discipline.

4. An elder who has served as a bishop up to the time of his retirement shall have the status of a retired bishop.

¶ 395. 1. A bishop shall be released from the obligation to travel through the connection at large and from residential supervision at the close of the regular session of his Jurisdictional Conference the first day of which next precedes his seventy-second birthday; *provided,* however, that a bishop retired from residential and presidential responsibilities in accordance with this rule shall receive full episcopal salary and house allowance in lieu of retirement benefits until he attains the mandatory retirement age for all ministers (¶ 361) if, during such period, he holds himself available for assignment by the Council of Bishops to some distinctive responsibility without further compensation. He shall be assigned to work with an agency of the Church only on specific invitation of that agency.

2. A bishop, at any age and for any reason deemed sufficient by his Jurisdictional Conference, may be released by that body from the obligation to travel through the connection at large and from residential supervision.

3. A bishop who has reached the age of sixty-five years and who for any reason deems it wise that he retire shall notify in writing the president (or secretary, in case he is the president) of the College of Bishops and the secretary of the standing Committee on Episcopacy of his jurisdiction. The college and committee shall convene in a joint meeting on the call of the president (or secretary) of the college within two months after receipt of the request to retire. If both, acting separately, approve the retirement by majority vote of those present and voting, the bishop shall be accorded the retired relation as soon as possible, but not later than two months from that date. The secretary of the Council of Bishops and the treasurer of the Episcopal Fund shall be notified. The college, in cooperation with the Council of Bishops when required by the Discipline, shall make provision for the supervision of the vacated area for the remainder of the quadrennium.

4. If one third or more of the members of the College of Bishops or of the standing Committee on Episcopacy of a jurisdiction have reason to believe that because of health impairment a bishop in the jurisdiction is no longer able to perform full work or render effective service and the bishop does not wish to retire, the college and committee shall convene jointly to consider the matter. If both, acting separately, by majority vote of those present and voting, decide that it is in the best interests of the Church that the bishop retire, he shall be so informed by the president (or secretary) of the college. If the bishop objects to this recommendation, he may request an examination by a panel of three doctors, not including his own physician, selected by the president (or secretary) of the college and the chairman of the committee. If he declines to take an examination, or if the doctors after such examination recommend his retirement, he shall be retired. The

bishop involved shall not be eligible to vote on any of the above items. The secretary of the Council of Bishops and the treasurer of the Episcopal Fund shall be notified of the action. The college, in cooperation with the Council of Bishops when required by the Discipline, shall arrange for the presidential supervision of the Annual Conferences of the vacated area for the remainder of the quadrennium.

5. A bishop who has been retired under § 1, 2, or 3 may, on vote of the Council of Bishops, be appointed to take charge of an episcopal area or parts of an area in case of the death, resignation, or disability of the resident bishop or because of judicial procedure; *provided* that the request is made by a majority of the bishops in the jurisdiction of the proposed change. This appointment shall not continue beyond the next session of his Jurisdictional Conference.

¶ 396. 1. A bishop who has been released from the obligation to travel through the connection at large in accordance with any of the foregoing provisions shall not preside thereafter over any Annual Conference, Provisional Annual Conference, or Mission, or make appointments, or preside at the Jurisdictional or Central Conference, but may take the chair temporarily in any conference if requested to do so by the bishop presiding. He may participate in the Council of Bishops, but without vote. In case, however, a retired bishop shall be appointed by the Council of Bishops to take charge of a vacant episcopal area or parts of an area under the provisions of ¶ 395.5, he may preside over sessions of an Annual Conference, Provisional Annual Conference, or Mission, make appointments, and participate and vote in the meetings of the bishops.

2. Each Central Conference shall determine the rules for retirement of its bishops; *provided* that the age of retirement shall not exceed that fixed for bishops in the jurisdictions. In the event of retirement allowances' being paid from the Episcopal Fund, these rules shall be subject to the approval of the General Conference.

¶ 397. *Bishops in Jurisdictions.*—1. Each jurisdiction having 500,000 church members or less shall be entitled to six bishops, and each jurisdiction having more than 500,000 church members shall be entitled to one additional bishop for each additional 500,000 church members or major fraction thereof; *provided,* however, that in those jurisdictions where this requirement would result in there being an average of more than 70,000 square miles per episcopal area, such jurisdiction shall be entitled to six bishops for the first 400,000 church members or less, and for each additional 400,000 church members or two thirds thereof shall be entitled to one additional bishop, and *provided* further that the General Conference may authorize any Jurisdictional Conference to elect one or more bishops beyond the quota herein specified in order to provide episcopal supervision for mission fields outside the territory of a Jurisdictional Conference.

2. In the event a bishop is transferred to a regional jurisdiction on the request of the Jurisdictional Conference, that conference may nevertheless elect bishops up to the limit of its regular quota whether or not the transfer becomes effective before the completion of such election.

3. Each Jurisdictional Conference may fix the episcopal residences within its jurisdiction and assign the bishops to the same. The bishops of the jurisdiction shall fix the boundaries of the episcopal area. It is recommended that in arranging the plan of episcopal supervision the bishops not assign to a newly elected bishop the Annual Conference of which he was a member at the time of election.

¶ **398.** *Bishops in Central Conferences.*—The Central Conferences shall elect bishops in the number determined by the General Conference, whose episcopal supervision shall be within the territory included in the Central Conference by which they have been elected, subject to such other conditions as the General Conference shall prescribe; *provided,* however, that a bishop elected by one Central Conference may exercise episcopal supervision in another Central Conference when so requested by such other Central Conference.

1. A bishop elected by a Central Conference shall be constituted by election in a Central Conference and consecrated by the laying on of hands of three bishops or at least one bishop and two elders.

2. A bishop elected by a Central Conference shall have, within the bounds of the Central Conference by which he is elected or within which he is administering, authority similar to that exercised by bishops elected by or administering in a Jurisdictional Conference.

3. A bishop elected by a Central Conference shall have the status, rights, and duties within his territory of a bishop elected by or functioning in a Jurisdictional Conference. A bishop elected by a Central

Conference shall have membership in the Council of Bishops and shall have the privilege of full participation with vote. Attendance at the annual meetings of the Council of Bishops by bishops elected by Central Conferences shall be left to the option of the bishops in each Central Conference.

4. In a Central Conference where term episcopacy prevails, a bishop whose term of office expires prior to the time of compulsory retirement because of age and who is not reelected by the Central Conference shall be returned to membership as a traveling elder in the Annual Conference (or its successor) of which he ceased to be a member when elected bishop. His term of office shall expire at the close of the Central Conference at which his successor is elected, and he shall therefore be entitled to participate as a bishop in the consecration of his successor. The credentials of his office as bishop shall be submitted to the secretary of the Central Conference, who shall make thereon the notation that he has honorably completed the term of service for which he was elected and has ceased to be a bishop of The United Methodist Church.

¶ 399. *Missionary Bishops.*—1. **A missionary bishop** is a bishop who has been elected for a specified foreign mission field with full episcopal powers but with episcopal jurisdiction limited to the foreign mission field for which he was elected.

2. Missionary bishops shall be included in all other provisions for the episcopacy, including relation to Jurisdictional Conferences, amenability, and provisions for support and retirement.

3. Notwithstanding the above definitions, in an emergency the Council of Bishops may assign a missionary bishop for specified service in any foreign field in consultation with the authorities, where such exist, of the Central Conference or the Provisional Central Conference concerned.

Chapter Three
THE LAY WORKER

¶ **501.** A **lay worker** in the Church is a person other than the clergy whose decision to make a career of work (either full-time or term) in the employed status in the Church or church-related agencies is accompanied by the meeting of standards of excellence in the chosen field of service and who has been consecrated by a bishop.

¶ 502. A lay worker shall be eligible for consecration by vote of the Annual Conference on recommendation of its Committee on the Lay Worker (¶ 667) after meeting the following conditions:

1. He must have been affirmed by the Charge Conference as a member in good standing (¶ 145.7).

2. He must have met the standards for lay workers (¶ 667.3c).

3. He must present a satisfactory certificate of good health on the prescribed form from a physician approved by the committee. The conference may require psychological tests to provide additional information on the candidate's fitness.

4. He must have been certified by the conference agency related to his career.

¶ 503. Consecration of the lay worker may be at the Annual Conference as a part of a single service with the ordination of ministers, with an order for each. If desired, the bishop may arrange for the consecration at another time or place.

¶ 504. A lay worker shall be commissioned, *i.e.* entrusted with work in a particular task in which a consecrated lay worker is to serve. The service of commissioning and any subsequent related act of installation or covenantal relationship with the employing church or church-related body shall be arranged in consultation with the certifying agency.

¶ 505. The lay worker shall be seated in the Annual Conference session and shall be given the privileges of the floor without vote.

¶ 506. The lay worker will hold a Charge Conference relationship.

¶ 507. 1. The employing agency shall include the lay worker in the retirement plan of the Lay Employee Pension Fund (¶ 1377.12) or other such appropriate plan as provided by the Board of Pensions or other boards or agencies of The United Methodist Church.

2. The employing agency in which a lay worker is serving shall provide guidance in lay employees' benefits in addition to the pension fund. It shall be the aim of the agency to insure for lay workers rights and conditions at least no less than those representative of enlightened

and Christian policies now commonly practiced by secular institutions.

¶ 508. 1. The lay worker may transfer his relationship from one Annual Conference to another on recommendation of the Committees on Lay Workers and the approval of the Annual Conferences involved.

2. The lay worker's relationship in the Annual Conference may be terminated by the Annual Conference on recommendation of the Committee on Lay Workers or for such reasons as the Annual Conference may determine.

Chapter Four
THE CONFERENCES

The United Methodist Church is a connectional structure maintained through its chain of conferences.

Section I.   The General Conference.

¶ 601. *Composition.*—The membership of the **General Conference** shall consist of an equal number of ministerial and lay delegates elected by the Annual Conferences as provided in the Discipline. Except in the case of Annual Conferences specified in ¶ 602, the number of delegates to which an Annual Conference is entitled shall be computed on a two-factor basis: the number of ministerial members of the Annual Conference and the number of resident church members in the Annual Conference, as follows:

1. One ministerial delegate for every 140 ministerial members of the Annual Conference and one additional ministerial delegate for each major fraction thereof, and

2. One ministerial delegate for the first 44,000 resident church members of the Annual Conference and one ministerial delegate for each additional 44,000 resident church members and an additional ministerial delegate for each major fraction of 44,000 resident church members, and

3. A number of lay delegates equal to the total number of ministerial delegates authorized as above.

Delegates to the General Conference shall be elected at the session of the Annual Conference held in the calendar year preceding the session of the General Conference.

This formula is designed to comply with the Constitution, Division Two, Section II, Article I, which defines the minimum and maximum number of delegates to a General Conference. Should the computations provided in this paragraph result in a figure below the prescribed minimum or above the prescribed maximum for delegates, the secretary of the General Conference shall be authorized to remedy the situation by adjusting up or down the fractions necessary to entitle an Annual Conference to elect additional delegates, any such adjustment to be the same for the factors of ministerial members and resident church members. In case of any such adjustments, the secretary of the General Conference shall notify the secretaries of the several Annual Conferences as promptly as possible. The term "ministerial members" as used above shall refer to both active and retired members of the Annual Conference. Every Annual Conference shall be entitled to at least one ministerial and one lay delegate. The secretaries of the several Annual Conferences shall furnish certificates of election to the delegates severally and shall send a certificate of such election to the secretary of the preceding General Conference immediately after the adjournment of the said Annual Conferences.

¶ **602.** *Representation.*—In order to carry out the intent and spirit of the constitutional provision (Division Two, Section III, Article VII) , the following special rules shall apply:

1. In any special session of the General Conference held during the quadrennium 1968-72 and in the General Conference of 1972, 13 percent of the delegates shall be chosen from among members coming from the Evangelical United Brethren membership and 87 percent from among members coming from the Methodist membership.

2. In any special session of the General Conference held during the quadrennium 1972-76 and in the General Conference of 1976, at least 6.5 percent of the delegates shall be chosen from among members coming from the Evangelical United Brethren membership and at least 43.5 percent from among members coming from the Methodist membership.

3. In General Conferences subsequent to the General Conference

of 1976 there shall be no requirements regarding representation from among the members coming from the constituent denominations.

4. For the purpose of this section the term "member coming from" a denomination shall mean a person who was a member of such denomination on the date the Plan of Union became effective.

5. It is anticipated that before 1976, through the uniting of Annual Conferences or otherwise, many Annual Conferences of the respective denominations may be materially changed as to boundaries, membership, or otherwise but that some of the Evangelical United Brethren and Methodist Annual Conferences existing at the time of union may continue to exist as such without material change. Accordingly, the secretary of the General Conference shall prepare and, subject to review and approval by the Council of Bishops, promulgate a schedule allocating to the Annual Conferences of the Church the number of delegates coming from The Evangelical United Brethren Church and The Methodist Church, respectively, which each Annual Conference shall elect. Such schedule shall attempt to allocate fairly the delegates to be elected as coming from the respective denominations among those Evangelical United Brethren and Methodist Annual Conferences which continue to exist as such without material change and among those Annual Conferences whose membership, because of mergers or otherwise, has been materially changed and consists of persons coming from both constituent denominations.

¶ 603. *Council of Secretaries.*—Members of the Council of Secretaries who were not elected members of the General Conference shall have the privilege of the floor on matters affecting the interests of their respective agencies, but without vote, and attendance shall be at the expense of their respective agencies. If an agency by formal action shall so request, it may be represented by an associate secretary rather than by the regularly elected general or executive secretary.

¶ 604. *Provisional Annual Conference.*—Each Provisional Annual Conference and Missionary Conference outside the United States may designate a member to meet with the standing committees and have the privileges of the floor of the General Conference on matters affecting the interest of his conference, but without vote and without expense to the General Conference except for the per diem during its sessions.

¶ **605.** *Presiding Officers.*—The bishops shall be the presiding officers at the General Conference.

¶ **606.** *Election of Secretary.*—The Council of Bishops shall present a nomination from the ministry or lay membership of The United Methodist Church for secretary. Other nominations shall be permitted from the floor. The election, if there be two or more nominees, shall be by ballot. Should the secretary not be a delegate, he shall have the privilege of the floor, but without vote. The General Conference shall elect, upon the nomination of the secretary, such assistant secretaries from the ministry or lay membership of The United Methodist Church as it may deem wise. If in the interim of the quadrennial sessions of the General Conference the office of secretary or assistant secretary shall for any reason be vacated, the Council of Bishops shall elect a successor to serve until the next session.

¶ **607.** *Rules of Order.*—The Plan of Organization and Rules of Order of the General Conference shall be the Plan of Organization and Rules of Order as published in the journal of the preceding General Conference until they have been altered or modified by the action of the General Conference.

¶ **608.** *Quorum.*—When the General Conference is in session, it shall require the presence of a majority of the whole number of delegates to the General Conference to constitute a quorum for the transaction of business, but a smaller number may take a recess or adjourn from day to day in order to secure a quorum and at the final session may approve the journal, order the record of the roll call, and adjourn sine die.

¶ **609.** *Petitions to General Conference.*—Any organization, minister, or lay member of The United Methodist Church may petition the General Conference by sending to the secretary a signed petition addressed to the members of the General Conference stating the local church of which each signer is a member. It is recommended that each petition meet the following requirements: (1) three copies of it should be supplied to the secretary in time to be received by him not later than thirty days before the opening day of the conference session, except that the thirty-day rule shall not apply in the case of Annual Conferences outside the United States or to Annual Conferences which meet less than thirty days prior to the opening day of the conference; (2) it should deal with only one subject and should propose revisions within only one chapter of the Discipline; (3) if it is one of a series, each petition should be written on a separate sheet; (4) all petitions timely received shall be processed by the secretary in order that they may be received by the appropriate legislative committees at their first meeting.

¶ 610. *Voting by Orders.*—The ministerial and lay members shall deliberate as one body and have equal rights. They shall vote as one body, but a separate vote shall be taken on any question when requested by one third of either order of delegates present and voting. In all cases of separate voting it shall require the concurrence of a majority of each order to adopt a proposed measure. However, in the case of changes in the Constitution, a vote of two thirds of the General Conference, as provided in the Constitution, shall be required.

¶ 611. *Speaking for the Church.*—1. No person, no paper, no organization has the authority to speak officially for The United Methodist Church, this right having been reserved exclusively to the General Conference under the Constitution.

2. Any individual member called to testify before a legislative body to represent The United Methodist Church shall be allowed to do so only by reading, without elaboration, the resolutions and positions adopted by the General Conference of The United Methodist Church.

Section II. The Jurisdictional Conference.

¶ 612. 1. The persons elected by their respective delegations to serve on the several jurisdictional Committees on Episcopacy shall meet jointly at the time of the General Conference, constituting an **Interjurisdictional Committee on Episcopacy,** not later than the fifth day of the conference session and at the time and place set for their convening by the president of the Council of Bishops and shall elect from their number a chairman, vice-chairman, and secretary. The function of this joint committee shall be to discuss the possibility of transfers of bishops across jurisdictional lines at the forthcoming Jurisdictional Conferences for residential and presidential responsibilities in the ensuing quadrennium. It shall elect an executive committee consisting of the officers named above and two ministers and two laymen from each jurisdictional committee, elected by that committee to conduct consultations with bishops and others interested in possible episcopal transfers. The executive committee shall be responsible to the interjurisdictional committee.

2. No bishop shall be transferred across jurisdictional lines unless he has consented to such transfer and has served at least one quadrennium in or under assignment by the jurisdiction in which he was elected and unless a concurrent transfer is effected into the jurisdiction from which he is transferring or unless the Jurisdictional Conference which is receiving him has voted to waive this right. Such a transfer shall not be concluded until the Committee on Episcopacy of each jurisdiction involved has approved the plan insofar as it affects its own jurisdiction, by majority vote of those present and voting, and the Jurisdictional Conferences, meeting concurrently, have also approved.

¶ 613.   All Jurisdictional Conferences shall have the same status and the same privileges of action within the limits fixed by the Constitution.

¶ 614.   The membership of each Jurisdictional Conference shall consist of an equal number of ministerial and lay delegates elected by the Annual Conferences as provided in the Discipline. Except in the case of Annual Conferences specified in ¶ 615, the number of delegates to which an Annual Conference is entitled shall be computed on a two-factor basis: the number of ministerial members of the Annual Conference and the number of resident church members in the Annual Conference, as follows:

1. One ministerial delegate for every seventy ministerial members of the Annual Conference and one additional ministerial delegate for each major fraction thereof, and

2. One ministerial delegate for the first 22,000 resident church members of the Annual Conference and one ministerial delegate for each additional 22,000 resident church members and an additional ministerial delegate for each major fraction of 22,000 resident church members, and

3. A number of lay delegates equal to the total number of ministerial delegates authorized as above; *provided* that no Annual Confer-

ence shall be denied the privilege of two delegates, one lay and one ministerial.

¶ **615.** In order to carry out the intent and spirit of the constitutional provision (Division Two, Section III, Article VII), the following special rules shall apply:

1. In any special session of a Jurisdictional Conference held during the quadrennium 1968-72 and in each Jurisdictional Conference of 1972, delegates shall be chosen from among members coming from the Evangelical United Brethren membership and the Methodist membership, respectively, as follows:

Northeastern ....22% and 78%
Southeastern .... 2% and 98%
North Central ....24% and 76%
South Central .... 5% and 95%
Western .... 8% and 92%

2. In any special session of a Jurisdictional Conference held during the quadrennium 1972-76 and in each Jurisdictional Conference of 1976, delegates shall be chosen from among members coming from the Evangelical United Brethren membership and the Methodist membership, respectively, using the following percentages as minimums:

Northeastern ....14.6% and 52.0%
Southeastern .... 1.4% and 65.0%
North Central .... 16.0% and 50.6%
South Central .... 3.3% and 63.3%
Western .... 5.3% and 61.3%

3. In any Jurisdictional Conference held subsequent to the General Conference of 1976 there shall be no requirements regarding representation from among the members coming from the constituent denominations.

4. For the purpose of this section the term "member coming from" a denomination shall mean a person who was a member of such denomination on the date the Plan of Union became effective.

5. It is anticipated that before 1976, through the uniting of Annual Conferences or otherwise, many Annual Conferences of the respective denominations may be materially changed as to boundaries, membership, or otherwise but that some of the Evangelical United Brethren and Methodist Annual Conferences existing at the time of union may

continue to exist as such without material change. Accordingly, the secretary of each jurisdiction shall prepare and, subject to review and approval by the College of Bishops, promulgate a schedule allocating to the Annual Conferences of the jurisdiction the number of delegates coming from The Evangelical United Brethren Church and The Methodist Church, respectively, which each Annual Conference shall elect. Such schedule shall attempt to allocate fairly the delegates to be elected as coming from the respective denominations among those Evangelical United Brethren and Methodist Annual Conferences which continue to exist as such without material change and among those Annual Conferences whose membership, because of merger or otherwise, has been materially changed and consists of persons coming from both constituent denominations.

¶ 616. The ministerial and lay delegates and reserves to the Jurisdictional Conferences shall be elected by ballot in accordance with the provisions of the Constitution.

¶ 617. The ministers and lay delegates shall deliberate in one body.

¶ 618. Each Jurisdictional Conference shall meet within the period prescribed by the Constitution at such time and place as shall have been determined by the preceding Jurisdictional Conference or by its properly constituted committee.

¶ 619. The Jurisdictional Conference shall adopt its own procedure, rules, and plan of organization. It shall take a majority of the whole number of delegates elected to make a quorum for the transaction of business; however, a smaller number may take a recess or adjourn from day to day and at the final session may approve the journal, order the record of the roll call, and adjourn sine die.

¶ 620. The Jurisdictional Conference shall provide for the expenses of its sessions.

¶ 621. 1. The Jurisdictional Conference may order a special session in such manner as it shall determine.

2. The College of Bishops of a jurisdiction by a two-thirds vote shall have authority to call a special session of the Jurisdictional Conference when necessary; *provided,* however, that if an episcopal area is left vacant by reason of death, retirement, or other cause within twenty-four months of the close of the preceding Jurisdictional Conference,

the College of Bishops may by majority vote convene within three months, after giving not less than thirty days' notice, a special session of the Jurisdictional Conference for the purpose of electing and consecrating a bishop and of considering any other matters specified in the call, and *provided* further that in such case the standing Committee on Episcopacy may recommend to the conference reassignment of one or more of the previously elected bishops.

3. The delegates to a special session of the Jurisdictional Conference shall be the delegates last elected by each Annual Conference.

4. A called session of the Jurisdictional Conference cannot transact any other business than that indicated in the call.

¶ 622. The Jurisdictional Conference shall be presided over by the bishops of the jurisdiction or a bishop of another jurisdiction. In case no bishop of the jurisdiction is present, the conference may elect a president from the ministerial delegates.

¶ 623. A bishop elected by or administering in a Jurisdictional Conference shall be amenable for his conduct to his Jurisdictional Conference. Any bishop shall have the right of appeal to the Judicial Council.

¶ 624. 1. The Jurisdictional Conference shall recognize as its standing **Committee on Episcopacy** a committee consisting of one ministerial and one lay delegate elected from each Annual Conference by the Annual Conference delegation.

2. The Committee shall review the work of the bishops, pass on their character and official administration, and report to the Jurisdictional Conference its findings for such action as the conference may deem appropriate within its constitutional warrant of power.

3. The committee shall recommend the boundaries of the episcopal areas, after consultation with the College of Bishops, and the assignment of the bishops to their respective residences for final action by the Jurisdictional Conference; *provided,* however, that it shall not reach any conclusion concerning residential assignments until all elections of bishops for that session are completed, except in the case of a bishop's being transferred into the jurisdiction, and *provided* further that no bishop shall be recommended for assignment to the same residence for more than twelve consecutive years not counting years served before 1960.

4. The committee shall not recommend assignment of nor shall the conference assign a newly elected bishop to a residence within the bounds of the Annual Conference of which he was a member at the time of his election, nor shall the conference recommend that he administer the area within which his membership was most recently held.

¶ **625.** The Jurisdictional Conference shall have powers and duties as described in the Constitution. It shall also have such other powers and duties as may be conferred by the General Conference, and in exercise thereof it shall act in all respects in harmony with the policy of The United Methodist Church with respect to elimination of discrimination based upon race.

¶ **626.** In all elections in a Jurisdictional Conference which are based on the number of church members within that jurisdiction, the number counted shall include lay members, ministerial members, and bishops assigned to that jurisdiction.

¶ **627.** The Jurisdictional Conference shall have authority to examine and acknowledge the journals of the Annual Conferences within its bounds and shall make such rules for the drawing up of the journals as may seem necessary.

¶ **628.** 1. The Jurisdictional Conference shall keep an official journal of its proceedings, duly signed by the secretary and president, to be sent for examination to the ensuing General Conference.

2. For the sake of convenience and uniformity the journal, when printed, should conform in page size and formation to the General Conference journal, and the printing should be done at the expense of the jurisdiction by The Methodist Publishing House.

Section III. The Central Conference.

¶ **629.** *Authorization.*—1. In territory outside the United States and Canada, Annual Conferences, Provisional Annual Conferences, Missionary Conferences, Mission Conferences, and Missions in such numbers as the General Conference by a two-thirds vote shall determine may be organized by the General Conference into Central Conferences or Provisional Central Conferences, with such duties, privileges, and powers as are hereinafter set forth and as the General Conference by a two-thirds vote shall prescribe.

2. There shall be such Central Conferences as have been authorized or shall be hereafter authorized by the General Conference; *provided* that a Central Conference shall have a total of at least thirty ministerial and thirty lay delegates on the basis of representation as set forth in this section, except as the General Conference may fix a different number. A Central Conference in existence at the time of union may be continued with a lesser number of delegates for reasons deemed sufficient by the Uniting Conference.

¶ 630. *Organization.*—1. The **Central Conference** shall be composed of ministerial and lay members in equal numbers, the ministerial members elected by the ministerial members of the Annual Conference and the lay members by the lay members thereof. Their qualifications and the manner of election shall be determined by the Central Conference itself, subject only to constitutional requirements. Each Annual Conference and Provisional Annual Conference shall be entitled to at least two ministerial and two lay delegates, and no other selection of delegates shall be authorized which would provide for more than one ministerial delegate for every six ministerial members of an Annual Conference, except that a majority of the number fixed by a Central Conference as the ratio of representation shall entitle an Annual Conference to an additional ministerial delegate and to an additional lay delegate. Each Missionary Conference and Mission is authorized to elect and send one of its members to the Central Conference concerned as its representative, said representative to be accorded the privilege of sitting with the committees of the Central Conference with the right to speak in the committees and in the regular sessions of the Central Conference but without the right to vote. Representatives of Missionary Conferences or Missions shall have the same claim for payment of expenses as is allowed to members of the Central Conference.

2. The first meeting of a Central Conference shall be called by the bishop or bishops in charge at such time and place as he or they may elect, to which members of the Annual Conferences, Provisional Annual Conferences, Missionary Conferences, and Missions concerned shall be elected on the basis of representation as provided herein. The

161

time and place of future meetings shall be determined by the Central Conference or its executive committee.

3. Each Central Conference shall meet within the year succeeding the session of the General Conference at such time and place as the Central Conference itself or its bishops may determine, with the right to hold such adjourned sessions as it may determine. The sessions of said conference shall be presided over by the bishops. In case no bishop is present, the conference shall elect a temporary president from among its own members. The bishops resident in a Central Conference or a majority of them, with the concurrence of the executive committee or other authorized committee, shall have the authority to call an extra session of the Central Conference to be held at the time and place designated by them.

4. The Council of Bishops may assign one or more of its number to visit any Central Conference or Provisional Central Conference. When so assigned, the bishop shall be an accredited representative of the general Church and when requested by a majority of the bishops resident in that conference may exercise therein the functions of the episcopacy.

5. The presiding officer of the Central Conference shall decide questions of order, subject to an appeal to the Central Conference, and he shall decide questions of law, subject to an appeal to the Judicial Council, but questions relating to the interpretation of the rules and regulations made by the Central Conference for the governing of its own session shall be decided by the Central Conference.

6. Each Central Conference within the bounds of which the Board of Missions has work shall maintain a cooperative and consultative relationship with the said board through a duly constituted executive committee, executive board, or council of cooperation; but the legal distinction between the Board of Missions and the organized Church on the field shall always be kept clear.

7. The journal of the proceedings of a Central Conference, duly signed by the president and secretary, shall be sent for examination to the General Conference.

8. A Provisional Central Conference may become a Central Conference upon the fulfillment of the necessary requirements and upon the authorization of the General Conference.

9. In the case of a Central Conference the rule of proportionate representation shall be applied by each Annual Conference, and in the case of the delegates to the Central Conference of Central and Southern Europe the rule shall be applied to delegates coming from the two Annual Conferences of Switzerland, and the membership of the other Annual Conferences shall not figure in the computation.

¶ 631. *Powers.*—1. To a Central Conference shall be committed for supervision and promotion, in harmony with the Discipline and interdenominational contractual agreements, the missionary, educational, evangelistic, industrial, publishing, medical, and other connectional interests of the Annual Conferences, Provisional Annual Conferences, Missionary Conferences, and Missions within its territory and such other matters as may be referred to it by said bodies or by order of the General Conference; and it shall provide suitable organizations for such work and elect the necessary officers for the same.

2. A Central Conference, when authorized by a specific enabling act of the General Conference, may elect one or more bishops from among the traveling elders of The United Methodist Church. The number of bishops to be elected by each Central Conference shall be determined from time to time by the General Conference.

3. When a Central Conference shall have been authorized to elect bishops, such elections shall be conducted under the same general procedure as prevails in the Jurisdictional Conferences for the election of bishops. A Central Conference shall have power to fix the tenure of bishops elected by the said Central Conference.

4. A Central Conference shall participate in the General Episcopal Fund on payment of its apportionment on the same basis as that fixed for Annual Conferences in Jurisdictional Conferences. When the total estimated support, including salaries and all allowances for the bishops elected by it, and the amount that it will be able to provide on apportionment have been determined by a Central Conference, these amounts in itemized form shall be submitted to the Council on World Service and Finance. This council, after consideration of the relative cost of living in various Central Conferences, shall determine the amount to be paid from the General Episcopal Fund in meeting the budget, after which the treasurer of the General Episcopal Fund shall

pay the amount established to the bishop concerned, or as the Central Conference may determine.

5. A minister who has served a term or part of a term as a bishop in a Central Conference where term episcopacy has prevailed shall upon his retirement from the effective relation in the ministry be paid an allowance from the General Episcopal Fund in such sum as the Council on World Service and Finance shall determine for the years during which he served as a bishop.

6. A Central Conference, in consultation with the bishops of that Central Conference, shall fix the episcopal areas and residences and make assignments to them of the bishops who are to reside in that Central Conference. The bishops of a Central Conference shall arrange the plan of episcopal visitation within its bounds.

7. The secretary of a Central Conference in which one or more bishops have been chosen shall report to the secretary of the General Conference the names of the bishop or bishops and the residences to which they have been assigned by the Central Conference.

8. A Central Conference shall have authority to elect and support general officers in all departments of the work of the Church within the boundaries of the Central Conference but may not determine the number of bishops.

9. A Central Conference shall have power to make such changes and adaptations as the peculiar conditions on the fields concerned require regarding the local church, ministry, special advices, worship, and temporal economy within its territory, including the authorizing of associate members to participate in the offices of the local church under such rules as it may see fit; *provided* that no action shall be taken which is contrary to the Constitution and the General Rules of The United Methodist Church.

10. A Central Conference shall have the authority to change the provisions for the ordination of ministers in such way that the ordination of an elder may follow immediately upon his ordination as a deacon; *provided* that other conditions are fully met.

11. A Central Conference shall fix the boundaries of the Annual Conferences, Provisional Annual Conferences, Missionary Conferences, and Missions within its bounds, proposals for changes first having been submitted to the Annual Conferences concerned as prescribed in the

Discipline of The United Methodist Church; *provided,* however, that the number of Annual Conferences which may be organized within the bounds of a Central Conference shall first have been determined by the General Conference. No Annual Conference shall be organized with fewer than thirty-five ministerial members except as provided by an enabling act for the quadrennium, which shall not reduce the number below twenty-five. Nor shall an Annual Conference be continued with fewer than twenty-five ministerial members except as provided by an enabling act for the quadrennium.

12. A Central Conference may advise its Annual Conferences and Provisional Annual Conferences to set standards of character and other qualifications for admission of lay members.

13. A Central Conference shall have power to make changes and adaptations in procedure pertaining to the Annual, District, and Charge Conferences within its territory and to add to the business of the Annual Conference supplementary questions considered desirable or necessary to meet its own needs.

14. A Central Conference shall have authority to examine and acknowledge the journals of the Annual Conferences, Provisional Annual Conferences, Missionary Conferences, and Missions located within its bounds and to make rules for the drawing up of the journals as may seem necessary.

15. A Central Conference may have a standing **Committee on Women's Work.** This committee should preferably be composed of the women delegates and such other persons as the Central Conference may elect. The duty of this committee shall be to study the relation of women to the Church and to devise ways and means of developing this portion of the church membership to the end that it may assume its rightful responsibilities in the extension of the kingdom. The committee shall make recommendations to the Central Conference regarding women's organizations within its areas. A Central Conference organization may become a member of the World Federation of Methodist Women and may elect a representative to the World Federation of Methodist Women within the provisions of the Federation.

16. A Central Conference may organize a women's unit, after consultation with the Committee on Women's Work, in connection with

any Annual Conference or Provisional Annual Conference within its bounds and provide a constitution and bylaws for it.

17. A Central Conference shall have authority to adopt rules of procedure governing the investigation and trial of its ministers, including bishops, and lay members of the Church and to provide the necessary means and methods of implementing the said rules; *provided,* however, that the ministers shall not be deprived of the right of trial by a ministerial committee and lay members of the Church of the right of trial by a duly constituted committee of church members, and *provided* also that the rights of appeal shall be adequately safeguarded.

18. A Central Conference is authorized to prepare and translate simplified or adapted forms of such parts of the Ritual as it may deem necessary, such changes to require the approval of the resident bishop or bishops of the Central Conference.

19. A Central Conference shall have the power to conform the detailed rules, rites, and ceremonies for the solemnization of marriage to the statute laws of the country or countries within its jurisdiction.

20. Subject to the approval of the bishops resident therein, a Central Conference shall have the power to prescribe courses of study, including those in the vernaculars, for its ministry, both foreign and indigenous, including local preachers, lay speakers, Bible women, deaconesses, teachers both male and female, and all other workers whatsoever, ordained or lay. It shall also make rules and regulations for examination in these courses.

21. A Central Conference shall have authority to edit and publish a Central Conference Discipline which shall contain, in addition to the Constitution of the Church, such sections from the general Discipline of The United Methodist Church as may be pertinent to the entire Church and also such revised, adapted, or new sections as shall have been enacted by the Central Conference concerned under the powers given by the General Conference, with the understanding that legislation passed by the General Conference becomes effective immediately throughout the entire Church except as provided in § 22.

22. In a Central Conference or Provisional Central Conference using a language other than English, legislation passed by a General Conference shall not take effect until six months after the close of that

General Conference in order to afford the necessary time to make adaptations and to publish a translation of the legislation which has been enacted, the translation to be approved by the resident bishop or bishops of the Central Conference. This provision, however, shall not exclude the election of delegates to the General Conference by Annual Conferences within the territory of Central Conferences or Provisional Central Conferences.

23. A Central Conference is authorized to interpret Article XXIII of the Articles of Religion so as to recognize the government or governments of the country or countries within its territory.

24. A Central Conference shall have power to authorize the congregations in a certain state or country to form special organizations in order to receive the acknowledgment of the state or country according to the laws of that state or country. These organizations shall be empowered to represent the interests of the Church to the authorities of the state or country according to the rules and principles of The United Methodist Church, and they shall be required to give regular reports of their activities to their respective Annual Conferences.

25. A Central Conference may, with the consent of the bishops resident in that conference, enter into agreements with churches or missions of other denominations for the division of territory or of responsibility for Christian work within the territory of the Central Conference.

26. A Central Conference shall have the right to negotiate with other Protestant bodies looking toward the possibility of church union; *provided* that any proposals for church union shall be submitted to the General Conference for approval before consummation.

27. A Central Conference, where the laws of the land permit, shall have the power to organize and incorporate one or more executive committees, executive boards, or councils of cooperation, with such membership and such powers as may have been granted by the Central Conference for the purpose of representing it in its property and legal interests and for transacting any necessary business that may arise in the interval between the sessions of the Central Conference or that may be committed to said boards or committees by the Central Conference.

28. A Central Conference, through a duly incorporated property-

holding body or bodies, shall have authority to purchase, own, hold, or transfer property for and on behalf of The United Methodist Church and of all the unincorporated organizations of The United Methodist Church within the territory of that Central Conference or on behalf of other organizations of The United Methodist Church which have entrusted their property to that Central Conference.

29. A Central Conference shall have authority to make the necessary rules and regulations for the holding and management of such properties; *provided,* however, that (*a*) all procedure shall be subject to the laws of the country or countries concerned, (*b*) no transfer of property shall be made from one Annual Conference to another without the consent of the conference holding title to such property, and (*c*) the status of properties held by local trustees or other holding bodies shall be recognized.

30. A Central Conference shall not, directly or indirectly through its incorporated property-holding body or bodies, alienate property or proceeds of property without due consideration of its trusteeship for local churches, Annual Conferences, the Board of Missions, and other organizations, local or general, of the Church.

31. A Central Conference or any of its incorporated organizations shall not involve the Board of Missions or any organization of the Church in any financial obligation without the official approval of said board or organization. All invested funds, fiduciary trusts, or property belonging to an Annual Conference, a Provisional Annual Conference, a Missionary Conference, or a Mission, or any of its institutions, acquired by bequest, donation, or otherwise and designated for a specific use, shall be applied to the purpose for which they were designated. They shall not be diverted to any other purpose except by the consent of the conference or mission involved, and with the approval of the Central Conference concerned, and civil court action when necessary. The same rule shall apply to similar funds or properties acquired by a Central Conference for specific objects. In cases involving the diversion of trust funds and properties within the territory of a Central Conference, the Central Conference concerned shall determine the disposition of the interests involved, subject to an appeal to the Judicial Court of the Central Conference.

Section IV. Provisional Central Conferences.

¶ **632.** Annual Conferences, Provisional Annual Conferences, Missionary Conferences, and Missions outside the United States which are not included in Central Conferences or in the territory of affiliated autonomous churches, and which because of geographical, language, political, or other considerations have common interests that can best be served thereby, may be organized into **Provisional Central Conferences** as provided in ¶ 629.1.

¶ **633.** The organization of Provisional Central Conferences shall conform to the regulations prescribed for Central Conferences insofar as they are considered applicable by the bishop in charge.

¶ **634.** The General Conference may grant to a Provisional Central Conference any of the powers of a Central Conference except that of electing bishops.

¶ **635.** In the interval between General Conferences the Board of Missions, upon the recommendation of the bishops in charge and after consultation with the Annual Conferences, Provisional Annual Conferences, Missionary Conferences, and Missions concerned, may make changes in the boundaries of a Provisional Central Conference and may grant to a Provisional Central Conference or to any of its component parts any of the powers of a Central Conference except that of electing bishops. All changes in boundaries and all grants of powers authorized by the Board of Missions shall be reported to the ensuing session of the General Conference and shall expire at the close of that session unless renewed by the General Conference.

¶ **636.** An Annual Conference or a Provisional Annual Conference in the field of a Provisional Central Conference shall have the power to set standards of character and other qualifications for admission of its lay members.

¶ **637.** To Annual Conferences, Provisional Annual Conferences, Missionary Conferences, and Missions which are outside the United States and are not included in Central Conferences or Provisional Central Conferences, the General Conference may grant any of the powers of Central Conferences except that of electing bishops; and in the interval between General Conferences the Board of Missions may grant such powers when requested to do so by the bishop in charge and by the Annual Conference, Provisional Annual Conference, Missionary Conference, or Mission concerned.

¶ **638.** The General Conference shall make provision for the episcopal supervision of work in the territory outside the United States which is not now included in Central Conferences.

¶ **639.** The Council of Bishops may provide, if and when necessary, for episcopal visitation of mission fields not included in Central or Provisional Central Conferences.

Section V.　Affiliated Autonomous Churches.

¶ **640.** A self-governing church in whose establishment The United Methodist Church or one of its constituent members has assisted and with which it is cooperating through its Board of Missions may be known as an **affiliated autonomous church.** Relations between The United Methodist Church and an affiliated autonomous church shall be such as may be mutually agreed upon by the two churches. The Board of Missions shall serve as the agent of The United Methodist Church in conferring with affiliated autonomous churches. The United Methodist Church assumes responsibility for all contractual agreements made by one of its constituent members with an affiliated autonomous church.

¶ **641.** Contractual agreements with The Methodist Church of Mexico, The Methodist Church of Brazil, Korean Methodist Church, United Church of Christ in Japan, Church of Christ in Okinawa, with united churches with which The Evangelical United Brethren Church has been affiliated, and with such other churches as may be added by action of the General Conference shall be continued until changed or modified by mutual agreement. The Board of Missions is authorized to harmonize and make uniform the present agreements and practices with respect to these churches by extending to each of them any provision contained in the present agreement with any one of them, if such change is desired by the affiliated autonomous church concerned and judged to be advisable by the Board of Missions.

¶ **642.** The contractual agreements between The United Methodist Church and the affiliated autonomous Methodist churches include the following provisions:

1. Certificate of church membership given by ministers in one church shall be accepted by ministers in the others.

2. Ministers may be transferred between Annual and Provisional Annual Conferences of The United Methodist Church and of affiliated autonomous Methodist churches with the approval and consent of the bishops or other appointive authorities involved.

3. Each affiliated autonomous church shall be entitled to two delegates, a minister and a layman, to the General Conference of The United Methodist Church, with all the rights and privileges of delegates, including membership on committees, except the right to vote. Such a church having more than seventy thousand full members shall be entitled to two additional delegates, at least one of whom shall be a woman, with the same rights and privileges. (*See* ¶ 1414.2.)

4. The United Methodist Church may be represented at the General Conference of each affiliated autonomous Methodist church by a member of the Council of Bishops and a delegate appointed by the Board of Missions, the delegate to be entitled to all the privileges of delegates except the right to vote.

¶ 643. When an Annual or Provisional Annual Conference becomes a part of an affiliated autonomous Methodist church, the Council of Bishops may at its discretion transfer its members who so desire to the conferences from which they went to the mission field. If any have not previously had membership in other conferences of The United Methodist Church, the Council of Bishops may at its discretion transfer them to conferences as it may determine.

¶ 644. The Council of Bishops may assign one or more of its members for episcopal visitation to the affiliated autonomous churches.

¶ 645. An affiliated united church which is a member of the World Methodist Council shall be entitled to two delegates, a minister and a layman, to the General Conference of The United Methodist Church, with all the rights and privileges of delegates, including membership on committees, except the right to vote. Such a church having more than seventy thousand full members shall be entitled to two additional delegates, at least one of whom shall be a woman, with the same rights and privileges. (*See* ¶ 1414.2.)

¶ 646. When the requirements of an unaffiliated autonomous Methodist church for its ministry are comparable to those of The

United Methodist Church, ministers may be transferred between its properly constituted ministerial bodies and the Annual and Provisional Annual Conferences of The United Methodist Church, with the approval and consent of the appointive authorities involved.

¶ 647. When conferences overseas related to the General Conference of The United Methodist Church desire to be autonomous, the procedures shall be as follows:

1. The conferences shall prepare a historical record, with reasons why autonomy is requested, and the Commission on the Structure of Methodism Overseas shall formally decide on the initiation of proceedings.

2. The commission and the conferences involved shall mutually agree on (*a*) the confession of faith and (*b*) the constitution of the new church. These shall be prepared with care and shall be approved by the conferences.

3. The commission shall request from the General Conference one of the following: (*a*) if proceedings are not well advanced, an enabling act authorizing autonomy when conditions are met, as determined by a special committee representing the commission, the Council of Bishops, the Board of Missions, and the Judicial Council; or (*b*) if agreement has been reached on the confession of faith and constitution as specified in § 2 above, enabling legislation formally authorizing the autonomous status.

4. When the autonomous status has been approved by the General Conference and the provisions for it have been met, the following shall sign the proclamation of autonomy: the president of the Council of Bishops, the secretary of the General Conference, the chairman of the Commission on the Structure of Methodism Overseas, and the president of the Board of Missions.

5. After the proclamation of autonomy has been signed, a delegation appointed by the Council of Bishops shall share in a service recognizing the new church. The delegation shall consist of five members: one from the Council of Bishops, one from an area contiguous to the new church, one nominated by the Commission on the Structure of Methodism Overseas, and two, at least one a woman, nominated by the Board of Missions.

6. Preparation of its Discipline is the responsibility of the auton-

omous church; if invited, the Commission on the Structure of Methodism Overseas shall provide assistance.

7. An autonomous church, Methodist or united, may become an affiliated autonomous church of The United Methodist Church by mutual agreement with the Commission on the Structure of Methodism Overseas and incorporation in its Discipline of provisions in accordance with ¶¶ 641-42.

8. The Board of Missions shall work out whatever agreements are needed to provide the basis of mutual support in the area of personnel, funds, and other patterns of relationship.

Section VI. Provisional Annual Conferences.

¶ 648. Any Missionary Conference or Mission established under the provisions of the Discipline may be constituted as a **Provisional Annual Conference** by the General Conference in consultation with the Central Conference, Provisional Central Conference, or Jurisdictional Conference within which the Mission is located; *provided* that no Provisional Annual Conference shall be organized with fewer than ten ministerial members, nor shall a Provisional Annual Conference be continued with fewer than six ministerial members.

¶ 649. A Provisional Annual Conference is authorized to exercise the powers of an Annual Conference, subject to the approval of the presiding bishop, and its members shall share pro rata in the produce of The Methodist Publishing House with members of the Annual Conferences. A Provisional Annual Conference within the territory of a Central Conference or of a Provisional Central Conference may elect delegates to a Central Conference or Provisional Central Conference on the same basis as an Annual Conference but may not elect delegates to a General Conference.

¶ 650. The bishop having episcopal supervision of a Provisional Annual Conference in a foreign or a home mission field may appoint a representative as **superintendent,** to whom may be committed specific responsibility for the representation of the Board of Missions in its relation to the indigenous church and also in cooperation with other recognized evangelical missions. Such duties shall be exercised so as not to interfere with the work of the district superintendent. This superintendent may also be a district superintendent; *provided* he is a member of the said conference. He shall be responsible directly to the bishop appointed to administer the work in that episcopal area, and he shall make adequate reports of the work and needs of his field to the bishop and to the secretaries of the Board of Missions immediately concerned.

¶ **651.** If there is no bishop present at an annual session of a Provisional Annual Conference, the superintendent shall preside; if there is no superintendent present, the presidency shall be determined as in an Annual Conference (¶ 661.5).

¶ **652.** Each Provisional Annual Conference or Mission at its annual session shall appoint a standing committee whose duty it shall be, with the concurrence of the president of the conference, to make an estimate of the amount necessary for the support of each pastoral charge, either in full or supplementary to the amount raised by the charge. Such estimates shall be subject to modification by the division of the Board of Missions immediately concerned.

¶ **653.** A charge within a Provisional Annual Conference, Missionary Conference, or Mission may receive aid from the Board of Missions without having been designated by the conference at its meeting.

¶ **654.** In a Provisional Annual Conference in the home field there shall be a conference Board of Missions constituted as in an Annual Conference and having the same duties and powers (¶¶ 1358-70).

Section VII. The Missionary Conference.

¶ **655.** *Definition.*—A **Missionary Conference** is a conference which because of its limited membership, ministry, financial strength, and property, requires administrative guidance and large financial aid from the Board of Missions.

¶ **656.** *Organization.*—A Missionary Conference shall be organized in the same manner and with the same rights and powers as an Annual Conference (¶¶ 660-62), but with the following exceptions:

1. The Board of Missions shall cooperate with the Council of Bishops in the selection of district or conference superintendent or superintendents and workers in the conference, who shall be appointed

by the Council of Bishops after consultation with the Board of Missions for such term as the Council of Bishops may determine.

2. The Board of Missions shall give close supervision and guidance in setting up the administrative and promotional budgets and advance projects within the conference and in the promotion of new mission projects. The conference, in making requests for appropriations for support and grants and loans for building projects, shall submit to the Board of Missions a statement of the proposed annual promotional and administrative budget and the proposed financial plan for new mission and building projects. New work and building projects involving increased appropriations from the Board of Missions shall first have the approval of the Board of Missions.

3. A Missionary Conference is not entitled to elect delegates to General, Jurisdictional, Central, or Provisional Central Conferences or to ministerial orders.

¶ 657. Only the General Conference can create a Missionary Conference or change a Missionary Conference to a Provisional Annual Conference or an Annual Conference. A petition to the General Conference for change in status from a Missionary Conference shall set forth details of the history and status of the conference and shall be accompanied by a report and recommendation of the Board of Missions.

Section VIII. Missions.

¶ 658. *In the Home Field.*—A Mission shall meet annually at the time and place appointed by the bishop in charge, who shall preside. In the absence of the bishop the superintendent of the Mission shall preside. The presiding officer shall bring forward the regular business of the meeting and arrange the work. For rules governing the administration of Missions in the home field see ¶¶ 652-53, 1336.

The Oklahoma Indian Mission shall have the same right as that given to Central Conferences in ¶ 631.9-.10 to make such changes and adaptations regarding the ministry and ordination of ministers as the effective use of indigenous leadership in the mission may require; *provided* that no action shall be taken which is contrary to the Constitution and the General Rules of The United Methodist Church. Any such ordination would be effective only within the bounds of the Indian Mission.

¶ 659. *In Foreign Fields.*—A foreign field outside an Annual Conference, working under the care of the Board of Missions and not having met the requirements for the organization of a Provisional Annual Conference, may be organized into a Missionary Conference or a Mission. For rules governing the administration of Missions in the foreign field see ¶¶ 637-39, 1315.

Section IX. The Annual Conference.

¶ 660. *Composition and Character.*—1. The ministerial membership of an Annual Conference (¶ 315) shall consist of members in full connection (¶ 331), probationary members (¶ 325), and associate members (¶ 322).

a) Members in full connection shall have the right to vote on all matters in the Annual Conference except in the election of lay delegates to the General and Jurisdictional Conferences (¶¶ 601.3, 614.3) and shall have sole responsibility for all matters of ordination, character, and conference relations of ministers (¶ 332).

b) Probationary members shall have the right to vote in the Annual Conference on all matters except constitutional amendments, election of delegates to the General and Jurisdictional or Central Conferences, and matters of ordination, character, and conference relations of ministers (¶ 325.2).

c) Associate members shall have the right to vote in the Annual Conference on all matters except constitutional amendments, election of delegates to the General and Jurisdictional or Central Conferences, and matters of ordination, character, and conference relations of ministers (¶ 322.2).

2. The following shall be seated in the Annual Conference and shall be given the privilege of the floor without vote: lay pastors who are in charge of pastoral appointments; lay missionaries, both men and women, regularly appointed by the Board of Missions in fields outside the United States; and deaconesses serving within the bounds of the Annual Conference. By authorization of a Central Conference national lay workers may be given the same privileges.

3. The lay member or alternate, whoever was last seated in the Annual Conference, shall be seated in a special session of the Annual Conference when convened; *provided* that no local charge shall be deprived of its lay member due to death, serious illness, or cessation of membership. Under such circumstances another lay member may be elected by the Charge Conference.

4. The lay members of the Annual Conference shall participate in all deliberations and vote upon all measures except on the granting or validation of license, ordination, reception into full conference membership, or any question concerning the character and official conduct of ministers. Lay members shall serve on all committees except those on ministerial relations and for the trial of ministers.

5. When at any time a lay member is excused by the Annual Conference from further attendance during the session, the alternate lay member may be seated in his stead. The lay member or alternate, whoever was last seated in the Annual Conference, shall be the lay member of the Annual Conference, and it shall be his duty to report on actions of the Annual Conference.

6. It is the duty of every member and all probationers and lay pastors of the Annual Conference to attend its sessions and furnish such reports in such form as the Discipline may require. Any such person unable to attend shall report by letter to the conference secretary, setting forth the reason for his absence. Should any minister in active service absent himself from the session of the Annual Conference without a satisfactory reason for his absence, the matter shall be referred by the conference secretary to the Board of the Ministry.

¶ 661. *Organization.*—1. Annual Conferences may become severally bodies corporate, whenever practicable, under the law of the countries, states, and territories within whose bounds they are located.

2. The bishops shall appoint the times for holding the Annual Conferences.

3. The Annual Conference or a committee thereof shall select the place for holding the conference, but should it become necessary for any reason to change the place of meeting, a majority of the district superintendents, with the consent of the bishop in charge, may change the place.

4. A special session of the Annual Conference may be held at such

time and in such place as shall have been determined by the Annual Conference after consultation with the bishop, or by the bishop, with the concurrence of three fourths of the district superintendents. A special session of the Annual Conference shall have only such powers as are stated in the call.

5. The bishop assigned shall preside over the Annual Conference or arrange for another bishop to preside in case of his inability. In the absence of a bishop the conference shall by ballot, without nomination or debate, elect a president pro tempore from among the traveling elders. The president thus elected shall discharge all the duties of a bishop except ordination.

6. The Annual Conference at the first session following the General Conference or Jurisdictional or Central Conferences (or, if it may desire, at the last session preceding the General, Jurisdictional, or Central Conferences) shall elect a secretary and statistician to serve for the succeeding quadrennium. In the case of a vacancy in any such office in the interim of the sessions, the bishop, after consultation with the district superintendents, shall appoint a person to act until the next session of the Annual Conference. (*See* ¶ 909 for election of the treasurer.)

7. The Annual Conference may designate a person who is a member in good standing of one of the local churches and who is a member of the bar of the state as **chancellor**. The chancellor, who shall be nominated by the bishop and elected by the Annual Conference, shall serve as legal advisor to the bishop and to the Annual Conference.

¶ **662.** *Powers and Duties.*—1. The Annual Conference for its own government may adopt rules and regulations not in conflict with the Discipline of The United Methodist Church; *provided* that in exercise of its powers each Annual Conference shall act in all respects in harmony with the policy of The United Methodist Church with respect to elimination of discrimination on the basis of race.

2. An Annual Conference cannot financially obligate The United Methodist Church or an organizational unit thereof except the Annual Conference itself.

3. The Annual Conference may admit into membership only those who have met all the Disciplinary requirements for membership and only in the manner prescribed in the Discipline.

4. The Annual Conference shall have power to make inquiry into the moral and official conduct of its ministerial members. Subject only to the provisions of ¶¶ 1720-60, the Annual Conference shall have power to hear complaints against its ministerial members and may try, reprove, suspend, deprive of ministerial office and credentials, expel, or acquit any against whom charges may have been preferred. The Annual Conference shall have power to locate a ministerial member for unacceptability or inefficiency.

5. The status of a ministerial member and of a probationer and the manner and conditions of a transfer of a ministerial member from one Annual Conference to another are governed by the section on the ministry (Chapter Two).

6. Every transfer of a traveling preacher is conditioned on the passing of his character by the conference to which he is amenable. The official announcement that a preacher is transferred changes his membership so that his rights and responsibilities in the conference to which he goes begin from the date of his transfer. Such member of an Annual Conference shall not vote twice on the same constitutional question, nor be counted twice in the same year in the basis for election of delegates, nor vote twice in the same year for delegates to the General, Jurisdictional, or Central Conferences.

7. Whenever a ministerial member, whether on trial or in full connection, is transferred to another Annual Conference, either in connection with a transfer of the pastoral charge to which he is appointed or by reason of the dissolution or merger of his Annual Conference, he shall have the same rights and obligations as the other members of the conference to which he is transferred.

8. The Annual Conference shall have power to make inquiry into the financial status of the local churches, and where there is a deficit in finances, it may require the minister and the lay member to appear before the appropriate committee and make explanation.

9. The Annual Conference shall have the power to make inquiry into the membership status of the local churches, and where no members have been received on confession of faith during the year, it may require the minister and the lay member to appear before the Committee on Evangelism and make explanation.

10. The Annual Conference shall give recognition to any new

179

churches that have been organized during the year and shall, through the presiding bishop and the secretary, send to each new church a **certificate of organization,** which the district superintendent shall, on behalf of the conference, present to the new church in an appropriate ceremony.

11. The Annual Conference shall secure, during the course of its annual session, the answers to the questions for conducting Annual Conference sessions, and the secretary of the Annual Conference shall include the answers to these questions in the conference record and in his report to the Council on World Service and Finance. (*See* ¶ 664.3.)

¶ **663.** *Business of the Conference.*—1. The session shall open with a period of devotions, followed by a call of the roll, including the roll of the lay pastors and deaconesses.

2. The Annual Conference, to expedite the transaction of its business, may adopt an agenda as a basis of its procedure. Such agenda shall be prepared by the bishop, the district superintendents, and such others as the conference may name, and shall be submitted to the conference for adoption.

3. Members for all standing committees, boards, and commissions of the Annual Conference shall be selected in such manner as the Annual Conference may determine or as the Discipline may specifically require.

For the purpose of adjusting tenure a certain number of members may be elected or appointed for particular terms. Members shall hold office until their successors are elected. For the Annual Conference agencies provided for by the Discipline see ¶ 665.1 and for the agencies established by the Annual Conference itself see ¶ 665.2.

4. The business of the Annual Conference shall include the receiving and acting upon reports from the district superintendents, the officers, the standing and special committees, the boards, commissions, and societies and also the making of such inquiries as the Council of Bishops shall recommend by the provision of a supplemental guide.

5. The Annual Conference shall make inquiry into the moral and official conduct of its ministers. In response to the inquiry whether all ministerial members of the conference are blameless in their life and official administration, the district superintendent may answer for all

the preachers in his district in one answer, or the Board of the Ministry may make inquiry of each district superintendent about each man in his district and make one report to the bishop and the conference in open session; *provided* that the conference or the bishop may order an executive session of the ministerial members to consider questions relating to matters of ordination, character, and conference relationships.

6. At the conclusion of the examination of the standing of the ministers in the conference or at such later times as the bishop may designate, the presiding bishop may call to the bar of the conference the class to be admitted into full connection and receive them into conference membership after asking the questions to be found in ¶ 334. This examination of the ministers and the passing of their characters may be the business of one session.

¶ 664. *Records and Archives.*—1. The Annual Conference shall keep an exact record of its proceedings according to the forms provided by the General, Jurisdictional, and Central Conferences. If there are no archives of the Annual Conference, the secretary shall keep the bound copy or copies to be handed on to his successor in office. The conference shall send to its Jurisdictional Conference or Central Conference a bound copy of the minutes of the quadrennium for examination and safekeeping.

2. Each Annual Conference shall send to the Council on World Service and Finance two printed or written copies of its annual journal signed by its president and secretary, one copy being for the Department of Records and the other for the Division of Coordination, Research, and Planning of the Program Council.

3. The Annual Conference journal shall include the following divisions, preferably in the following order:
    a) Officers of Annual Conference
    b) Boards, commissions, committees; rolls of conference members
    c) Daily proceedings
    d) Disciplinary questions
    e) Appointments
    f) Reports as ordered by the Annual Conference
    g) Memoirs as ordered by the Annual Conference

   h) Roll of dead—deceased ministerial members
   i) Historical
   j) Miscellaneous
   k) Pastoral record (including the records of accepted lay pastors in such manner as the conference may determine)
   l) Statistics
   m) Index

4. An Annual Conference in the United States shall include in its journal a list of the deaconesses and missionaries, ministerial and lay, active and retired, who have gone from the conference into the service of the Church in mission fields.

5. The secretary of each Annual Conference shall keep a service record of every ministerial member of the Annual Conference together with the date of marriage and the birth dates of the member, his wife, and children.

6. All records of secretaries, statisticians, and treasurers shall be kept according to the forms prepared by the Council on World Service and Finance so that all statistical and financial items shall be handled alike in all conferences and that uniformity of reporting shall be established as a churchwide policy.

¶ **665.** *Conference Agencies.*—1. The Annual Conference at the first session following the General Conference or the Jurisdictional or Central Conferences shall appoint or elect such quadrennial boards, commissions, or committees as shall be ordered by the General Conference or the Jurisdictional or Central Conferences of which the said Annual Conference is a part. The powers and duties of these agencies shall be prescribed by the conference authorizing them or as defined in certain paragraphs of the Discipline.

2. The Annual Conference may appoint additional committees for the purpose of promoting the work of The United Methodist Church within the bounds of the said Annual Conference and may prescribe their membership and their powers and duties.

3. In the appointment or election of Annual Conference boards, commissions, and committees the provisions of the Discipline concerning membership requirements shall be held to be the *minimum* requirements; each Annual Conference may make its agencies of such size as its work may require. Full-time lay pastors serving charges are

eligible for election or appointment to such agencies, except those dealing with qualifications, orders, and status of ministers and lay pastors.

4. (*a*) Each Annual Conference at the first session following the General Conference shall elect for a term of four years a **Board of the Ministry**, consisting of not fewer than six ministers in full connection in the conference, nominated by the presiding bishop after consultation with the chairman of the board of the previous quadrennium, or with a committee of the board, and with the Cabinet. It is recommended that the conference Board of Education have due representation and that at least two thirds of the members be graduates of colleges and schools of theology accredited or approved by the University Senate. Vacancies shall be filled by the bishop after consultation with the chairman of the board.

b) The board shall organize by electing from its membership a chairman, a registrar, and such other officers as it may deem necessary.

c) The board shall convene at the seat and time of the Annual Conference, preferably the day before the session opens, to review and complete the work of the past year and to plan for the future, and at such other times during the conference year as its work may require.

d) The board shall select for each of the district Committees on the Ministry an official representative, who need not reside within the district, to serve as a member of the committee.

e) The board shall work in cooperation with the Department of the Ministry.

5. The duties of the Annual Conference Board of the Ministry shall be:

a) To study problems of ministerial supply in the Annual Conference and to cooperate with the conference director of recruiting, district superintendent (s) , and ministers of the conference in every effort to enlist suitable persons for the Christian ministry; to list all persons who have declared their purpose to prepare for the Christian ministry as ministerial students; and to provide contact with and counsel for all ministerial students while in preparation for the ministry.

b) To urge and encourage in every practical way all ministerial students to attend theological schools of The United Methodist Church to complete the course leading to the Bachelor of Divinity or equivalent degree and to guide and counsel them in this course.

c) To receive annual reports on the progress made by each ministerial student enrolled in a theological school and to record credit for work satisfactorily completed.

d) To guide the ministerial candidate who is not enrolled in a theological school and who is pursuing the course of study as adopted by the Department of the Ministry.

e) To cooperate with the Department of the Ministry in administering its program of recruiting and training and in maintaining its standards.

f) To inquire into the educational and spiritual qualifications of each candidate for the ministry.

g) To examine each candidate to be advanced to membership in the Annual Conference and to orders and each minister from another church seeking entrance into our fellowship according to the provisions of the Discipline and report its recommendations to the Annual Conference.

h) To cooperate with other conference agencies and the Department of the Ministry in providing support, guidance, and programming for continuing education of ministers.

i) To study matters pertaining to the status and relationships of ministers in the Annual Conference and to interpret the high ethical standards of the ministry set forth in the Discipline.

j) To make recommendations to the conference concerning: (1) changes from the effective relation to the superannuate and supernumerary relations, (2) return to the effective relation from other relations, (3) locations, (4) readmission of located persons, (5) sabbatical leave, (6) disability leave, and (7) appointment as a student, and to report to the conference all transfers into and out of the conference, withdrawals, and other changes in conference relations.

6. The board shall seek, in cooperation with the Commission on Enlistment for Church Occupations, with the bishop, district superintendents, pastors, and laymen of the conference, and with the Department of the Ministry and the United Methodist schools of theology, to enlist suitable candidates for the Christian ministry. It shall seek in every way practicable to provide guidance and counsel to them in

their training and preparation for the ministry, recommending colleges and schools of theology accredited or approved by the University Senate. It shall cooperate with our schools of theology by recommending from the Annual Conference students with definite ministerial promise.

7. For the purpose of making financial assistance available to students for the ministry, it is recommended that each Annual Conference and/or Jurisdictional Conference have a seminary loan fund or seminary student-aid fund under the direction of the conference Board of the Ministry.

8. The board shall examine all applicants (*a*) for employment as lay pastors and (*b*) for admission on trial as to their fitness for the ministry, and shall make full inquiry as to the fitness of candidates for admission into full connection. This must include an examination as to character, habits of life, conversion, call to the ministry, Christian experience, evangelistic and missionary concern, age, educational qualifications, domestic situation, cooperation with others, ability to lead a service of worship, and understanding of the Church's mission. The answers to the examination questions may be submitted in writing. The board shall also report recommendations concerning: (*a*) candidates for the office of deacon, (*b*) candidates for ordination as elders, (*c*) those to be received from other churches, (*d*) those to be transferred into the conference, and (*e*) students, not yet elders in full connection, to be appointed to attend school and assigned to a Charge Conference.

9. The board shall certify all information and recommendations concerning each candidate to the Annual Conference in duplicate. One copy of this record is to be kept by the registrar of the board, and one copy is to be mailed after each conference session to the Department of the Ministry.

10. In all cases involving discontinuance of membership on trial or termination of lay pastor status, the board shall file with the office of the resident bishop for permanent record a copy of the circumstances relating thereto.

11. The board shall urge all members on trial to attend colleges and schools of theology related to The United Methodist Church and accredited or approved by the University Senate and shall encourage

and assist them in every practicable way to complete the preparation recommended in ¶ 333.3-.4. It shall require and assist all who are not attending an approved school of theology to pursue promptly the courses of study in an approved courses-of-study school.

12. The **registrar** of the board shall keep a full personnel record, including transcripts of academic credit, for all ministerial candidates within the bounds of the conference.

13. He shall keep a permanent record of the standing of the students in the course of study and report to the conference when required. This record shall include the credits allowed students for work done in accredited schools of theology, in approved schools, in approved courses-of-study schools, and by correspondence.

14. The registrar or some other designated officer of the board shall keep a record of the educational history and interests of each minister serving in the conference. This material shall be furnished to the board by active ministers. Such records are the property of the conference and shall be carefully preserved.

15. The board shall be directly amenable to the Annual Conference for its actions. It shall cooperate with and be responsible to the Department of the Ministry in all matters relating to the ministry.

16. The Annual Conference Board of the Ministry shall cooperate with and be amenable to the Annual Conference in all matters relating to the development and promotion of program for local churches. It shall cooperate with the Annual Conference Program Council in order that its program emphasis may be integrated into the total unified program of the council. It shall promote the total program of the Church or aspects of it which are particularly related to the board as it may be directed by the Program Council. Field work plans which relate to the promotion of program in the Annual Conference or the local church shall be cleared through the Program Council.

17. There shall be a **district Committee on the Ministry** composed of the district superintendent as chairman, five other traveling preachers of the district nominated annually by him and approved by the Annual Conference, and one representative from and appointed by the Board of the Ministry. Interim vacancies may be filled by the chairman.

18. The committee shall examine each person who applies in writing for a license to preach or for a renewal of such license. Where there is evidence that his gifts, graces, and usefulness warrant and that he is qualified under ¶¶ 318-20, on recommendation of his Charge Conference (¶ 145.5), the committee shall recommend to the District Conference to issue or renew his license to preach; *provided,* however, that where no District Conference exists, final action may be taken by the committee, and *provided* further that before the ballot for licensing a person to preach is taken he shall have agreed to the condition set forth in ¶ 318.7.

19. The committee shall recommend to the Board of the Ministry of the Annual Conference suitable candidates for acceptance or continuance as lay pastors, for admission on trial, and for restoration of credentials.

20. The vote of the committee in all such matters shall be by individual written ballot, and a three-fourths majority vote of the committee shall be required for license or approval.

21. The committee shall report its work to the District Conference for approval, where such conference exists.

22. The chairman and another representative of the committee shall meet annually with the **Board of the Ministry,** on call of the chairman of the board, either separately or with representatives of all the districts.

23. The committee shall designate an official spokesman other than the chairman to confer with the board when so requested about any candidate recommended to it by the committee.

24. There shall be a **Joint Committee on Disability** in each Annual Conference. It shall be composed of a minimum of two representatives each from the Board of the Ministry and the conference Board of Pensions, who may be elected by those boards at the beginning of each quadrennium and at other times when vacancies occur, and a district superintendent appointed from time to time by the bishop to represent the Cabinet. If the Annual Conference has entered the Ministers' Reserve Pension Fund, the General Board of Pensions may name any ministerial member of the conference in full connection and in the effective relation as its representative on the committee. Unless and until other members are elected, the chairman and registrar of the

187

Board of the Ministry and the chairman and secretary of the conference Board of Pensions, or others designated by them, shall be authorized to represent their respective boards. The committee shall organize
at the beginning of each quadrennium by the election of a chairman
and a secretary. The duties of the Joint Committee on Disability shall
be:

a) To study the problems of disability in the Annual Conference.

b) To provide for a continuing personal ministry to any disabled
ministers of the conference and to aid them in maintaining fellowship
with their brethren of the conference.

c) To determine what medical doctor or doctors it will approve
for medical examinations and reports regarding disabled ministers
and what medical doctor or doctors it will recommend to the General
Board of Pensions for that purpose.

d) To make recommendations to the Board of the Ministry, the
conference Board of Pensions, and the Cabinet on matters related to
disability, including steps for its prevention, disability leave, benefits,
and programs of rehabilitation.

e) To cooperate with and give assistance to the General Board
of Pensions in its administration of disability benefits through the
Ministers Reserve Pension Fund.

¶ 666.   1. In each Annual Conference there shall be a **Commission on Enlistment for Church Occupations** composed of a representative of the Cabinet; the executive secretary of the conference Program
Council or the conference Board of Education; the conference directors
of youth work and of adult work; the chairman or another member of
the Board of the Ministry; one representative each from the conference
Boards of Christian Social Concerns, Education, Evangelism, Health
and Welfare Ministries, Laity, and Missions; the chairman of missionary education of the conference Women's Society of Christian Service;
a representative of the Campus Ministry; a deaconess (in conferences
where deaconesses are at work); one youth not over eighteen years of
age; and the district secretaries of enlistment for church occupations.
The Cabinet or the commission may appoint other members when
advisable. The agency representative shall be responsible for representing church-related occupations in their respective organizations.

2. It shall be the duty of this commission: (*a*) to cooperate with

the Interboard Committee on Enlistment for Church Occupations (¶ 1084) and with the district secretaries and the local church secretaries of enlistment for church occupations; (*b*) to promote among youth and adults a philosophy of Christian vocation that recognizes the potential sacredness of all useful work and all opportunities for Christian service; (*c*) to organize a program for presenting to youth and adults the opportunities and claims of the pastoral ministry and other church occupations; (*d*) to take into account the basic interest and aptitudes of interested youth and adults and to inform them of the necessary preparation for specific church occupations; (*e*) to keep accurate and useful records of each youth who has indicated an interest in church occupations from the time of his first commitment until he is appointed to full work in the Church or until such time as responsibility for him is accepted by the proper conference board or commission.

3. Each Annual Conference, in whatever way it may decide, shall make adequate provision for the financial support of the work of its Commission on Enlistment for Church Occupations so that the commission may be able to carry forward an effective program of promotion and guidance in the field of Christian vocations.

4. Each district superintendent shall appoint a district secretary of enlistment for church occupations who shall work with the conference Commission on Enlistment for Church Occupations and the Interboard Committee on Enlistment for Church Occupations. He shall maintain contact with local church secretaries of enlistment for church occupations and seek to establish counseling and guidance programs with public schools.

¶ 667. 1. In each Annual Conference there shall be a **Committee on the Lay Worker** composed of no fewer than six nor more than fifteen members, of whom two thirds shall be laity. It shall include one representative from the Board of the Ministry. The committee shall be nominated by the bishop and elected by the Annual Conference on a quadrennial basis with due consideration to the boards and agencies related to the occupations for which the Church has established standards.

2. The committee shall organize by electing from its membership a chairman and such other officers as may be necessary.

3. It shall be the duty of this committee:

a) To receive the list of persons certified for lay careers by the agencies.

b) To review qualifications of these persons as lay workers.

c) To examine candidates in terms of personal, church, and professional standards for the lay worker in The United Methodist Church. Personal standards include: commitment to Christian standards; integrity; concern for persons; willingness to work with persons of various social, religious, and ethnic backgrounds; openness to new thinking; and sensitivity to change. Church standards include: membership in a local congregation, a functional knowledge of the data of the Christian faith, a willingness to see professional improvement, and an enabling approach to leadership with persons in groups. Professional standards include competency norms for performance in lay careers developed from standards established by the particular professions concerned.

d) To recommend candidates to the Annual Conference for consecration as lay workers.

e) To process and report to the Annual Conference for action on matters of transfer and termination of the lay-worker relationship.

f) To keep the Annual Conference advised concerning the lay worker, the careers included in this relationship for which the Church has established standards, and ways in which the Annual Conference may be supportive of the work of persons who serve as lay workers.

¶ **668.** *Transfer of a Local Church.*—A local church may be transferred from one Annual Conference to another in which it is geographically located by a two-thirds vote of those present and voting in each of the following: (1) the Charge Conference, (2) a congregational meeting of the local church, and (3) each of the two Annual Conferences involved. Upon announcement of the required majorities by the bishop or bishops involved, the transfer shall immediately be effective. The votes required may originate in the local church or either of the Annual Conferences involved and shall be effective regardless of the order in which taken. In each case a two-thirds vote of those present and voting shall remain effective unless and until rescinded prior to the completion of the transfer by a vote of a majority of those present and voting.

Section X. The District Conference.

¶ 669. A District Conference shall be held if directed by the Annual Conference of which it is a part and may be held upon the call of the district superintendent, which call shall specify the time and place.

¶ 670. 1. A District Conference shall be composed of all the preachers—traveling, including retired and supernumerary, and local —the deaconesses, the church lay leader, church-school superintendent, president of the Women's Society of Christian Service, and president of the chartered United Methodist Men from each local church in the district, the district stewards, the district trustees, the district lay leader and associate district lay leaders, the lay member of the Annual Conference from each charge, the president of the district Women's Society of Christian Service, the district directors of children's, youth, adult, and general church-school work, and such other persons as the Annual Conference may determine.

2. The District Conference may choose its own order of business. The secretary duly elected shall keep an accurate record of the proceedings and submit it to the Annual Conference for examination.

3. The District Conference shall vote on issuing or renewing licenses to preach on recommendation of the district Committee on the Ministry and shall consider for approval the reports of this committee.

Chapter Five

ADMINISTRATIVE ORDER

Section I. General Provisions.

¶ 801. The administrative work of The United Methodist Church shall be defined, authorized, and structured by the General Conference. The agencies of administration are the Council of Bishops, the Council of Secretaries, the Council on World Service and Finance, and the general agencies.

¶ 802. 1. The general agencies of The United Methodist

Church are the regularly established councils, boards, commissions, and committees which have been constituted by the General Conference. Not included are Boards of Trustees, interagency committees, such commissions and committees as are created by the General Conference to fulfill a special function within the ensuing quadrennium, ecumenical groups on which The United Methodist Church is represented, or committees related to the quadrennial sessions of the General Conference.

2. Each world service agency, so far as possible, shall adopt the following levels in agency organization:

a) **Board** or **division**—the general organization of staff responsibility.

b) **Section**—a broad subdivision of responsibility in a board or division.

c) **Department**—a specific phase of service to the field.

d) **Bureau**—a subdivision of responsibility within a department.

3. Each world service or other general agency, so far as possible, shall adopt the following titles for staff executives:

a) **General secretary**—head of a council or board. Each council or board is entitled to only one general secretary.

b) **Associate general secretary**—head of a division of a council or board.

c) **Executive secretary**—head of a commission or interboard committee. The United Methodist Committee for Overseas Relief is considered a commission.

d) **Assistant general secretary**—head of a section.

e) **Director**—head of a department.

f) **Superintendent**—head of a bureau.

¶ 803. When the membership of an agency is determined in part by the size of the church membership of the jurisdictions, the jurisdictional membership according to the latest official report preceding the General Conference, as shown in the General Minutes, shall be used to determine the size of the jurisdictional representation for the ensuing quadrennium.

¶ 804. No person other than a bishop shall serve at the same time on more than one agency, and no bishop shall serve at the same time on more than three agencies (including any agency on which he serves as a liaison member from another agency); *provided,* however, that if this limitation would deprive a jurisdiction of episcopal representation on an agency, it may be suspended to the extent necessary to permit such representation; *provided* further, that this limitation shall not apply to a division of a board, to an interagency body, or to a Commission on Chaplains and Related Ministries, or a Committee for Overseas Relief; and *provided* that a bishop elected to the Council on World Service and Finance shall not serve on any other agency during his term on this council.

¶ 805.   No person shall serve as president or chairman of more than one general agency or division thereof.

¶ 806.   No elected member of the staff of a general agency shall be eligible for voting membership on any general or jurisdictional agency except where the Discipline specifically provides for such interagency representation.

¶ 807.   No person who receives compensation for services rendered or commissions of any kind from an agency shall be eligible for voting membership on that agency.

¶ 808.   1. Tenure on any general agency shall be limited to twelve consecutive years; *provided,* however, that this limitation shall not affect staff representatives of general agencies serving on other agencies in accordance with the Discipline's requirements. To provide a continuing membership on these agencies it is recommended that each nominating and electing body give special attention to rotation of its representatives.

2. If a general agency is merged with another agency, the years served by members prior to the merger shall be counted as part of the maximum specified in § 1 above.

3. Should a person be elected bishop while serving on any agency, the years which he has served prior to election shall be counted as part of the maximum specified in § 1 above.

4. The years served by members of the corresponding agencies of The Methodist Church and The Evangelical United Brethren Church shall be counted as part of the maximum specified in § 1 above.

5. The twelve-year-tenure rule shall not apply to the Board of Publication for the quadrennium 1968-72.

6. Service on a prior agency of the former Evangelical United

Brethren and Methodist churches shall not be counted as part of the twelve-year limitation in determining eligibility for service on the Program Council *(see also ¶ 827.1)*.

¶ **809.** 1. No person who has passed the age of seventy shall be nominated for, or elected to, membership on any general agency.

2. A minister serving as a member of a general agency who takes the retired relationship shall cease to be a member thereof at the time of his retirement. The vacancy shall be filled in accordance with the appropriate provisions of the Discipline.

3. A general agency may, by majority written ballot, elect quadrennially as a nonvoting honorary member a person who has previously served on it with distinction and who has passed the age of seventy; *provided,* however, that not more than one honorary member may be elected for every twenty-five regular members or major fraction thereof. An honorary member shall receive an expense allowance in the same manner as regular members.

¶ **810.** When a minister who has been elected as a representative of a jurisdiction to a general agency is transferred to an Annual Conference in another jurisdiction or a layman who has been so elected changes his legal residence to another jurisdiction, he shall cease to be a member of that agency at the time of his transfer or removal. The vacancy shall be filled in accordance with the appropriate provisions of the Discipline.

¶ **811.** If a member of a general agency is absent from two consecutive regular meetings without a reason acceptable to the agency, he shall cease to be a member thereof. In that case he shall be so notified, and his place shall be filled in accordance with the appropriate provisions of the Discipline.

¶ **812.** When a bishop is unable to attend a meeting of an agency of which he is a member, the Council of Bishops may name an alternate representative to attend that meeting with the privilege of vote.

¶ **813.** Unless otherwise specified, vacancies on boards and other agencies occurring during the quadrennium shall be filled as follows: an episcopal vacancy shall be filled by the Council of Bishops; a vacancy in jurisdictional representation shall be filled by the College of

Bishops of that jurisdiction; a vacancy in the membership at large shall be filled by the agency itself.

¶ 814. 1. It shall be the policy of The United Methodist Church that all administrative agencies and institutions, including hospitals, homes, and educational institutions, shall: (*a*) recruit, employ, utilize, recompense, and promote their professional staff and other personnel without regard to race, color, or sex; (*b*) fulfill their duties and responsibilities in a manner which does not involve racial segregation or discrimination; and (*c*) secure adequate representation by laymen and laywomen.

2. Elected staff personnel of a general agency shall be retired at the first regular meeting of the agency within the quadrennium in which the person shall become seventy-two years of age. All other staff personnel shall be retired not later than their seventieth birthday. An agency may retire its personnel at an earlier but not a later age than specified above. Nothing in this or any part of Part IV of the Discipline shall prevent the general church treasurers of The Evangelical United Brethren Church and The Methodist Church, respectively, from continuing their respective employments, under the general direction of the Council on World Service and Finance, until December 31, 1968, for the purpose of closing the accounts of their respective churches.

¶ 815. *Relative Representation.*—In order to carry out the intent and spirit of the Constitution (Division Two, Section III, Article VII) :

1. All General Conference boards and agencies:

a) Regardless of size shall have, during the first three quadrenniums following union, at least one member coming from The Evangelical United Brethren Church membership.

b) During the quadrennium 1968-72 shall have approximately 13 percent of the members coming from The Evangelical United Brethren Church membership and 87 percent coming from The Methodist Church membership.

c) During the quadrennium 1972-76 shall have at least 8.7 percent from The Evangelical United Brethren Church membership and 58 percent from The Methodist Church membership.

d) During the quadrennium 1976-80 shall have at least 4.3 percent from the Evangelical United Brethren Church membership and 29 percent from The Methodist Church membership.

e) Members of General Conference boards and agencies are elected in various ways: some by the General Conference, some by Jurisdictional Conferences, and some by the boards and agencies themselves. As promptly after the close of each General Conference as possible, the secretary of the General Conference shall make a tabulation of all General Conference boards and agencies showing the members already elected by the General Conference and the denomination from which each came, and, further, he shall prepare and, subject to review and approval by the Council of Bishops or such subcommittee of the council as the council may designate, promulgate a schedule allocating to each jurisdiction and to each board or agency the number of members to be elected as coming from the former Evangelical United Brethren Church and the former Methodist Church, respectively, and each jurisdiction and each board or agency shall elect in accordance with such allocation. The allocation shall take into consideration the relative number of members coming from the former Evangelical United Brethren Church, shall be made as fair and equitable as possible, and shall be designed to carry out the intent and spirit of the constitutional provision regarding representation.

2. All jurisdictional boards and agencies:

a) Regardless of size shall have, during the first three quadrenniums following union, at least one member coming from The Evangelical United Brethren Church membership.

b) During the quadrennium 1968-72 shall have members coming from The Evangelical United Brethren Church membership and The Methodist Church membership, respectively, approximately as follows:

Northeastern	22% and 78%
Southeastern	2% and 98%
North Central	24% and 76%
South Central	5% and 95%
Western	8% and 92%

c) During the quadrennium 1972-76 shall have members coming from The Evangelical United Brethren Church membership and The Methodist Church membership, respectively, at least approximately as follows:

Northeastern .... 14.6% and 52.0%
Southeastern .... 1.4% and 65.0%
North Central .... 16.0% and 50.6%
South Central .... 3.3% and 63.3%
Western .... 5.3% and 61.3%

d) During the quadrennium 1976-80 shall have members coming from The Evangelical United Brethren Church membership and The Methodist Church membership, respectively, at least approximately as follows:

Northeastern .... 7.3% and 26.0%
Southeastern .... .7% and 32.7%
North Central .... 8.0% and 25.3%
South Central .... 1.7% and 32.7%
Western .... 2.7% and 30.7%

3. All boards and agencies of united Annual Conferences shall, when practicable, during the first three quadrenniums following union:

a) Regardless of size have at least one member coming from The Evangelical United Brethren Church membership.

b) Recognize the principle of at least twice the number of members coming from The Evangelical United Brethren Church membership, in relation to the number coming from The Methodist Church membership, as the relative numerical membership in the Annual Conference coming from the respective denominations would indicate; subject to the constitutional provisions and further subject to the fact that over the period of the three quadrenniums many persons will come into membership of The United Methodist Church without prior membership in either of the two uniting denominations and that, therefore, the fixed membership on boards and agencies to come from membership in the two uniting denominations should, over the period, be scaled down, in each case proportionately.

4. The membership of boards, committees, and agencies of The United Methodist Church, at the level of the General and Jurisdictional Conferences and insofar as possible at the level of the Annual Conference and the local church, shall insure adequate representation of racial minority members; further, all such boards, committees,

197

and agencies whose membership is set forth in the Discipline shall be authorized to elect as many additional members at large as may be necessary to meet this requirement.

5. For the purpose of this section the term "member coming from" a denomination shall mean a person who was a member of such denomination on the date the Plan of Union became effective.

6. The College of Bishops of the jurisdiction shall have power to pass upon the facts concerning, and application of this section to, any situation arising under this section, and in such case the action of the College of Bishops shall be binding on all parties, subject only to appeal to the Judicial Council on matters within its jurisdiction. It is recognized that application of these provisions may prove difficult in many instances, but Annual Conferences are urged to comply so far as possible with the spirit and intention of the provisions regarding relative representation.

¶ **816.** The boards, committees, or commissions elected, authorized, or provided for by the General Conference shall have full power and authority to remove and dismiss at their discretion any member, officer, or employee thereof:

1. Who has become incapacitated so as to be unable to perform his official duties.

2. Who is guilty of immoral conduct or breach of trust.

3. Who for any reason is unable to, or who fails to, perform the duties of his office, or for other misconduct which any of said boards, committees, or commissions may deem sufficient to warrant such dismissal and removal.

In the event that any member, officer, or employee of such board, committee or commission, elected, authorized, or provided for by the General Conference, is found guilty of any crime involving moral turpitude by any federal, state, or county court or pleads guilty thereto, then and in that event, the board, committee, or commission of which he is a member, officer, or employee shall be and is hereby authorized to remove such member, officer, or employee so charged or convicted; and the place so vacated shall be filled as provided in the Discipline. The action of such board, committee, or commission in removing such member, officer, or employee in the circumstances above set forth shall be final; and such member, officer, or employee so removed shall have no further authority to participate in any way in the affairs of such board, committee, or commission.

¶ 817. *Fiscal Policy.*—1. The regular fiscal year for The United Methodist Church shall be the calendar year.

2. Apportionments shall be submitted to former Methodist Annual Conferences based upon the new budget adopted for The United Methodist Church at Dallas, Texas, for a seven-month period from June 1, 1968, to December 31, 1968.

3. The former Evangelical United Brethren Annual Conferences shall be asked to continue to pay apportionments now in force through December 31, 1968.

4. The present central treasurer's office of The Methodist Church shall receive and disburse receipts from former Methodist Annual Conferences through 1968, and the treasurer's office of The Evangelical United Brethren Church shall receive and disburse funds from former Evangelical United Brethren Annual Conferences through 1968.

5. Apportionments based upon the budget adopted at the Uniting Conference shall be given to all Annual Conferences on January 1, 1969, and the Church shall begin operating on the calendar year as its fiscal year.

6. The fiscal quadrennium for The United Methodist Church shall be adjusted so that it begins as a regular practice on January 1 and continues through four calendar years. This adjustment is to be effected as follows:

a) The first fiscal quadrennium of The United Methodist Church shall begin on June 1, 1968, and continue through December 31, 1972.

b) The second fiscal quadrennium shall begin on January 1, 1973, and continue through the next four calendar years.

¶ 818. *Evangelical United Brethren Council of Administration.* —The Council on World Service and Finance shall take steps to preserve the corporate existence of the Evangelical United Brethren Council of Administration until such time as attorneys shall advise its dissolution. The Council on World Service and Finance shall nominate for election the Board of Trustees of the Evangelical United Brethren Council of Administration.

¶ 819. *Church Name Outside the United States of America.—*

1. The name of The United Methodist Church may be translated by any Central Conference into languages other than English.

2. The United Methodist Church in the Central and Southern Europe Central Conference and the Germany Central Conference may use the name *Evangelisch-methodistische Kirche.*

3. The United Methodist Church in the Northwest Canada Annual Conference may use the name "The Evangelical Church—Northwest Canada Annual Conference, affiliated with The United Methodist Church."

¶ 820. *Church Founding Date.*—The United Methodist Church has become the legal and ecclesiastical successor to all property, property rights, powers, and privileges of The Evangelical United Brethren Church and The Methodist Church; the two churches, from their beginnings, have had a close relationship.

The Methodist Church, the first of the two churches to organize, dates from the Christmas Conference of 1784. Therefore, The United Methodist Church recognizes as its founding date the year 1784.

All General Conferences shall be designated not in numerical sequence from any particular date, but merely by the calendar years in which they are respectively held. An Annual Conference, local church, or other body within The United Methodist Church which is composed of uniting units with differing dates of origin, shall use as the date of its founding the date of founding of the older or oldest of the uniting units, or it may use such other founding-date formula as it may determine.

¶ 821. *Interim Responsibilities of the Boards of the Former Churches.*—1. The boards and agencies of The Evangelical United Brethren Church and The Methodist Church shall continue to function until such time as their respective responsibilities shall be taken over by the designated board or agency of The United Methodist Church. During this interim period authorizations of treasurers and other executive officers and staff of the two denominations and of their boards and agencies shall remain in force.

2. Former agencies which are beneficiaries of the World Service Fund, the General Administration Fund, the Episcopal Fund, and the Interdenominational Cooperation Fund shall continue to receive their share of the receipts of contribution from former Methodist Annual

Conferences until the merger of cognate units in The United Methodist Church. The beneficiaries of the Christian Service Fund of the former Evangelical United Brethren Church shall continue to receive their proportionate share of the receipts of that fund.

3. When cognate units are united prior to January 1, 1969, the united unit shall be the beneficiary of all the funds which the uniting units had been receiving from their separate sources.

4. Assets and liabilities of the uniting units shall become the assets and liabilities of the united unit.

5. At the time of the establishment of the Program Council in The United Methodist Church, the budget allocation and the assets and liabilities of the General Council of Administration, the Program Council, and the Reserve Fund of The Evangelical United Brethren Church shall be transferred to the Program Council; except that if it should become essential to continue the General Council of Administration of The Evangelical United Brethren Church beyond the time of the organization of the Program Council in The United Methodist Church, the budget allocation and the assets and liabilities of the General Council of Administration and the Reserve Fund shall not be transferred until the Council on World Service and Finance declares that its work is completed.

6. The allocation to the Contingent Fund of the General Council of Administration, and its assets and liabilities, shall be transferred 50 percent to the Interdenominational Cooperation Fund and 50 percent to the Council on World Service and Finance when the General Council of Administration has completed its work.

7. Apportionments for all major funds for the general Church in The United Methodist Church, including the World Service Fund, the Episcopal Fund, the General Administration Fund, and the Interdenominational Cooperation Fund, shall be computed by using the factors which are now used by The Methodist Church.

8. All increases in salary which may be voted for bishops by the General Conference shall become effective on June 1, 1968.

9. The salary of the bishops of the former Evangelical United Brethren Church shall be adjusted to the level of the salary voted for a bishop of The United Methodist Church on June 1, 1968.

10. Increases in salaries of general secretaries and staff persons

which may be voted by boards shall become effective on June 1, 1968.

11. The salary of general officers and staff persons of the general boards of the former Evangelical United Brethren Church and The Methodist Church shall be adjusted on June 1, 1968, to the level of salary which they would have received on June 1, 1968, had they held the position in which they shall be placed in a United Methodist agency. In the event that this salary is not known as of June 1, 1968, the salary shall be paid retroactive to that date from the funds of the board by which the person is employed before its funds are merged with its cognate unit.

12. The date for membership of former general officers and staff persons of the general boards of the former Evangelical United Brethren Church in the pension plans of the boards of The United Methodist Church by which they are employed shall be retroactive to June 1, 1968.

13. The general secretaries and staff persons of all general agencies of The United Methodist Church shall be covered by any insurance plans which may be adopted by the agencies of The United Methodist Church from the date of their employment by their board, and in those instances where present group insurance plans must be terminated because of the realignment of staff persons of present boards to the new boards of The United Methodist Church or the moving of boards from one city to another, steps shall be taken to see that no person now covered by such a policy is left without coverage as long as he continues in the service of the board to which he was related. This agreement shall include retired persons now covered by such group insurance policies. Cost of the continuation of a group policy which must be phased out shall be borne by the agencies covered by the policy or their successor agencies until such time as the policy can be terminated. It is expected that no present group policy which must be phased out shall continue beyond January 1, 1969.

Section II.   Program Council.

¶ 822. The aims of the Program Council are:

1. To provide a consultation process wherein the Council of Bishops, the Council of Secretaries, and representative laymen and

pastors may discuss, choose, and coordinate program emphases of The United Methodist Church.

2. To provide services to assist in the selection and coordination of the program emphases and in the interpretation and promotion of them in the Annual Conferences and local churches.

ORGANIZATION

¶ 823. *Name.*—The name of this organization shall be the **Program Council** of The United Methodist Church, hereinafter called the council.

¶ 824. The council is an organizational union of the Commission on Promotion and Cultivation; the Coordinating Council; the Interboard Commission on the Local Church; the Television, Radio, and Film Commission; and the Department of Research of the Council on World Service and Finance of The Methodist Church and the Program Council of The Evangelical United Brethren Church.

¶ 825. *Incorporation.*—The council shall be incorporated. Divisions of the council may be incorporated. These corporations shall be successor corporations to the corporations whose functions are assigned to them. The council and its divisions shall be incorporated in such state or states as the council may elect.

¶ 826. *Amenability.*—The council shall be responsible directly to the General Conference.

¶ 827. *Council Organization.*—The management, business, property, and all affairs of the council shall be governed and administered by the council, which shall be organized as follows:

1. *Membership.*—Membership of the council shall consist of fifteen active members of the Council of Bishops resident in the United States—three from each jurisdiction, elected by the Council of Bishops —plus the following elected by each Jurisdictional Conference: four ministers of whom at least three shall be pastors of charges at the time of their election and seven laymen of whom at least one shall not be over twenty-one years of age at the time of election and of whom at least two shall be women. All members of the Council of Secretaries shall be members with privilege of the floor but without vote. Any

other bishop having any interest in an agenda item of a particular meeting shall have the privilege of the floor but without vote.

Under the twelve-year-tenure rule (¶ 808) service on a prior agency of the former Evangelical United Brethren and Methodist churches shall not be counted in determining eligibility for service on the Program Council.

2. *Meetings.*—Within three months after the adjournment of the last Jurisdictional Conference to meet in any General Conference year, the elected members of the council shall be assembled by a convener designated by the Council of Bishops to organize the council.

The council shall hold at least one meeting in each calendar year. It shall convene at such other times as are necessary on call of the president or on written request of one fifth of the members. Thirty-five members shall constitute a quorum.

3. *Officers.*—The council shall have a president who shall be a bishop, three vice-presidents, and a recording secretary, each elected from the membership of the council, and a treasurer. Each division shall have a chairman, a vice-chairman, and a recording secretary elected from the membership of the council. The chairmen of the divisions shall be the vice-presidents of the council. The president of the council and the chairmen of the divisions shall be presiding, not administrative, officers. Officers shall be elected for the quadrennium and will continue in office until their successors are duly elected and qualified.

4. *Council Executive Committee.*—There may be an **executive committee** consisting of the officers of the council and of its divisions, and additional members elected by the council.

5. *Nominating Committee.*—A **nominating committee** shall be established, consisting of one bishop from each jurisdiction and one other person selected by the members from that jurisdiction. The nominating committee shall nominate members of the council for election by the council as (*a*) a president and a recording secretary, (*b*) members of the council executive committee, if any, as provided in § 4 above, and (*c*) members of the constituent divisions of the council in the following approximate ratios: Division of Coordination, Research, and Planning, 40 percent; Division of Interpretation, 35 percent; and Division of Television, Radio, and Film Communication,

25 percent; and the members of the Committee on Review as per ¶ 836.

6. *Elected Staff.*—The council shall elect a **general secretary** quadrennially and such other staff personnel annually as may be needed. The general secretary shall sit on the council and its executive committee, if any, and with each division and division executive committee, if any, at all sessions and shall have right to the floor without the privilege of voting.

¶ **828.** *Divisions.*—The council shall conduct its activities both directly and through three divisions: the Division of Coordination, Research, and Planning; the Division of Interpretation; and the Division of Television, Radio, and Film Communication; and through the Committee on Review.

¶ **829.** *Amenability.*—The divisions shall be amenable to and report regularly to the council and its executive committee, if any, to keep the same fully informed concerning divisional plans and activities.

¶ **830.** *Organization of Divisions.*—The divisions shall be organized as follows:

1. *Membership.*—The divisions shall be composed of council members as provided in ¶ 827.5c. Divisions shall have authority to elect members at large to the divisions in a total number not to exceed one third of the total number of members of the division elected by the council in order to provide for division members with special qualifications.

2. *Meetings.*—Each division shall meet at least once annually.

3. *Officers.*—Each division shall elect as its officers a chairman, who shall be a vice-president of the council, a vice-chairman, a recording secretary, and such other officers as it shall deem necessary. Vacancies shall be filled by the divisions or their executive committees. The divisions shall determine the powers and duties of their officers.

4. *Executive Committee.*—Each division may elect an **executive committee** and establish rules for its meetings and the carrying out of its duties.

5. *Elected Staff.*—Each division shall elect an **associate general secretary** quadrennially and such other staff personnel annually as may be needed. The associate general secretary shall sit with the coun-

cil and its executive committee, if any, and with the division and its executive committee, if any, at all sessions and shall have the right to the floor without the privilege of voting.

6. *Secretariat.*—The general secretary of the council and the associate general secretaries of its divisions shall constitute the **Secretariat** of the council, and the general secretary of the council shall be the chairman of the Secretariat.

FUNCTIONS

¶ **831.**   The functions of the council shall be:

1. To give leadership in, participate in, and coordinate research and planning for The United Methodist Church as specified in ¶ 832.

2. To study the program emphases of The United Methodist Church, especially the emphases projected by the general agencies, and with those agencies to develop a coordinated program for use in the Annual Conferences and local churches as specified in ¶ 832.

3. To assist the general agencies in the interpretation and promotion of the coordinated program and of other programs of the agencies as specified in ¶ 833.

4. In order to fulfill its function as a communication agency within the United States, to present the faith and work of the Church to the general public by radio and television broadcasting and by such other audio or visual media as may be available as assigned and specified in ¶ 834.

5. To participate in and receive reports from all interboard agencies and activities of The United Methodist Church.

6. To coordinate and harmonize the work of its divisions and other interboard agencies and activities.

7. To receive program recommendations from the general agencies and other sources and also to make program recommendations to the same.

8. To receive and act upon reports of the divisions, the committees, the general secretaries, and the treasurer.

9. To establish appropriate organization of the council, its divisions, its committees, and its staff in order to accomplish its aims and perform its duties.

10. To create or discontinue, as deemed necessary, committees (including interboard committees), task forces, and consultations to carry out the regular or special duties of the council.

11. To determine the need for a special program for any particular quadrennium and, if such is deemed desirable, to formulate the same and present it to the General Conference for determination and action.

12. Upon request of a general board or agency or of an Annual Conference, or on its own initiative, to study and review questions involving overlapping in activity or lack of cooperation among or within general agencies and to make recommendations to the boards or agencies involved for resolving such issues. A record of all decisions shall be kept, and a report of each shall be forwarded to the Council of Bishops and the Council on World Service and Finance.

13. To keep under constant review the several and combined plans of the general agencies for the production and distribution of all free literature and promotional and resource materials (except church-school literature) for the purpose of coordinating the content, distribution, and timing of the release of such materials to the end that duplication of activity and of material may be avoided. Plans for the production of free literature shall be submitted to the Section on Coordination for approval.

14. To review the plans of any general agency or board proposing to acquire real estate or erect a building or enter into a lease in the continental United States and determine whether the proposed action is in the best interest of The United Methodist Church. On the basis of that determination it shall approve or disapprove all such proposed actions, except that nothing in the foregoing shall include the operational requirements of the Board of Publication.

15. To designate the agency which shall undertake any special study authorized by the General Conference when such agency has not been indicated by the General Conference.

16. To consult with the general agencies of The United Methodist Church in regard to publishing policy. It shall lead to a continuing consultation with all editors of all publications and the president and publisher of The Methodist Publishing House and shall suggest such steps as may seem advisable to minimize unnecessary

duplication and overlappings of content, emphasis, and coverage and where deemed desirable, to recommend the combining of periodicals.

17. To report to each session of the General Conference. The report shall include a list of all decisions and recommendations made and a statement concerning the response to each.

DIVISION OF COORDINATION, RESEARCH, AND PLANNING

¶ 832. The **Division of Coordination, Research, and Planning** shall perform its functions both directly and through three sections:

1. *The Section of Coordination.*—In order to coordinate program emphases proposed by general boards and agencies for transmission to and implementation by the Annual Conferences and the local churches, there shall be a **Section of Coordination,** which shall have the following functions:

a) To study the total program of The United Methodist Church as projected by the council and the general agencies with a view to preventing overlapping of emphases and/or program resources and for the purpose of developing a coordinated program. The general agencies shall present regularly to the Section of Coordination, for review and suggestions, program proposals for the Annual Conferences and local churches. The Section of Coordination shall harmonize the special program plans of each agency for the year ahead and shall present the same to the annual meeting of the Program Council for its endorsement and transmission to the churches.

b) To assist the council and the general agencies in the promotion of the coordinated program as adopted by the council, utilizing the facilities of the Division of Interpretation to communicate the program to the Annual Conferences and the local churches through regular channels.

c) To cooperate with the Division of Interpretation in providing a free program journal for pastors and other leaders of local churches.

d) To organize, give leadership to, participate in, and report to the council for a **Continuing Coordinating Committee,** consisting of the staff personnel of the division and representative staff personnel assigned to the committee by the Boards of Christian Social Concerns, Education, Evangelism, Health and Welfare Ministries, Laity, and

Missions and the Commissions on Ecumenical Affairs and Worship.

This committee shall cooperate with the general agencies in providing workbooks, manuals, filmstrips, and other training and guidance materials as needed by leaders in local churches. This shall not contravene the responsibility of a board or agency to provide separate materials within its own field.

2. *The Section of Research.*—There shall be a **Section of Research.** Its functions are:

a) To establish standards for conducting research for The United Methodist Church and to review and evaluate research projects in terms of these standards.

b) To initiate, on approval of the division or its executive committee, if any, such research as may be deemed essential; *provided* that due care is taken not to duplicate similar research being made by other general agencies.

c) To analyze, interpret, and evaluate facts gathered through research, making them available to the general agencies.

d) To cooperate with specialized research personnel associated with other agencies of the Church in the development of a comprehensive and coordinated research program. This shall be accomplished by the creation of an **Interagency Staff Committee on Research,** which shall meet as often as is necessary to accomplish its work.

e) To establish and convene, at least annually, an **Interagency Committee on Research,** which shall be advisory to the section. This committee shall include: representatives from the general agencies; research specialists and theologians from schools of theology; general research specialists; physical, political, and social scientists; economists; and other qualified personnel from educational institutions and industry in order to consider, develop, and evaluate proposed research projects.

f) To assist the Interagency Committee on Research in discovering and choosing research projects which merit support from the reserve for research projects as provided in the General Administration Fund of the Council on World Service and Finance. This reserve shall be administered by the Division of Coordination, Research, and Planning in harmony with the decisions of the Interagency Committee

on Research and in cooperation with the Council on World Service
and Finance.

g) To establish a procedure whereby the research data developed
in the Church can be effectively coordinated and communicated to the
Church and its policy makers.

h) To make research services available to any other official agency
of the Church; *provided,* however, that where the research requested
by an agency requires postage, supplies, temporary additional staff,
or other necessary expense, the requesting agency shall enter into an
agreement with the section and the division for this additional cost
before such service is undertaken.

i) To maintain a roster of competent research personnel associated with other agencies of the Church.

j) To maintain a research library and an index including a listing and a cataloging of past and current research made by or for the
several agencies of the Church.

3. *The Section of Planning.*—There shall be a **Section of Planning.** Its functions are:

a) To establish standards for short-range and long-range planning
in The United Methodist Church.

b) To review and evaluate plans in terms of these standards.

c) To serve in an advisory capacity to any general agency or official personnel on such matters as may properly come before such a
section.

d) To engage in planning for the continuing ministry of The
United Methodist Church through cooperation with staff planners
from other agencies in the Church in order to develop coordinated
plans which can be recommended to The United Methodist Church
and its agencies. This shall be accomplished by the creation of an
Advisory Staff Committee on Planning, which shall meet as often
as necessary to accomplish its work.

e) To establish and convene, at least annually, an **Advisory
Committee on Planning** to advise the section and the division concerning long-range plans of the boards and agencies of The United
Methodist Church. Such a committee may include theologians, social
and physical scientists, economists, and other qualified personnel in

order to develop and test assumptions concerning trends in American life and to assess the implications of these trends for the Church.

f) To cooperate in the planning activities of the World Council of Churches, the National Council of Churches, the World Methodist Council, and the denominations having headquarters in the United States and to the extent feasible to coordinate with other work being done in this field.

DIVISION OF INTERPRETATION

¶ 833. In order to coordinate the promotion of the program and the general benevolence causes of The United Methodist Church to the end that our people may be informed about and may adequately support the work of the general agencies, there shall be a **Division of Interpretation.**

The associate general secretary, under the authority and direction of the division, on a churchwide basis shall coordinate and promote world service and all other general benevolence causes except as otherwise directed by the General Conference. He shall direct the work of the staff of the division, making provision for salaries and office facilities within the policies established by the Program Council. The associate general secretary shall cooperate with the Secretariat of the Program Council, its divisions, and the Council on World Service and Finance. He shall, by such plans as shall be authorized by the division, promote the general benevolence causes of the Church with the assistance of the bishops, district superintendents, pastors, lay officials, and General, Jurisdictional, and Annual Conference boards and agencies.

Functions of the division are:

1. To establish and maintain a central promotional office, operating under the division's authority and direction, for the purpose of promoting throughout the Church the program of world service, Advance specials (¶¶ 871-73, 876), One Great Hour of Sharing (¶¶ 875-76), the Fellowship of Suffering and Service (¶ 877), the Interdenominational Cooperation Fund (¶ 892), and other general benevolence causes except as otherwise directed by the General Conference.

2. To employ all available means of communication in carrying out its purposes throughout The United Methodist Church. In pre-

paring its materials the division shall give attention to the inseparable relationship between giving for benevolence and education in Christian stewardship. Appeals for giving that are made to United Methodists shall be consistent with the aims of Christian stewardship. The division shall cooperate with the Board of the Laity to the end that stewardship education materials of that board and promotional materials of this division shall be in harmony.

3. To publish a free program journal for pastors and local church leaders, the name to be selected by the Division of Interpretation, which shall present to the local church for its use the program and promotional materials of the general agencies in a coordinated manner and shall be in lieu of general agency promotional periodicals. The principal editors of the journal shall be elected quadrennially by the division. They shall be responsible to the associate general secretary of the division for publishing procedures but shall themselves be responsible for the content of the journal. The division shall obtain from the churches or the district superintendents the names of church officials entitled to receive the journal so as to compile a subscription list compatible with post office department regulations.

4. To conduct, as early as practicable in each new quadrennium, a district superintendents' convocation to lift up the general benevolence causes, the quadrennial program, and other program interests of the Church. The division shall provide district superintendents with ongoing assistance in the performance of their duties through printed resources, counsel, and training.

5. To maintain a calendar of meetings in behalf of all agencies of The United Methodist Church as an aid to the agencies in regulating the number and timing of such meetings.

6. To recommend to the General Conference, through the Program Council and after consultation with the Council of Bishops and the Council on World Service and Finance, the number and timing of special days which are to be observed on a churchwide basis, except that the Council of Bishops and the Council on World Service and Finance may authorize a special financial appeal in an emergency.

7. To undertake the promotion of any cause or undertaking, financial or otherwise, not herein mentioned, demanding churchwide promotion or publicity; *provided* that such action shall have been

previously approved by the Council of Bishops, by the Council on World Service and Finance, and by the Program Council, or by their respective executive committees.

8. To design and supervise the use of an official insignia for The United Methodist Church, which may be used by any official agency of the Church or any Annual Conference thereof to identify the work, program, and materials of The United Methodist Church. The design of the official insignia shall be approved by the Division of Interpretation. The official insignia shall be registered as a trademark in behalf of The United Methodist Church by the Division of Interpretation, and the division shall supervise the use of the official insignia in order to preserve the integrity of its design and to protect it against unauthorized use. The division shall provide patterns of the insignia for purposes of their use by any board or agency of The United Methodist Church and its Annual Conferences.

9. To maintain a shipping and service operation, including addressing, packaging, mailing, and duplicating services, as may be deemed necessary. The services of this operation shall be available to all general agencies. The associate general secretary is authorized and directed to make equitable charges to the agencies using their services.

10. To prorate on a monthly basis to the several promoted funds on the basis of receipts for each fund, the expenses of the division, including the editing, publishing, and distribution of the journal of program and promotion, world service leaflets, and other publications or visual aids for the promoting of general benevolence causes authorized by the General Conference. The budget of the division, as recommended by the Program Council and approved by the Council on World Service and Finance, shall be a prior claim against the World Service Fund and the other promoted funds.

DIVISION OF TELEVISION, RADIO, AND FILM COMMUNICATION

¶ 834. The functions of the **Division of Television, Radio, and Film Communication** are:

1. To unify and coordinate the audio-visual programs of all United Methodist agencies dealing with projected pictures, recordings,

transcriptions, radio and television programs, and other audio-visual materials. The division is assigned the responsibility in the United States for presenting the faith and work of the Church to the general public by radio and television broadcasting and by such other audio or visual media as may be available.

2. To make the studies necessary for the development of a unified and comprehensive program of resources to serve all age groups in the home, church, and community and to represent the causes of the Church.

3. To produce and distribute such programs and materials in the area of the work of member agencies as the agencies may request and finance and such other resources as are needed to serve the causes of the Church. Insofar as practical, the rental or sale of materials for use in United Methodist churches shall be handled through The Methodist Publishing House.

4. To represent The United Methodist Church in the Broadcasting and Film Commission of the National Council of Churches and in other interdenominational agencies working in the area of mass communication.

5. To provide funds for scholarships and other training opportunities to prepare qualified persons for full-time Christian service in this field, and to work with other United Methodist agencies in providing training opportunities for ministers and lay leaders so that resources provided may be effectively used.

¶ 835. *Financial Support.*—The financial support of the division shall be determined as follows: the General Conference shall determine and provide from world service funds, on the recommendation of the Council on World Service and Finance, the budget of the division. The budget shall include provision for necessary staff and administrative costs and such funds as may be deemed necessary to enable the division to fulfill its stated functions. Additional contributions may be accepted from member agencies which are not supported by world service funds.

The General Conference, on recommendation of the Council on World Service and Finance and of the division, shall allot such funds as it deems wise to the Broadcasting and Film Commission of the National Council of Churches. If this apportionment is included in a total church budget for the National Council of Churches, it shall be paid only after annual approval by the division.

COMMITTEE ON REVIEW

¶ **836.** Within the Program Council there shall be a **Committee on Review,** composed of twenty-one of the voting members of the Program Council, elected for a term of four years upon nomination of the council's nominating committee and eligible for reelection. One member shall be a bishop, and the remainder shall consist of two laymen and two ministers from each jurisdiction, none of whom, other than the bishop, shall be a member of any other general board or agency.

The functions of the Committee on Review shall be:

1. Upon request of the Division of Coordination, Research, and Planning, a general board or other agency, or an Annual Conference, or on its own initiative, to review questions involving overlapping in function or lack of cooperation among or within general boards or agencies and to make recommendations for resolving such issues.

2. To consider the plans of any general agency to publish a promotional periodical. Any board or agency proposing to publish a promotional periodical shall submit its request to the Committee on Review. If the committee disapproves, the agency shall delay such publication and circulation until the proposal can be submitted to the next General Conference for determination; *provided,* however, that the foregoing shall not apply to periodicals exempted in ¶ 966 or to church-school curriculum materials.

3. To consider the plans of any general agency proposing to acquire real estate or erect a building or enter into a lease as prescribed in ¶ 831.14 and to determine whether the proposed action is in the best interest of The United Methodist Church. On the basis of that consideration it shall approve or disapprove. If the Committee on Review disapproves, the agency shall delay the project until it can be considered by the next General Conference.

4. To consult with general agencies of The United Methodist Church in regard to duplication or overlapping in their publishing policies which may be identified by the other divisions of the Program

Council and to suggest steps for minimizing duplication or overlapping of content, emphasis, and coverage; and where desirable the committee shall recommend the combining of periodicals.

5. To keep under review the effectiveness of the general boards and agencies in terms of their concurrence with the social principles of The United Methodist Church and for the purpose of encouraging modern, efficient policies of planning, operation, and evaluation.

6. To evaluate the effectiveness of procedures to orient overseas delegates on both the operation of the General Conference and the materials which it will consider and, where possible, to devise and implement measures to assure full, effective representation and participation of overseas members in the work of The United Methodist Church and the General Conference.

7. The Committee on Review shall elect a chairman, a vice-chairman, and a secretary, who shall keep a permanent record of its meetings and of any decisions reached. Certified copies of the minutes shall be filed with the secretary of the Program Council, the secretary of the General Conference, the Council on World Service and Finance, and the secretary of the Council of Bishops. An annual written report shall be submitted to the Program Council, the Council of Bishops, and the secretary of the General Conference, and a quadrennial report shall be submitted by the committee to the General Conference.

Jurisdictional Program Council

¶ 837. In each jurisdiction there may be a **jurisdictional Program Council** designed to coordinate and make the work of the boards and agencies of the Church effective within the jurisdiction and organized as the jurisdiction may determine.

¶ 838. In each jurisdiction there may be a **jurisdictional Committee on Coordination,** auxiliary to the Division of Coordination of the General Program Council and the jurisdictional Program Council.

¶ 839. In each jurisdiction there may be a **jurisdictional Committee on Interpretation** auxiliary to the Division of Interpretation of the General Program Council and the jurisdictional Program Council.

¶ 840. In each jurisdiction there may be a **jurisdictional Committee on Television, Radio, and Film Communication,** auxiliary to the Division of Television, Radio, and Film Communication of the General Program Council and the jurisdictional Program Council.

ANNUAL CONFERENCE PROGRAM COUNCIL

¶ **841.** In each Annual Conference of The United Methodist Church an **Annual Conference Program Council** shall be organized; *provided* that such council or any component thereof may be organized on an area basis.

1. *Purpose.*—The purpose of the Program Council shall be (*a*) to receive program recommendations from the local churches, the district agencies, the Annual Conference agencies, and the jurisdictional and General Program Councils; (*b*) to develop these recommendations into a coordinated program to be recommended to the Annual Conference for consideration, amendment, and adoption as the Annual Conference program; and (*c*) to provide implementation for and administration of the coordinated program as adopted by the conference.

2. *Membership.*—The membership of the Annual Conference Program Council shall consist of the presiding bishop; the district superintendents; representatives of conference agencies as determined by the conference; the conference secretary; two representatives of the conference youth organization; two representatives of the conference Women's Society of Christian Service, one of whom shall be the president; the conference lay leader; one layman from each district; chairmen of age-level and family departments; and such additional members as the Annual Conference may determine.

The following shall be members of the council without vote: salaried and volunteer Annual Conference staff, the conference treasurer, and one or more members of the Commission on World Service and Finance.

3. *Officers.*—The officers of the council shall be a chairman, a vice-chairman, a secretary, and a treasurer. They shall be elected by the council.

4. *Executive Committee.*—There may be an **executive committee** consisting of the officers, the bishop, at least one district superintendent chosen by the Cabinet, the director of the council, and other members

as the Annual Conference may determine. Approximately one half of the members of the executive committee shall be laymen.

5. *Committees, Task Forces, and Consultations.*—The council shall appoint a Committee on Interpretation; a Committee on Television, Radio, and Film Communication; and a Committee on Publishing Interests (¶ 979). It may appoint such other committees, task forces, and consultations as may be deemed essential to the effective discharging of its responsibilities.

6. *Age-Level and Family Departments.*—The council may appoint age-level and family departments as it deems necessary to the performance of its duties.

7. *Director.*—The council shall elect, upon nomination by the bishop and district superintendents, an executive officer to be known as the **conference program director.** He shall be in consultative relationship to the conference Cabinet on matters relating to coordination, implementation, and administration of the conference program.

8. *Staff.*—All Annual Conference program staff may be employed by, directed by, and amenable to the Annual Conference Program Council. Ordained ministers on the staff are subject to being appointed by the presiding bishop.

9. *Relationships.*—The council shall have the following relationships, including the amenabilities indicated:

a) All District and Annual Conference agencies shall submit the elements of program which are to be promoted in, supported by, or implemented by the local churches of the conference to the council for consideration, coordinating, and calendaring prior to presentation to the local churches. The council may request District or Annual Conference agencies to implement a program for the entire conference.

b) The council staff shall be responsible, in cooperation with the district superintendents, for the implementation of the conference program.

10. *Functions.*—The functions of the Annual Conference Program Council are:

a) To study the mission of the Annual Conference and the local churches of the conference and to determine program emphases which will assist the conference and the local churches to perform their mission.

b) To describe, coordinate, and organize opportunities to serve within the mission.

c) To receive program recommendations from the local churches, the District and Annual Conference agencies, and the jurisdictional and General Program Councils; to evaluate these recommendations; and to formulate a coordinated conference program to be presented to the Annual Conference for consideration.

d) To provide for implementation and administration of the program adopted by the conference.

e) To provide program resources and assistance in program planning and implementation for local churches.

f) To provide staff personnel for implementing and administering the conference program.

g) To provide channels of communication between Annual Conference agencies and local churches.

h) To give leadership in research and planning for the conference and to cooperate with other research and planning agencies.

i) To cooperate in ecumenical projects and events which have been approved by the conference.

j) To study and coordinate the budget askings of the conference agencies as they relate to the conference program and to make recommendations regarding the same to the Commission on World Service and Finance, understanding that an Annual Conference may direct that the accounting service for the conference treasurer shall be provided by a centralized office under the direction of a business manager.

k) To interpret the conference program to the local churches with a view toward gaining the financial support needed in order to implement that program.

¶ 842. In each Annual Conference Program Council, chosen by it and amenable to it, there shall be a **Committee on Interpretation.**

1. *Functions.*—It shall, in cooperation with the council, promote the program of world service and other general benevolence causes in the pastoral charges of the conference in cooperation with the Division of Interpretation of the General Program Council. It shall coordinate the promotion of all approved general and conference benevolence causes, including general and conference Advance specials, the One Great Hour of Sharing, the Fellowship of Suffering and Service, the

Interdenominational Cooperation Fund, and other general benevolence causes except as otherwise directed by the General Conference, and shall assign the responsibility for the promotion of approved causes that do not clearly belong to an existing agency.

2. *Finance.*—The budget for the committee shall be provided by the conference through its Commission on World Service and Finance.

¶ 843. In each Annual Conference Program Council, chosen by it and amenable to it, there shall be a **Committee on Television, Radio, and Film Communication,** which in cooperation with the program boards and other agencies in the conference shall have as its purpose the serving of the conference in the field of communication by:

1. Promotion of the principles of good communication.

2. Promotion of the use of mass-communication methods and materials by the local churches.

3. Where necessary, establishment of audio-visual libraries and assistance in training audio-visual librarians.

4. Production and distribution of programs for conference-wide use.

5. Cooperation with the conference Board of Education and other conference agencies in providing training opportunities for leaders in the use of audio-visual methods and materials.

6. Service to other agencies of the conference and close cooperation with the conference or area public relations office.

7. Cooperation with other agencies in the organization and training of local-church Audio-visual Committees.

8. Cooperation with the Division of Television, Radio, and Film Communication in the promotion and placement of television and radio programs within the conference.

District Program Council

¶ 844. Where desired, a **district Program Council** may be organized to coordinate programs within the district.

Local Church Council on Ministries

¶ 845. There shall be a **Council on Ministries** in each local church (*see also* ¶¶ 153-60) which shall consider, initiate, develop, and coordinate proposals for the church's strategy for mission (¶¶ 153-54). It shall receive and, where possible, utilize resources for mission provided by the District, Annual, Jurisdictional, and General Conference Program Councils, boards, and agencies, and shall coordinate these resources with the church's plan for ministries in its local and other settings. The council shall be amenable to the Administrative Board, to which it shall submit its plans for review and appropriate action. Upon adoption of the program by the Administrative Board, the council shall implement the plans which are assigned to it.

¶ 846. The Council on Ministries shall make recommendations to the Committee on Finance requesting financial resources needed to undergird the ministries which it has developed, using local and connectional program suggestions, and which it recommends to the Administrative Board.

¶ 847. In the local church the Council on Ministries may organize an **Audio-visual Committee,** composed of at least one representative from each work area commission and, where organized, a representative from age-level and program agencies. This committee shall give counsel in the selection, purchase, and use of audio-visual materials and equipment and in the evaluation and use of radio and television programs related to the program of the church, and it shall serve as the contact group for the Television, Radio, and Film Commission. It shall develop a library of audio-visual materials (which may be a part of the general church library) and train the librarian responsible for its supervision. It shall report to the Council on Ministries. When it is impractical to have a representative committee, an audio-visual counselor may be appointed by the Council on Ministries. He shall then be responsible for the duties indicated in this paragraph.

Section III. Council on World Service and Finance.

CHURCH FINANCE

¶ 848. *General Statement on Church Finance.*—The work of the Church requires the support of our people, and participation therein through service and gifts is a Christian duty and a means of grace. In order that all members of The United Methodist Church may share in its manifold ministries at home and abroad and that the work committed to us may prosper, the following financial plan, including the causes supported by the Christian Service Fund of the former Evangelical United Brethren Church, has been duly approved and adopted.

¶ 849.   The various causes, funds, and budgets of The United Methodist Church shall be known and designated as follows: (1) **world service,** the general benevolences of The United Methodist Church, approved by the General Conference and included in the world service budget; (2) **conference benevolences,** the Annual Conference benevolences and causes, approved by the conference and included in the conference benevolence budget; (3) the **world service budget,** the **general administration budget,** the **episcopal budget,** the **interdenominational cooperation budget,** the amounts approved or estimated by the General Conference for these causes respectively; (4) **conference benevolence budget,** the amounts approved for Annual Conference causes respectively and included in one budget; (5) **world service and conference benevolence budget,** the world service apportionment to any Annual Conference plus its conference benevolence budget, included in one sum and distributed among the charges of the conference; (6) the **World Service Fund,** including the retirement allowance for bishops, general church officers, and staff personnel of the former Evangelical United Brethren Church, the **General Administration Fund,** the **Episcopal Fund,** the **Interdenominational Cooperation Fund,** the **Committee for Overseas Relief Fund,** the **Fellowship of Suffering and Service Fund,** the **Temporary General Aid Fund,**[9] all causes presently included in the Christian Service Fund of the former Evangelical United Brethren Church, funds received into the central treasury for these causes respectively.

---

[9] The United Methodist General Conference of 1968 continued the Temporary General Aid Fund to provide grants-in-aid to raise the level of pensions and minimum salaries in the former Central Jurisdiction and the Rio Grande Annual Conference and assist the Annual Conferences in geographical jurisdictions receiving transfers from the former Central Jurisdiction where major differences in annuity and minimum salary rates are involved. The pension portion of this fund is to be administered by the General Board of Pensions, and the minimum salary portion by the Council on World Service and Finance. The apportionment and distribution are to be made by the Council on World Service and Finance in accordance with action of the 1968 General Conference.

ORGANIZATION

¶ 850. There shall be a **Council on World Service and Finance,** which shall be incorporated. Its members shall be elected quadrennially by the General Conference as follows: two bishops, nominated by the Council of Bishops; two ministers and two lay persons from each jurisdiction, nominated by the bishops of that jurisdiction; seven members at large, at least three of whom shall be women, nominated by the Council of Bishops without reference to jurisdictions; and a proportionate number of ministers and laymen from the former Evangelical United Brethren Church as agreed upon in the Plan of Union. The members, including bishops, shall not be eligible to membership on, or employment by, any other general agency except the Board of Trustees of The United Methodist Church. They shall serve until their successors are elected and qualified. Vacancies occurring between sessions of the General Conference shall be filled by the council on nomination of the bishops of the jurisdiction concerned or, in the event of a vacancy among the members at large, on nomination of the Council of Bishops. For the quadrennium 1968-72 there shall be, in addition to the members specified above, one bishop from the former Evangelical United Brethren Church.

¶ 851. The officers of the council shall be a president, a vice-president, a recording secretary, and a general secretary, who shall also be the treasurer of the council, all of whom shall be elected by the council. They shall serve until the adjournment of the next succeeding quadrennial session of the General Conference after their election and until their successors are duly elected and qualified. The president, vice-president, and recording secretary shall be elected from the membership of the council. The general secretary shall sit with the council and its executive committee at all sessions and shall have right to the floor without the privilege of voting. The employed personnel of the council shall be selected by and shall work under the direction of the general secretary.

¶ 852. The council shall convene annually and at such other times as are necessary on call of the president or on written request of one fifth of the members. Sixteen members shall constitute a quorum.

¶ **853.** There shall be **an executive committee** of the council consisting of officers of the council and six members to be elected annually by the council. The executive committee shall meet on call of the president or of a majority of the membership and shall act for the council and exercise its powers in the interim of the meetings of the council, but it shall not take any action contrary to or in conflict with any action or policy of the council. A copy of the minutes of each meeting of the executive committee shall be sent from the central office to each member of the council as soon after the meeting as practicable.

¶ **854.** The council shall maintain and supervise under the direction of its general secretary three sections and their respective departments, as follows:

1. *The Central Treasury.*—The duties of the **Central Treasury** shall be to receive and disburse, in accordance with budgets approved by the General Conference or its properly authorized agency, the general funds of the Church as set forth in ¶¶ 858-60 and to administer funds as outlined in ¶¶ 848-49, 856-60.

2. *Administrative Departments.*—The **administrative departments** shall require each world service agency to follow uniform policies and practices in the employment and remuneration of personnel, recognizing differences in local employment conditions, to establish titles for the employed executive staff of world service agencies in the interest of uniformity and consistency, to provide legal counsel where necessary in order to protect the interest of the Church and at the request of a world service agency or of a bishop, other action as the council deems advisable. It shall also maintain the following departments under its section:

a) A **Transportation Office** to represent the Church in its relation with the responsible persons or concerns operating the several modes of public transportation. The purchase of tickets and the securing of space reservations for travel shall be placed as nearly as possible on a self-supporting basis. The costs of the Transportation Office shall be a charge against the General Administration Fund.

b) A **Convention Bureau** to offer its services to all general agencies of the Church.

3. *Records and Statistics Departments.*— (*a*)   The **Department of**

Records shall have the function of maintaining an accurate record of the mail addresses of all bishops; ministers in the effective relation; lay pastors, including retired ministers serving charges; and conference lay leaders and such lists of general, jurisdictional, conference, and district boards, commissions, and committees, and officers of the same, and of local-church commission chairmen as may be deemed necessary. No one other than authorized bodies or officers of the Church shall be permitted to use these records.

b) The **Department of Statistics** shall have the duty of preparing the important statistics relating to The United Methodist Church for the General Minutes, The Fact Book, and such other publications and releases as may be authorized by the council.

c) The expenses of these departments, including the printing of the General Minutes, The Fact Book, and such other publications and releases as may be authorized by the council, shall be borne by the General Administration Fund. The number and qualifications of the regularly employed staff shall be determined by the council.

¶ 855. The council shall maintain and supervise under the direction of its general secretary a **Committee on Official Forms and Records,** which shall have the duty of preparing and editing all official statistical blanks, record forms, and record books for use in the Church, including the preparation and circulation of the manual for conducting Annual Conferences. The committee shall consist of one bishop elected by the Council of Bishops and nine persons elected by the Council on World Service and Finance, as follows: one member of the council from each jurisdiction and one conference secretary, one conference treasurer, one conference statistician, and one district superintendent. The following persons shall be consultants to this committee ex officio without vote: a staff representative of the council, the director of the Department of Statistics, a representative elected by the Interagency Committee on Research, a representative of The Methodist Publishing House, and representatives of other general agencies when their programs are directly involved. All official statistical blanks, record forms, and record books required for use in The United Methodist Church shall be printed and published by The Methodist Publishing House.

¶ 856. *Function of the Council.*—The General Conference at

each quadrennial session shall elect a Council on World Service and Finance which shall through its central office receive and disburse, in accordance with the directions hereinafter set forth, all funds raised throughout the Church for: (1) the World Service Fund, including world service special gifts and Advance special gifts, (2) the General Administration Fund, (3) the Episcopal Fund, (4) the Interdenominational Cooperation Fund, (5) the Committee for Overseas Relief Fund, (6) the Fellowship of Suffering and Service Fund, (7) the One Great Hour of Sharing Fund, and (8) any other fund or funds as directed by the proper authority, including funds supported by the Christian Service Fund of the former Evangelical United Brethren Church. (For the authority and responsibility of the council in non-fiscal matters see ¶¶ 854.2-.3.)

¶ **857.** The council shall be elected and organized in accordance with the provisions of ¶¶ 850-55.

¶ **858.** The council shall have the authority and responsibility to perform the following functions:

1. It shall submit to each quadrennial session of the General Conference, for its action and determination, a budget of annual expense for its own operation and for the world service agencies for the ensuing quadrennium. The expenses of the council, including the expense of the central office, shall be a first claim against the World Service Fund, the General Administration Fund, the Episcopal Fund, and the Interdenominational Cooperation Fund; and the total expense shall be prorated annually to each in proportion to the amount received on the account of each during the fiscal year. Out of funds thus provided the treasurer shall pay the expenses of the council, including the expense of the central office, and shall keep a true and accurate account thereof.

2. It shall require annually, one month in advance of its annual meeting, or as is deemed necessary, statements of proposed budgets of all agencies receiving general church funds. It shall also require certified public accountant audits annually of all treasuries receiving general church funds through the Central Treasury. (See ¶ 893.) It shall review in each such agency budget the amount for administration, service, and promotion with a view to maintaining a proper balance among the various parts of the budgets.

3. It shall withhold approval of any item or items for inclusion

in the budget or budgets receiving general church funds which in its judgment represents unnecessary duplication of activities or programs within an agency or between two or more agencies. (*See* ¶ 895.)

4. It shall recommend to the General Conference for its action and determination a world service program outlining the general financial objectives of the Church for the forthcoming quadrennium and proposing the ratio of distribution of world service funds among the participating agencies. It shall indicate the proportion of world service funds to be used for administration, service, and promotion. It shall recommend apportionments to the Annual Conferences, subject to the approval of the General Conference.

5. It shall consult with the Council of Bishops relative to the number and timing of all special days which are to be observed on a churchwide basis. After such consultation the council shall make appropriate recommendations to the General Conference. Between sessions of the General Conference the Council of Bishops and the Council on World Service and Finance may in an emergency authorize a financial appeal.

6. It shall have authority to employ a comptroller. It shall require all agencies receiving general church funds to follow uniform accounting classifications and procedures for reporting and to submit a yearly audit following such auditing procedures as it may specify. It shall have authority to pass on the acceptability of any auditing firm proposed by an agency for handling such yearly audit. All general agencies of the Church shall observe a uniform fiscal year ending on December 31. It shall provide direction and coordination in the design and implementation of operating systems in order to maximize the efficiency of operating personnel, equipment, and resources between and within world service agencies.

7. It shall review the investment policies of all agencies receiving general church funds with respect to permanent funds and shall require that Christian as well as sound economic principles be observed in the handling of investment funds.

8. After consultation with the agency it shall perform or arrange facilities for handling the treasury functions for any general agency which is not large enough to have a full-time treasurer and the finan-

cial policies of which are not approved by the council. The cost of such service shall be charged to the agency.

9. On the request of a general agency it shall hold and invest funds allocated to it when such funds are not intended for current expenditure by that agency. It shall also hold and invest funds for any general agency which does not have an investment program approved by the council.

10. It shall establish standardized annuity rates and formulate policies for the writing of annuities by institutions and agencies operating under the auspices of The United Methodist Church.

11. It shall receive bequests and memorial gifts in the interests of world service or one or more of the world service agencies. The moneys from these sources, where not otherwise designated, shall be invested by the council and the income therefrom distributed annually according to the world service ratio; the local church of the testator or donor shall receive a world service special gift voucher. (*See* ¶ 867.)

12. It shall administer the General Administration Fund (¶¶ 879-82), the Episcopal Fund (¶¶ 883-91), the Interdenominational Cooperation Fund (¶ 892), the Temporary General Aid Fund (*see* ¶ 849, note 9), and other funds, including the causes supported by the Christian Service Fund of the former Evangelical United Brethren Church.

13. It shall receive from the Board of Trustees a report of the distributable income from undesignated funds held by the board and shall recommend to the General Conference how such income should be distributed.

14. It shall withhold approval of the entire budget of any agency or any church-related institution receiving general church funds until such agency or church-related institution certifies to the council in writing that it has established and has complied with a policy of (*a*) recruiting, employing, utilizing, recompensing, and promoting professional staff and other personnel without regard to race, color, or sex, and (*b*) fulfilling its duties and responsibilities in a manner which does not involve racial segregation or discrimination.

¶ 859. The treasurer of the Council on World Service and Finance shall, not less than thirty days prior to the session of each Annual Conference, transmit to the presiding bishop thereof, to the president of the conference Commission on World Service and Finance, and to the conference treasurer a statement of the apportionments to the conference for the World Service Fund, the General Administration Fund, the Episcopal Fund, the Interdenominational Cooperation Fund, and such other funds as may have been apportioned by the General Conference. (*See* ¶¶ 870, 881, 885, 892.) He shall keep an account of all amounts remitted to him by the conference treasurers and from other sources intended for: (1) the World Service Fund, including world service special gifts and Advance special gifts, (2) the General Administration Fund, (3) the Episcopal Fund, (4) the Interdenominational Cooperation Fund, (5) the Committee for Overseas Relief Fund, (6) the Fellowship of Suffering and Service Fund, (7) the One Great Hour of Sharing Fund, (8) the Temporary General Aid Fund, and (9) any other fund so directed by the proper authority, including funds supported by the Christian Service Fund of the former Evangelical United Brethren Church, and shall disburse the same as authorized by the General Conference and directed by the council. A separate account shall be kept of each such fund, and none of them shall be drawn on for the benefit of another fund. The fiscal year for the council and for the several funds, boards, and agencies related to it, shall be from January 1 to December 31 inclusive.

¶ 860. The treasurer shall report annually to the council and to the respective conference commissions as to all amounts received and disbursed during the year. He shall also make to each quadrennial session of the General Conference a full report of the financial transactions of the council for the preceding quadrennium. The treasurer shall be bonded for such an amount as may be determined by the council. The books of the treasurer shall be audited annually by a certified public accountant approved by the executive committee.

THE WORLD SERVICE FUND

¶ 861. The **World Service Fund** is basic in the financial program of The United Methodist Church. World service on apportionment (¶ 870) represents the minimum needs of the general agencies of the Church. Payment in full of these apportionments by local

229

churches and Annual Conferences is the first benevolent responsibility of the Church.

¶ 862. 1. Prior to each quadrennial session of the General Conference the council shall make a diligent and detailed study of the needs of all the general causes or authorized agencies of the Church asking to be included in the world service budget.

2. The general secretary or other duly authorized representative of each agency of The United Methodist Church requesting support from the World Service Fund and the authorized representative of any other agency for which askings are authorized by the General Conference shall appear before the council at a designated time and place to represent the cause for which each is responsible.

¶ 863. The council shall make a diligent effort to secure full information concerning the general benevolence and service causes of the Church in order that none may be neglected, jeopardized, or excluded. It shall study in relation to each other the proposed programs of the several agencies as presented to it (¶ 862.2) and shall withhold approval of any item or items for inclusion in the world service budget which in its judgment represent unnecessary duplication of activities or programs. Basing its judgment of needs upon the programs of the several agencies as approved by it, the council shall recommend to the General Conference for its action and determination the amount to be apportioned in the annual world service budget for each authorized agency of the Church. The total amount thus designated by the council for the several agencies, when approved by the General Conference, shall be the annual world service budget for the ensuing quadrennium. The council shall recommend also to the General Conference for its action and determination a plan and schedule for the distribution of the receipts for the world service budget among the several agencies. During the quadrennium the council shall have full authority to correlate the work of the world service agencies in the interest of cooperation, economy, and effectiveness as these relate to the financial interests of the Church.

¶ 864. Any general board, cause, agency, or institution or any organization, group, officer, or individual of The United Methodist Church desiring or proposing to make a special churchwide financial appeal during the quadrennium or at any time in the interim of the quadrennial sessions of the General Conference shall present a request for authorization to make such appeal to the Council on World Service and Finance when the askings of the regular agencies are presented as provided in ¶ 862.2. The council shall then report such request to the General Conference with a recommendation for its action thereon. "Special appeal" shall be understood to mean any appeal other than the general appeal for support of the world service program as represented in the world service budget. (*See* ¶ 863.) "Churchwide appeal" shall be understood to mean any appeal to the Church at large except appeals to such special groups as alumni of an educational institution.

¶ 865. The world service agencies shall not solicit additional or special gifts from individual donors or special groups, other than foundations, unless approval for such solicitation is first secured from the Council on World Service and Finance.

¶ 866. Individual donors or local churches may make **special gifts** to the support of any cause or project which is a part of the work of any one of the world service agencies. Such gifts may be sent directly to the agency concerned or to the Central Treasury of the Council on World Service and Finance. They shall not apply on the benevolence apportionment of any local church and shall not be charged against the agency or agencies receiving them in the ratio distribution of the on-apportionment benevolences. Bequests, gifts on the annuity plan, gifts to permanent funds, and gifts of property shall be classified as special gifts. (*See* ¶ 867.5.)

¶ 867. 1. All special gifts made to or administered by a general agency, except as provided in § 5 below, shall be acknowledged by **special-gift vouchers.**

2. The vouchers acknowledging such gifts to world service agencies shall be entitled "world service special-gift vouchers"; *provided,* however, that vouchers for such gifts to the World and National Divisions of the Board of Missions or the Committee for Overseas Relief (except as provided in ¶ 1311.1*f*) shall be entitled "Advance special-gift vouchers" (¶ 873) ; and *provided* further, that vouchers for the One Great Hour of Sharing offering (¶ 875) and Fellowship of Suffering and Service offerings (¶ 877) shall bear the respective names of these appeals.

3. All special-gift vouchers shall be credited in their respective special columns in the Annual Conference minutes. The agency or office issuing each voucher shall send at the same time a duplicate voucher to the Central Treasury for forwarding to the conference treasurer.

4. A world service agency or any individual or agency authorized to make a churchwide appeal for funds, but not equipped to issue special-gift vouchers, shall channel all special gifts through the Central Treasury. Individuals soliciting such funds shall channel the money received through the Central Treasury or the treasurer of the appropriate agency, which shall issue the proper vouchers.

5. Bequests, gifts on the annuity plan at maturity, and gifts of real property shall be reported to the Central Treasury as **supplemental contributions** and shall not be included among the promoted funds chargeable under ¶ 833.10.

¶ **868.**   The council shall also recommend to the General Conference the days in connection with the churchwide observance of which the taking of special offerings shall be authorized, and in the case of each shall recommend whether or not the receipts derived therefrom shall be credited to the contributing local church as a part of its world service apportionment and charged against the claims of the agency receiving the same. All such recommendations are subject to the approval of the General Conference.

¶ **869.**   The General Conference having determined the budgeted amounts and the plan and schedule of distribution to the participating boards and agencies as provided in ¶ 863, thereafter no benevolence interest shall be allowed to have a prior or preferred claim or increased ratio participation in the world service budget during the quadrennium except to meet an emergency, and then only by a three-fourths vote of those present and voting at a regular or called meeting of the Council on World Service and Finance, the Council of Bishops concurring in this action by a three-fourths vote of those present and voting; nor shall the total world service budget be changed in the interim between the quadrennial sessions and then only by a three-fourths vote of those present and voting at a regular or called meeting of the council, the Council of Bishops concurring in this action by a three-fourths vote of those present and voting. No general board, cause, agency, or institution or any organization, group, officer, or individual employed by The United Methodist Church or any of the authorized groups of The United Methodist Church shall make a churchwide financial appeal in the interim of the quadrennial sessions of the General Conference unless authorized as provided in ¶ 864 except with the approval of the Council on World Service and Finance and the Council of Bishops. In case of emergency the executive committee of either of these bodies may act in such matter for the body itself but only by a three-fourths vote. *(See* ¶ 864.)

¶ 870. The council shall, after careful study, prepare an equitable schedule of apportionments by which the total world service budget (¶ 863) shall be distributed to the several Annual Conferences and shall present the same to the General Conference for its action and determination. *(See* ¶ 861.)

THE ADVANCE

¶ 871. For the more adequate support of the missionary program of the Church the **Advance** shall be organized and administered as hereinafter set forth, to the end that opportunity may be given each local church, through its Charge Conference, to participate in such support over and above its world service contributions, as each may determine. The Advance program shall include all special gifts (¶ 866) to missionary causes, which shall be designated as general Advance specials (¶ 873) or conference Advance specials (¶ 874), and One Great Hour of Sharing offerings (¶ 875).

¶872. 1. There shall be a **General Advance Committee,** organized under the authority and direction of the Division of Interpretation of the Program Council. It shall consist of ten members, representing equally all five jurisdictions and including at least two bishops, two ministers, and two laymen, named by the Division of Interpretation of the Program Council from its membership. In addition the associate general secretaries of the World and National Divisions and Joint Commission on Education and Cultivation of the Board of Missions, associate general secretary of the Division of Interpretation of the Program Council, the executive secretary of the United Methodist Committee for Overseas Relief, and the general secretary of the Council on World Service and Finance shall be ex officio members.

2. The committee shall have general oversight of the Advance program in accordance with the plan and procedure hereinafter described.

¶ 873. 1. **A general Advance special** is a designated gift made by an individual, local church, organization, or District or Annual Conference to a specific project in missions or overseas relief that has been authorized by the General Advance Committee. Agencies authorized to receive funds for their projects as general Advance specials shall be the World and National Divisions of the Board of Missions and the United Methodist Committee for Overseas Relief.

2. As far as practicable these specials shall be solicited for specific objects that may be visualized and described. Each such special object shall be approved by the Advance Committee (or by a Committee on Specials appointed by it) on recommendation of the agency concerned. An Annual Conference, local church, or individual may assume responsibility for an undesignated foreign, home, or overseas relief special; in which case the agency concerned shall determine where such special shall be allocated, shall inform the donor where his gift has been invested, and shall as far as practicable establish communication between donor and recipient. All specials authorized by the Advance Committee and solicited for special projects shall be reported in duplicate to the associate general secretary of the Division of Interpretation of the Program Council and to the treasurer of the Council on World Service and Finance.

3. Receipts for general Advance specials shall be remitted by the local church treasurer to the conference treasurer, who shall make remittance each month to the general treasurer. The general treasurer shall remit monthly to the respective participating agencies the amount received for each; *provided,* however, that when a donor church or individual so elects, remittance may be made directly to the treasurer of the agency administering such special, whereupon the agency receiving such remittance shall send to the Central Treasury a voucher for the central treasurer and a voucher for the conference treasurer.

4. Each participating agency shall administer the general Advance specials received by it in harmony with procedures approved

by the Advance Committee and shall report them to the Advance Committee at such intervals and in such detail as the committee may request.

5. Each participating agency shall, on receipt of a general Advance special, communicate with the donor, whether conference, local church, or individual, and as far as practicable establish communication between donor and recipient.

¶ 874. Each Annual Conference is authorized to initiate and promote **conference Advance specials** for missionary and church-extension objects within the conference, as follows:

1. Proposed conference Advance specials shall be approved and promoted by the conference Board of Missions; *provided,* however, that such approval shall be given only to projects or programs administered as provided in §§ 2, 3, and 4 below.

2. Conference Advance specials may be administered by the conference Board of Missions or by the National Division of the General Board of Missions on request of the Annual Conference concerned.

3. An Annual Conference may undertake a conference-wide campaign for a lump sum to be applied to its missionary and church-extension needs. The funds so received shall be designated as conference Advance specials and shall be administered by the conference Board of Missions. Local churches shall report their respective contributions as conference Advance specials.

4. Unless the Annual Conference directs otherwise, a district within the conference may authorize and promote Advance specials for church-extension and missionary needs within the district, such funds to be administered by a district missionary society organized for that purpose or by a similar body set up by the District Conference. Such specials secured and administered on a district level shall be reported by each local church to the Annual Conference as conference Advance specials.

5. Annual Conference report forms shall include separate spaces designated as "Advance specials, general," and "Advance specials, conference," and local churches shall report accordingly.

6. It is recommended that each Annual Conference or district administering conference Advance specials set aside each year 10 percent of the amount received for that purpose for aid to the weaker and

more urgent situations outside the conference and that such amount be remitted to the National Division of the General Board of Missions, to be administered by it as a general Advance special.

¶ **875.** The annual observance of the **One Great Hour of Sharing** shall be under the general supervision of the Division of Interpretation of the Program Council, in accordance with the following directives:

1. The One Great Hour of Sharing shall be observed annually on or about the fourth Sunday in Lent. All local churches shall be fully informed and encouraged to contribute a freewill offering in behalf of the crusade scholarship program, the overseas relief program, the ministry to servicemen overseas program of The United Methodist Church, and such capital-funds emergency projects of the National Division of the Board of Missions as may be authorized by the Division of Interpretation of the Program Council.

2. In connection with the One Great Hour of Sharing there shall be an emphasis on the spiritual implications of Christian stewardship.

3. The following participating agencies shall administer the funds in accordance with the ratios determined by the division: the Crusade Scholarship Committee for the Crusade Scholarship Fund, the United Methodist Committee for Overseas Relief for the Overseas Relief Fund, the World Division of the Board of Missions for the Servicemen Overseas Fund in cooperation with the cooperative committee of the National Council of Churches, and the National Division for the capital-funds emergency projects.

4. The One Great Hour of Sharing offering shall be promptly remitted by the local church treasurer to the conference treasurer, who shall remit monthly to the general treasurer. The general treasurer shall distribute these funds to the participating agencies in accordance with the ratios determined by the Division of Interpretation of the Program Council.

5. A One Great Hour of Sharing special-gift voucher shall be issued (¶ 867), and a space for reporting the amount of the offering shall be included in the form for the pastor's report to the Annual Conference.

6. The expense budget for promoting the One Great Hour of Sharing shall be subject to approval annually by the Division of In-

terpretation of the Program Council and shall be a prior charge against receipts from these offerings.

¶ 876. The following general directives shall be observed in the promotion and administration of the Advance and One Great Hour of Sharing:

1. In the appeal and promotion of Advance specials and One Great Hour of Sharing offerings there shall be no goals or quotas except as they may be set by the Annual Conferences for themselves.

2. The treasurer of the Council on World Service and Finance shall be treasurer of the Advance and One Great Hour of Sharing.

3. The expense of promotion for Advance specials shall be borne by the respective participating agencies in proportion to the amount received by each in Advance specials. The causes of the Advance shall be coordinated with other financial appeals and shall be promoted by the central promotional office of the Division of Interpretation of the Program Council.

4. The appeal for Advance specials shall be channeled through bishops, district superintendents, and pastors, the details of the procedure to be determined by the Division of Interpretation of the Program Council in consultation with the Joint Commission on Education and Cultivation of the Board of Missions and the Advance Committee.

5. In each Annual Conference the conference Board of Missions, in cooperation with the General Board of Missions, shall promote Advance specials and One Great Hour of Sharing offerings through district missionary secretaries, conference and district missionary institutes, and other effective means as it may determine.

6. Should a clear emergency arise, any feature of the structure and administration of the Advance may be altered on the approval of a majority of the Council of Bishops and of the Council on World Service and Finance.

¶ 877. The **Fellowship of Suffering and Service** appeal shall be continued until it is deemed no longer needed, either by the General Conference or between its sessions by a three-fourths vote of the Council of Bishops and of the Council on World Service and Finance meeting separately. Each local church shall be requested to transmit, either through its conference treasurer or directly to the treasurer of the Council on World Service and Finance, under designation of the

Fellowship of Suffering and Service, all the Communion offering received on Worldwide Communion Sunday (the first Sunday in October) and a portion of the Communion offering received at subsequent observances of the Sacrament of the Lord's Supper. A Fellowship of Suffering and Service special gift voucher shall be issued (¶ 867), and a space for reporting the amount of the offerings shall be included in the form for the pastor's report to the Annual Conference. The treasurer of the Council on World Service and Finance is authorized to distribute these receipts on the basis of 50 percent to the United Methodist Committee for Overseas Relief and 50 percent to the Commission on Chaplains and Related Ministries.

¶ **878.** The Division of Interpretation of the Program Council may organize special committees from its membership for the effective promotion of special days and other special appeals referred to it for promotion by the Council of Bishops and the Council on World Service and Finance.

The General Administration Fund

¶ **879.** The **General Administration Fund** shall provide for the expenses of the sessions of the General Conference, the Judicial Council, the Departments of Records and Statistics and the Transportation Office and the Convention Bureau of the Council on World Service and Finance, the Committee on Family Life, the Commission on Worship, the Commission on Ecumenical Affairs, the Commission on Public Relations and Methodist Information, the Commission on Archives and History, the World Methodist Council, Religion in American Life, such special commissions and committees as may be constituted by the General Conference, including causes supported by the Christian Service Fund of the former Evangelical United Brethren Church, and such interchurch causes and other activities as may be authorized by the General Conference, other than those provided for under the Interdenominational Cooperation Fund. Any agency or institution requiring or desiring support from the General Administration Fund shall present its case for the same to the council at a time and place which shall be indicated by the officers of the council. The council, having heard such requests, shall report the same to the

General Conference with recommendations for its action and determination.

¶ 880. The council shall submit to each quadrennial session of the General Conference an annual general administration budget, including such items as in the judgment of the council should be provided for out of this fund for the ensuing quadrennium. The council shall likewise recommend to the General Conference what prior or preferred claims shall be allowed in the general administration budget and by what plan or ratios the causes included in the budget shall share in the funds collected. The general administration budget thus submitted, including all recommendations, shall be subject to the action and determination of the General Conference.

¶ 881. The council shall apportion among the several Annual Conferences of the Church the total general administration budget, as approved by the General Conference, by such ratio and percentage to the total giving (not including the payment of debts or for church buildings) as recorded in the General Minutes for the first three years of the quadrennium closing with the current session of the General Conference, as is necessary to raise the approved annual budget. The apportionments for the general administration budget shall not be subject to change or revision either by the Annual Conference or by the charge or local church.

¶ 882. The treasurer of the council shall disburse the funds received by him for the General Administration Fund as authorized by the General Conference and as directed by the council. Where the General Conference has not allocated definite sums to agencies receiving money from the General Administration Fund, the council or its executive committee shall have authority to determine the amount to be allocated to each.

THE EPISCOPAL FUND

¶ 883. The **Episcopal Fund**, raised separately from all other funds, shall provide for the salary and expenses of effective bishops and for the support of retired bishops and of the widows and minor children of deceased bishops. Subject to the approval of the Council on World Service and Finance, the treasurer shall have authority to borrow for the benefit of the Episcopal Fund such amounts as may be necessary for the proper execution of the orders of the General Conference.

¶ **884.** The council shall recommend to each quadrennial session of the General Conference for its action and determination: (1) the amounts to be fixed as salaries of the effective bishops; (2) a schedule of such amounts as may be judged adequate to provide for their expense of house, office, and travel; (3) the amounts to be fixed as annual pensions for the support of retired bishops; and (4) a schedule of allowance for the widows and for the support of minor children of deceased bishops. From the facts in hand the council shall estimate the approximate total amount required annually during the ensuing quadrennium to provide for the items of episcopal support above mentioned and shall report the same to the General Conference. This amount as finally determined shall be the estimated episcopal budget.

¶ **885.** The council shall estimate what percentage of the total salaries paid pastors and associate pastors by the entire Church will yield an amount equal to the estimated episcopal budget and shall make recommendations to the General Conference concerning the same for its action and determination. When such percentage has been approved by the General Conference, it shall be the basis of the annual apportionment to each Annual Conference for the Episcopal Fund. The apportionment to each Annual Conference shall be an amount equal to the approved percentage of the total cash salaries paid to the pastors and associate pastors serving charges under episcopal appointment or as lay pastors, as reported to the current session of the Annual Conference. This apportionment shall be distributed to the pastoral charges as the conference may determine. In every case the amount apportioned to a charge for the Episcopal Fund shall be paid in the same proportion as the charge pays its pastor.

¶ **886.** The treasurer of the Council on World Service and Finance shall remit monthly to each effective bishop one twelfth of his annual salary and also one twelfth of his house rent or maintenance, and office expenses as approved by the council. Allowances for retired bishops and for the widows and minor children of deceased bishops shall be paid to them severally in equal monthly installments.

¶ **887.** The treasurer of the council shall pay monthly the claim for the official travel of each bishop or missionary bishop upon presentation of an itemized voucher. "Official travel" of an effective bishop shall be interpreted to include all visitations to local churches within his area and to institutions or enterprises of The United Methodist Church where he is called in the performance of his official duties and such journeys outside his area as are within the meaning of "travel through the connection at large" (¶ 390.10). No part of the expense and no honoraria for any such visitations shall be accepted from local churches or enterprises or institutions of The United Methodist Church, such expense being a proper claim against the Episcopal Fund; *provided* that when a bishop who is a member of an agency of the Church is called to a meeting of the same or to a meeting of a committee thereof, the expenses incident to such journey shall be paid by the said agency.

¶ **888.** Nothing in this interpretation is intended to preclude special or nonofficial engagements of a bishop, other than the oversight of the temporal and spiritual affairs of the Church, such as series of lectures in educational institutions, baccalaureate addresses, and preaching missions of several days' duration, when such engagements do not interfere with his official duties, nor does it preclude the acceptance of honoraria for such services.

1. The pensions for the support of retired bishops elected by General or Jurisdictional Conferences and the surviving widows and minor dependent children of such deceased bishops shall be provided by means of a contributory reserve pension fund, to be held and administered by the Council on World Service and Finance in consultation with the General Board of Pensions.

2. The amounts of the annual pensions payable to such persons shall be determined by the General Conference on recommendation of the council.

3. Each bishop in active service shall contribute annually to the fund an amount equal to 3 percent of his cash salary. The treasurer of the Episcopal Fund is authorized and instructed to withhold from each bishop's salary the amount of his required contribution and pay it to the fund.

4. Any and all benefit derived from the contributions required of a bishop shall be regarded as a part of the total amount of the pension payable to said bishop upon his retirement and to his surviving widow and minor dependent children.

5. The remainder of the cost of the reserve funding of such pensions shall be provided from the Episcopal Fund in accordance with such program and procedure as may from time to time be determined by the Council on World Service and Finance with the approval of the General Conference.

¶ 889. Should any effective bishop in the interim of the quadrennial sessions of his Jurisdictional Conference be relieved by the College of Bishops of his jurisdiction from the performance of regular episcopal duties on account of ill health or for any other reason, the president of the said College of Bishops shall so notify the treasurer of the Episcopal Fund. Beginning ninety days after such notification, he shall receive the regular pension allowance of a retired bishop, and such pension allowance shall continue until he resumes the regular duties of an effective bishop or until his status shall have been determined by his Jurisdictional Conference. Assignment of another bishop or bishops to perform the regular episcopal duties of a bishop so disabled or otherwise incapacitated, for a period of sixty days or more, shall be interpreted as a release of the said bishop from the performance of his regular episcopal duties.

¶ 890. Should any retired bishop, in the interim of the quadrennial sessions of his Jurisdictional Conference, be called into active service by the Council of Bishops and assigned to active episcopal duty (¶ 390), he shall be entitled to remuneration for such service out of the Episcopal Fund. In the event of such assignment of a retired bishop to active episcopal duty, the president of the Council of Bishops shall notify the treasurer of the Episcopal Fund, giving full information as to the nature and scope of the work assigned him. On the basis of this information the Council on World Service and Finance or its executive committee shall determine what salary remuneration and what expense allowance shall be allowed the bishop concerned during the period of his active service. The treasurer of the Episcopal Fund shall make remittance to him accordingly.

¶ 891. In determining the schedule of allowances for the widows of deceased bishops the following rules shall apply: each beneficiary who prior to the death of her husband had been his wife for not less than fifteen years while he was engaged in the effective ministry of The United Methodist Church, whether bishop or traveling preacher, shall receive the full allowance for the widow of a deceased bishop as ordered by the General Conference. The allowance of the widow of a deceased bishop who prior to the death of her husband had been his wife for less than fifteen years while he was an effective minister of The United Methodist Church shall be determined on the basis of that fraction of fifteen years during which she was his wife while he was an effective minister of The United Methodist Church, whether bishop or traveling preacher; *provided* that the Council on World Service and Finance may at its discretion increase the said allowance if special need exists, but in no instance shall the allowance of the widow of a deceased bishop exceed the full allowance as hereinbefore set forth.

INTERDENOMINATIONAL COOPERATION FUND

¶ 892. The council shall recommend to the General Conference the sum which the Church shall undertake to provide as its share of the budget of the National Council of Churches, the General Commission on Chaplains and Armed Forces Personnel, and the World Council of Churches and shall recommend the sum to be provided for the expenses of delegates of The United Methodist Church to official meetings of the National Council of Churches and the World Council of Churches except when such expenses are paid by a board or agency of The United Methodist Church. The sum approved by the General Conference for this purpose shall be the interdenominational cooperation budget. The council shall recommend to the General Conference for consideration and determination appropriate measures to be employed in order to provide the approved sum. The money contributed by the local churches, boards, or other agencies for this purpose shall be known as the **Interdenominational Cooperation Fund** and shall be received and held by the treasurer of the Council on World Service and Finance and disbursed as the General Conference shall direct. Promotion shall be by the Division of Interpretation of the Program Council.

MISCELLANEOUS

¶ **893.** All boards and other agencies receiving financial support from the World Service Fund, the General Administration Fund, or any authorized churchwide appeal shall make to the Council on World Service and Finance audited reports of all receipts and disbursements in such detail and at such times as the council may direct. (*See* ¶ 858.2.)

¶ **894.** During the quadrennium these agencies shall study their respective functions, programs, and internal operations and institute such improvements and economies in their work as they find to be feasible and practicable. They shall cooperate with the council in working out, in advance of these studies, the general areas to be included and methods of carrying out this objective. They shall report their accomplishments in improvements and economies at the close of each fiscal year to the council, which shall prepare from this information a combined report for the General Conference.

¶ **895.** In the event of any interboard disagreement on matters of policy and program involving world service funds, the Council on World Service and Finance shall act as arbiter. It shall also consider any complaints from contributors, whether individuals or organizations. If it shall discover what in its judgment is unnecessary duplication of activities or lack of correlation in the programs of the several agencies in relation to each other, it shall promptly direct the attention of the agencies involved to the situation and shall cooperate with them in correcting the same and may decline to supply from the world service treasury money to continue activities which have been held by the council to duplicate each other unnecessarily or plainly violate the principle of correlation as applied to the total benevolence program of the Church. (*See* ¶ 858.3.)

¶ **896.** The council may receive, take title to, collect, or hold, absolutely or in trust for the benefit of the World Service Fund, the General Administration Fund, the Episcopal Fund, the Interdenominational Cooperation Fund, the Committee for Overseas Relief Fund, the Fellowship of Suffering and Service Fund, the One Great Hour of Sharing Fund, the Temporary General Aid Fund of The United Methodist Church, or any other fund or funds properly committed to its care, or for proper distribution among the causes supported by these funds, any and all donations, bequests, and devises of any kind or character, real or personal, that may be given, devised, bequeathed, or conveyed unto said Council on World Service and Finance, and to administer the same and the income therefrom in accordance with the directions of the donor, trustor, or testator.

The Council on World Service and Finance shall also have power to invest, reinvest, buy, sell, transfer, and convey any and all funds and properties which it may hold absolutely or in trust, subject always to the terms of the legacy, devise, or donation.

¶ 897. The council shall recommend to each conference Commission on World Service and Finance a uniform procedure for presenting its report to the Annual Conference and shall prepare a form for the guidance of the conference treasurer in making his annual statement in the conference journal.

THE CONFERENCE COMMISSION ON WORLD SERVICE AND FINANCE

¶ 898. Each Annual Conference shall elect, at its session next succeeding the General Conference, a **Commission on World Service and Finance,** nominated by the district superintendents or a nominating committee, as the conference may determine, and composed of five ministers and six lay persons; *provided* that in smaller conferences the number may be reduced to not less than two ministers and three lay persons. Their term of service shall begin with the adjournment of the said conference session, and they shall serve for the quadrennium and until their successors shall have been chosen. No member or employee of any conference board and no employee, trustee, or director of any agency or institution participating in the funds of the conference benevolence budget shall be eligible for membership on the commission. Any vacancy shall be filled by action of the commission until the next conference session, at which time the Annual Conference shall fill the vacancy.

¶ 899. The commission shall elect a president, a vice-president, and a secretary. The conference treasurer (¶ 909) shall be the treasurer of the commission. As an employee of the commission he shall not be a member of it but may sit with the commission and its executive committee at all sessions and have the privilege of the floor but without vote. He shall be bonded in a surety company approved by the commission and for an amount which the commission judges to be adequate.

¶ **900.** The chairman of each conference agency, or other duly authorized representative, shall have opportunity to represent the claims of his agency before the commission. The commission shall make diligent effort to secure full information regarding all conference benevolence and service causes that none may be neglected, jeopardized, or excluded, and shall recommend to the Annual Conference for its action and determination the total amount to be apportioned for conference causes and included in the conference benevolence budget. All agencies receiving financial support from conference benevolences or from any other authorized conference-wide appeal shall make audited reports to the commission concerning all such receipts and the disbursements thereof in such detail and at such times as the commission may direct.

¶ **901.** The commission shall also recommend to the Annual Conference for its action and determination the amount or the percentage of the total sum of the conference benevolence budget which shall be apportioned to each cause included in the said budget.

¶ **902.** The commission, on receiving from the treasurer of the Council on World Service and Finance a statement of the amount apportioned that Annual Conference for world service, shall combine the world service apportionment and the approved conference benevolence budget (¶ 900) in one total sum to be known as **world service and conference benevolences.** The total world service and conference benevolence budget thus established shall include a statement of the percentage for world service and the percentage for conference benevolences and shall be distributed annually among the districts or charges by the method determined by the conference (¶ 903) and by such divisions and ratios as the conference may approve. A like distribution shall be made of Jurisdictional Conference apportionments and any other apportionments that have been properly made to the Annual Conference. The distribution of all apportionments mentioned in this paragraph shall be subject to the approval of the Annual Conference.

¶ **903.** The commission shall recommend to the Annual Conference for its action and determination whether the apportionments referred to in ¶ 902 shall be made by the commission to the districts only or to the charges of the conference. If the apportionments are made by the commission to the districts only, then the distribution to the charges of each district shall be made as provided in ¶ 904. The conference may order that the entire distribution to all the charges of the conference be made by the district superintendents.

¶ 904. Should the Annual Conference make the apportionments to the districts only, the distribution to the charges of each district shall be made by its **district Board of Stewards,** composed of the district superintendent as chairman and the district stewards elected by the several Charge Conferences (¶ 145.3). In that case it shall be the duty of the district superintendent to call a meeting of the board as soon as practicable after the adjournment of the Annual Conference, and the board shall make the distribution to the charges of the district, using such methods as it may determine, unless the Annual Conference shall have determined the method of distribution to the charges.

¶ 905. The commission shall include in its recommendations to the Annual Conference the amounts computed by the conference Board of Pensions as necessary to meet the needs for pension and benefit programs of the conference.

¶ 906. The commission shall report to the Annual Conference at each session the standard percentage approved by the General Conference for the Episcopal Fund as an apportionment to the Annual Conference, as described in ¶ 885. This apportionment shall be distributed to the pastoral charges as the conference may determine.

¶ 907. The commission, on receiving from the Council on World Service and Finance a statement of the amount apportioned to the Annual Conference for the General Administration Fund (¶ 879), the Interdenominational Cooperation Fund (¶ 892), and the Temporary General Aid Fund (*see* ¶ 849, note 9), shall apportion the same to the several districts or charges as the conference may direct.

¶ 908. It shall be the duty of the commission, unless otherwise provided, to estimate the total amount necessary to furnish a sufficient and equitable support for the district superintendents of the conference, including salary and suitable provision for dwelling, travel, and office expense. The commission shall recommend to the Annual Con-

247

ference for its action and determination the amount estimated, including the salary and other allowances specified above, for each of the several district superintendents. The commission shall also recommend to the Annual Conference for its action and determination the basis and method by which the total amount shall be apportioned to the districts or charges in harmony with ¶ 920. The conference treasurer shall, as far as practicable, remit monthly to the several district superintendents the amounts due them, respectively, and with the approval of the Annual Conference the commission or the treasurer, as the conference may determine, may borrow the funds necessary to make this possible. If an Annual Conference adopts the basic salary plan (¶ 925) for ministerial support, the support for the several district superintendents thereof shall be included therein. The amounts necessary to provide for suitable dwelling, travel, and office expense may be included in the basic salary budget or apportioned separately as the conference may determine.

¶ 909. Each Annual Conference, on nomination of its Commission on World Service and Finance, shall at the first session of the conference after the General Conference elect a **conference treasurer.** He shall serve for the quadrennium or until his successor shall be elected and qualify. If a vacancy should occur during the quadrennium, the commission shall fill the vacancy until the next session of the Annual Conference. The commission shall have authority and supervision over the treasurer. After consultation with the bishop in charge, it may remove him from office for cause and fill the vacancy until the next session of the conference. The commission shall have the accounts of the conference treasurer for the preceding conference year audited by a certified public accountant within ninety days after the close of each session of the Annual Conference.

¶ 910. All amounts contributed in each local church for world service and conference benevolences shall be remitted monthly by the local church treasurer to the conference treasurer, who shall each month divide the total amount thus received, setting aside the proper amount for world service and the proper amount for conference benevolences, according to the ratio of each established by the Annual Conference in the total world service and conference benevolence budget. He shall make monthly remittances of the share received by him for conference benevolences to the treasurers of the several agencies for conference work according to the rightful share and proportion of each. He shall remit monthly to the treasurer of the Council on World Service and Finance the total share received by him for world service. When the amount contributed during the year for world service and conference benevolences exceeds the amount apportioned to or accepted by the Annual Conference, the entire share contributed for world service shall be remitted in regular order to the treasurer of the Council on World Service and Finance before the end of the fiscal year.

¶ 911. The conference treasurer shall remit monthly to the treasurer of the Council on World Service and Finance the amounts received and payable for the General Administration Fund, the Episcopal Fund, the Interdenominational Cooperation Fund, and the Temporary General Aid Fund. He shall also transmit all amounts received for world service special gifts, Advance special gifts, the Fellowship of Suffering and Service, the One Great Hour of Sharing, the United Methodist Committee for Overseas Relief, and all other general causes not otherwise directed.

¶ 912. The conference treasurer shall make each month a full report of all general funds handled by him to the treasurer of the Council on World Service and Finance, and annually a report of all receipts, disbursements, and balances of all funds under his direction, which report shall be printed in the conference journal. The reports shall be made on forms authorized by the council (*see* ¶ 897) so that all financial items going outside the local church shall be handled alike in all districts and conferences, and uniformity of financial reporting shall be established as a churchwide policy.

¶ 913. The commission shall provide a suitable bond for the conference treasurer and shall designate a depository or depositories for conference funds. It shall require the treasurers of all conference boards and agencies to be properly bonded in companies approved by the commission and shall require that their books be properly audited at least annually. The commission shall recommend to the Annual Conference the amount in which the treasurers of all unincorporated boards or commissions shall be protected by fidelity insurance, and application for such fidelity bonds shall be made by the corporate body of the Annual Conference, and the costs shall be provided for out of the funds held by the unincorporated board or commission so insured. Institutions and organizations that are incorporated under the laws of the state shall secure fidelity bonds for the treasurers of their funds and shall pay the cost of the premium required.

¶ **914.** For the sake of economy and efficiency the Annual Conference may constitute the conference treasury as a depository for funds designated for any or all conference boards and agencies participating in the conference benevolences, eliminating as far as possible the necessity of a treasurer for each. In this event the conference treasurer shall keep a separate account for each such conference board or agency, enter the proper credits in each at the end of each month's business, and disburse the same on proper order from each board or agency, respectively. None of the above-designated accounts shall be drawn on for the benefit of another.

¶ **915.** The commission shall cooperate with the Council on World Service and Finance and with the General Board of the Laity in promoting and standardizing the financial system in the local churches of the conference.

¶ **916.** No Annual Conference board or interest, such as a school, college, university, or hospital, shall make a special conference-wide appeal to the local churches for funds without the approval of the Annual Conference except in case of an extreme emergency, when such approval may be given by a two-thirds vote of the district superintendents and of the commission, acting jointly.

¶ **917.** When application is made to the conference for the privilege of a special conference-wide financial appeal, whether by special collections, campaigns, or otherwise, the application shall be referred to the commission before final action is taken thereon. The commission shall investigate the application and its possible relation to other obligations of the conference, and in the light of the facts make recommendations to the conference for its action and determination. Such application for privilege of a special appeal may be made directly to the commission for recommendation to the Annual Conference.

¶ **918.** The various conference agencies shall report each year to their respective Annual Conferences the salaries and other expenses allowed each secretary in their employ, and they shall be published in the conference journal.

MINISTERIAL SUPPORT

¶ 919. Assumption of the obligations of the itinerancy, required to be made at the time of admission into the traveling connection, puts upon the Church the counter obligation of providing support for the entire ministry of the Church. In view of this the claim for ministerial support in each pastoral charge shall include provision for the support of pastors, district superintendents, bishops, and conference claimants.

¶ 920. Each Annual Conference shall determine what plan and method shall be used in distributing the apportionments to its several districts and charges for the Episcopal Fund (¶ 883), for the support of district superintendents and conference claimants, and for the minimum salary fund (¶ 924), whether by percentages based on the current cash salary paid to the ministers serving pastoral charges under episcopal appointment and to lay pastors or by some other method.

¶ 921. When the apportionments for bishops, district superintendents, conference claimants, and the Minimum Salary Fund for the several districts and charges have been determined, payments made to the same in each pastoral charge shall be exactly proportional to the amount paid on the ministerial salary or salaries. (*See* ¶ 885.) The treasurer or treasurers of each pastoral charge shall accordingly make proportional distribution of the funds raised in that charge for the support of the ministry and shall remit monthly if practicable and quarterly at the latest, the items for bishops, district superintendents, conference claimants, and the Minimum Salary Fund to the proper treasurer or treasurers.

¶ 922. The several Charge Conferences shall determine the pastors' salaries according to the provisions of ¶ 145.9.

¶ 923. No pastor shall be entitled to any claim for unpaid salary against any church or charge he has served after his pastoral connection with the church or charge has ceased.

¶ 924. *Minimum Salaries.*—1. Each Annual Conference shall adopt a schedule of minimum salaries for pastors and shall create a

Commission on Minimum Salaries, composed of ministers and laymen, to administer it. The commission shall carefully study the number and extent of the needs for additional ministerial support within the conference and the sources of income and with the approval of the Commission on World Service and Finance shall present to the conference for adoption a schedule of minimum salaries, subject to such rules and regulations as the conference may adopt so long as the rules do not conflict with the provisions of this legislation. The schedule may allow for differences in living conditions, number of dependents in pastor's family, and any other variants the conference may direct.

2. In so far as practicable this schedule of minimum salaries shall be observed by the bishops and district superintendents in arranging charges and making appointments.

3. The Commission on Minimum Salaries shall present its estimate of the amount required to comply with the schedule of minimum salaries for the pastors, as adopted by the conference, to the Commission on World Service and Finance, which shall apportion the amount as an item of ministerial support to the districts or the charges as the conference may direct.

4. The Minimum Salary Fund, secured as described in § 3, shall be used to provide each pastor who receives less than the minimum salary with an additional amount sufficient to make the salary approved by the pastoral charge plus the supplemental aid or income from other sources equal to the minimum salary approved by the conference; *provided* that nothing in this paragraph shall be construed as limiting the right of an Annual Conference to set a maximum amount to be used in attaining such minimum salary in any given case.

5. The Commission on Minimum Salaries shall see that the amounts for minimum salaries are collected and disbursed.

¶ **925.** *Basic Salary Plan.*—1. An Annual Conference may by a two-thirds majority vote at any regular session adopt a **basic salary plan** for the support of its active itinerants and lay pastors who are giving their full time to the ministry of the Church; *provided,* however, that it shall not institute the basic salary plan until the plan has been approved and ratified by a majority vote of the members of the Charge Conferences present and voting in 75 percent of the pastoral charges of such conference. The district superintendents shall certify to the conference secretary the results of the votes taken in the several Charge Conferences.

2. The basic salary plan shall provide an established salary schedule for the support of the regular active itinerants and lay pastors giving their full time to the ministry of the Church, which may allow for differences of living conditions, number of dependents in the family, and other variants. On recommendation of the Commission on World Service and Finance the basic salary schedule may be changed from time to time by a majority vote of the Annual Conference.

3. The Commission on World Service and Finance shall estimate the amount necessary to provide such ministerial support as may be required by the schedule adopted, which amount shall be distributed as an apportionment to the districts or pastoral charges by a method to be determined by the conference.

4. The amounts due from the pastoral charges on apportionment shall be paid to a conference treasury established for that purpose, and all basic salaries due shall be paid from that treasury. The basic salary provided for each minister concerned shall constitute his entire salary except as hereinafter provided.

5. Any pastoral charge which has made adequate provision for paying its apportionments for all ministerial support items in full may augment the basic support of its pastor.

6. The Commission on World Service and Finance shall administer the basic salary plan and shall be responsible for collecting and disbursing the funds.

¶ 926. *Sustentation Fund.*—An Annual Conference may establish a **Sustentation Fund,** which shall be administered by the Commission on World Service and Finance or some other agency created or designed for the purpose of providing emergency aid to the ministers of the conference who may be in special need. On recommendation of the commission the amount needed for this purpose may be apportioned to the pastoral charges as the conference may determine.

¶ 927. The total of all travel, automobile, and other expenses allowed and paid to a pastor in addition to his salary shall be reported for insertion in the journal of the Annual Conference, in a separate column from that of pastor's salary and adjacent thereto. These expenses shall be distinguished from the moving expenses of a new appointee to a pastoral charge, which shall be reported as provided in ¶ 145.9.

¶ **928.** Every ministerial member of an Annual Conference appointed to any other field than the pastorate or district superintendency shall furnish annually to the conference secretary, at the time of the conference session, a statement of his remuneration, and the salaries or remuneration of all ministers in special service shall be published in the journal of the Annual Conference.

Section IV.　The Publishing House.

¶ **929.**　*Publishing Interests.*—The General Board of Publication comprises the publishing interests of The United Methodist Church and shall hereafter be designated as The Methodist Publishing House. It shall have responsibility for and supervision of the publishing and printing for The United Methodist Church. The General Board of Publication shall through agencies or instrumentalities it deems necessary achieve the objectives set forth in ¶ 943. The General Board of Publication shall provide publishing and printing services for other boards and agencies of The United Methodist Church and shall share with other boards and agencies of The United Methodist Church in the total program of The United Methodist Church.

¶ **930.**　*Organization.*—The **General Board of Publication,** hereinafter called the board, constituted coincident with or next following the Declaration of Union of The Evangelical United Brethren Church and The Methodist Church, shall consist of forty-five members, including two bishops selected by the Council of Bishops. Five members shall be members at large elected by the board. The remaining members shall be elected by the Jurisdictional Conferences on a ratio which will provide for an equitable distribution among the various jurisdictions, based on the memberships thereof; *provided* that no jurisdiction shall be represented by fewer than two members. Membership on the board shall be equally divided, as far as practicable, between ministers and laymen. Membership shall also be by classes based on term of office for one, two, or three quadrenniums, attention being given to the principle of rotation so that, as far as practicable, one third of the membership shall be elected each quadrennium. It shall be the duty of the secretary of the General Conference to inform the various jurisdictional secretaries of the number of members to be elected from their jurisdictions, the ratio of such representation being computed on the basis of the latest official membership statistics available. In case a vacancy occurs between sessions of the Jurisdictional Conferences for any cause, the board shall fill the vacancy for the unexpired term from that jurisdiction in the representation of which the vacancy occurs, except in the case of members at large where such vacancies would be filled by the board in the prescribed manner without regard to geographic or jurisdictional relationship. The publisher of The United Methodist Church (¶ 944) shall be an ex officio member of the board without vote.

¶ **931.** In order to conform to the provision relating to relative representation (¶ 815) the following special rules, rather than the rules above so far as they relate to elections by jurisdictions and the filling of vacancies relating thereto, shall apply to elections for the quadrennium beginning with the Uniting Conference of 1968: The special session of the Evangelical United Brethren General Conference of 1968 shall elect six members, two each for terms of one, two, and three quadrenniums respectively. The Methodist General Conference of 1968 shall authorize thirty-two members to be elected by the Jurisdictional Conferences as outlined in the preceding paragraph. At the end of the 1968-72 quadrennium this paragraph shall be automatically deleted from the Discipline.

¶ **932.** The board shall meet annually. The place and time of all meetings shall be designated by the board, but if it fails to do so, then the time and place shall be designated by the chairman. Special meetings may be called by the chairman on his own initiative or by the board or by the executive committee. Special meetings shall be called by the chairman on written request of one third of the members of the board. At all meetings of the board a majority of the members shall constitute a quorum.

¶ **933.** The board shall keep a correct record of its proceedings and make written report thereof to the Church through the General Conference.

¶ **934.** The members of the board and all officers of the board elected by it shall hold office until their successors are chosen and the new board is duly organized.

¶ **935.** The board is authorized to perfect its organization from its membership, including the offices of chairman, vice-chairman, and secretary. The board shall elect from its membership an **executive committee** of sixteen members, including the chairman, vice-chairman, and secretary of the board, who shall serve respectively as chairman, vice-chairman, and secretary of the committee. Not more than four members of the executive committee shall be from any one jurisdiction, and for the first three quadrenniums following the Declaration of Union two members shall be from the former Evangelical United Brethren Church. The bishops serving on the board shall be ex officio members and the publisher of The United Methodist Church (¶ 944) shall be an ex officio member without vote. Any vacancy occurring in the membership of the executive committee shall be filled by it, subject to confirmation by the board at its next meeting.

¶ **936.** The executive committee shall have and may exercise all the powers of the board except those expressly reserved by the board and/or by the Discipline for board action. It shall meet quarterly to examine the affairs under its charge and shall keep and submit to the board correct records of its proceedings. Special meetings may be called by the chairman on his own initiative and shall be called on the written request of five members of the executive committee. A majority of the members shall constitute a quorum.

¶ **937.** The board shall be the successor to and carry on the work of the Board of Publication of The Evangelical United Brethren Church and the Board of Publication of The Methodist Church.

¶ **938.** The board shall cause all legal and moral obligations of the former Board of Publication of The Evangelical United Brethren Church and the former Board of Publication of The Methodist Church now existing to be met, fulfilled, and performed.

¶ **939.** *The Methodist Publishing House.*—1. The board is empowered and authorized in its discretion to cause the general operations, if any, of the seven existing corporations to be conducted under the name of **The Methodist Publishing House.** The corporations are: The Methodist Book Concern, a corporation existing under the laws of the State of New York; The Methodist Book Concern, a corporation

256

existing under the laws of the State of Ohio; The Board of Publication of The Methodist Protestant Church, a corporation existing under the laws of the State of Pennsylvania; Book Agents of the Methodist Episcopal Church, South, a corporation existing under the laws of the State of Tennessee; Board of Publication of The Methodist Church, a corporation existing under the laws of the State of Illinois; The Otterbein Press, a corporation existing under the laws of the State of Ohio; and The Evangelical Press, a corporation existing under the laws of the State of Pennsylvania.

2. The board is authorized and empowered at any time it may deem such action to be desirable or convenient to take corporate action in the name of said corporations to surrender the charter or charters of one or several or all of said corporations or to merge, consolidate, or affiliate such corporations, or any of them, in compliance with appropriate state corporation laws; *provided,* however, that nothing contained in this subparagraph shall supersede, change, or affect the provisions of ¶¶ 951 and 954, which shall remain in full force and effect.

¶ **940.** The members of the board shall serve and act as directors or trustees of the corporations named in ¶ 939.

¶ **941.** The corporations named in ¶ 939 are agencies or instrumentalities through which The United Methodist Church conducts its publishing, printing, and distribution in the name of The Methodist Publishing House in accordance with the objectives set forth in ¶ 943. Each of these corporations shall comply with the policies set forth in ¶ 814.

¶ **942.** The board shall examine carefully the affairs of The Methodist Publishing House and make written report thereof to the Church through the General Conference.

¶ **943.** *Objectives.*—The objectives of The Methodist Publishing House shall be: the advancement of the cause of Christianity by disseminating religious knowledge and useful literary and scientific information in the form of books, tracts, and periodicals; the promotion of Christian education; the transaction of any and all business properly connected with the publishing, manufacturing, and distribution of books, tracts, periodicals, materials, and supplies for churches and church schools; and such other business as the General Conference may direct.

¶ **944.** *Direction and Control.*—The Methodist Publishing House shall be under the direction and control of the board, acting through an executive officer elected quadrennially by the board, who shall be the publisher of The United Methodist Church, and such other officers as the board may determine.

¶ **945.** The net income from the operations of The Methodist Publishing House, after providing adequate reserves for the efficient operation of the business and allowing for reasonable growth and expansion, shall be appropriated by the board and distributed annually on the basis of an equitable plan provided by the General Board of Pensions to the several Annual Conferences for the persons who are and shall be conference claimants.

¶ **946.** The net income from the operations of The Methodist Publishing House shall be appropriated to no other purpose than its own operating requirements and for persons who are or shall be conference claimants as provided in ¶¶ 20 and 945.

¶ **947.** The members of the board and their successors in office are declared to be the successors of the incorporators named in the charters of The Methodist Book Concern issued by the states of New York and Ohio and in the charter of The Board of Publication of The Methodist Protestant Church issued by the state of Pennsylvania. The executive officer of the board, elected from time to time under this or any subsequent Discipline, is declared to be the successor in office of the Book Agents of the Methodist Episcopal Church, South, named in the charter issued to the corporation of that name by the State of Tennessee.

¶ **948.** Subject to the provisions of ¶ 944 and to the continuing control and direction of the General Conference of The United Methodist Church as set forth from time to time in the Discipline, the board is authorized and empowered to cause the operations of The Methodist Publishing House to be carried on and the objectives defined in ¶ 943 to be achieved in such manner, through or by means of such agencies or instrumentalities, and by use of such procedures as the board may from time to time determine to be necessary, advisable, or appropriate, with full power and authority in the premises to take all such action and to do all such other acts and things as may be required or found to be advisable. In particular, and without limiting the generality of the foregoing, the board is authorized and empowered, for the purposes of this section:

1. To use, manage, operate, and otherwise utilize all property and assets of every kind, character, and description of four corporations—namely The Methodist Book Concern, a corporation existing under the laws of the State of New York; The Methodist Book Concern, a corporation existing under the laws of the State of Ohio; The Board of Publication of The Methodist Protestant Church, a corporation existing under the laws of the State of Pennsylvania; and Book Agents of the Methodist Episcopal Church, South, a corporation existing under the laws of the State of Tennessee—as well as all income from such property and assets and the avails thereof, all with liability or obligation to account for such property and assets, the use thereof, the income therefrom, and avails thereof, only to the General Conference of The United Methodist Church or as it shall direct.

2. To cause each of the said corporations to take all such action and to do all such things as the board may deem necessary or advisable to carry out the intent and purposes of this ¶ 948. The governing body of each of the said corporations from time to time shall take all action which the board deems necessary or advisable to carry out the intent and purposes of this ¶ 948. The board shall cause all legal obligations of said four corporations, now existing or hereafter incurred, to be met, fulfilled, and performed.

3. To continue to exercise the powers and administer the duties and responsibilities conferred on it as an agency of The United Methodist Church through the corporation named Board of Publication of The Methodist Church, incorporated under the laws of the State of Illinois in accord with authority delegated to it by the General Conference of 1952, or through such other means and agencies as it may from time to time determine to be expedient and necessary in order to give full effect to the purposes expressed in this section.

¶ 949. 1. The property, assets, and income of the Illinois corporation shall be held by it, under the direction of the board, as an agency of The United Methodist Church and shall at all times be subject to the control and direction of the General Conference of The

United Methodist Church as set forth from time to time in the Discipline.

2. In carrying out and executing its operations and functions, the Illinois corporation shall be entitled to hold, use, manage, operate, and otherwise utilize all property and assets of every kind, character, and description of each of the four corporations identified in ¶ 948.1 (other than its corporate powers and franchises) and all income therefrom and avails thereof for the purposes and objectives defined in this section.

3. The governing body of each of the five existing corporations under the direction of the board shall from time to time take all such action as the board deems necessary or advisable to carry out the intent and purposes of this paragraph and section.

4. The Illinois corporation shall be liable for and shall execute and satisfy all legal obligations of each of the four corporations named in ¶ 948.1, but neither it nor the board shall have or be under any obligation to account for principal and income to any such other corporation or to otherwise report to any of them.

¶ 950.   Pursuant to the Declaration of Union of The Evangelical United Brethren Church and The Methodist Church and subject to the provisions of ¶ 944 and to the control and direction of the General Conference of The United Methodist Church as set forth from time to time in the Discipline, the board is empowered and authorized to use, manage, operate, and otherwise utilize all property and assets of every kind, character, and description of the Board of Publication of The Evangelical United Brethren Church (unincorporated) and the two corporations—namely The Otterbein Press, an Ohio corporation, with offices in Dayton, Ohio, and The Evangelical Press, a Pennsylvania corporation, with offices in Harrisburg, Pennsylvania—as well as all income from such property and assets and the avails thereof, all without liability or obligation to account for such property and assets, the use thereof, the income therefrom, and the avails thereof, only to the General Conference of The United Methodist Church or as it shall direct. The governing body of each of the two said corporations shall take all such action and do all such things as the board may deem necessary or advisable to carry out the intent and purposes of this paragraph.

¶ **951.** The board is empowered and authorized at its discretion to transfer to the Board of Publication of The Methodist Church, an Illinois corporation, all property and assets of every kind, character, and description of the Board of Publication of The Evangelical United Brethren Church (unincorporated), exclusive of any property and assets of The Otterbein Press, an Ohio corporation, and any property and assets of The Evangelical Press, a Pennsylvania corporation. The Board of Publication of The Methodist Church, an Illinois corporation, shall be liable for and shall execute and satisfy all legal obligations of the Board of Publication of The Evangelical United Brethren Church (unincorporated). The Board of Publication of The Evangelical United Brethren Church shall take all such action and do all such things as the board may deem necessary or advisable to carry out the intent and purposes of this paragraph.

¶ **952.** The Board of Publication of The Methodist Church, an Illinois corporation; The Otterbein Press, an Ohio corporation; and The Evangelical Press, a Pennsylvania corporation, shall be presently continued, the members of the board serving and acting as directors or trustees of each of said corporations. The board shall have full authority and discretion to make to and between these several corporations such allocation and distribution of printing, binding, and publishing for the Church as it shall from time to time determine to be fair and in the best interests of The United Methodist Church.

¶ **953.** The members of the board and their successors in office are declared to be the successors of the incorporators named in the charters of The Otterbein Press and The Evangelical Press.

¶ **954.** The property and assets of The Otterbein Press, an Ohio corporation, and The Evangelical Press, a Pennsylvania corporation, shall be held by each of said corporations under the direction of the board as an agency of The United Methodist Church and shall at all times be subject to the control and direction of the General Conference of The United Methodist Church as set forth from time to time in the Discipline.

¶ **955.** *Officers of the Corporations.*—The officers of each corporation under the direction of the board shall be elected annually in accordance with its charter and bylaws.

¶ **956.** The executive officer (publisher) elected pursuant to

¶ 944 shall also be elected the president of each corporation under the direction of the board.

¶ 957. The board shall fix the salaries of the officers of the corporations and shall report the same quadrennially to the General Conference.

¶ 958. The board shall require the president to submit quarterly to the executive committee and annually to the board written reports of the financial condition and operating results of The Methodist Publishing House.

¶ 959. The president (publisher) and the board shall have authority to extend the activities of The Methodist Publishing House in such manner as they may judge to be for the best interests of the Church.

¶ 960. The board shall require the president and other corporate officers to give bond conditioned on the faithful discharge of their respective duties. It also shall authorize the execution of a blanket bond covering all staff personnel whose responsibilities justify such coverage. The amount of the bonds shall be fixed by the board, and the bonds shall be subject to the approval of the board. The premiums shall be paid by The Methodist Publishing House, and the chairman of the board shall be the custodian of the bonds.

¶ 961. The board shall have power to suspend, after hearing, and to remove, after hearing, the president or any of the officers for misconduct or failure to perform the duties of their offices.

¶ 962. *Book Editor.*—The board shall elect quadrennially a book editor, who shall have joint responsibility with the publisher for approving manuscripts considered for publication. He shall edit all the books of our publication, and the quarterly *Religion in Life.* In the case of materials authorized by the Program-Curriculum Committee in the field of Christian education which are to be edited by the editor of church-school publications, he shall collaborate with that editor whenever such collaboration is necessary or desired. He shall perform such other editorial duties as may be required of him by the board. He shall not have responsibility for materials issued by other agencies of the Church for program or promotional purposes.

¶ 963. The board, at its discretion, may continue the publication of the quarterly *Religion in Life,* with the book editor responsible for its editorial content.

¶ **964.** The board shall fix the salary of the book editor.

¶ **965.** The board shall have power to suspend or remove, after hearing, the book editor for misconduct or failure to perform the duties of his office.

¶ **966.** *General Church Periodicals.*—1. The board is authorized to publish a periodical for pastors and other church leaders and a periodical for the family, which shall be a general magazine, informative and vital to the religious life of all United Methodists. The board may, at its discretion, issue such editions of the official periodicals as in its judgment may be deemed advisable. In consultation with the Program Council it shall explore ways and means of making the pages of these periodicals available to other general agencies to the extent possible, either through acceptable editorial channels or by paid insertion as the need may indicate. It shall make available to the council the operating statements of these periodicals and shall furnish such other relevant information as the council may request. (*See* ¶ 831.16.)

2. The editors of these periodicals shall be elected quadrennially by the board after consultation with the Program Council through a joint committee composed of the chairman and two other members of the council and the chairman and two other members of the board, one of whom shall be a bishop. The editors shall be responsible to the publisher for ongoing publishing procedures but shall themselves be responsible for the editorial content of their respective publications.

3. All other details relating to the publishing and distribution of these periodicals, not specifically delegated to the editors, shall be under the direction of the publisher.

4. The board shall fix the salaries of the editors.

5. The board shall have power to suspend or remove, after hearing, any editor for misconduct or failure to perform the duties of his office.

¶ **967.** *Church-School Publications.*—There shall be an editor of church-school publications, elected as set forth in ¶ 1097.

¶ **968.** The editor of church-school publications shall be responsible for the preparation of all curriculum materials as set forth in ¶ 1100.

¶ **969.** The curriculum of the church school shall be determined by the Program-Curriculum Committee, which shall include in its membership the editor of church-school publications, the book editor, and the publisher, as set forth in ¶ 1086.2.

¶ **970.** The board shall fix the salary of the editor of church-school publications and shall have full financial responsibility for all expenses connected with his work.

¶ **971.** The publications of the General Board of Education shall be manufactured, published, and distributed through The Methodist Publishing House. In matters involving financial responsibility the final determination in every case shall lie with the board. After consultation with the publisher, the editor of church-school publications shall prepare a complete budget for his work, including salaries of assistants and office secretaries and travel, etc., to be effective when approved by the board, and shall direct its operation from year to year.

¶ **972.** There shall be one complete, coordinated system of literature published by the board for the entire United Methodist Church. This literature is to be of such type and variety as to meet the needs of all groups of our people.

¶ **973.** The board and the publisher shall have authority to decline to publish any item of literature when in their judgment the cost would be greater than should be borne by The Methodist Publishing House.

¶ **974.** The editor of church-school publications and the chairman of the Division of Curriculum Resources of the General Board of Education shall have the right to sit with the board and shall have the privilege of the floor without vote for the consideration of matters pertaining to the joint interests of the board and the Board of Education.

¶ **975.** The provisions of this section shall not apply to the program and promotional materials of the Division of Higher Education or of the Division of the Local Church.

¶ **976.** *Printing for Church Agencies.*—It is recommended that the general agencies and institutions of The United Methodist Church have all their printing done by The Methodist Publishing House. (*See* ¶¶ 628, 855.)

¶ 977. *Real Estate and Buildings.*—The Methodist Publishing House shall not buy, sell, or exchange any real estate except by order of the General Conference or, between sessions of the General Conference, by a two-thirds vote of all the members of the board; nor shall the board authorize any new buildings or make any improvements, alterations, or repairs to existing buildings to cost in excess of $500,000 except by order of the General Conference or, between sessions of the General Conference, by a two-thirds vote of all members of the board. In either case such vote shall be taken at a regular or called meeting of the board, and if at a called meeting, the purpose of this meeting shall have been stated in the call.

¶ 978. The erection of a new building or the improvement, alteration, or repair of an existing building involving an expenditure of not more than $500,000 may be authorized by the vote of a majority of the executive committee. These provisions shall not prevent the making of investments on mortgage security or the protection of the same or the collection of claims and adjustments. (*See* ¶ 977 for additional requirements and restrictions.)

¶ 979. *Annual Conference Committee.*—1. There shall be organized in each Annual Conference Program Council a **Committee on Publishing Interests** (¶ 841.5), consisting of no fewer than three nor more than five members at large. The resident bishop, the conference or area director of public relations and Methodist information, the conference director of the Annual Conference Board of Education, and any resident member of the Board of Publication shall be members ex officio. There may be also one additional person from each district, to be designated **district secretary of publishing interests.**

2. The committee shall meet at least once before or during every regular conference session and shall act in cooperation with the board in promoting the work of the board within the bounds of the conference.

Section V. Board of Christian Social Concerns.

¶ 980. *Name.*—In keeping with the historic concerns of The Evangelical United Brethren Church and The Methodist Church,

265

there shall be a **General Board of Christian Social Concerns** in The United Methodist Church. This board shall be incorporated.

¶ **981.** *Purpose.*—Its purpose shall be to relate the gospel of Jesus Christ to the members of the Church and to the persons and structures of the communities and world in which they live. It shall seek to bring the whole life of man, his activities, possessions, and community and world relationships, into conformity with the will of God. It shall show the members of the Church and the society that the reconciliation which God effected through Christ involves personal, social, and civic righteousness. To achieve this purpose the board shall project plans and programs that challenge the members of The United Methodist Church to work through their own local church, through ecumenical channels, and through society toward such righteousness; to analyze the issues which confront the person, the local community, the nation, and the world; and to encourage Christian lines of action which assist mankind to move toward a world where peace and justice are achieved.

¶ **982.** *Authority.*—It shall be the responsibility of the board and its executives to give forthright leadership and witness on those social issues that call Christians to action as forgiven men for whom Christ died. The board shall speak to the Church, and to the world, its convictions, interpretations, and concerns, recognizing the freedom and responsibility of all Christian men to study, interpret, and act on any or all recommendations in keeping with their own Christian calling.

¶ **983.** *Organization.*—The first General Board of Christian Social Concerns, hereinafter referred to as the board or the general board, constituted coincident with or next following the Declaration of Union of The Evangelical United Brethren Church and The Methodist Church, shall be composed as follows: ten bishops elected by the Council of Bishops, with representation from each jurisdiction; *provided* that at least one bishop shall be from the former Evangelical United Brethren Church; one minister and one lay person for each 400,000 members or major fractions thereof, elected by the Jurisdictional Conference; *provided* that there shall be no fewer than three ministers and three laymen from each jurisdiction; three young persons who shall be members of the United Methodist Church, two of whom shall be eighteen years of age or younger at the time of their election, nominated by the United Methodist Council of Youth Ministry, and one student who shall be enrolled in a college or university, elected by the board from nominations submitted by the Department of Campus Ministry after consultation with students who are members of The United Methodist Church; nine members at large, elected by the board, on nomination of the executive committee, which shall in turn receive nominations from the divisions, as provided in ¶ 991.3. In addition, the board shall take account of the number of members of the former Evangelical United Brethren Church elected to the board from the jurisdictions and, in order to provide that at least seven persons, including one youth from the former Evangelical United Brethren Church, are included in the membership of the board, may elect up to seven additional members at large upon nomination of the executive committee. In addition, there shall be three liaison members with vote from the Women's Division of the Board of Missions, one of whom shall be the chairman of the Section of Christian Social Relations and one of whom shall be a member of the former Evangelical United Brethren Church. In order that there may be an established liaison relationship with certain other boards of the Church, there shall be eight liaison members with privilege of the floor, but without vote: two persons named by the Board of Missions, one each from the World and National Divisions; three by the Board of Education, one from each of its divisions; one by the Board of Evangelism; one by the Board of the Laity; and one by the Board of Health and Welfare Ministries. No member of the board shall be a salaried officer thereof.

¶ **984.** *Vacancies.*—If a vacancy occurs in the board by death or resignation, it shall be filled as follows: in the case of a bishop, by the College of Bishops of the jurisdiction; in the case of a ministerial or lay representative from a jurisdiction, by the board on nomination of the College of Bishops of the jurisdiction, such member to serve until the next meeting of the Jurisdictional Conference; in the case of a youth or student member or a member at large, as provided in ¶ 983.

¶ **985.** *Officers.*—The board shall elect a president, who shall be a bishop; three vice-presidents, each of whom shall serve as the chairman of one division; a recording secretary; and such other officers as it may determine.

¶ **986.** *Executive Committee.*—The board shall elect an **executive committee,** which shall consist of the officers of the board and four additional members from each of the three divisions of the board, one of whom shall be the recording secretary of the division. Not more than four members of the executive committee shall be from one jurisdiction. This committee shall have the power ad interim to fill any vacancies occurring in the elected staff and to transact such business as is necessary between the meetings of the board. It shall report all of its actions for confirmation at the next meeting of the board.

¶ **987.** *Nominating Committee.*—A **nominating committee** of six members shall be constituted. It shall be composed of one member, ministerial or lay, from each jurisdiction, chosen by the board members from that jurisdiction, and one bishop chosen by the bishops who are board members. The bishop shall serve as convener. This committee shall nomiante the officers of the board (¶ 985) and assign each member of the board, including the vice-presidents, to one of the three divisions (¶ 991).

¶ **988.** *Meetings.*—1. The board shall meet quadrennially for purposes of organization and other necessary actions after the adjournment of the General Conference and not later than October 15 of that year. The organizational meeting shall be convened by the bishop designated by the Council of Bishops for that purpose, and he shall fix the time and place.

2. The board shall hold an annual meeting, at a time and place to be determined by its executive committee, and such other meetings as its work may require, and shall enact suitable bylaws governing the activities of the board and its employees. A majority of the membership shall constitute a quorum.

¶ **989.** *Predecessor Boards.*—The members of the board shall constitute the membership of its predecessor boards, namely the Board of Temperance of The Methodist Church and all its legal predecessors, the Board of World Peace of The Methodist Church and all its legal predecessors, the Board of Social and Economic Relations and the Board of Christian Social Concerns of The Methodist Church, and the

Department of Christian Social Action of The Evangelical United Brethren Church.

¶ **990.** *Financial Support.*—1. The work of the board shall be supported from the general benevolences of the Church, the amount to be determined by the General Conference, on recommendation of the Council on World Service and Finance. The board shall present quadrennially to the council a statement of the amount required for its general expense and for the support of each of its divisions.

2. Either on behalf of its total work or on behalf of one or more of its divisions, the board may solicit and create special funds, receive gifts and bequests, hold properties and securities in trust, and administer all these financial affairs in accordance with its own rules and the provisions of the Discipline. (*See* ¶¶ 864, 869.) Funds vested in any of the predecessor boards shall be conserved for the specific purposes for which such funds have been given.

¶ **991.** *Divisions.*—1. The board shall be organized into three divisions: the Division of General Welfare, the Division of World Peace, and the Division of Human Relations. The members of the board shall be assigned to divisions by the nominating committee (¶ 987), subject to the approval of the board. It shall be the duty of this committee to assign the membership, other than members at large, to the three divisions so that the three shall as nearly as possible be of the same size and shall have members from each jurisdiction and from ministerial and lay groups in as nearly as possible equal proportion. No member shall belong to more than one division, except that the president of the board shall be a member ex officio of each division.

2. Each division shall organize itself under the chairmanship of a vice-president of the board and shall elect a recording secretary. It shall also elect three of its own number by written ballot who, together with the chairman and recording secretary, shall constitute the executive committee of that division. The members of the divisional executive committee shall be members of the executive committee of the board.

3. Each division shall nominate for election by the board three members at large, selected on the basis of their specialized skills and

knowledge relevant to the work of the division, to be members of that division and of the board. (*See* ¶ 983.)

¶ **992.** Each division shall meet at the same time and place as the board. A special meeting of the division may be held on the call of its chairman or of three members of its executive committee or of ten of its members. All expenses of such special meetings shall be chargeable to the budget of the division.

¶ **993.** 1. The members assigned to each division shall have the responsibility of establishing policies relating to the work of that division and its staff, subject to the approval of the board.

2. The divisions shall carry forward cooperatively the total work of the board through the Annual Conferences and districts, in the local churches, and in such other places and by such means as they may have opportunity to present the witness of Christian social concern.

¶ **994.** *Staff.*—The board shall elect quadrennially a general secretary, three associate general secretaries, and a staff treasurer, on nomination of the executive committee. Other staff personnel shall be approved by the executive committee of the board, on nomination of the president and the general secretary. The executive committee of the board may, at its discretion, assign this responsibility to the executive committee of a division. At least one staff member shall be from the former Evangelical United Brethren Church. The salaries and duties of all employees of the board shall be fixed by the board.

¶ **995.** *General and Associate General Secretaries.*—1. The **general secretary** shall be an ex officio member of the board, of its executive committee, and of the executive committee of each division, without vote. He shall be the chief administrative officer of the board, responsible for the coordination of the total program of the board and for the general administration of the headquarters office and of such facilities and functions as serve all three divisions of the board.

2. Under the supervision of the general secretary there shall be a **staff treasurer,** who shall have charge of the financial operations of the board, property management, the service department, purchasing, and such other duties assigned by the board. The general secretary shall also have under his supervision such other staff persons as are deemed necessary by the board.

3. Each of the **associate general secretaries** shall have primary responsibility for those Christian social concerns which are assigned to his particular division. Within this area and under the direction of the division and its executive committee, he, with his staff, shall develop a program of research, education, and action, bringing these concerns to the attention of the denomination and all its churches and of the communities they serve. He shall be responsible, under the direction of the division and its executive committee, for the administration of the budget, including the income from trust funds allocated to his division. The three associate general secretaries shall cooperate with one another and with the general secretary to prevent undue overlapping in the work of the divisions and to avoid conflicts in scheduling of meetings and conferences.

4. The general secretary and the associate general secretaries shall be members of the Council of Secretaries.

¶ **996.** *Headquarters.*—1. The headquarters of the board and of its divisions shall be in Washington, D. C.

2. In addition to the general headquarters there shall be a New York United Nations office, conducted in cooperation with the Women's Division of the Board of Missions. In the operation of this office the Division of World Peace shall represent the board and shall carry the board's responsibility for staffing and budget.

DIVISION OF GENERAL WELFARE

¶ **997.** 1. It shall be the responsibility of the **Division of General Welfare** to conduct a program of research, education, and action, centering around the following Christian social concerns: alcohol problems, tobacco, drug abuse, gambling, sex and moral values and pornography, juvenile delinquency, crime and rehabilitation, mental health, medical care, problems of the aging, population problems, family life, planned parenthood, public safety, morality and mass media, community welfare policies and practices, and such other related concerns as the board may specify. For clarification of responsibility in relation to other boards see ¶ 1170.

2. The work assigned to the division shall be carried forward by the associate general secretary and such other staff members as the

division shall determine, subject to budget allocations. The staff shall report to the division at the time of the annual board meeting concerning the work of the past year and plans proposed for further implementation of its assigned responsibilities.

3. To implement United Methodist concern for the problems of alcohol and drug abuse as expressed in the Social Creed and the resolution on "The Addictive Society" (See *The Book of Resolutions*), the second Sunday in November will be set aside to emphasize drug and alcohol concerns for the purpose of:

a) Educating the constituency on the nature and extent of alcohol and drug abuse problems from theological, ethical, and sociological perspectives.

b) Fostering understanding and acceptance of the dimensions of Christian responsibility in one's decisions about alcohol and drugs and in the Church's concern for the personal and social problems related to alcohol and drugs, especially the addictive and dependency disorders.

c) Enlisting United Methodists and others for effective action to alleviate social problems that contribute to and issue from alcohol and drug abuse; to work in the development of new and improved services and facilities for the treatment and rehabilitation of individuals suffering from alcohol and drug abuse problems; to develop a healing, reconciling, and sustaining community in the Church for such persons; to strengthen the resources of family, Church, and community to help persons grow into the kind of maturity which makes it possible to cope with the tensions of life without undue dependence upon alcohol and drugs; and to foster a social and cultural environment conducive to responsible decision-making.

d) Encouraging abstinence from the use of alcoholic beverages as one form of personal and social witness to God's liberating love for mankind.

Division of World Peace

¶ **998.** 1. It shall be the responsibility of the **Division of World Peace** to conduct a program of research, education, and action, centering around the following Christian social concerns: American foreign policy; United Nations and related international organizations; disarmament and nuclear weapon control; space control; foreign aid, tariffs, and trade; immigration and naturalization; military policy and conscription legislation; conscientious objectors and the draft; and such other concerns as the board may specify. The general policies shall be established by the division, subject to the approval of the board.

2. The work assigned to the division shall be carried forward by the associate general secretary and such other staff members as the division shall determine, subject to budget allocations. The staff shall report to the division at the time of the annual board meeting concerning the work of the past year and plans proposed for further implementation of its assigned responsibilities.

3. To enlist United Methodists and encourage others to promote international brotherhood and good will and to challenge church members to creative action for world order, the Sunday preceding Reformation Sunday shall be observed as **World Order Sunday.**

Division of Human Relations

¶ 999. 1. It shall be the responsibility of the **Division of Human Relations** to conduct a program of research, education, and action, centering around the following Christian social concerns: race relations, extremist movements, civil liberties, application of democratic principles related to voting, public policy on education, church and state relations, labor-management relations, agriculture, conservation, government and private economic policy and practice, technological and social change, employment, poverty, urbanization, housing, and such other concerns as the board may specify. The general policies shall be established by the division, subject to the approval of the board.

2. The work assigned to the division shall be carried forward by the associate general secretary and such other staff members as the division shall determine, subject to budget allocations. The staff shall report to the division at the time of the annual board meeting concerning the work of the past year and plans proposed for further implementation of its assigned responsibilities.

3. To enlist United Methodists and encourage others to cooperate in studies and discussions and to work toward a better understanding in all human relations, the divisions shall seek to enlist all churches to cooperate fully in the observance of Labor Sunday, Race Relations Sunday, and other days related to this area of concern.

Miscellaneous Provisions

¶ **1000.** *Amenability.*—The Board of Christian Social Concerns is amenable to the General Conference, to which it shall report. It shall work with the Program Council in all matters relating to the development and promotion of program for jurisdictional boards, conference boards, and local churches, in order that its program emphasis may be integrated into the total unified program of the Church. It shall promote the total program of the Church or aspects of it which are particularly related to the board.

¶ **1001.** *Bylaws.*—The Board of Christian Social Concerns shall provide its own bylaws, which shall not violate any provisions of the constitution or the Discipline, and which may be amended by a two-thirds vote of the members present and voting thereon at a regular or special meeting; *provided* that notice of such amendment has previously been given to the members.

¶ **1002.** *Amendments.*—The constitution of the Board of Christian Social Concerns can be amended only by the General Conference of The United Methodist Church.

¶ **1003.** *Jurisdictional Boards.*—In each jurisdiction there may be a **jurisdictional Board of Christian Social Concerns,** auxiliary to the general board, as the Jurisdictional Conference may determine. (*See* ¶¶ 26.3, 625.)

¶ **1004.** *Annual Conference Boards.*—1. Each Annual Conference shall elect, on nomination of the nominating committee of the conference, or otherwise, as the conference may direct, a **conference Board of Christian Social Concerns.** It shall have no fewer than fifteen nor more than sixty members, with an approximately equal number of laymen and ministers. The lay members shall include a youth eighteen years of age or younger at the time of his election, nominated by the conference youth organization, a student enrolled in a college or university, nominated by the Department of Campus Ministry after consultation with students who are members of The United Methodist Church, and the chairman of Christian social relations of the conference Women's Society of Christian Service. The remaining lay members shall consist of an approximately equal number of men and women. All district directors of Christian social concerns and any members of the general and jurisdictional boards living within the bounds of the conference shall be ex officio members. Additional members, either clerical or lay, may be nominated at any time during the quadrennium by the board, as it may deem advisable, for election by the conference. Vacancies in the elected membership between conference sessions may be filled by the executive committee of the board, pending action of the next conference session.

2. The conference board, in cooperation with the general board and the Annual Conference Program Council, shall develop and promote programs on Christian social concerns within the bounds of the conference. To this end it may divide its membership into three committees of approximately equal size, patterned after the divisions of the general board. They shall have responsibility to cooperate with one another to advance the concerns of their respective divisions.

3. The board shall estimate annually the amount necessary for support of its work and shall report this amount according to the procedure of the Annual Conference. The work of the board may be considered a benevolence interest of the Church within the conference.

4. The Annual Conference may employ a person or persons to further its purposes. Two or more Annual Conferences may cooperate in developing their programs and in employing one or more persons.

¶ 1005. *District Committees.*—The district superintendent, after consultation with the conference board, shall appoint a district director of Christian social concerns and, if desired, a **district Committee on Christian Social Concerns** of laymen and ministers to work with him to further the purposes of the conference board. The chairman of Christian social relations of the district Women's Society of Christian Service shall be an ex officio member. If the Annual Conference so orders, three district directors shall be appointed, each to represent the interests of one of the divisions within the general board.

¶ **1006.** *Local Church Commissions.*—For the program of Christian social concerns in the local church see ¶ 158.4.

Section VI. Board of Education.

¶ **1007.** *Purpose.*—Christian education is rooted in the nature of the Christian gospel. The objective of the Church as manifested through its educational ministry is that all persons be aware of and grow in their understanding of God, especially of his redeeming love as revealed in Jesus Christ, and that they respond in faith and love, to the end that they may know who they are and what their human situation means, increasingly identify themselves as sons of God and members of the Christian community, live in the Spirit of God in every relationship, fulfill their common discipleship in the world, and abide in the Christian hope. The divisions of the Board of Education shall develop standards and programs consistent with this purpose.

GENERAL BOARD ORGANIZATION

¶ **1008.** The program and work of Christian education, as directed by the General Conference, shall be under the supervision of the **General Board of Education,** the Jurisdictional and Annual Conference Boards of Education, and the Jurisdictional and Annual Conference Councils on Local Church Program and Boards of the Ministry, as provided for in the Discipline.

¶ **1009.** The total Christian educational program of The United Methodist Church for use in local churches shall be developed by the Division of the Local Church for incorporation in the total church program, which is integrated and unified through the Program Council. It shall include the educational emphases and activities of all the general departments and interests of the denomination, such as evangelism, stewardship, missions, Christian social action, and Bible instruction. It shall be developed as a comprehensive, unified, and coordinated Christian educational program for children, youth, and adults in local churches and shall be promoted and administered by the Boards of Education of the general Church and the Annual Conferences in cooperation with their Councils on Local Church Program and Program Councils in the local churches.

¶ **1010.** *Organization.*—1. There shall be a Board of Education of The United Methodist Church, hereinafter referred to as the General Board of Education or the board. The board shall have general oversight of the educational interests of the Church in the United States and Canada as directed by the General Conference. It may cooperate with the Board of Missions for the advancement of Christian education in other lands.

2. The General Board of Education shall be incorporated under the laws of whatever state the board may determine.

3. The board shall meet annually at such time and place as it may determine, subject to the provisions of the act of incorporation, and may hold such special meetings as may be necessary. A majority of the members of the board shall constitute a quorum.

4. The board shall appoint such committees as may be necessary for the proper discharge of its business. It may adopt such bylaws for the regulation of the affairs of the board and its divisions and committees as are consistent with the act of incorporation or with General Conference legislation.

5. The board shall be organized quadrennially, and its members and all officers elected by it shall hold office until their successors have been chosen.

6. Within three months after the adjournment of the last Jurisdictional Conference to meet in any General Conference year, the elected members of the board shall be assembled by a convener, designated by the Council of Bishops, to organize.

¶ **1011.** *Membership of the General Board.*—1. Membership of the board shall consist of fifteen bishops resident in the United States, representing all the jurisdictions, elected by the Council of Bishops, together with additional members elected as follows: each Jurisdictional Conference shall elect to the membership of the Board of Education, on nomination of its Committee on Education, one minister and one layman, without regard to the number of members within the jurisdiction, and in addition, one minister and one layman for each 500,000 members or major fraction thereof within the jurisdiction; *provided* that not more than two shall be from any one Annual Conference.

2. There shall be elected a sufficient number of members at large

without respect to jurisdictions or Annual Conferences to bring the membership to a total of ninety-one; *provided* that three members at large shall be young adult churchmen (eighteen to thirty years of age). These shall be persons of demonstrated competence in the field of education in the Church, community, and/or higher education, elected by the board, on nomination of its nominating committee.

3. There shall be four youth and two student members. Three youth shall be nominated for election by the board on recommendation of the national youth organization, in accordance with ¶¶ 1081-82; one youth shall be a member of the council of the national youth organization. Two students, members of The United Methodist Church and presently enrolled in a college or university, shall be chosen from nominations submitted by the Department of Campus Ministry after consultation with students who are members of The United Methodist Church.

4. If any vacancy occurs in the membership of the board, it shall be filled in the following manner: in the case of a bishop, by the Council of Bishops; in the case of a ministerial or lay representative of a jurisdiction, by the board, on nomination of the College of Bishops of the jurisdiction, such member to serve until the next meeting of the Jurisdictional Conference; in the case of a member at large, by the board, on nomination of its nominating committee; in the case of a youth member, by the board, on nomination of the council of the national youth organization (¶ 1081); in the case of a student member, on nomination of the Department of Campus Ministry.

¶ **1012.** *Committees of the General Board.*—1. A **nominating committee** shall be elected, which shall be composed of one member from each jurisdiction, chosen by the members of said jurisdiction, and one bishop, chosen by the bishops who are members of the board.

2. The nominating committee shall nominate for election by the board: (*a*) members of the constituent divisions of the board as follows: Division of Higher Education, thirty-three; Division of the Local Church, thirty-three; Division of Curriculum Resources, twenty-four; (*b*) a president and a recording secretary for the board; (*c*) members at large as provided in ¶ 1011.2.

¶ **1013.** 1. The **executive committee** of the board shall be composed of the president and recording secretary of the board and the members of the advisory committees of the constituent divisions as provided in ¶ 1025.2. A majority of the members shall constitute a quorum.

2. The executive committee shall manage the funds of the board under such regulations as the board may adopt; appoint finance and investment committees, which shall render to it detailed reports at each meeting; fix the official bond of the treasurer and of any other officers entrusted with the handling of funds; and consider and approve the administrative budgets of the board and its divisions, except the Division of Curriculum Resources.

3. The board may commit to the executive committee such other powers and duties as it may determine. Minutes of the executive committee shall be sent to the members of the board and submitted to the annual meeting of the board for approval. Meetings of the committee shall be held at least once each year, not including meetings held in connection with the annual meetings of the board.

¶ **1014.** *Officers of the General Board.*—The members of the divisions, the president, and the recording secretary shall be elected from the membership of the board. The president, who shall be a presiding, not an administrative, officer, shall preside over the meetings of the board and of the executive committee. Each division shall elect a chairman, and these chairmen shall be vice-presidents of the board. The officers of the board and members of the divisions, together with the officers of each division, shall hold office for the quadrennium.

¶ **1015.** 1. The treasurer shall be elected by the board, on nomination of the executive committee. An associate treasurer may be elected by the board, on nomination of the executive committee in consultation with the treasurer.

2. The treasurer of the board shall be the custodian of all the funds of the board. He shall keep the accounts of the assets, liabilities, receipts, and disbursements of the board and of the Division of Higher Education and the Division of the Local Church. He shall pay out funds on order of the general secretaries of these divisions. He shall report annually to the board and to the executive committee as requested by it.

¶ **1016.** The general secretaries of the Division of Higher Education and the Division of the Local Church shall be elected for the quadrennium by the board from nominations made by the respective divisions. A vacancy in either office shall be filled by election by the board. The general secretary of the Division of Curriculum Resources shall be elected as provided in ¶ 1097.

¶ 1017. No member of the board shall be a salaried officer of the board.

¶ 1018. The salaries and duties of all employees of the board, except those of the Division of Curriculum Resources, shall be fixed by the board.

¶ 1019. *Powers of the General Board.*—The board is authorized to solicit and create special funds, to receive gifts and bequests, to hold properties and securities in trust, and to administer all these financial affairs in accordance with its own rules and the provisions of the Discipline.

¶ 1020. All assets and liabilities existing at the time of union in the funds of the boards of education of the two uniting churches shall be the assets and liabilities of the corresponding divisions in the new Board of Education.

¶ 1021. The Division of Higher Education and the Division of the Local Church shall present quadrennially to the Council on World Service and Finance a statement of the amounts required for their general expenses and for the support of their work, and the appropriations of the council shall be made to each division. The Division of Curriculum Resources shall be financed as provided in ¶¶ 970-71. In all cases the purposes for which funds are committed to the board shall be strictly observed.

¶ 1022. The Board of Education shall be the legal successor and successor in trust of the General Board of Christian Education of the Methodist Episcopal Church, South; the Board of Education of the Methodist Episcopal Church; the Board of Education of the Methodist Protestant Church; the Board of Education for Negroes of the Methodist Episcopal Church; the Board of Sunday Schools of the Methodist Episcopal Church; the Epworth League of the Methodist Episcopal Church; the Board of Christian Education of The Evangelical United Brethren Church; the Board of Christian Education of the Church of the United Brethren in Christ; the Board of Christian

Education of the Evangelical Church; the Board of Education of The Methodist Church; and such educational boards and societies as may have been merged to constitute these boards; and it is authorized and empowered at any time it may deem such action to be desirable or convenient to take corporate action in the name of said corporations to surrender the charter or charters of one or several or all of said corporations (including a transfer of all the properties of said corporations to the Board of Education if necessary or desirable) or to merge, consolidate, or affiliate such corporations, or any of them, with the Board of Education in compliance with appropriate state corporation laws, so as to accomplish as nearly as may legally be possible the end result that the Board of Education shall be the one legal entity authorized to act on behalf of the interest heretofore or hereafter in the name of one or the other of said corporations.

¶ **1023.** As a means of assisting the Church to fulfill its commitment to be an inclusive Church and to support the schools historically related to education for Negroes, Race Relations Sunday shall be observed in all the congregations.

¶ **1024.** The board may have authority to make provision for cooperation with any of the general boards or other agencies of the Church, or with other agencies, in matters within its field; *provided* that nothing in the foregoing shall be construed to limit the Annual Conference. Each Annual Conference shall determine for itself to what extent it will undertake to cooperate with other denominations or agencies in its own territory.

¶ **1025.** 1. The board shall conduct its work through the constituent divisions, each of which shall be responsible for the specific areas assigned to it by the board.

2. Each of the divisions shall elect from its members an **advisory committee,** consisting of its chairman, recording secretary, and other members to the following totals: Division of Higher Education, eight; Division of the Local Church, eight; Division of Curriculum Resources, five. In addition, the president of the board shall be an ex officio member of each advisory committee. These committees shall assist in the conduct of the work and serve as members of the executive committee of the board. (*See* ¶ 1013.1.)

3. The **general secretaries** of the divisions shall be the administrative officers of their respective divisions, under such regulations as the board may make. Reports of the work of the respective divisions, including organization and budget, except the budget of the Division of Curriculum Resources, shall be presented annually by them to the board. Assistants to the general secretaries of the Division of Higher Education and the Division of the Local Church shall be elected annually by the divisions on nomination of the respective general secretaries. Assistants to the general secretary of the Division of Curriculum Resources shall be appointed by him and reported to the board.

4. Each of the divisions shall provide for a review of its work, pass upon recommendations of its general secretary and staff, and make recommendations to the board concerning its needs and programs.

5. The general secretaries shall attend the meetings of the board, the executive committee, and their respective divisions, participating in their deliberations, but without vote.

6. The general secretaries shall form a **Secretarial Council,** which shall choose annually in rotation from its members a presiding officer and which shall meet as necessary to coordinate the work of the divisions.

DIVISION OF HIGHER EDUCATION

¶ **1026.** 1. Higher education is part of both our Wesleyan heritage and our present task. In establishing and maintaining educational institutions and in ministering to students without respect to race or national origin, the Church continues its historic work of uniting knowledge and vital piety.

2. There shall be a **Division of Higher Education,** which shall represent The United Methodist Church in all activities connected with secondary and higher education, ministerial education, and campus ministry. The division shall have responsibility for establishing and coordinating denominational policy for higher education and shall have an advisory relationship to all educational institutions in the United States and Canada affiliated with The United Methodist Church: universities, schools of theology, colleges, secondary schools,

Wesley Foundations and similar units, and the regularly organized interdenominational campus ministry groups. On request it may serve in an advisory capacity to the several agencies of the Church owning or administering educational institutions.

3. Its principal objectives shall be: (*a*) to develop an educational plan and purpose which shall definitely relate the educational institutions of the Church to the Church; (*b*) to foster within them the highest educational standards and soundest business practices; (*c*) to interpret to them their place and function in the life and work of the Church; (*d*) to encourage them in their commitment to Christian standards and ideals in their teaching, policies, and practices; (*e*) to interpret to the membership of the Church the distinctive services rendered by these educational institutions and their functions in the Church and society; and (*f*) to lead the Church in a program designed to assure their permanence, efficiency, academic excellence, and Christian commitment.

4. It shall operate through three constituent departments: the Department of Educational Institutions, the Department of the Ministry, and the Department of Campus Ministry.

5. It shall elect, on nomination of the general secretary, directors for each of the departments and such other staff members as are needed for the operation of the division.

6. It shall engage personnel and appoint such commissions and committees and adopt such regulations as necessary for the discharge of its responsibilities.

¶ 1027. The specific responsibilities of the Division of Higher Education are:

1. To devise ways and means to interpret and aid the higher education program of the Church. (*See* ¶ 1031.2.)

2. To cooperate with Annual Conferences in establishing and conducting institutions of higher education in the United States and Canada in areas in which facilities for Christian higher education are not adequately provided. (*See* ¶ 1064.1.)

3. To promote Christian instruction, afford opportunities for Christian service, and offer guidance in Christian vocations for students at educational institutions of The United Methodist Church and for

United Methodist students at tax-supported and other institutions not related to The United Methodist Church.

4. To make use, insofar as is practicable, of the existing church organization and publications for carrying out its work of interpretation, setting up such conferences and producing such materials as will strengthen the interrelation of the Church, its educational institutions, and its campus ministry units.

5. To study the financial status of United Methodist educational institutions, encourage the Church to give them continuing and conscientious support, provide guidance and leadership in their special financial campaigns, and formulate procedures by which they can approach United Methodist members and constituents for gifts and bequests.

6. To direct attention to the work and needs of educational institutions which stand in special relationship to the Church at large and to request support for them, with due recognition of the needs of schools and colleges historically related to education for Negroes.

7. To furnish guidance, plans of procedure, personal leadership, and plans for special gifts to be known as **educational specials** in the promotion of the work of higher education in the Annual Conferences and in the local churches.

8. To devise methods of credit for local-church giving to educational institutions and campus ministry units related to the division, including the listing of all such giving in appropriate columns in the statistical reports of the Annual Conference minutes.

¶ 1028. The **Department of Educational Institutions** shall have primary responsibility for the work of the division as outlined in ¶¶ 1026-27 and hereafter described in ¶¶ 1029-34 insofar as the provisions thereof relate to the universities, colleges, secondary, and other schools of The United Methodist Church.

¶ 1029. 1. The division shall appropriate such of its funds as are available for the support of educational institutions related to The United Methodist Church, under such rules as it may adopt.

2. In making appropriations for the support of educational institutions, the division shall give due consideration to their current financial needs as shown in carefully prepared reports presented by them on forms provided. Appropriations to institutions from funds

at the disposal of the division shall not bar those institutions from soliciting aid from their supporting conferences or from other sources. (*See also* ¶ 1052.2.)

3. The division shall cooperate with the General and Annual Conferences in their efforts to provide the institutions related to them adequate financial income for the operation of accredited educational programs.

4. The division shall recommend to Jurisdictional and Annual Conference Boards of Education concerned with the appropriation of conference funds those institutions whose educational and religious aims and programs are in active accord with the policies of the Church as expressed in the Discipline and through special General Conference enactments. (*See* ¶¶ 1039, 1058.)

5. The division shall have power to administer under the rules and regulations of the board any and all funds, gifts, and bequests which have been or may be committed to it, and subject to the approval of the board, it may solicit or create special funds for its projects. The purposes for which the funds are given and accepted shall be faithfully observed.

6. The division shall take such action as is necessary to protect or recover the investment which it or an Annual Conference has made in capital funds to any institution founded, organized, developed, or assisted under the direction or with the cooperation of The United Methodist Church should any such institution discontinue operation or move to sever or to modify its connection with the Church or violate the terms of any such grant of new capital funds made by The United Methodist Church.

¶ 1030. 1. The division shall, in cooperation with the University Senate, study population growth and trends and make recommendations to the Annual Conferences concerning the needs for new institutions of learning and the discontinuance, reopening, relocation, and merger of existing institutions.

2. No educational institution hereafter establish or acquired shall be qualified for classification as an institution related to The United Methodist Church or be aided by the division unless the division shall have been consulted and shall have approved the expenditures in-

volved in the establishment or acquisition of such institution. *(See* ¶¶ 1039, 1064.)

3. When any change in sponsorship or in cooperating territory and relationships is desired relative to any of these institutions, such proposed change shall be subject to approval by the division.

¶ 1031. 1. The division, through such officers, committees, and commissions as it may deem necessary, shall provide for the cooperative study of plans for maximum coordination of the work of United Methodist educational institutions with the Church's entire program of Christian education.

2. In cooperation with the Annual Conferences and the pastors and Commissions on Education of local churches, the division shall bring to the attention of church members the contribution of United Methodist educational institutions to the life and character of youth and the place the institutions have in the preservation and propagation of Christianity. *(See* ¶ 1027.1.)

¶ 1032. 1. The division shall foster and aid through a special offering the United Methodist institutions historically related to education for Negroes. It shall have authority to institute plans by which schools sponsored by the division may cooperate with or may unite with schools of other denominations or under independent control; *provided* that the interests of The United Methodist Church are adequately protected.

2. The division shall encourage such schools to secure adequate endowments for their support and maintenance. Whenever the division is assured that their support will be adequate and the property will be conserved and perpetuated for Christian education under the auspices and control of The United Methodist Church, it may transfer the schools to Boards of Trustees under such conditions as the General Board of Education may prescribe, including the right of reversion to the General Board of Education.

¶ 1033. 1. The division shall promote and administer the **United Methodist Student Loan Fund,** the **United Methodist Scholarship Fund,** and other grants and bequests made to the division for the aid of students in accordance with regulations recommended by the division and adopted by the board.

2. The division shall be responsible for promoting United Methodist Student Day.

Note: For the participation of the division in the crusade scholarship program see ¶ 1355.

¶ **1034.** Educational societies or foundations created by Annual Conferences for the promotion of work in Christian higher education may be recognized as auxiliaries of the Division of Higher Education when their objects and purposes, their articles of incorporation, and their methods of administration shall have been approved by the Annual Conference within whose bounds they are incorporated. All auxiliaries thus approved may be required to make an annual report of their fiscal and administrative affairs to the division.

¶ **1035.** The **Department of Campus Ministry** shall have administrative responsibility for the work of the division in promoting a campus Christian movement and a ministry to the educational community as this work shall be defined by the division and in accordance with policies and procedures of the board. It shall also adopt whatever administrative and program relationships with the Young Adult Ministry as may seem desirable.

¶ **1036.** The Department of Campus Ministry shall give direction and encouragement to local churches, Annual Conferences, and church-related educational institutions in the establishment and expansion of an effective policy and program with regard to the campus Christian movement of the Church and the concern for the mission of the Church within all campus communities.

The responsibility of the department for the campus Christian movement and for the campus ministry shall include the following:

1. It shall describe the general nature and purpose and assist the functioning of the several expressions of movement and ministry related to the division, including: (a) the local-church Commission on Education, (b) the Annual Conference and interconference Committee/Commission on Christian Higher Education and Campus Ministry, (c) the United Methodist–related colleges and universities, (d) colleges and universities not related to The United Methodist Church, (e) the Wesley Foundations, (f) the intercollegiate campus Christian movement, and (g) such other expressions of movement and ministry as shall be approved by the division.

2. It shall provide for necessary representation in such agencies as: (a) the Council for Policy and Strategy of United Ministries in Higher Education, (b) the Committee of Administrators of United Ministries in Higher Education, and (c) the Department of Higher Education of the National Council of Churches and its related units.

¶ 1037. The United Methodist Church affirms its commitment to an ecumenical approach to campus ministry. It urges local, campus, state, and regional units of that ministry to work toward such ecumenical programming and structures as may most fully express the commitment in their respective areas of ministry.

There shall be a governing body for the campus ministry in every college community where The United Methodist Church is at work, as follows:

1. For each Wesley Foundation and interdenominational campus ministry related to The United Methodist Church there shall be a Board of Directors.

2. The division shall encourage each United Methodist–related college or university to establish a **Committee on Campus Religious Life,** which may serve also as a Campus-Church Relations Committee, and to state qualifications and define duties of the committee in consultation with the division.

3. For each other institution there shall be a **Campus-Church Relations Committee,** nominated by a local United Methodist body and elected by the conference Board of Education.

4. The governing body for the campus ministry on a local campus, in cooperation with the Annual Conference, may unify its ministry with others in ecumenical organization, program, and procedure.

¶ 1038. A Wesley Foundation or a regularly organized interdenominational campus ministry unit is the form through which The United Methodist Church makes possible a unified ministry to the tax-supported or independent college or university. The nature of such ministry shall be defined and evaluated by the division.

¶ 1039. 1. The division's evaluation of the ministry of a Wesley Foundation and of interdenominational campus ministries related to The United Methodist Church shall be the responsibility of a **Commission on Standards for Campus Ministry,** appointed by the division.

The commission shall be composed of six members of the division and five other persons who are not members of the General Board of Education but who are actively engaged in the campus ministry of The United Methodist Church, and all of whom are qualified by training and experience to evaluate the functions and structure of the campus ministry and to establish standards for such ministry.

On the recommendation of the commission the department shall report annually to the division and to the Annual Conferences those Wesley Foundations and interdenominational campus ministries which meet the standards it has established.

2. Each Wesley Foundation and comparable ministry approved by the commission and each such unit seeking approval shall submit annually to the division reports of program and financial status.

¶ 1040. 1. In carrying out its responsibility for the operation, support, and expansion of campus ministry among United Methodists and other persons involved in institutions of higher education, the Department of Campus Ministry may seek to relate campus Christian organizations on Methodist campuses, Wesley Foundations at tax-supported and independent colleges and universities, and such other forms of ministry as may be developed, to the intercollegiate Christian movement.

Through such agencies The United Methodist Church shall seek to further the mission of the Church within the campus community. There shall be such state or similar area units, regional and national, as the department shall see fit to maintain in order to serve the students, faculty, and administrative personnel of the colleges and universities. The department shall publish such materials as are necessary to develop this work.

2. Among the purposes of the campus Christian movements, defined in § 1 above, shall be:

a) To lead all members of the college and university community to accept the Christian faith in God, according to the Scriptures; to live as true disciples of Jesus Christ; and to become members of Christ's Church.

b) To deepen, enrich, and mature the Christian faith of college and university men and women through commitment to Jesus Christ and his Church and to assist them in their service and leadership to the world, in and through the Church.

c) To witness in the campus community to the mission, message, and life of the Church.

¶ **1041.** 1. The intercollegiate Christian movement represents an ecumenical approach to the campus ministry. The United Methodist Church recognizes this movement as represented nationally in the **University Christian Movement** and internationally in the **World Student Christian Federation.**

2. In carrying on its work in national and international fields, the department recognizes the University Christian Movement and the World Student Christian Federation as appropriate expressions of the intercollegiate Christian movement.

3. The department shall cooperate with the Annual Conferences in serving United Methodist students through such state, area, or regional units as the Annual Conference desires to maintain.

¶ **1042.** The **Department of the Ministry** shall have primary responsibility for the work of the division in relation to the schools of theology and the preparation of the ministry of the Church and shall be responsible for promoting theological education in the Church.

¶ **1043.** The purpose of the Department of the Ministry shall be:

1. To study the problems of ministerial supply for The United Methodist Church, to cooperate with other denominational agencies in programs seeking to recruit young men for the Christian ministry, and to promote Ministry Sunday.

2. To study the needs of United Methodist ministry in the field of education and training and to make recommendations for meeting them.

3. To provide the ministerial courses of study.

4. To cooperate with the Boards of the Ministry of the Annual Conferences by providing guidance in the counseling and examination of ministerial students on the high school and college levels.

5. To recommend courses of reading and study for all the ministers subsequent to ordination and to devise means of in-service training.

6. To maintain the educational, moral, and religious standards of

the ministry of The United Methodist Church and to study problems relating to ministerial ethics and moral principles.

7. To consider problems relating to the ecclesiastical status of ministers so far as these problems may affect denominational policies concerning the ministry and to make recommendations accordingly.

¶ **1044.** 1. The division shall elect, on nomination of the general secretary, a **director** of the department, who shall be responsible for that part of the program of the board concerned with the enlistment and educational preparation of candidates for the ministry and with the conference relations of the ministers. In matters pertaining to ministerial education he shall serve as liaison officer between the general boards and other agencies and the schools of theology of the Church.

2. The division shall elect, on nomination of the general secretary, such associate directors as are deemed necessary to assist in the program of the department.

¶ **1045.** The department shall be responsible for: maintenance of the educational standards for the ministry (*see* ¶¶ 301-80), development and promotion of a program of ministerial enlistment and guidance (in cooperative relationship with the Interboard Committee on Enlistment for Church Occupations), the educational preparation of candidates for the ministry, relationships with the Annual Conference Boards of the Ministry (¶ 665.4), schools and programs of continuing education and inspiration for ministers, supervision of the courses of study as described in ¶ 1046; standards and procedures in regard to conference relations, and interdenominational relationships that relate to the ministry, such as with the Department of Ministry of the National Council of Churches.

¶ **1046.** 1. The department shall prescribe the ministerial courses of study which shall include studies required for license to preach, introductory studies, and the **four-year course of study.** It shall also provide advanced courses of study for preachers who have finished the above courses and must meet the requirements of ¶ 333.3.

2. It shall provide and administer special courses of study and examinations in United Methodist history, doctrine, and polity for candidates who are theological school graduates lacking seminary credits in these fields (¶ 333.3.).

3. It shall cooperate with the Boards of the Ministry and other conference boards in organizing, financing, and conducting **pastors' schools** (short-term schools to provide programs of inspiration and instruction for all ministers) and in the development of other opportunities for continuing education.

4. All work in the courses of study for candidates for elder in full connection (¶¶ 331-37) and for lay preachers and deacons seeking renewal of license (¶ 320), including lay pastors qualifying for appointment (¶¶ 348-49), shall be taken under the direction of the Department of the Ministry in an approved course-of-study school. (For exceptional provisions for taking the ministerial course of study by correspondence see ¶ 348.1.)

5. It shall, in cooperation with the United Methodist schools of theology, administer **correspondence work** in the courses of study described in § 1 above.

¶ 1047.   The department shall certify the course offerings in non–United Methodist seminaries for meeting the requirements in United Methodist history, doctrine, and polity specified in ¶ 333.3 and shall provide the Boards of the Ministry with a list of the courses approved. It shall consult with the United Methodist schools of theology in regard to courses meeting these requirements (¶ 1053).

¶ 1048.   The department shall develop and promote a program of selective enlistment and guidance of candidates for the ministry in cooperation with the Interboard Committee on Enlistment for Church Occupations, the United Methodist schools of theology, the Boards of the Ministry, and the bishops, district superintendents, counselors with preministerial students in the colleges and universities, and directors of Wesley Foundations. It shall also sponsor and promote conferences on the ministry in the Annual Conferences in cooperation with the Interboard Committee on Enlistment for Church Occupations and the respective bishops, conference Committees or Commissions on Christian Higher Education and Campus Ministry, conference Boards of Education, and Boards of the Ministry.

¶ 1049.   The department shall be responsible for a continuing study of the ministry, and a report of its findings shall be given to each General Conference.

¶ 1050.   1. The Department of the Ministry shall maintain active relationship with the Boards of the Ministry of the Annual Conferences and with the theological schools of The United Methodist Church.

2. It shall also be affiliated with the appropriate departments of interdenominational bodies.

¶ 1051. The work of the department shall be supported from the general benevolences of the Church. The division shall recommend to the Council on World Service and Finance, as items apart from its own budget, the amounts of financial support which should be allocated for ministerial education.

Schools of Theology

¶ 1052. 1. The **schools of theology** of The United Methodist Church are established and maintained for the education of ministers. They exist for the benefit of the whole Church, and support shall be provided by the Church as a part of its general benevolent giving. (*See* ¶ 1029.2.)

2. For the purpose of providing for the better support of these schools, the Division of Higher Education, in consultation with their administrative officers, shall establish budget askings for their adequate support, and the amount necessary for such support shall be added as a separate item in the askings of the General Board of Education from the benevolence funds as determined by the authoritative body; *provided*, however, that the receiving of appropriations of such funds through the division shall not debar the schools from soliciting additional funds from the Annual and Jurisdictional Conferences as a part of the program of Christian higher education.

3. No school of theology or department of theology in a college or university shall be established without first submitting its proposed organization and classification to the University Senate for prior approval. (*See* ¶ 1064.)

¶ 1053. United Methodist schools of theology, in addition to preparing their students for effective service for Christ and the Church, shall acquaint them with the current programs of The United Methodist Church, such as its educational, missionary, social, and other service programs, and with the organizations and terminology of the Church. Each school of theology, in consultation with the Department of the Ministry, shall provide in its curriculum the courses in United Methodist history, doctrine, and polity specified in ¶ 333.3. *(See also* ¶ 1047.)

¶ **1054.** The United Methodist schools of theology share with the Boards of the Ministry the responsibility for the selection and education of young people for admission to the Annual Conferences.

1. It is recommended therefore that these schools, before admitting a candidate for the United Methodist ministry as a divinity student, shall *(a)* inquire into his personal character and promise of usefulness in the ministry and *(b)* require a letter of recommendation from the Board of the Ministry of the Annual Conference in which he resides.

2. It is further recommended that when such a candidate has been admitted, the school shall give careful attention to his progress in studies and his personal and religious development to determine whether he should be continued in his preparation for the ministry. When a candidate's progress is adjudged to be unsatisfactory, he should not be permitted to continue. Notification of the termination of his relationship in the school shall be given by the school to the registrar of the Board of the Ministry where his Annual Conference relations are recorded.

UNIVERSITY SENATE

¶ **1055.** The **University Senate** shall be the accrediting and standardizing agency for all the educational institutions related to The United Methodist Church.

¶ **1056.** 1. The senate shall be composed of twenty-one persons, not members of the General Board of Education, who are actively engaged in the work of education and are fitted by training and experience for the technical work of establishing standards and evaluating educational institutions in accordance with such standards. Eleven of these members shall be elected quadrennially by the General Board of Education, and ten shall be appointed by the Council of Bishops. Due regard shall be given to representation from the various types of institutions included in the senate's classification of educational institutions. If in consequence of the retirement of a member from educa-

tional work or for any other cause a vacancy occurs during the quadrennium, it shall be filled by the agency by which the retiring member
was elected at its next meeting.

2. The general secretary of the Division of Higher Education
shall be the **executive secretary** of the senate. He shall convene
it for organization at the beginning of each quadrennium. The senate
shall elect its own officers, including a president, a vice-president, and
a recording secretary, and may appoint such committees and may
delegate to them such powers as are incident to its work. Thereafter it
shall meet annually at such time and place as it may determine. Special
meetings may be called on the written request of five members or at the
discretion of the president and the executive secretary.

¶ 1057. The senate shall establish and assist in maintaining
standards for the educational institutions related to The United Methodist Church and shall sustain an advisory relation to the Division of
Higher Education in matters of educational institutions. It shall prepare and publish annually a proper classification of all educational
institutions in the United States and Canada which are related to The
United Methodist Church. Such classification shall comprise the official
senate list of educational institutions related to the Church in the
United States and Canada, and on the basis of this list the division
shall be governed in its work.

¶ 1058. At its discretion the senate shall investigate the objectives, academic programs, educational standards, personnel, plant and
equipment, business and management practices, financial program,
public relations, student personnel services, religious life, and church
relations of any designated educational institution claiming or adjudged to be related to The United Methodist Church and shall report
to the sponsoring board or agency through the Division of Higher
Education decisions as to whether or not the institution is such as to
justify its official recognition and continued financial support by the
Church.

¶ 1059. The senate shall act as consultant and counselor on all
educational matters to all educational institutions related to the
Church and as it deems necessary shall make to the sponsoring board
or other agency of the Church through the Division of Higher Education, to the conference Boards of Education or to other constituent

bodies, recommendations leading to their improvement or accreditation. Failure of any educational institution to make reasonable progress in complying with said recommendations of the senate may render the institution ineligible for further support by the Division of Higher Education or by its related board or other agency, Annual Conference or Conferences.

¶ **1060.** The senate, as the accrediting agent for all educational institutions of the Church, may investigate on its own initiative or at the written request of any general board of the Church, conference Board of Education, or institutional Board of Trustees, the educational work of an institution related to said board and shall report to the board concerned its recommendations as to what specific changes or improvements should be made.

¶ **1061.** After consultation with the officers of the senate the Division of Higher Education shall provide in its annual budget for the expense of the senate as it may deem sufficient, except that expenses incurred by the senate on behalf of any other board of the Church shall be borne by that board.

¶ **1062.** It shall be the duty of the senate to classify educational institutions in the United States and Canada related to The United Methodist Church as follows:

1. Universities
2. Schools of theology
3. Four-year colleges
4. Two-year colleges
5. Secondary schools
6. Other schools

The senate shall be consulted before any change in the classification of an institution is proposed.

¶ **1063.** It shall be the duty of the executive secretary of the senate to secure from each educational institution related to The United Methodist Church such information as may be needed by the senate for an understanding of the status, work, and progress of the institution. This information shall be supplied on forms approved by the senate.

¶ **1064.** 1. In cooperation with the Division of Higher Education, the senate shall study population growth and trends and consider recommendations to the Annual Conferences concerning the need for new institutions of learning and the discontinuance, reopening, relocation, and merger of existing institutions. (*See* ¶ 1030.)

2. There shall be only as many institutions of higher education as can be supported adequately on a fully accredited basis, as determined by the University Senate.

3. All institutions of higher education should be adequately endowed. Endowment funds shall be kept sacred for the purpose for which they are given.

4. Within the United States and Canada no educational institution or foundation of The United Methodist Church shall hereafter be established or reopened until its plans and organization shall have been approved by the senate. No Annual or Provisional Annual Conference shall acquire or affiliate with a school, college, university, or other educational institution through any board or society unless the approval of the senate shall have been obtained previously and unless in the judgment of the Division of Higher Education there is reasonable assurance of financial support sufficient to equip and maintain the institution in the classification approved for it by the senate. (*See* ¶ 1030.2.)

Division of the Local Church

¶ **1065.** 1. There shall be a **Division of the Local Church,** which shall be responsible for the development and promotion of a comprehensive and unified educational ministry for the Church. The division shall devote itself to studying, supervising, strengthening, and extending the educational ministry of the Church. The educational work of the Church shall be developed and function through the structure adopted for the local church.

2. The ministry of Christian education shall be comprehensive and unified and shall seek to encourage persons to commitment to Christ and membership in his Church and to a knowledge of the Holy Scriptures, the Christian religion, and the Christian church. The educational ministry shall provide for study, worship, fellowship, and service including social, recreational, evangelistic, stewardship, and missionary activities as education in the Christian way of life.

3. The division shall establish and maintain standards and shall give direction to the program of Christian education in the local church in accordance with ¶ 158.1, in camps, in conferences, and elsewhere.

4. The division, in cooperation with the Division of Curriculum Resources, shall seek to inform the Church on all phases of church-school work.

5. The division shall provide for instruction concerning the significance and work of the Church and the functions of its various officers and boards, and for education for churchmanship with the cooperation of other agencies.

6. The division shall seek ways and means of promoting the membership and attendance of children, youth, young adults, and adults in all Christian education activities.

7. The division shall promote observance of special days and other occasions related to Christian education.

8. The division shall organize as may be necessary for carrying on its educational ministry throughout the whole life-span of persons.

¶ **1066.** 1. The division shall establish standards defining membership and attendance in the church school and governing the maintenance of the membership roll.

2. It shall develop standards governing the work of local-church directors, ministers, and associates of Christian education and educational assistants and concerning their certification as provided in ¶ 1115. It is authorized to cooperate with the Christian Educators Fellowship of The United Methodist Church.

3. It shall develop standards governing the work of local-church directors, ministers, and associates of music and music assistants and shall serve as may be possible in advancing this field of work in the Church. It shall cooperate with the **National Fellowship of Methodist Musicians of The United Methodist Church.**[10]

4. It shall develop standards governing all types of camping in regard to physical facilities, program, and leadership. All camps shall be available to persons without regard to race or national origin.

---

[10] A change in the name of this organization will be voted by the entire membership at their biennial convocation meeting in August, 1969.

5. It shall provide guidance for local churches in equipment, arrangement, and design for church-school buildings or rooms.

¶ **1067.** 1. The division shall have supervision of all the training processes of the Church, both for lay and ministerial workers, except where these have been specifically delegated to other agencies.

2. It shall provide programs for the training of pastors, parents, teachers, officials, and others in the work of the local church and shall promote these programs through various types of training schools, correspondence work, and such other agencies as it may see fit to establish. It shall have authority also to promote and conduct educational conferences, councils, assemblies, and other meetings in the interest of church schools and Christian education of children, youth, and adults, and in the interest of improved leadership.

¶ **1068.** The division shall cooperate with other agencies as follows:

1. It shall cooperate with other general boards and agencies in the promotion of stewardship, evangelism, missionary education, and social action.

2. It shall plan and provide education in communication processes and the use of learning resources.

3. It shall, in cooperation with the Interboard Committee on Enlistment for Church Occupations and the Division of Higher Education, recruit and give guidance to volunteers for Christian service. It shall offer training courses and other aids designed to provide vocational guidance.

4. It shall, with the cooperation of the Division of Higher Education, give guidance in the training of directors and ministers of education and of music (¶ 1066.2-.3).

5. It shall, with the Division of Curriculum Resources and the Division of Higher Education, work through the Program-Curriculum Committee in determining and developing the curriculum for the educational ministry of the Church, including courses of leadership education.

¶ **1069.** 1. The division shall have authority to cooperate with the Jurisdictional and Annual Conference Boards of Education, the Division of Curriculum Resources, the Division of Higher Education, and other agencies in the promotion of the **United Methodist Conference on Christian Education.**

2. It shall have authority to sponsor and participate in general conventions or convocations on Christian education, holding at least one during each quadrennium.

¶ **1070.** The division shall have authority to develop within the Church organizations of youth, nationally and in conferences, districts, and/or subdivisions of districts; *provided,* however, that such organizations shall include all groups within a given age range within the local church. (*See* ¶ 1081.)

¶ **1071.** The division shall be authorized to project and promote plans for church-school extension throughout the Church and to contribute to the support of Christian education in mission territory.

¶ **1072.** The division shall have responsibility to develop, in cooperation with jurisdictional Boards of Education, a general program and plan to further within the Annual Conferences all the interests of Christian education within the purview of the division.

¶ **1073.** 1. The division shall have authority to receive and administer funds, gifts, or bequests that may be committed to it for any portion of its work and to solicit, establish, and administer any special funds that may be found necessary for the carrying out of its plans and policies.

2. The division may solicit special contributions in the church schools in its own area of work. Only such special solicitations as are approved by the advisory committee of the Division of the Local Church of the Board of Education may be promoted in the church schools.

COOPERATION WITH OTHER BOARDS

¶ **1074.** 1. There shall be an Interboard Committee on Town and Country Ministries. (*See* ¶ 1353.)

2. There shall be an Interboard Committee on Christian Education. (*See* ¶¶ 1347-49.)

3. There shall be a Joint Committee on Architecture. (*See* ¶ 1354.)

4. There shall be a Joint Commission on Cooperation and Counsel (*see* ¶ 1356) to continue the historic relationship between The

Methodist Church and The Christian Methodist Episcopal Church.

¶ **1075.** There shall be an Interboard Committee on Missionary Education for the purpose of promoting effective cooperation between the Board of Missions and the Board of Education. (*See* ¶¶ 1350-52.)

¶ **1076.** In the discharge of its responsibility for Christian education in The United Methodist Church, the Division of the Local Church may establish, and provide for participation by church-school groups in, a fund (or funds) for missions and Christian education in the United States and overseas. Plans for the allocation of, administration of, and education for this fund (s) shall be developed cooperatively by such means as the Board of Missions and the Division of the Local Church of the Board of Education shall determine.

¶ **1077.** 1. There shall be a **General Committee on Family Life,** which shall be related administratively to the Division of the Local Church and shall cooperate with its staff for Christian family program development to promote activities of a creative nature that can be most efficiently engaged in by the boards working together, including the planning of national, regional, and area conferences on family life. (*See* ¶ 1117.)

2. The committee shall be composed of four bishops, one of whom shall be designated chairman, three ministers, and three laymen elected by the Council of Bishops, and staff members or other representatives elected by general agencies, as follows: five from the Division of the Local Church and two from the Division of Curriculum Resources of the Board of Education; two from the Board of Evangelism; one each from the World and National Divisions, and one staff and one board member from the Women's Division of the Board of Missions; one from each division of the Board of Christian Social Concerns; and one each from the Board of the Laity, the Division of Television, Radio, and Film Communication, the Board of Health and Welfare Ministries, the Commission on Chaplains and Related Ministries, and The Methodist Publishing House. In addition three ministers and three laymen at large shall be elected by the committee.

3. The program of the committee shall be financed by the General Administration Fund according to the budget adopted by the General Conference.

¶ **1078.** 1. The **Joint Committee on Confirmation Resources** shall be created by the Board of Education and the Board of Evangelism. The purpose of the committee shall be to prepare resources for use in the local church. This committee shall annually report its actions to the Board of Education and the Board of Evangelism. All confirmation resources shall be coordinated with the church-school curriculum through the representatives of this committee on the Program-Curriculum Committee. These resources shall be designed for use in special classes for various age groups and for various lengths of time, and there shall be ample resources for extended courses.

2. The committee shall be composed of two bishops, the general secretaries of the Division of the Local Church and of the Division of Curriculum Resources of the Board of Education, the general secretary and an additional staff member of the Board of Evangelism, two representatives named by the Program-Curriculum Committee, the book editor, the director of the Department of the Ministry, one representative from the Commission on Worship, and six other qualified persons, three of whom shall be elected by the Board of Evangelism and three by the Board of Education.

¶ **1079.** There shall be a **Joint Committee on Architecture,** composed of staff personnel as follows: four staff members of the National Division of the Board of Missions, including representatives of the work of church extension and architecture; the executive secretary of the Section of Program Development; the staff member responsible for design of church-school buildings; one representative elected by the General Commission on Worship; and two others elected by the Division of the Local Church of the Board of Education. It shall have authority to prepare standards for the architecture of churches, parsonages, and religious educational buildings and to recommend them to the cooperating boards and is authorized, under such provisions as the boards may agree on, to offer counsel in the erection of such buildings. It shall meet annually and at such other times as its work may require. (*See* ¶ 1354.)

¶ **1080.** The youth ministry of The United Methodist Church shall include all persons from the seventh grade through senior high school (approximately twelve through eighteen years of age), who are currently or potentially associated with the Church or any of its activities. This ministry shall take into account all the interests of youth and all the interests of the Church so that youth may be conscious that together their lives are identified with the total life of the Church. The Division of the Local Church shall be responsible for providing guidance in organizing and aiding the varied forms of this ministry in the Annual Conferences and local churches. Provision shall be made for ministry with United Methodist youth to be expressed through organized groups, classes, and projects, and other appropriate ways. The statistical record shall include only youth who are members of a class or group within this ministry.

¶ **1081.** 1. The Division of the Local Church, with the cooperation of the other agencies of The United Methodist Church which have an interest in youth work, is authorized to sponsor a **national youth organization,** whose functions shall include the following:

a) Initiating and supporting special plans and projects at the national level which are of particular interest to youth.

b) Providing for the free expression of the convictions of the Church's youth on issues vital to them.

c) Cooperating with the United Methodist Council on Youth Ministry in making recommendations regarding the youth ministry of the Church.

d) Requesting suggestions from Annual Conference youth organizations and making recommendations to general board nominating committees of youth for membership on general boards.

2. The membership of such an organization should represent the youth of the Annual Conferences and the staff of the participating agencies. Details of membership and organization shall be determined by a group called for this purpose by the sponsoring agencies.

3. Its financial support shall be provided by the general agencies which cooperate in sponsoring it.

4. For administrative purposes the organization (and staff, if any) shall be related to the Division of the Local Church of the Board of Education.

¶ **1082.** The **United Methodist Council on Youth Ministry** shall be responsible for unifying the ministry with youth throughout the Church.

¶ **1083.** 1. In the discharge of its responsibility for youth work in The United Methodist Church, the Division of the Local Church shall establish and provide for participation of youth in local churches and on every level of youth ministry in the **Youth Service Fund.** Local treasurers shall send the full amount of the Youth Service Fund offerings to the treasurer of the Annual Conference, by whom it shall be sent monthly to the treasurer of the General Board of Education, to be directed for missions and youth work as follows: 45 percent for missions through the World and National Divisions of the Board of Missions; 25 percent for Christian education in mission fields; 15 percent returned to the Annual Conferences for youth work therein; 15 percent for Christian education through the Division of the Local Church.

2. There shall be an **Administrative Committee on the Youth Service Fund,** consisting of the associate general secretaries of the three divisions and joint commission of the Board of Missions, the general secretary and the directors of youth ministries of the Division of the Local Church, the executive secretary of the Interboard Committee on Missionary Education, and the staff member responsible for Youth Service Fund education. The committee shall meet at least once a year. It shall have responsibility for annual review of the plans for Youth Service Fund education and of the distribution of funds, making recommendations to the responsible agencies for necessary adjustments within the allocations set forth in § 1 above. It shall give special attention to creative and new developments relative to the use of the fund and to the requests of youth thereon, making provision for youth and adult workers with youth to function in advisory capacities. It shall review and recommend the annual budget to be used for Youth Service Fund education by the Youth Service Fund office and shall nominate for election by the General Board of Education and confirmation by the Board of Missions such staff as may be necessary. The office shall be lodged in the Division of the Local Church. The staff shall hold membership within this division and likewise in the Joint Commission on Education and Cultivation of the Board of Missions. The committee shall report annually to the two boards and for information annually to the Interboard Committee on Missionary Education.

3. The policies under which the Youth Service Fund office op-

erates shall be those agreed on by all the agencies related thereto. Youth Service Fund education shall be planned and carried out in harmony with the philosophy of missionary education expressed through the program and work of the Interboard Committee on Missionary Education and also with the philosophy of unity in the total youth program of the church. (*See* ¶¶ 1080, 1351.)

¶ **1084.** 1. There shall be an **Interboard Committee on Enlistment for Church Occupations,** which shall give leadership in initiating, correlating, and maintaining for the Church a comprehensive enlistment program with appropriate record systems and in developing a philosophy of Christian vocation. It shall develop plans and educational procedures for the effective enlistment and guidance of persons in church-related occupations and shall seek to interpret to the Church through its several agencies the total field of vocation in Christian terms. It shall lead in discovering and making known the various needs of the Church at home and abroad and shall be responsible for the development of a recruiting procedure which shall seek, through and in cooperation with all the appropriate agencies of the Church, to enlist persons for Christian service.

2. The committee shall be composed of four bishops, named by the Council of Bishops; five representatives from the Board of Education (two from the Division of the Local Church, one from the Division of Curriculum Resources, the director of the Department of Campus Ministry, and the director of the Department of the Ministry); four from the Board of Missions; two from the Board of Health and Welfare Ministries; and one each from the National Association of Schools and Colleges of The United Methodist Church, the Methodist Association of Theological Schools, the Division of Stewardship and Finance of the Board of the Laity, the Board of Christian Social Concerns, the Board of Evangelism, and the Commission on Chaplains and Related Ministries, elected by the respective agencies. The committee may elect five persons at large, three of whom shall be pastors serving local churches.

3. The committee shall select from its membership an **executive committee,** consisting of its chairman, the executive secretary of the committee, one bishop (unless the chairman is a bishop), one pastor from the members at large, one representative from the Department

of the Ministry, one from the Board of Health and Welfare Ministries, two from the Board of Education, and two (one a woman) from the Board of Missions.

4. There shall be an **executive secretary** for the committee, elected by the Board of Education on nomination of the committee. He shall be administratively related to the Division of the Local Church. He shall supervise and administer the work of the committee. He shall have staff relationship with the participating agencies of the committee as shall be necessary for the effective promotion of the program.

5. The expenses of the committee shall be met by the participating agencies on such ratio as developed by the committee and approved by the agencies.

CURRICULUM FOR THE EDUCATIONAL PROGRAM OF THE CHURCH

¶ **1085.** The educational program of the Church calls for a curriculum that is graded and based on sound educational principles and on the universal gospel of the living Christ. Such a curriculum shall be integrally related to the traditions, purposes, programs, and movements of the Church. It shall include the heritage of the faith, personal and social ethics, and mission through churchmanship, including worship, leadership education, stewardship, witness, and service.

¶ **1086.** *Program-Curriculum Committee.*—1. (*a*) There shall be a **Program-Curriculum Committee** of the General Board of Education. It shall formulate the philosophy and design for a curriculum for The United Methodist Church and for elements of program related to this curriculum. In its curriculum function the committee shall develop descriptions of teaching-learning units for use by children, youth, and adults in educational settings such as the church school, outdoor experiences, family life, leadership education, and others, formal and informal. In its program function the committee shall develop underlying assumptions and recommend plans concerning grouping, grading, educational settings, leadership enterprises, and teaching-learning theory as these are related to the curriculum.

b) The committee shall be administratively responsible to the Secretarial Council. The recommendations of the committee shall be presented to the General Board of Education for action.

c) The preparation of curriculum resources based on the descriptions of teaching-learning units developed by the committee shall be the responsibility of the Division of Curriculum Resources. The committee shall receive recommendations for study materials from the Board of the Laity, the Board of Missions, and other agencies that develop teaching-learning units.

d) Primary responsibility for implementation of program plans developed by the committee shall reside in the Division of the Local Church.

2. The Program-Curriculum Committee shall consist of thirty-five voting members selected as follows:

a) Thirteen members at large (one of whom shall be a bishop) chosen on the basis of training and experience in Christian education. The members at large shall be elected by the Board of Education on nomination of the Secretarial Council. Recommendations for members at large may be made to the Secretarial Council of the Board of Education by the general secretaries of the Boards of Evangelism, Laity, Missions, and Christian Social Concerns, and by other agencies of the Church.

b) One representative each from the Boards of Missions, Evangelism, Laity, and Christian Social Concerns. Appointments shall be made by the general secretary of each of these boards after consultation between the general secretary of each of the boards and the Secretarial Council of the Board of Education.

c) Eighteen ex officio members as follows: general secretary, Division of the Local Church, and five other members of his staff appointed by him; general secretary, Division of Higher Education; general secretary, Division of Curriculum Resources, and five other members of his staff appointed by him; executive secretary, Interboard Committee on Missionary Education; executive secretary, Interboard Committee on Enlistment for Church Occupations; publisher, The United Methodist Church; vice-president in charge of publishing, The Methodist Publishing House; book editor, The United Methodist Church.

3. The general secretaries of the Boards of Education, Evangelism, Laity, Missions, and Christian Social Concerns, and other agencies, may nominate staff members and other competent persons as consulting

members of the committee. These nominees are subject to election by the General Board of Education. Consulting members shall have full privilege of membership except for voting on final recommendations presented in plenary sessions.

4. The work of the Program-Curriculum Committee shall be financed by the Division of the Local Church, the Division of Curriculum Resources, and the Division of Higher Education in amounts to be mutually agreed upon.

EDUCATION IN THE LOCAL CHURCH

¶ 1087. The program for education in the local church is described in ¶¶ 158.1 and 159.1.

DIVISION OF CURRICULUM RESOURCES

¶ 1088. There shall be a **Division of Curriculum Resources,** which shall have responsibility for the development of curriculum resources for use in the educational ministry of the Church. Curriculum resources, which are the study and related materials used in Christian education, are distinguished from program guidance resources for carrying out the procedures of Christian education. The curriculum resources shall be designed to help guide the development of a balanced, comprehensive, and unified curriculum in the local church in order that all persons may "be aware of and grow in their understanding of God, especially of his redeeming love as revealed in Jesus Christ, and that they respond in faith and love—to the end that they may know who they are and what their human situation means, increasingly identifying themselves as sons of God, in every relationship, fulfill their common discipleship in the world, and abide in the Christian hope." [11]

¶ 1089. The division shall participate with the Program-Curriculum Committee in the development of statements of theological positions and of Christian education philosophy and in curriculum planning and building.

---

[11] From *Foundations of Christian Teaching in United Methodist Churches* (Nashville: General Board of Education of The United Methodist Church, 1969).

¶ **1090.** The division shall reflect through its resources the official positions of The United Methodist Church as authorized by the General Conference. It shall give appropriate support and guidance through its resources to the total life and work of the Church.

¶ **1091.** The division shall issue a list of the curriculum materials that are approved by the Program-Curriculum Committee for use in United Methodist church schools. Such materials shall include the resources prepared through the Board of Education and may include resources prepared by other agencies.

¶ **1092.** The division may cooperate with other denominations through the National Council of Churches of Christ in the United States of America or in other ways in curriculum planning. It may explore cooperative publication wherever both the division and the publisher find this to be practicable and in harmony with editorial and publishing policies.

¶ **1093.** The division may cooperate in curriculum planning and building with Christian bodies overseas through such groups as the Interboard Committee on Christian Education, the National Council of Churches of Christ in the United States of America, the World Council of Christian Education and Sunday School Association, and the World Council of Churches.

¶ **1094.** The division is authorized to cooperate with the Jurisdictional and Annual Conference Boards of Education and with organizations of United Methodist Church educational workers.

¶ **1095.** The division shall cooperate through its representatives in the work of the Interboard Committee on Missionary Education (¶ 1350), the Interboard Committee on Christian Education (¶ 1347), the Interboard Committee on Enlistment for Church Occupations (¶ 1084), the General Committee on Family Life (¶ 1077), the Joint Committee on Confirmation Resources (¶ 1078), The United Methodist Council on Youth Ministry (¶ 1082), and the Division of Television, Radio, and Film Communication (¶¶ 834-35).

¶ **1096.** The division shall work through a **Department of Children's Publications, a Department of Youth Publications, a Department of Adult Publications, a Department of General Publications,** and such other departments as may be determined.

¶ **1097.** The **general secretary** of the division, who shall be the editor of church-school publications (¶ 1016), shall be elected quadrennially by the Board of Education upon nomination of a joint committee composed of the president of the Board of Education and two members from the Division of Curriculum Resources and the chairman and two other members of the Board of Publication. The election of the editor shall be subject to confirmation by the Board of Publication. A vacancy in this office shall be filled by the same procedure.

¶ **1098.** The general secretary shall appoint his assistants and report the same to the board. He shall be responsible for the administration of the work of the division.

¶ **1099.** In the development of formats and types of curriculum resources the Division of Curriculum Resources shall work cooperatively with the Board of Publication, which agency has final responsibility in relation to publishing and financial matters. The division shall recommend additions or changes in the publications to be produced, within the provisions of ¶ 971. These resources may include a variety of types, such as periodicals, books, booklets, graphic resources, recordings, and other audio-visual resources.

¶ **1100.** The editor of church-school publications and his staff shall be responsible for the content of resources and shall work cooperatively with the publisher in the design, the layout, and the handling of proofs and equivalent steps in the case of nonprinted resources. The editor shall be responsible to the Board of Education through the Division of Curriculum Resources regarding editorial policies and content of resources. In matters of publication and financing he shall be responsible to the Board of Publication.

¶ **1101.** The resources of the Division of Curriculum Resources shall be published, manufactured, and distributed by The Methodist Publishing House as set forth in ¶¶ 967-75. The interpretation and promotion of these resources shall be a joint responsibility of the Board of Education and the Board of Publication.

¶ **1102.** The publisher or his representative shall sit with the Division of Curriculum Resources for the consideration of matters pertaining to the joint interests of the Division of Curriculum Resources and the Board of Publication and shall have the privilege of the floor without vote.

Jurisdictional Boards

¶ **1103.** In each jurisdiction there may be a **jurisdictional Board of Education,** auxiliary to the general board, as the Jurisdictional Conference may determine. (*See* ¶¶ 26.3, 625.)

Annual Conference Boards

¶ **1104.** 1. In each Annual Conference there shall be a **conference Board of Education,** elected by the conference to foster and direct a plan of Christian education that encourages an experience of Christ and the development of a well-rounded Christian character and that gives children, youth, young adults, and adults a knowledge of and experience in the Christian faith as motivation for Christian service in the Church, the community, and the world; to promote the cause of higher education under Christian auspices; and to aid persons in their preparation for the Christian ministry and other church occupations. It shall promote church-school extension, the program of Christian education, and the use of church school literature approved by the General Board of Education.

2. The board shall be auxiliary to the jurisdictional board, if any, and to the general board and shall cooperate with them and the Annual Conference Program Council.

3. The board may be incorporated under the laws of the state (or all the states) within whose bounds the conference is located. The board may receive gifts for its work. It may hold title to property for use in its work and to housing for its personnel. It shall report to each session of the conference on the legal and financial status and physical condition of all such property.

4. Each conference shall set apart a portion of a session in which the interests of Christian education shall be adequately considered.

¶ **1105.** The board shall be composed of: (1) an equal number of laymen and ministers elected quadrennially, the number and manner of election to be determined by the conference; (2) three youth, one of whom shall be president of the conference Council on Youth Ministry, and two others elected biennially by the conference youth organization, all of whom shall be eighteen years of age or younger at the time of their selection, and one student chosen by the state or regional student organization operating within the conference territory; (3) the president of the conference Young Adult Fellowship, or in the absence of a fellowship, one young adult churchman between the ages of eighteen and thirty; (4) one certified director or minister of Christian education employed in a local church within the conference and one director or minister of music; and (5) additional members, either clerical or lay, nominated at any time during the quadrennium by the board in such numbers as it may deem advisable, for election by the conference. Vacancies in the elected membership between conference sessions may be filled by the executive committee of the board, pending action of the next conference session. Care shall be taken to elect persons who by training and experience are qualified for the work of the board. The staff of the board, including the directors of education, shall have the privilege of the floor without vote. A majority of the members shall constitute a quorum. The members shall continue in office until their successors have been elected and the successor board organized.

¶ 1106. The officers of the board shall be a president, vice-president, recording secretary, and treasurer, all of whom shall be elected by the board for the quadrennium. The retiring board shall complete the business and make its annual report to the conference and shall make such recommendations as it may desire to the new board.

¶ 1107. The president shall be a presiding, not an administrative, officer. The treasurer, who shall be adequately bonded, shall receive and receipt for all funds of the board and shall disburse them by check as ordered by the board.

¶ 1108. There shall be an **executive committee** of the board, of which the president shall be a member. The executive committee shall meet on the call of the president or of one third of the members and shall transact all necessary business of the board ad interim under such regulations as the board may adopt. Its acts shall be reported to the annual meeting of the board. The executive committee shall act as the finance committee of the board and shall prepare a statement of its financial needs for the next year.

¶ 1109. 1. The board may elect a conference **director of educa-**

tion, after consultation with the bishop and his Cabinet, who shall then become a member of the Annual Conference Program Council staff (¶ 841.8) and who may serve two or more contiguous conferences. The conference program director (¶ 841.7) or another staff person may also serve as the director of education. The director shall have responsibility for the general oversight and promotion of all the work of the board and for the direction and supervision of age-level and family-life responsibilities of the conference Program Council. (*See* § 4 below.) He shall make a full report annually both to the board and to each of the three general secretaries of the general board.

2. The director shall give leadership and direction to (*a*) the ministries with children, youth, adults, and families; (*b*) the program of Christian education; (*c*) the chairman of the work area on education; and (*d*) the Commission on Education and the superintendent of the study program in the local churches.

3. The director shall actively cooperate in the promotion of knowledge about and support for all schools, colleges, universities, and seminaries related to the conference, the campus Christian movement, and campus ministry of the conference, region, or area. He shall assist in the establishment and support of such forms of this program as shall be approved by the conference board or boards in harmony with policies and procedures of the General Board of Education.

4. The director shall nominate, for election annually by the conference Program Council, staff persons who are to be responsible for age-level and family ministries. The director shall consult with the responsible officers of the conference youth organization before nominating conference directors of youth work.

5. The director shall nominate annually, after consultation with each district superintendent, the district directors, as provided in ¶ 1123.

¶ 1110. 1. The board shall be responsible for developing and promoting a conference program of Christian education which will provide guidance and help for all the agencies of Christian education within the bounds of the conference, such as: coordinators and councils of age-level and family ministries; the chairmen of the work areas and the Commission on Education; the superintendents of the study program; the church schools; and the related agencies of Christian education, including leadership training schools, Bible conferences, camps, assemblies, and institutes. It shall encourage and give help in the use of United Methodist curriculum resources. It shall promote and support those agencies which direct the cause of higher education under Christian auspices and shall provide for the campus Christian movement and campus ministry related to the conference.

2. The board shall see that the first Sunday of Christian Education Week, or some other day designated by the Annual Conference, is observed in each local church as **Christian Education Sunday**, for the purpose of emphasizing the importance of Christian education and for receiving an offering for the program of its local-church division. (*See* ¶¶ 158.1 and 162.1*c*.)

¶ **1111.** 1. The board, in cooperation with other conference agencies, shall be responsible for developing and recommending to the Annual Conference long-range plans for the procurement of camp and conference properties in accordance with standards of camping developed by the General Board of Education. The development and operational policies of all camp and conference properties shall be under the direction of the conference board, or organizations delegated by it, in cooperation with other conference agencies.

2. On recommendation of the board and in cooperation with other conference agencies, the Annual Conference may constitute a **conference Committee on Camps and Conferences,** composed of the director and three or more members of the board, of whom one shall be a youth and one a young adult; the conference directors of camps and conferences, children's ministry, youth ministry, and adult ministry; one or more district superintendents elected by the Cabinet; the chairmen of district Committees on Camps and Conferences (¶ 1124) ; a representative of the trustees of any camp or conference properties of the board (*see* § 1 above) ; one representative each from the conference Board of Trustees and any other incorporated trustees holding title to properties used extensively in the Christian education program of camping, conferences, and related enterprises of the Annual Conference or of the districts and a representative each from the conference Women's Society of Christian Service and the conference Board of the Laity. Other persons may be added on the basis of qualifications to meet specific needs.

3. The committee may select, develop, and operate properties as charged by the board and authorized by the Annual Conference; develop and recommend to the board policies and long-range plans for the selection, development, and operation of campsites and facilities to meet program needs; recommend fund-raising procedures for the purchase and development of sites and facilities; and work with district Committees on Camps and Conferences and with other denominations and agencies as directed by the board.

¶ **1112.** The president, or someone designated by him, shall present to the Commission on World Service and Finance of the conference the financial needs for adequate support of the schools, colleges, universities, seminaries, campus Christian movements, Wesley Foundations, and other campus ministries related to the conference, as approved by the board on the recommendation of its Committee/Commission on Christian Higher Education and Campus Ministry. In accordance with the financial plan of the Church, an apportionment shall be allotted to the churches within the conference for the work of the conference Board of Education. Other sources of income shall be gifts, returns from special days, and receipts from missionary offerings in the church school. The board shall determine the distribution of the funds thus received to each of the general interests under the care of the board.

Note: For a description of the United Methodist Student Day offering, see ¶ 162.1e.

¶ **1113.** 1. A **Wesley Foundation,** as defined by the Board of Education, shall have a **Board of Directors** composed of members from the local campus-church community and members at large representing the interests of the Annual Conference or Conferences. They shall be elected by the Annual Conference or Conferences on nomination of the conference Board or Boards of Education.

2. The Board of Directors shall be responsible for the direction and administration of the foundation in accordance with the policies and standards established by the conference board or boards and the General Board of Education. The foundation shall be related functionally and cooperatively through its Board of Directors to the United Methodist local church or churches in the immediate vicinity of the college or university. The Board of Directors, when incorporated, may

hold property, according to the laws of The United Methodist Church and the state in which the foundation is located.

¶ **1114.** 1. The board shall constitute a **conference Committee on Christian Higher Education and Campus Ministry,** composed of not fewer than eight of its members. This committee shall have specific responsibility for developing knowledge of and support for the schools, colleges, universities, seminaries, Wesley Foundations, and other campus ministries related to The United Methodist Church and particularly those related to the conference.

2. An Annual Conference, at its discretion, may constitute a **conference Commission on Christian Higher Education and Campus Ministry,** which shall include the members of the Committee on Christian Higher Education and Campus Ministry, the bishop, Cabinet representatives, the conference director of education, secretary of the board, the state or regional director of the student movement and/or campus ministry within the conference, and up to twenty members at large elected by the commission for their experience and ability in the fields of education and campus ministry. They shall serve four years, except that ex officio membership shall coincide with term of office. The commission shall elect its officers quadrennially, and they shall serve until their successors are duly elected and qualified. It may employ such staff members as are deemed necessary for its work. The Annual Conference shall make provision for its expense as the conference may determine.

3. Two or more Annual Conferences may, on recommendation of their Boards of Education, join in constituting an **area or regional Committee or Commission on Christian Higher Education and Campus Ministry,** the membership of which shall be determined by the cooperating conferences, in consultation with their bishop or bishops, and shall include representatives of the conference Committee on Christian Higher Education and Campus Ministry.

4. The committee or commission shall:

a) Cooperate with the Division of Higher Education in the achievement of its objectives.

b) Make provision for such conferences, training courses, and study groups as will assist in meeting its responsibilities.

c) Report annually to the board and the Annual Conference on the programs of those institutions of learning, Wesley Foundations, campus Christian movements, and campus ministries related to the conference and supported by it, including a statement concerning the capital and current needs of each and their program of service in behalf of The United Methodist Church.

d) Recommend annually to the board, for presentation to the Annual Conference, a minimum goal for the support of educational institutions and Wesley Foundations, campus Christian movements and campus ministries or, if none are related to the conference, recommend the method of distributing to United Methodist educational institutions and campus ministries, either directly or through the Division of Higher Education, the funds raised for higher education and campus ministry.

e) The duties of the commission (area or regional Committee or Commission on Christian Higher Education and Campus Ministry) with reference to the campus ministry shall be: (1) to evaluate the campus ministry within its region; (2) to report its evaluation to the conference Board of Education; (3) to recommend improvements in facilities, program, finance, and personnel; (4) to approve the purchase or sale of property and the plans for any new building, including a parsonage, proposed by the Wesley Foundation (or its equivalent) and the financial program covering the liquidation of its cost (where deemed advisable, the commission may invite the chairman of the district Board of Church Location and Building in which the foundation making the proposal is located to serve in an advisory capacity as the commission studies the proposal and makes its recommendations); and (5) to cooperate in interpretation of the intercollegiate campus Christian movement. It shall be the task of this commission to work with the Commission on Education of the local church to assist the latter commission in defining its duties and discharging its responsibilities.

¶ 1115. 1. It shall be the duty of the board to determine whether applicants meet the standards of the general board for directors and ministers of Christian education and directors and ministers of music and to certify and keep a record of those who do. The board shall set up a committee or committees on these offices whose duties shall be (*a*) to review the credentials of candidates and make recommendations to the board for certification in harmony with the said standards and (*b*) to recommend to the board plans for institutes, conferences, and other occasions for fellowship and training for directors and ministers of Christian education, associates, and educational assistants, and for directors and ministers of music, associates, and music assistants, and others responsible for music in the local church. Whenever directors or ministers of Christian education and of music are serving in the Annual Conference, they shall be represented on this committee. All persons certified shall furnish to the board, on blanks provided by the general board, information for purposes of annual review and approval of status.

2. A roster of certified directors, associates, ministers of Christian education, educational assistants, and certified directors, associates, ministers of music, and music assistants shall be included in the annual report of the board and published in the conference journal. A person so certified may move to another Annual Conference and be recorded there without reestablishing status.

3. Certified directors and associates of Christian education and music may be consecrated and commissioned at a conference session or other suitable time.

¶ **1116.** The board may constitute a Committee on Leadership Development.

¶ **1117.** The board may constitute a **conference Committee on Family Life,** composed of the conference director of education and two members of the board; the conference directors of children's, youth, and adult ministry; one representative each from the conference Youth Fellowship and Young Adult Fellowship and from the conference Boards of the Laity and Evangelism; the secretary of Christian social relations of the conference Women's Society of Christian Service; and one district superintendent elected by the Cabinet. Special resource persons may be added as the committee shall determine. Its duty shall be to study the forces which affect family life within the conference and recommend to the board plans to strengthen family life. It shall be administratively related to the board and shall report to it annually. (*See* ¶ 1077.)

¶ **1118.** The board may constitute a **Committee on Use of**

United Methodist Curriculum Materials, composed of the conference director of education and one member of the board from each district. This committee shall encourage the adoption of United Methodist curriculum materials by any classes, groups, or church schools not now using them.

¶ **1119.** The board shall have authority, in cooperation with the conference Committee on Television, Radio, and Film Communication, to provide training conferences for selected persons in the District and Annual Conferences and local churches in the effective use of audio-visual materials and other learning resources.

¶ **1120.** The board shall have authority to cooperate with other conference boards in matters of common interest. It shall also have authority to cooperate with the General and jurisdictional Boards of Education and other agencies in the holding of the United Methodist Conference on Christian Education. (*See* ¶ 1069.)

¶ **1121.** The board shall report its proceedings and policies to the Annual Conference, including the treasurer's report showing all resources and liabilities of the board, its income, and its expenditures. Immediately following the conference session it shall report to the jurisdictional Board of Education, through its executive secretary, a summary of its acts and the names of its officers and salaried workers. It shall transmit to the jurisdictional board the names and addresses of superintendents of the study program and the officers of the district and conference organizations operating under the conference board and of youth assemblies and other organizations.

¶ **1122.** In each Annual Conference there shall be a **conference Council on Youth Ministry,** composed of both youth and adults. Its purpose shall be to strengthen the youth ministry of The United Methodist Church in the Annual Conference. It shall be under the sponsorship and the responsibility of the conference Board of Education, to which it shall report, and of the General Board of Education. It shall cooperate with the conference Program Council, with other agencies with which youth are concerned within the conference, and with the national youth organization (¶ 1081). The conference director of education of the conference board and the conference director of youth ministry shall be advisers to it.

DISTRICT ORGANIZATIONS

¶ **1123.** 1. In each district the Annual Conference shall elect annually a district director of adult ministry, of youth ministry, of children's ministry, and of family ministry and such others as may be desired, who, with the district superintendent, shall constitute the **district staff of Christian education** and shall be members of any district organization set up for the purpose of coordinating program. They shall be nominated by the director of the conference Board of Education, after consultation with the district superintendent, and the nominations shall be reported to the board for confirmation and transmittal to the Annual Conference. Interim vacancies shall be filled by the director in consultation with the district superintendent. These directors may be coordinate with the age-level and family-life directors in the local church (*see* ¶ 155).

2. The staff should consult with local churches, assisting them to design a program of Christian education, develop leadership, interpret resources, and evaluate local church activities.

¶ **1124.** 1. The District or Annual Conference may constitute a **district Committee on Camps and Conferences** on recommendation of the district staff of Christian education, in cooperation with other district agencies. The chairman shall be nominated and confirmed in the same manner as the district directors (¶ 1123). The committee shall include the district superintendent and other members of the district staff, at least one camp director or institute dean representing each age group actively involved in camps and conferences and related enterprises in the district, and other persons to meet specific needs.

2. Its responsibilities shall be: (*a*) to cooperate with the conference Committee on Camps and Conferences (¶ 1111.2) ; (*b*) to make available to pastors and superintendents of the local-church study program information as to suitable locations and recommended guidance materials relating to camping, conferences, and retreats; (*c*) to encourage and initiate training for such enterprises; (*d*) to interpret and assist the local church in implementing standards relating to program and leadership and to the use and care of any sites or facilities used for camping, planning conferences, and retreats; and (*e*) to refer to the district staff, for confirmation by the District Conference, nomi-

nations by the age-level directors of persons to serve as directors or deans of summer camps, institutes, or conferences sponsored by the district.

3. If the committee is charged with the development and/or operation of camp or conference facilities held in trust by the conference or district Board of Trustees, there shall be added to its membership a representative from such board. The selection, development, or improvement of any such properties, or of conference- or district-owned property, the title to which is vested in other incorporated boards but which is used primarily for Christian education enterprises of the district, shall be in harmony with the policies and standards of the conference and General Boards of Education.

4. District property may be acquired for use in the program of camps and conferences when authorized by the District or Annual Conference on recommendation of the district staff of Christian education after consultation with the conference Board of Education and in keeping with the standards of the general board.

Section VII. Board of Evangelism.

¶ 1125. *The Aim of Evangelism.*—The aim of evangelism is to bring all persons into living, active fellowship with God through Jesus Christ as divine Savior and Lord, and through the regenerating power of the Holy Spirit to gather them into the fellowship of the Church and lead them to express their Christian discipleship in every area of human life that the kingdom of God may be realized.

¶ 1126. *Evangelism Defined.*—Evangelism is the winning of persons to Jesus Christ as Savior and Lord. It is an attitude, a spirit, and a living faith that finds expression in a continuous cooperative effort on the part of the Holy Spirit and man to bring the individual into vital relationship with God and his fellowmen through faith in Jesus Christ, God's Son. It results in a definite personal experience of salvation, a growing sensitivity to the social relevance of the gospel, and a progressive building of Christlike character. It seeks to bring man into complete harmony with the will of God, into the fellowship of the Church, and into involvement in the world to be God's servant of reconciliation. It helps him to grow spiritually through the means of grace and to serve God in daily living.

Evangelism is the task of the whole Church. Every minister, department, agency, local church, and member of The United Methodist Church is responsible for its accomplishment.

¶ **1127.** *Incorporation.*—There shall be an incorporated **General Board of Evangelism** of The United Methodist Church, hereinafter called the board. It shall be incorporated under the laws of the state in which its headquarters are established by the General Conference. This corporation shall be the successor corporation to all prior corporations of the Board of Evangelism of The Methodist Church and of the Board of Evangelism of The Evangelical United Brethren Church.

Constitution

¶ **1128.** *Article 1. Name and Objectives.*—The name of this organization shall be the General Board of Evangelism of The United Methodist Church. Its objectives are evangelistic and are designed to diffuse the blessings of the gospel of the Lord Jesus Christ to all men by the promotion and support of all forms and phases of evangelism; to promote evangelistic understanding, interest, and zeal throughout the membership of The United Methodist Church; to promote the practice of intercession and of individual and family worship; and to stimulate the entire membership of the Church in worship, in prayer, and in Christian service.

¶ **1129.** *Article 2. Authority.*—The board shall organize quadrennially at its first meeting following the General Conference and shall have authority to regulate its own proceedings in accordance with its constitution and charter; to buy, acquire, receive (by gift, devise, or bequest), hold, sell, and dispose of property—real, personal and mixed; to secure, appropriate, and administer funds for its work; to sue and be sued; to elect the necessary officers and members of its staff, remove them for cause, and fill vacancies; to make bylaws in harmony with the Discipline of The United Methodist Church and the charter of the board. It shall have the right to do any and all things which shall be authorized by its charter; *provided* that in case of devises or gifts of real estate to this board in states where such devises or gifts are not valid when made to religious corporations, the board shall be empowered to name trustees for the purpose of receiving and taking title to such gifts or devises for the benefit of the board.

¶ 1130.   *Article 3.*—1. *Membership.*—The membership of the board shall be composed of one bishop from each jurisdiction, elected by the Council of Bishops; four lay persons (of whom at least two are to be women) and four ministers from each jurisdiction, elected by the Jurisdictional Conferences; a representative of the Women's Division of the Board of Missions, nominated by the Women's Division and elected by the board; a representative of the Board of the Laity, nominated by the Board of the Laity and elected by the board; a youth representative, nominated by the national youth organization and elected by the board; a student representative, nominated by the Department of Campus Ministry in consultation with United Methodist student leaders in the University Christian Movement and elected by the board; a seminary professor from among those teaching in United Methodist seminaries, elected by the board; and five lay persons and five ministers from the Church at large, elected by the board.

2. *Tenure of Office.*—The members of the board and the officers elected by the board shall serve for the quadrennium or until such time as their successors shall be elected.

¶ 1131.   *Article 4. Officers.*—The board shall elect from its membership the following officers for the quadrennium:

1. A president, who shall be a bishop. He shall make a report and present a program of work for the board to the Council of Bishops.

2. A vice-president, who shall be a bishop.

3. A recording secretary.

¶ 1132.   *Article 5. General Secretary.*—On nomination of the executive committee the board shall elect a **general secretary** for the quadrennium, who shall have general direction of the total program of evangelism. He shall acquaint himself with, and bring to the attention of The United Methodist Church, tested and approved methods of evangelism, and under the board's direction he shall foster experimentation and demonstration of additional evangelistic approaches consistent with the nature of the Christian gospel and the Church. He shall be the executive officer of the board.

He shall report annually to the board and quadrennially to the General Conference and shall promote and administer the various phases of work as developed and adopted by the Board of Evangelism.

¶ 1133. *Article 6. Other Executive Staff.*—On nomination by the general secretary and the executive committee the board shall elect such **associate** and **assistant general secretaries** as may be needed and the editor of *The Upper Room.*

¶ 1134. *Article 7. Treasurer.*—On nomination of the executive committee a **treasurer** shall be elected by the board for the quadrennium. He shall be a member of the executive staff and shall be properly bonded. He shall receive and hold all moneys of the board, deposit the same in a bank approved by the executive committee, disburse the same on order of the board, and make such investments and loans as are approved by the executive committee. He shall report the financial status of the board from time to time to the board and its executive committee, as he may be directed.

The general secretary, the treasurer, and the president of the board shall have power to execute on behalf of the board legal papers such as conveyances of real estate, releases or mortgages, transfers of securities, contracts, and all other legal documents.

¶ 1135. *Article 8. Meetings.*—1. The board shall meet for the purposes of organization and other necessary action quadrennially after the adjournment of the General Conference and not later than ninety days following the Jurisdictional Conferences of that year. The organizational meeting shall be convened by the bishop designated by the Council of Bishops for that purpose, and he shall fix the time and place.

2. There shall be a **temporary nominating committee,** composed of the bishop designated to convene the organizational meeting of the board and one lay person and one minister from each jurisdiction, chosen from among and by the members of the board elected by such jurisdiction. The committee shall consult with the executive staff.

3. The temporary nominating committee shall prepare the following nominations for the organizational meeting of the board: the ten members at large and a seminary professor from among those teaching in United Methodist seminaries; *provided* that other nominations may be made by the board. After the ten members at large and the seminary professor have been elected and seated, the temporary nominating committee shall nominate the officers of the board, the chairmen of

324

the divisions of the board, and the executive committee; *provided* that other nominations may be made by the board. When the election of the above nominees is completed, the temporary nominating committee shall be discharged. The executive committee shall then become the nominating committee of the board to serve for the remainder of the quadrennium.

4. The board shall hold an annual meeting. Special meetings may be held at the call of the board or its executive committee.

¶ **1136.** *Article 9. Duties.*—The board shall endeavor to create an intelligent conception of, an interest in, and a passion for evangelism among ministers and lay persons.

It shall give particular emphasis to the promotion of full, well-rounded, and practical programs of evangelism on the conference, district, and local-church levels. To this end it shall give guidance and help to the jurisdictional Boards of Evangelism, the conference Boards of Evangelism, the district Committees on Evangelism, and the Commissions on Evangelism in local churches (¶ 158.2). The board shall give guidance to the Church in using the appropriate days and seasons of the Christian calendar for special evangelistic emphasis.

¶ **1137.** *Article 10. Executive Committee.*—1. The board shall elect from its members an **executive committee**, which shall consist of the officers of the board, the section chairmen, one representative from each jurisdiction of the Church, and two lay persons. The executive staff shall be advisory members of the executive committee.

2. The executive committee shall have power to transact the business of the board in the interim of its meetings, unless otherwise provided, and as outlined in the bylaws. It shall report its proceedings to the board for ratification.

3. The executive committee shall meet at least quarterly at such time and place as it may determine. A majority of the members shall constitute a quorum.

4. Special meetings may be held upon the call of the chairman or the general secretary or at the request of five members of the committee. The officers shall designate the time and place. Notice shall be given ten days prior to the meetings. A majority of the members shall constitute a quorum.

¶ **1138.** *Article 11. Cooperation.*—The board shall cooperate with the various agencies of the Church in the training of ministers and lay persons for leadership in the field of evangelism, in creating new congregations, in initiating new forms of ministry, and in the creation and distribution of literature to serve the cause of evangelism.

Representation in departments of evangelism of interdenominational agencies shall be determined by the board.

¶ **1139.** *Article 12. Financial Support.*—The financial support of the general work of the board shall be derived from the general benevolence funds of the Church and that of *The Upper Room* as provided for in ¶ 1161. When special evangelistic missions are conducted or special projects undertaken by the board, freewill offerings may be received toward defraying their expenses.

¶ **1140.** *Article 13. Conference Evangelists.*—Evangelism as a full-time ministerial service is recognized by The United Methodist Church. An elder who feels called of God to be a full-time evangelist should prepare definitely for such service under the guidance of the Annual Conference to which he belongs, according to the standards established by the board. The board shall send copies of these standards annually to the bishops, the district superintendents, the conference Boards of Evangelism, and the conference evangelists. Only elders who feel so called and who meet these standards should be considered eligible for appointment as conference evangelists.

¶ **1141.** *Article 14. Chaplains.*—The board and its staff shall cooperate closely with the Commission on Chaplains and Related Ministries. It shall attempt to help United Methodist chaplains in every possible way, informing them concerning all forms and phases of evangelism, including evangelistic and devotional literature.

¶ **1142.** *Article 15. Amenability.*—The board is amenable to the General Conference, to which it shall report and submit the record of its proceedings.

¶ **1143.** *Article 16. Bylaws.*—The board shall provide its own bylaws, which shall not violate any provisions of the constitution or the Discipline and which may be amended by a two-thirds vote of the members present and voting thereon at a regular or special meeting; *provided* that written notice to such amendment has been given to the members and the vote thereon shall be delayed at least one day.

¶ **1144.** *Article 17. Amendments.*—This constitution can be amended only by the General Conference of The United Methodist Church.

JURISDICTIONAL BOARD OF EVANGELISM

¶ 1145. In each jurisdiction there may be a **jurisdictional Board of Evangelism,** auxiliary to the general board, as the Jurisdictional Conference may determine. (*See* ¶¶ 26.3, 625.)

ANNUAL CONFERENCE BOARD OF EVANGELISM

¶ 1146. *Article 1. Name and Objectives.*—Each Annual Conference shall elect for the quadrennium a **conference Board of Evangelism,** which shall plan and promote a program of evangelism throughout the conference in cooperation with the Annual Conference Program Council. The board shall endeavor to create an intelligent conception of, interest in, and passion for evangelism, and shall promote various types, phases, and methods of evangelism throughout the conference. It shall cooperate with the general and jurisdictional boards. It shall seek to enlist the cooperation of ministers and lay persons throughout the Annual Conference in promoting the work of evangelism. It shall develop and promote a conference program of evangelism, which shall include the training of ministers and lay persons in that program, the distribution of promotional literature, and the encouragement of local church participation in the year-round program of evangelism. It shall foster prayer, private devotions, and family worship and encourage attendance and participation in the prayer and worship services of the local church. It shall give guidance to the district Committees on Evangelism and to local-church Commissions on Evangelism in carrying out their purposes and responsibilities as outlined in ¶ 158.2.

¶ 1147. *Article 2. Membership.*—The board shall include in its membership at least one district superintendent; the conference secretary or director of evangelism; the district secretaries of evangelism; one pastor and one layman from each district, nominated by the conference nominating committee; such members of the general and jurisdictional boards as reside within the bounds of the conference; a laywoman, nominated by the conference Women's Society of Christian Service; a layman, nominated by the conference Board of the Laity; a representative of the conference United Methodist Youth Fellowship, nominated by the conference United Methodist Youth Fellowship; and such other representatives of conference organizations as determined by the conference, nominated by the organization. The conference board, when organized, may elect to the board not more than ten additional members at large whose special knowledge or experience would increase the competence of the board. The board shall meet annually at such time and place as it may designate. Special meetings may be held at the call of the president and the conference secretary or director of evangelism.

¶ 1148. *Article 3. Officers.*—The board shall elect its own chairman, vice-chairman, recording secretary, and treasurer, who may be the conference treasurer, quadrennially, together with such other officers and executive committee members as desired, and shall fill vacancies throughout the quadrennium as they occur. At the end of the quadrennium the retiring board shall complete its business and make its report to the Annual Conference and its recommendations to the new board. The new board shall organize immediately, formulate plans for an ongoing evangelism, and also make its report and recommendations to the Annual Conference.

¶ 1149. *Article 4. Chairman.*—The **chairman** shall be the presiding, not the administrative, officer of the board, and shall not be the conference secretary or director of evangelism. His duties shall be to preside over all board and executive committee meetings, to present the report of the board to the Annual Conference, and to support the evangelistic causes and programs of the conference. In cooperation with the secretary or director he shall annually present the askings of the board to the Commission on World Service and Finance.

¶ 1150. *Article 5. Conference Secretary of Evangelism.*—1. Each Annual Conference, on nomination of its Board of Evangelism, shall elect quadrennially a **conference secretary of evangelism** (except as provided in § 2), to be publicly assigned by the bishop, who shall promote the policies and program of the General, jurisdictional, and conference Boards of Evangelism in the Annual Conference in cooperation with the conference Program Council. He shall be the administrative and executive officer of the board. It shall be his duty to lead in program planning, to implement and execute the plans and programs adopted, and to carry the leadership of evangelism throughout the conference, working closely with the board, the bishop, the district superintendents, district secretaries of evangelism, the district committees on Evangelism, and the conference Program Council. He shall direct the expenditure of the funds of the board, faithfully adhering to its program and financial policies.

2. The board may elect, after consultation with the bishop and his Cabinet, a full-time **conference director of evangelism,** subject to approval by the Annual Conference; *provided* that in filling a vacancy, confirmation shall not be required for the interim period. He shall serve as the administrative and executive officer of the board, instead of a conference secretary of evangelism, and shall assume all the duties assigned to that office (*see* § 1). Additional duties shall be carefully outlined by the board, to which he shall be amenable. He shall have no vote in board or executive committee meetings.

¶ 1151. *Article 6. Standing Committees.*—The board shall divide itself into such committees as it may deem necessary.

¶ 1152. *Article 7. Conference Evangelists.*—The board may recommend to the Annual Conference and to the bishop in charge the appointment of certain effective members of the conference as **conference evangelists;** *provided* that such persons shall meet the standards set up by the general board and the conference board for conference evangelists (¶ 1140).

1. When an individual meets the standards for evangelists of The United Methodist Church, the Annual Conference, upon recommendation of the Board of Evangelism, may vote him the designation of evangelist and grant him a certificate as such as an expression of confidence in him. Such certificate, to remain valid, must be renewed annually by vote of the Annual Conference upon recommendation of the Board of Evangelism on the basis of review and approval of his work methods and financial plans.

2. When an elder receives assignment as an evangelist in his own conference, he shall submit to the conference board a complete annual report of his work in triplicate, one for his district superintendent, one

for the conference board, and one for the general board. These forms shall be prepared by the general board.

3. The board shall assist ministers who may need help in planning their evangelistic programs for the year. It shall encourage ministers to be their own evangelists. It shall help plan for mutual pastoral exchanges in evangelistic endeavors when feasible. It shall assist the local church in the choice of recognized United Methodist evangelists.

4. No pastor shall engage for an evangelist any person who is not a conference evangelist, a regular member of an Annual Conference, a lay pastor, a local preacher, or a lay speaker in good standing in The United Methodist Church without first obtaining written consent of his district superintendent.

¶ **1153.** *Article 8. Amenability.*—The board is amenable to the Annual Conference, to which it shall report annually. It shall send to the general board a copy of its annual report.

¶ **1154.** *Article 9. Bylaws.*—The board may adopt bylaws consistent with this constitution.

¶ **1155.** *Article 10. Amendments.*—This constitution can be amended only by the General Conference of The United Methodist Church.

DISTRICT COMMITTEE ON EVANGELISM

¶ **1156.** *Purpose.*—1. In those Annual Conferences which are organized into districts there may be a **district Committee on Evangelism,** which shall promote the program of evangelism in cooperation with the conference Board of Evangelism.

2. The conference Board of Evangelism shall determine the membership of the district Committees of Evangelism when such committees are desired. These committees shall include the district superintendent and the district secretary of evangelism along with any other persons desired, including laity.

3. The committee, under the leadership of the district superintendent, the conference secretary or director of evangelism, and the district secretary of evangelism, shall seek to work out areas of evangelistic responsibility, geographic or otherwise, in whatever manner

may seem to be most feasible in each situation, so that no person may be omitted from the responsibility of some local church. (*See* ¶ 105.)

¶ 1157. The committee shall divide itself into such committees as it may deem necessary.

¶ 1158. There shall be a **district secretary of evangelism** in each district, nominated by the district superintendent and publicly assigned by the bishop. The district secretary of evangelism shall be a member of the conference Board of Evangelism.

LOCAL-CHURCH COMMISSION ON EVANGELISM

¶ 1159. Each local church may have a Commission on Evangelism. (*See* ¶ 158.2.)

¶ 1160. *Minister of Evangelism.*—1. If a **minister of evangelism** is desired in the local church, the Charge Conference shall request through the district superintendent that the bishop appoint one, and shall fix his salary.

2. If the employment of a layman as director of evangelism is desired, the pastor, in consultation with the district superintendent and with the concurrence of the commission, shall recommend a proper person to the Charge Conference, which shall have the power to employ him, fix his salary, and terminate his service.

3. The minister or director of evangelism shall be administratively responsible to the pastor and, in cooperation with the pastor and the chairman of the commission, shall guide the evangelistic program of the church.

THE UPPER ROOM

¶ 1161. The General Board of Evangelism is hereby instructed to assume the management and publication of *The Upper Room* and to produce and distribute such literature as that now represented by *The Upper Room* for the cultivation of the devotional life; *provided,* however, that no funds either now in hand or hereafter accumulated by *The Upper Room* or other devotional and related literature hereafter produced shall be used for the support of other features of the board's work, but that all net income from the sale of such publications shall be conserved by the board for the purpose of preparing and circulating such literature; *provided,* however, that this shall not prevent the setting up of a reserve fund out of such income as a protection against unforeseen emergencies.

Section VIII.　Board of Health and Welfare Ministries.

CONSTITUTION

¶ **1162.**　*Article 1. Name, Purpose, and Policy.*—1. There shall be a **General Board of Health and Welfare Ministries** of The United Methodist Church, which shall have an advisory relationship to all United Methodist philanthropic health and welfare interests, institutional and noninstitutional, such as hospitals, extended-care agencies, services for the aging, agencies for children and youth, and Jurisdictional and Annual Conference Boards of Health and Welfare Ministries.

2. All health and welfare agencies and programs operated by, or under the auspices of, or related to any connectional unit of, The United Methodist Church shall make their programs and services available to all persons regardless of race.

¶ **1163.**　*Article 2. Incorporation.*—The Board of Health and Welfare Ministries of The United Methodist Church shall be duly incorporated according to the laws of Illinois. Its headquarters shall be located at Evanston, Illinois.

¶ **1164.**　*Article 3. Management.*—The management of the board shall be vested in a **Board of Directors** of twenty-one persons: five bishops, one from each jurisdiction, elected by the Council of Bishops; one minister and one lay member from each jurisdiction, elected by the Jurisdictional Conference, at least one of whom shall be an active administrator of an institution or agency under the general supervision of the board; and six members at large, elected by the board, three of whom may be active administrators of institutions under the general supervision of the board. All the Board of Directors shall be members of The United Methodist Church. Should a vacancy occur among those elected by the jurisdictions, the College of Bishops where such vacancy occurs shall elect the person to fill the unexpired term. All other vacancies shall be filled by the electing body.

¶ **1165.** *Article 4. Officers.*—1. The officers of the Board of Directors shall be a president, elected by the board from the bishops who are members; a vice-president; a recording secretary; and a treasurer. All these officers shall be elected by the board for the quadrennium. In addition there shall be such other officers and agents as the board may from time to time determine.

2. The board shall elect a **general secretary** and shall provide for his salary and necessary help. The general secretary shall be subject to the authority and control of the board.

¶ **1166.** *Article 5. Meetings.*—1. An annual meeting of the board shall be held at such time and place as the board may determine.

2. An **executive committee** of nine members shall be elected by the board, to include the officers of the board and five additional members to be elected by the board, with the provision that each jurisdiction shall be represented on the committee by an elected member, the general secretary being a member of the executive committee ex officio without vote. Five members of the executive committee shall constitute a quorum.

¶ **1167.** *Article 6. Affiliation.*—In order that United Methodist philanthropic activities may be professionally competent and Christian, hospitals, homes, or other health and welfare service programs which are known as institutions or agencies of The United Methodist Church and which maintain Christian standards or which look to United Methodist constituency for support and which are not affiliated with any other board of the Church shall be expected to affiliate with the Board of Health and Welfare Ministries.

¶ **1168.** *Article 7. Financial Support.*—Since the Board of Health and Welfare Ministries is empowered to act only in an advisory, educational, and cooperative capacity, its support shall be derived as follows: (1) from such share in the general benevolences of the Church as the General Conference may determine and (2) from gifts, devises, wills, and bequests, and from the administration of trust funds.

¶ **1169.** *Article 8. Powers.*—1. The board may make surveys, disseminate information, suggest plans for securing funds, maintain a bureau for the purpose of securing experts in all lines of work, provide architectural data, and render assistance, other than financial assistance, in the promotion and establishment of new institutions. (*See* ¶ 1170.) It shall make appraisals and advise as to the validity and wisdom of accepting or rejecting institutions, such as hospitals and homes, which may benefit in any way from the approval or support of The United Methodist Church. It may suggest plans for Annual Conferences regarding their religious ministry to state and non–United Methodist hospitals and homes needing such ministry. It shall give counsel to local pastors and churches in dealing with health and welfare services to children, youth, and adults.

2. The board shall formulate standards—spiritual, financial, and scientific—to protect the aims and ideals of The United Methodist Church and shall encourage and assist institutions in attaining these standards.

3. The board is authorized to establish a **Certification Council**, under such rules and regulations as it may determine, to develop criteria and to implement a program for the classification and certification of institutions and agencies of philanthropic service related to The United Methodist Church.

4. The board shall provide for conference boards the consultative services regarding proposed new institutions specified in ¶¶ 1173.4, 1181.

5. The board may organize a **Personnel Service** under such rules and regulations as it may determine: (*a*) to help institutions or agencies of philanthropic service in The United Methodist Church to find adequately trained Christian personnel to conduct the various types of work represented by United Methodist hospitals, homes, or other health and welfare service programs; (*b*) to encourage United Methodist youth desirous of investing their lives in some form of Christian health and welfare work; and (*c*) to cooperate in the work of the Interboard Committee on Enlistment for Church Occupations (¶ 1084).

6. The board shall cause to be established a **code of ethics** to serve as a standard and guide for service institutions of The United

Methodist Church in developing Christian and professionally competent characteristics.

7. The board is empowered to act as trustee for the administration of bequests or endowments for institutions of the Church and as a result of said trusts to assist designated Christian social welfare work anywhere throughout the Church.

8. As an advisory, standardizing, and educational agency of The United Methodist Church, the board is empowered to prepare interpretive literature which can be used in a practical manner throughout the Church for the Golden Cross Fund or other appeals.

9. The Board of Directors is authorized to organize committees, set up financial accounts, assist institutions in efforts to secure funds, and perform such other functions as the normal work of the board may require.

10. The Board of Health and Welfare Ministries shall not be responsible, legally or morally, for the debts, contracts, or obligations, or for any other financial commitments of any character or description, created, undertaken, or assumed by any institution, agency, or interest of The United Methodist Church, whether or not such institution, agency, or interest shall be approved, accepted, or recognized by the board, or shall be affiliated with the board, or whether or not the promotion or establishment of the same shall be approved, under any of the provisions of this constitution, or otherwise. No such institution, agency, or interest of The United Methodist Church and no officer or member of the Board of Directors of this board shall have any authority whatsoever to take any action, directly or by implication, at variance with, or deviating from, the limitation contained in the preceding sentence hereof.

11. The board shall be responsible for fostering the continued financial support of any Annual-Conference-related home whose support may be adversely affected by the union of the Methodist and Evangelical United Brethren churches. Homes of the former Evangelical United Brethren Church which have been supported on an area basis fall into this category because the homes in The United Methodist Church will regularly be supported by an Annual Conference or Conferences in a relatively small geographical area.

The board shall encourage conferences of the former Evangelical United Brethren Church and uniting Annual Conferences to accept continuing financial responsibility for the support of the homes of the former Evangelical United Brethren Church until they are informed by the board that such help is no longer needed.

The Central Treasury of the Council on World Service and Finance shall receive all contributions for the support of these homes from the Annual Conferences and shall distribute the same to the homes of the former Evangelical United Brethren Church on a formula basis which shall be reviewed and adopted annually by the homes involved after consultation with the board.

The board shall also counsel with the homes receiving such financial support in order to assist each of them to move toward a program of benevolent care which can be supported by the territory that will accept responsibility for the home on a regular basis. It shall also seek to develop support for a home in such a territory so that the transition to the regular base of support can be accomplished at the earliest possible time.

¶ 1170. *Clarification of Responsibility.*—1. In the field of United Methodist health and welfare the Board of Health and Welfare Ministries carries primary responsibility for direct services, and the Board of Christian Social Concerns carries primary responsibility for affecting public policy. Both boards carry a joint responsibility for community health and welfare planning. This clarification of responsibility shall not be interpreted as affecting the function and role of the Board of Missions.

2. The terms used in § 1 above shall be understood as follows: "Direct services" includes advising and administering the operation of organized services to persons in need, whether through an institution or a local church. "Community health and welfare planning" refers to the assessing of needs for health and welfare services and the development of support for needed public and church-related services. "Affecting public policy" encompasses the representation of the Church in developing public support for legislation and rules of procedure relating to public agencies in health and welfare ministries.

¶ 1171. *Interboard Consultation.*—The Board of Health and

Welfare Ministries is authorized to initiate or participate in relationships with other boards where common interests are evident.

JURISDICTIONAL BOARDS

¶ **1172.** In each jurisdiction there may be a **jurisdictional Board of Health and Welfare Ministries,** auxiliary to the general board, as the Jurisdictional Conference may determine. (*See* ¶¶ 26.3, 625.)

ANNUAL CONFERENCE BOARDS

¶ **1173.** 1. Each Annual Conference shall promote within its bounds a **conference Board of Health and Welfare Ministries,** composed as follows: (*a*) at least one ministerial and one lay member, elected from each district of the conference; *provided* that there shall be a minimum of four ministers and four lay members; (*b*) any member of the general board within the conference, ex officio; and (*c*) administrators of hospitals and homes related to the conference, ex officio, without vote.

2. The board in former Annual Conferences of The Evangelical United Brethren Church and in united Annual Conferences shall assume responsibility for the continued support of the homes of the former Evangelical United Brethren Church until such time as it shall be released from this responsibility by the General Board of Health and Welfare Ministries. The Annual Conference shall channel money raised for the support of these homes through the Central Treasury of the Council on World Service and Finance.

3. The board shall meet at least once before or during each regular conference session and shall act in cooperation with the general board and the Annual Conference Program Council to promote the interests of the hospitals and homes, for which the conference has responsibility, within the bounds of the conference. It may aid in planning and developing a religious ministry, wherever practicable, in state and non–United Methodist hospitals and homes needing such ministry. Where civil law requires the election of Boards of Trustees or managers by the Annual Conference, it may nominate the persons for such election.

4. The board, in cooperation with the general board, shall help lift spiritual, financial, and scientific standards in United Methodist health and welfare ministries in the Annual Conference. It shall seek to strengthen the ties between related hospitals and homes and the Church. It shall make recommendations to the Annual Conference regarding establishment of new institutions and changes in existing institutions, as provided in ¶ 1181. In so doing it shall use the consultative services of the general board. The charter, constitution, and bylaws of any proposed new institution or agency, and in due course of time the architectural plans and program of financing, shall first be submitted to the general board for suggestions before Annual Conference approval and action are requested.

5. The board shall organize with a chairman, who may become a voting member of the National Association (¶ 1180). He shall be expected to take as much interest as possible in the program of Christian philanthropy in United Methodism as represented by the association.

District Directors

¶ 1174. In each district the district superintendent may designate one of the representatives of the district on the conference board (¶ 1173.1) as district director of health and welfare ministries.

Local-Church Committee

¶ 1175. The Committee on Health and Welfare Ministries in the local church shall promote, in cooperation with the General, Jurisdictional, and Annual Conference Boards of Health and Welfare Ministries, the health and welfare ministries of The United Methodist Church. (*See* ¶ 161.4.)

Golden Cross

¶ 1176. The Golden Cross symbolizes the ministry with Christian compassion to persons in need through deeds of love, care, help, and service by The United Methodist Church, its members, its congregations, and its health and welfare institutions and agencies.

¶ **1177.** There shall be a **Golden Cross Society** of The United Methodist Church, which shall promote the work of health and welfare ministries under the direction of the Board of Health and Welfare Ministries and which shall collect moneys and afford other material assistance in providing care for the sick, older persons, children, and youth. The enrollment in the Golden Cross Society shall be held annually in order to secure interest in, and support of, health and welfare ministries in every congregation in such manner and on such date as determined by the patronizing Annual Conference or Conferences. The week following Golden Cross Enrollment Sunday shall be known as **Health and Welfare Ministries Week.** Funds raised through this enrollment shall be used as directed by the Annual Conference through its Board of Health and Welfare Ministries, in keeping with the policies of the society.

¶ **1178.** Each Annual Conference shall employ such methods for financing its philanthropic institutions as it may decide upon recommendation of the Annual Conference board. The Annual Conference board may promote a **Golden Cross Fund,** which shall support the work of health and welfare ministries for which the conference has responsibility. An annual offering shall be received on a Sunday (to be known as **Golden Cross Sunday**) to be determined upon recommendation of the Annual Conference board.

¶ **1179.** There shall be a **Golden Cross Fellowship** of The United Methodist Church, membership in which shall be open to all Methodists who are seeking to fulfill their Christian vocation through a life of service in one of the helping and healing occupations. It shall be auxiliary to the Board of Health and Welfare Ministries and shall have as its purposes: (1) in cooperation with Annual Conference Commissions on Enlistment for Church Occupations, the recruitment and guidance of others into the helping and healing professions as an expression of Christian vocation; (2) the provision of a questing fellowship which seeks to clarify and deepen the understanding of how the Christian faith relates to the healing process and of how the theological dimensions of United Methodist belief relate to the life of service; and (3) the provision of a place where lay and professional persons may exchange dialogue to the end that a better understanding of the helping and healing process in its relation to faith may be the result for both. There may be student membership in each Annual Conference chapter of the fellowship.

NATIONAL ASSOCIATION

¶ **1180.** There shall be organized a **National Association,** to be composed of the representatives of institutions and the presidents of jurisdictional and conference boards who are connected with United Methodist philanthropy. This association shall have its own constitution and bylaws, shall meet in convention once a year, and shall establish its requirements for membership and have such membership dues as it may require. It shall work under the general direction of the Board of Health and Welfare Ministries, whose general secretary shall be an ex officio member of the association's executive committee. The aim and purpose of this association, in cooperation with the board, shall be to help lift the spiritual, scientific, and financial standards of our church hospitals and homes.

SUNDRY PROVISIONS

¶ **1181.** No new United Methodist helping and healing institution shall be established, nor shall an existing institution alter its major purpose and functions nor add any new facility in another location, without first receiving the approval of the Annual Conference, on recommendation of the conference Board of Health and Welfare Ministries, after consultation with the general board, as provided in ¶ 1173.3. This restriction shall not apply to institutions of the Board of Missions.

¶ **1182.** **Women's auxiliaries** connected with the various philanthropic institutions of United Methodism may be organized under, or given approval on compliance with, established standard requirements and procedures, such as the adoption of a constitution and bylaws fixing the identity, responsibility, and relationship of such organization as an auxiliary of a United Methodist institution. Such an auxiliary, when so organized and when request is made by the Board of Trustees of the institution which it represents, shall be granted a certificate of recognition from the Board of Health and Welfare Ministries.

Section IX. Board of the Laity.

THE GENERAL BOARD

¶ **1183.** *Name.*—There shall be a **General Board of the Laity** of The United Methodist Church.

¶ **1184.** *Incorporation.*—The General Board of the Laity of The United Methodist Church shall be incorporated under the laws of the State of Illinois. It shall be the successor to the General Board of Lay Activities of the former The Methodist Church and the Department of Christian Stewardship and the general organization of Evangelical United Brethren Men of the former The Evangelical United Brethren Church. It shall operate under the charter of its incorporation and the Discipline of The United Methodist Church to hold and administer trust funds and assets of every kind and character, real, personal or mixed, held by it, and to develop and promote a program in keeping with its objective and functions.

¶ **1185.** *Headquarters.*—The headquarters of the board shall be fixed by the General Conference.

¶ **1186.** *Objective.*—The basic objective of the Church as accepted by the General Board of the Laity is that all persons be aware of and grow in their understanding of God, especially of his redeeming love as revealed in Jesus Christ, and that they respond in faith and love to the end that they may know who they are and what their human situation means, increasingly identify themselves as sons of God and members of the Christian community, live in the spirit of God in every relationship, fulfill their common discipleship in the world, and abide in the Christian hope.

¶ **1187.** *Scope of Work.*—The Board of the Laity implements its objective in cooperation with other boards and agencies of The United Methodist Church. In this cooperative endeavor the scope of work of the General Board of the Laity includes:

1. The support of all members of The United Methodist Church as they seek to lead persons to accept Jesus Christ as Lord and Savior.

2. Engagement in research, consultation, and experimentation in search of an understanding of what it means to be Christian, to love the world, to identify with its need, to go into the world to meet God

341

at work there, to live in redemptive fellowship in the world, and to be in mission in the world.

3. The development of settings for conversation between laity and clergy in which understanding of the common ministry of witness and service of all Christians is sought.

4. Participation in the study of lay movements, union with ecumenical movements for action, and experimentation with new forms of expressing the lay movement and with new methods of educating the laity.

5. The interpretation of the nature of the lay ministry.

6. The proclamation of the call of God to all persons to be good stewards of the gifts of life, time, abilities, and possessions; to all congregations to be faithful stewards of the resources at their disposal; and to members to provide adequate financial support for the Church's ministries.

7. The interpretation of the leadership functions of Christians in the world and in the Church and the support of congregations as they call and educate persons for designated leadership responsibilities.

8. The assistance of Jurisdictional, Annual, District, and Charge Conferences as they establish and maintain the structures which are essential to vital lay witness and service.

9. The provision of resources for the laity which interpret the nature of lay witness and service, motivate obedient response to God's call, and assist the laity in developing their skills for witness and service.

¶ 1188. *Membership.*—The board shall be composed of five effective bishops, elected by the Council of Bishops; twenty Annual Conference lay leaders, present or immediate past, elected by the Jurisdictional Conferences on nomination of the Committees on the Laity, each jurisdiction entitled to a proportionate number of the whole determined on the basis of church membership; one effective minister; one conference associate lay leader for lay life and work; and one conference associate lay leader for stewardship and finance, elected by each Jurisdictional Conference on nomination of its committee on the laity; five lay members at large from within the United States, elected by the General Conference on nomination of the Council of Bishops; one lay member at large from outside the United

States, elected annually by the Council of Bishops; one student elected biennially by the Department of Campus Ministry; three representatives of the Women's Division of the Board of Missions, elected by that division; and such other representatives as the board may deem essential to achieve ethnic representation. The directors of adult, youth, and children's work of the General Program Council shall be ex officio members without vote.

¶ **1189.** *Tenure.*—All members of the general board shall be elected for a quadrennium unless otherwise specified and shall serve until their successors are elected and installed.

¶ **1190.** *Interim Agreement.*—During the first two quadrenniums of The United Methodist Church the following members of the General Board of the Laity shall be members coming from the former Evangelical United Brethren Church: one of the bishops and one of the members at large; one of the members of the board representing conference lay leaders or immediate past conference lay leaders from each of the North Central, Southeastern, and South Central Jurisdictions shall be a former member of the Board of Managers of Evangelical United Brethren Men or a former conference president of Evangelical United Brethren Men; one of the members of the board representing the ministers of the Northeastern Jurisdiction shall be a former Evangelical United Brethren minister; and one of the members of the board representing the conference associate lay leaders for stewardship and finance of the Western Jurisdiction shall be a former Evangelical United Brethren conference director of Christian stewardship. At the termination of the second quadrennium following union this paragraph shall be automatically deleted.

¶ **1191.** *Jurisdictional Conferences.*—Jurisdictional Conferences shall not elect to the board more than one representative from any one Annual Conference regardless of category.

¶ **1192.** *Vacancies.*—If a vacancy occurs in the board by death, resignation, or for disciplinary reasons, it shall be filled as follows: in the case of a bishop, by the Council of Bishops; in the case of a jurisdictional representative, lay or clergy, or member at large, by the board itself; in the case of a representative from a cooperating board or agency, by that board or agency.

¶ **1193.** *Officers.*—The officers of the General Board of the Laity shall be a president, a vice-president, a recording secretary, and the division chairmen.

¶ 1194. *Election.*—The board shall elect its officers at the first annual meeting following the session of General Conference. The chairman of each division shall be nominated by his respective division and elected by the board.

¶ 1195. *Term of Office.*—All officers provided for in ¶ 1193 shall be elected for the quadrennium and shall remain in office until their successors are duly elected and installed. Vacancies occurring in any office shall be filled by the board.

¶ 1196. *Divisions and Sections.*—The General Board of the Laity shall function through the **Division of Lay Life and Work** and the **Division of Stewardship and Finance.** The Division of Lay Life and Work shall function through the **Section on Lay Ministries,** the **Section on United Methodist Men,** and such other sections as the board shall determine. The Division of Stewardship and Finance shall function through the **Section on Stewardship Education,** the **Section on Financial Resources,** and such other sections as the board shall determine.

¶ 1197. *Division Membership.*—The board shall assign its members to the divisions so that each shall be approximately the same size and shall have members from each jurisdiction and from both clergy and laity. Members shall be appointed to the divisions on the basis of their major interest. The executive committee of the board shall review the division membership annually and recommend such changes as it deems advisable.

¶ 1198. *Staff of the General Board.*—The board shall elect for the quadrennium a general secretary, an associate general secretary for each division, and a business manager. The general board or its executive committee shall determine the number of staff persons to be employed, define their assignments, and elect other personnel upon the recommendation of the General Staff Administrative Committee.

1. The **general secretary** shall be the chief administrative officer of the board and shall serve under its direction. He shall be an ex officio member, without vote, of the general board and its executive committee. He shall supervise the divisions of the board, coordinate the total program of the board, and administer the affairs of the head-

quarters office and of such other facilities as the board may direct. He is responsible for recommending the annual budget and administering the finances of the board. The general secretary shall represent the board on the Council of Secretaries, the General Program Council, and such other councils and boards as the board or its executive committee may direct.

2. The **associate general secretaries** shall be the chief administrative officers of their respective divisions. They shall be ex officio members, without vote, of the general board and its executive committee. They shall serve under the direction of the division and the general secretary; shall be responsible for the general supervision of their divisions; and shall coordinate the program development and field work of their divisions, the development and administration of the division budget, and in cooperation with the General Staff Administrative Committee supervise the staff of the division. The associate general secretaries shall report to the annual meetings of their divisions and the board and shall cooperate with one another and with the general secretary to prevent undue overlapping in the work of the divisions and to avoid conflicts in scheduling meetings and conferences. The associate general secretaries shall represent their divisions of the board on the Council of Secretaries, the General Program Council, and such other councils and boards as the general board or its executive committee may direct.

3. The **business manager** shall receive, account for, and disburse all funds in accordance with the procedures established by the Staff Administrative Committee. He shall cooperate with the Staff Administrative Committee in the preparation and administration of the annual budget. He shall be responsible for purchasing, for the management of nonprofessional personnel, and for the operation of the production, shipping, and order departments. He shall be an ex officio member, without vote, of the the general board and its executive committee.

¶ 1199. *Committees.*—1. There shall be an **executive committee**, composed of the elected officers of the board, one bishop, one minister, and a representative of the Women's Division of the Board of Missions. Each jurisdiction shall be represented on this committee, and should any jurisdiction not have representation, a representative from that jurisdiction shall be added by and from the general board.

The officers of the board shall be the officers of the executive committee. The executive committee is authorized and empowered to act for the General Board of the Laity in the interim between its annual sessions to implement the actions of the board. It shall present its records to the annual meeting of the board for approval.

2. There shall be a **Staff Administrative Committee,** consisting of the general secretary, the associate general secretaries, and the business manager of the board. It shall be responsible for developing all staff recommendations for presentation to the board.

3. The board shall have such **functional committees** as it deems advisable and shall determine their duties and relations.

¶ **1200.** *Meetings.*—The board shall meet annually at the time and place which it shall determine. The executive committee of the board shall meet at such times and places as necessary.

¶ **1201.** *Finances.*—The work of the board shall be considered a benevolent interest of the Church, and the Council on World Service and Finance shall include in the appropriation recommended for adoption by the General Conference such sum as may be necessary for the proper support of the board and its program. The board shall report to said council an estimate of the amount needed annually for its work.

The board is authorized to solicit and receive gifts, special memberships, bequests, annuities, special offerings, and money raised in special projects or collected in meetings held in the interest of the program; to hold properties and securities in trust; and to administer all these financial affairs in accordance with its own rules and the provisions of the Discipline.

¶ **1202.** *Laymen's Day.*—**Laymen's Day** shall be observed annually in every church on the Sunday which will be designated by the General Program Council. Its purpose shall be to interpret the role of the laity in the world and to provide laymen with opportunity to witness to their faith in Jesus Christ and their commitment to his mission in the world. A conference Board of the Laity may promote and receive an offering on Laymen's Day for such benevolent purpose or project as it shall deem worthy.

¶ **1203.** *Bylaws.*—The board may adopt bylaws consistent with the provisions of the Discipline. The bylaws may be amended at any regular meeting of the board, a quorum being present, by a two-thirds vote of the members present and voting thereon; *provided* that notice of the proposed amendment has been given in writing to the members of the board at least thirty days in advance of the meeting.

DIVISION OF LAY LIFE AND WORK

¶ **1204.** *Organization.*—The Division of Lay Life and Work shall be organized as specified in ¶¶ 1196-97.

¶ **1205.** *Objective.*—The objective of the General Board of the Laity shall be implemented by the Division of Lay Life and Work.

¶ **1206.** *Scope of Work.*—The scope of work for the Division of Lay Life and Work shall include:

1. The search for an adequate understanding of the theological and biblical basis for lay life and work, consistent with the doctrines of The United Methodist Church, and the development of methods and settings for the involvement of the laity in this search.

2. Cooperation with other program agencies of the Church in supporting and equipping the laity for their life and ministry in the Church and in the world.

3. Developing United Methodist Men as a part of the total program of The United Methodist Church.

4. Engaging in study, research, experimentation, analysis, and evaluation for the enrichment of lay life and work and for the creation of more effective lay ministry.

5. The provision of resources for the program of the division and for programs assigned to it by the General Program Council.

6. Promoting the observance of Laymen's Day throughout the Church.

¶ **1207.** *Membership.*—Membership of the division shall be determined as outlined in ¶ 1197.

¶ **1208.** *Officers.*—Officers of the Division of Lay Life and Work shall be a chairman, a vice-chairman, a recording secretary, and the chairman of each organized section of the division. The division shall elect its officers, except its chairman and the section chairmen, who shall be nominated by the division and elected by the board.

¶ **1209.** *Term of Office.*—All officers shall be elected for a quadrennium and shall remain in office until their successors are elected and installed. Vacancies occurring in any office shall be filled by the division, except the division chairman and the section chairmen, who shall be elected by the board.

¶ **1210.** *Sections.*—The Division of Lay Life and Work shall function through the Section on Lay Ministries, the Section on United Methodist Men, and such other sections as the board shall establish. The division shall assign members to each section so that each jurisdiction is represented. The number of members shall be approximately the same in each section. The division shall review the membership of each section annually and recommend changes as it deems advisable.

¶ **1211.** *Committees.*—There shall be an **executive committee,** consisting of the division chairman and chairmen of the organized sections, and such other committees as the division deems necessary.

¶ **1212.** *Meetings.*—The division shall meet at the same time and place as the board. Special meetings of the division may be called only when authorized by the board or its executive committee.

¶ **1213.** *Finance.*—The associate general secretary of the division shall present the interests of the division to the Staff Administrative Committee when it develops the annual budget for presentation to the board for adoption. The associate general secretary is responsible for administering the budget of the division.

SECTION ON LAY MINISTRIES

¶ **1214.** *Scope of Work.*—The Section on Lay Ministries shall implement their objective through a scope of work which shall include:

1. *Research and Experimentation.*—By creative thinking, study, and conversation, the section shall keep abreast with the latest trends in the ministry of the Church through its laity, within the ecumenical movement, the educational forum, and the published literature. It shall consult with other program agencies and initiate conversations of clergy and laity of The United Methodist Church at all levels. Those facets of the movement which deserve further consideration shall be the subject of experimentation by pilot projects, suitably placed within the Church to yield reliable data upon which to consider widespread application.

2. *Study, Survey, Analysis, and Evaluation.*—Within the framework cited above will be the need for careful and unbiased evaluation of the results from pilot projects by scientific measures and experienced judgment. The board shall be responsible for such complete evaluation before action can be recommended. Only after such study shall new ventures be deemed worthy.

3. *Resources.*—The section shall continually appraise recommended resource material that has already been offered to the laity to ascertain its validity for further use. It shall be aware of the opportunity to provide new and stimulating reference material for the benefit of all segments of the laity. It shall make available through the variety of media at its command the resource materials selected.

The section shall attempt to be creative within itself to produce materials of specific reference value to the laity of The United Methodist Church. These shall be appropriately integrated within the framework of experimentation and within the continued opportunities offered to the total laity of The United Methodist Church. The section shall promote opportunity for lay response through age-level groups and men's and women's groups.

4. *Interpretation.*—As required, the section shall interpret the objectives cited above. This shall be done within the concept of the call of Christ to all persons to minister to the needs of humanity without and within the gathered Church. Interpretation shall be a consistent expression of value for guidance of the laity.

5. *Field Service.*—That the section may be certain that its program has the maximum opportunity for acceptance by the laity, it shall offer the services of its members and of such professional personnel as it may select to all levels of the Church for consultation, interpretation, training, and promotion. It shall keep a close liaison with the other program agencies of the Church in an effort to provide a united approach, particularly at the local level.

¶ 1215. *Services.*—1. These services will support the lay ministries of the Boards of the Laity in the Jurisdictional, Annual, and District Conferences through:

a) Consultations, conferences, workshops, retreats, lay schools of theology, and opportunities for lay-clergy dialogue.

b) Educational opportunities for Jurisdictional, Annual, and District Conference Boards of the Laity.

c) Opportunities for world service by laymen.

d) Experimental projects in lay life and work.

e) Printed resources.

f) Consultation for Annual Conference lay leaders.

2. These services will support the lay ministry of the local church through:

a) Provision of resources for consultations of the laity: retreats, lay schools of theology, lay-clergy dialogue.

b) Opportunities for laymen to support and engage in world service.

c) Resources and designs for the improvement of leadership in local churches, especially those who serve as members of pastor-parish relations committees, Administrative Boards, Charge Conferences, Boards of Trustees, and nominating committees and those who serve as lay leaders, lay members of Annual Conferences, and members of Committees on Lay Personnel.

d) Resources and designs for the interpretation of the nature of Christian leadership and witness in the world and the improvement of the same.

e) Provision of resources for lay speaker courses and certification procedures for lay speakers.

f) Discovering, developing, and recommending resources for lay study groups.

g) Encouraging the laity in all churches to use resource materials which are provided by all boards and departments of The United Methodist Church.

h) Developing procedures for voluntary service projects and encouraging local congregations to initiate the same.

i) Encouraging local congregations to provide counseling services for those who volunteer for unordained church careers and supplying resources which will enable congregations to render effective service in this area.

j) Supporting local congregations as they seek to provide other ministries which will enable the laity to be more effective servants of Jesus Christ in the world.

¶ **1216.** *Membership.*—The membership of the section is specified in ¶ 1210.

¶ **1217.** *Officers.*—The officers of the section shall be a chairman, nominated by the division and elected by the board, and a vice-chairman and a recording secretary, elected by the section at the first annual meeting of each quadrennium. They shall serve until their successors have been elected and installed.

¶ **1218.** *Committees.*—There shall be such committees as the section deems necessary.

¶ **1219.** *Meetings.*—The section shall meet at the same time and place as the board. Special meetings of the section may be called only when authorized by the board or its executive committee.

SECTION ON UNITED METHODIST MEN

¶ **1220.** *Name.*—United Methodist Men is the name of the authorized organization of the men of the Church.

¶ **1221.** *Scope of Work.*—The Section on United Methodist Men shall strive to provide essential services for United Methodist Men at all levels. Its principal areas of service shall be:

1. To define and interpret the purposes of United Methodist Men.

2. To apply the findings and utilize the resources of the Section on Lay Ministries for improvement of the quality of the men's fellowship and for the increased effectiveness of the ministry of Christian men in the world.

3. To anticipate the nature of the ministry which the Church must provide for its men who are called to be servants of Christ in the world.

4. To engage in projects which will challenge United Methodist Men.

5. To evaluate the need for national meetings of United Methodist Men and to plan, promote, and conduct them.

6. To assist the work of United Methodist Men on Jurisdictional, Annual, and District Conference levels.

7. To encourage the organization and chartering of local fellowships of United Methodist Men and maintain liaison with them, and

to encourage the formation of county, metropolitan, and subdistrict groups when there is a mission to be served.

8. To provide program resources for local fellowships of United Methodist Men which are coordinated with other program resources of the Church.

9. To relate United Methodist Men to ecumenical activities.

10. To engage in related phases of men's work as the board or division may authorize.

¶ 1222. *Membership.*—The membership of the section is specified in ¶ 1210.

¶ 1223. *Officers.*—The officers of the section shall be a chairman, nominated by the division and elected by the board, and a vice-chairman and a recording secretary, elected by the section at the first annual meeting of each quadrennium. They shall serve until their successors have been elected and installed.

¶ 1224. *Committees.*—There shall be such committees as the section deems necessary.

¶ 1225. *Meetings.*—The Section on United Methodist Men shall meet at the same time and place as the board. Special meetings of the section may be called only when authorized by the board or its executive committee.

DIVISION OF STEWARDSHIP AND FINANCE

¶ 1226. *Organization.*—The Division of Stewardship and Finance shall be organized as specified in ¶¶ 1196-97.

¶ 1227. *Objective.*—The stewardship implications of the objective of the General Board of the Laity shall be implemented by the Division of Stewardship and Finance.

¶ 1228. *Scope of Work.*—The scope of work for the Division of Stewardship and Finance shall include:

1. The interpretation of the biblical and theological basis for stewardship as consistent with the doctrines of The United Methodist Church and informing the Church of the same through educational channels and study materials.

2. Communication with other agencies in whose programs the subject matter of stewardship should be included, to provide counsel,

guidance, and resources for the implementation of such programs, also cooperation with the Division of Curriculum Resources of the Board of Education for the inclusion of stewardship concepts in local-church curriculum materials.

3. Development of program resources and training materials for local-church Commissions on Stewardship and committees in the areas of stewardship education and financial resources, including Every-Member Commitments.

4. Counseling of Jurisdictional and Annual Conference Commissions of Stewardship and Finance relative to their organizational structure and program responsibilities and assisting them in their interpretation of program and resources.

5. Taking action as necessary to encourage United Methodists to provide for their continued participation in world service, or in one or more of the world service agencies, through wills and special gifts. The division shall give leadership to local-church committees on wills and legacies and with conference Committees on Wills and Special Gifts in such ways as may be deemed mutually helpful.

6. Seeking to motivate, through stewardship education and guidance, sound financial methods to aid local churches, areas, District and Annual Conferences, institutions, and general benevolent causes in raising funds for current expenses and capital needs. When projects of this nature are so extended as to exceed the conventional amount of service rendered by a general agency, a fee may be charged.

7. Providing guidance for groups or organizations responsible for making decisions regarding the corporate stewardship of their resources.

8. Seeking to assure adequate financial support for all United Methodist ministers and church-related employees.

9. Giving guidance and consultation in the area of local-church business administration, including establishment of professional standards, a training program, certification of administrators, sponsorship of an association of United Methodist administrators, and placement services.

10. Furnishing guidance and consultation to Boards of Trustees and related committees and to local church officials in financial matters.

¶ **1229.** *Membership.*—Membership of the division shall be determined as outlined in ¶ 1197.

¶ **1230.** *Officers.*—Officers of the Division of Stewardship and Finance shall be a chairman, a vice-chairman, a recording secretary, and the chairman of each organized section of the division. The division shall elect its officers, except its chairman and the section chairmen, who shall be nominated by the division and elected by the board.

¶ **1231.** *Term of Office.*—All officers are elected for a quadrennium and shall remain in office until their successors are elected and installed. Vacancies occurring in any office shall be filled by the division, except the division chairman and the section chairmen, who shall be elected by the board.

¶ **1232.** *Sections.*—The Division of Stewardship and Finance shall function through the Section on Stewardship Education, the Section on Financial Resources, and such other sections as the board may establish. The division shall assign its members to each section so that each jurisdiction is represented and the sections are of approximately equal size. The division shall review the membership of each section annually and make changes as it deems advisable.

¶ **1233.** *Committees.*—There shall be an **executive committee,** composed of the division chairman and section chairmen, and such other committees as the division deems necessary.

¶ **1234.** *Meetings.*—The division shall meet at the same time and place as the board. Special meetings of the division may be called only when authorized by the board or its executive committee.

¶ **1235.** *Finance.*—The associate general secretary of the division shall present the interests of the division to the Staff Administration Committee when it develops the proposed annual budget for presentation to the board for adoption. The associate general secretary is responsible for administering the budget of the division.

SECTION ON STEWARDSHIP EDUCATION

¶ **1236.** *Functions.*—The Section on Stewardship Education shall concern itself with the following functions and such others as may be assigned to it by the division:

354

1. To develop literature, audio-visual aids, and other educational materials.

2. To bring United Methodists to an understanding of the theological meaning of Christian stewardship and its application to the entire life of the Christian, including the use of time, influence, personal abilities, and material resources.

3. To emphasize Christian motivation in regard to acquiring, investing, and spending material resources.

4. To develop a program which will arouse concern for the conservation of natural resources.

5. To participate in schools of training for pastors and laymen in cooperation with other agencies where stewardship is desired.

¶ 1237. *Membership.*—The membership of the section is specified in ¶ 1232.

¶ 1238. *Officers and Tenure.*—The officers of the section shall be a chairman, nominated by the division and elected by the board, and a vice-chairman and a recording secretary, who shall be elected by the section at the first annual meeting of each quadrennium. They shall serve until their successors have been elected and installed.

¶ 1239. *Committees.*—There shall be such committees as the section deems necessary.

¶ 1240. *Meetings.*—The section shall meet at the same time and place as the board. Special meetings of the section may be called only when authorized by the board or its executive committee.

SECTION ON FINANCIAL RESOURCES

¶ 1241. *Functions.*—The Section on Financial Resources shall concern itself with the following functions and such others as may be assigned to it by the division:

1. To provide materials and give leadership in training Jurisdictional, Annual, and District Conference Commissions on Stewardship and Finance and local church Commissions on Stewardship and Committees on Finance.

2. To provide materials and give leadership in training Jurisdictional, Annual, District, and local-church Committees on Wills and Special Gifts.

3. To aid in motivating United Methodists to increased support of world service.

4. To provide local churches, Annual Conferences, and church institutions with special services, including the Every-Member Commitment, fund raising, and expansion programs.

5. To prepare materials and provide training for local church treasurers, financial secretaries, and any other officers related to the financial operation of the local church.

6. To provide counsel and advice to the United Methodist Association of Church Business Administrators.

¶ **1242.** *Membership.*—The membership of the section is specified in ¶1232.

¶ **1243.** *Officers and Tenure.*—The officers of the section shall be a chairman, nominated by the division and elected by the board, and a vice-chairman and a recording secretary, who shall be elected by the section at the first annual meeting of each quadrennium. They shall serve until their successors have been elected and installed.

¶ **1244.** *Committees.*—There shall be such committees as the section deems necessary.

¶ **1245.** *Meetings.*—The section shall meet at the same time and place as the board. Special meetings of the section may be called only when authorized by the board or its executive committee.

Jurisdictional Boards

¶ **1246.** In each jurisdiction there may be a **jurisdictional Board of the Laity,** auxiliary to the general board, as the Jurisdictional Conference may determine.

Annual Conference Boards

¶ **1247.** *Name.*—There shall be in every Annual Conference a **conference Board of the Laity,** which shall be auxiliary to the General and jurisdictional Boards of the Laity. It shall cooperate with the Annual Conference Program Council.

¶ **1248.** *Objective and Scope of Work.*—The objective and scope of work of the conference Board of the Laity shall be related to those set forth for the General Board of the Laity and its divisions. (*See* ¶¶ 1186-87, 1206, 1214-15, 1221, 1227-28, 1236, 1241.)

¶ 1249. *Membership.*—The board shall be composed of the conference lay leader, who shall be chairman; the associate conference lay leaders; the district lay leaders; the associate district lay leaders; the district superintendents; members of the General and jurisdictional Boards of the Laity residing within the Annual Conference; conference directors of program activities, as the board shall determine; directors of adult, youth, and children's ministries of the conference Program Council; the conference director or president of United Methodist Men; the conference president of the Women's Society of Christian Service; the conference president of United Methodist Youth; and such other persons as the conference Board of the Laity may authorize.

¶ 1250. *Officers.*—The conference lay leader shall be elected annually by the Annual Conference on nomination of the board. The nomination shall be by written ballot. The associate conference lay leader for lay life and work, the associate conference lay leader for stewardship and finance, the secretary, the treasurer, and such other officers as the conference board may authorize, shall be elected annually by the Annual Conference or the board.

¶ 1251. *Tenure and Vacancies.*—All elections of board members shall be for the term of one year. Any vacancy occurring in the office of conference lay leader or in any other office elected by the board shall be filled by the board.

¶ 1252. *Commissions.*—The conference Board of the Laity shall function through two commissions: the Commission of Lay Life and Work and the Commission of Stewardship and Finance.

¶ 1253. *Commission Membership.*—The conference Board of the Laity shall assign its members to the two commissions in a manner similar to that in ¶ 1197 and shall have members from each of the districts.

¶ 1254. *Committees.*—1. There shall be an **executive committee,** consisting of the conference lay leader, who shall be chairman; associate conference lay leaders; the secretary and the treasurer of the board; the conference director or president of United Methodist Men; the conference president of the Women's Society of Christian Service; the conference directors of special program activities, elected by the board; a district superintendent, selected by the Cabinet; and one or more district lay leaders as selected by the board.

2. There shall be such other committees as the board may from time to time find necessary.

¶ 1255. *Meetings.*—The board shall hold an annual meeting in connection with or immediately after the Annual Conference session, at which time it shall elect its officers. It shall hold such other meetings as are deemed advisable by the board or its executive committee.

¶ 1256. *Finances.*—1. The work of the board shall be considered a benevolent interest of the Church, and the conference Commission on World Service and Finance shall include in the appropriations recommended for adoption by the Annual Conference such sum as may be necessary for the proper support of the board.

2. The board, through its officers, shall report annually its proposed budget to the conference Commission on World Service and Finance.

¶ 1257. *Conference Lay Leader.*—The **conference lay leader** is the designated leader of the conference laity, with responsibility for becoming increasingly aware of the work of the laity in achieving the mission of the Church. He shall guide the deliberations of the board in developing long-range and annual objectives, direct the implementation of these objectives, and represent the board in other conference agencies as determined by the Discipline. He shall guide the work of the board so that it will be coordinated with the comprehensive program of the conference. He shall present a written report annually to the board and to the Annual Conference. The conference lay leader shall be seated in the Annual Conference as a voting member.

¶ 1258. *Associate Conference Lay Leaders.*—The **associate conference lay leader of lay life and work** and the **associate conference lay leader of stewardship and finance** are co-workers with the conference lay leader responsible for the same general concerns. They shall provide leadership for their respective commissions as each commission shall determine.

¶ 1259. *Commission of Lay Life and Work.*—There shall be an **Annual Conference Commission of Lay Life and Work,** auxiliary to the General, jurisdictional, and conference Boards of the Laity.

1. *Objective and Scope of Work.*—The objective and scope of

work of the Commission of Lay Life and Work shall be related to those set forth for the Division of Lay Life and Work of the General Board of the Laity. (*See* ¶¶ 1186-87.)

2. *Officers.*—The associate conference lay leader for lay life and work shall serve as chairman of the commission. The commission shall elect annually a vice-chairman and a recording secretary.

3. *Committee on United Methodist Men.*—There may be a con-ference **Committee on United Methodist Men,** whose objective and scope of work shall be related to those set forth for the Section on United Methodist Men of the General Board of the Laity (¶ 1221). The committee shall be composed of the district directors of United Methodist Men. The chairman, who shall be nominated by the com-mittee and elected by the board, shall serve as the conference director or president of United Methodist Men. The committee shall elect its vice-chairman and recording secretary and shall function as authorized by the conference Commission of Lay Life and Work.

4. *Additional Committees.*—There shall be such additional com-mittees as the commission deems necessary.

5. *Meetings.*—The commission shall meet during the annual ses-sions of the conference Board of the Laity. Additional meetings may be held when authorized by the conference board or its executive com-mittee.

6. *Finance.*—The commission shall present annually its proposed budget to the conference Board of the Laity.

¶ **1260.** *Commission of Stewardship and Finance.*—There shall be a **Commission of Stewardship and Finance** of the Annual Confer-ence Board of the Laity, which shall be auxiliary to the General, juris-dictional, and conference Boards of the Laity.

1. *Objective and Scope of Work.*—The objective and scope of work of the Commission of Stewardship and Finance shall be related to those set forth for the Division of Stewardship and Finance of the General Board of the Laity in ¶¶ 1186-87, 1227-28, 1236, and 1241.

2. *Officers.*—The commission shall elect annually a chairman, a vice-chairman, and a recording secretary, who may be either laymen or ministers.

3. *Conference Director of Stewardship.*—Each Annual Conference shall elect a **conference director of stewardship and finance.** He may

be a full-time or part-time employee of the conference, or he may serve on a voluntary basis. In any case, he shall be the liaison person between the Annual Conference and the Division of Stewardship and Finance of the General Board of the Laity. He shall attend at conference expense, and fully participate in, the meetings of the Division of Stewardship and Finance of the general board.

The conference director of stewardship and finance shall be nominated by the Commission of Stewardship and Finance and elected by the Annual Conference. He shall be publicly assigned to his responsibility by the bishop. The director shall serve as the executive officer of the conference Commission of Stewardship and Finance.

4. *Committees.*—There shall be such committees as the commission or board deems necessary.

5. *Meetings.*—The commission shall meet during the annual sessions of the conference Board of the Laity. Additional meetings may be held when authorized by the conference board or its executive committee.

6. *Finance.*—The commission shall present annually its proposed budget to the conference Board of the Laity.

District Boards

¶ **1261.** *Name.*—There shall be in every district a **district Board of the Laity,** which shall be auxiliary to the General, Jurisdictional, and Annual Conference Boards of the Laity.

¶ **1262.** *Objective and Scope of Work.*—The objective and scope of work of the district Board of the Laity shall be related to those adopted by the General Board of the Laity as shown in ¶¶ 1186-87, 1206, 1214-15, 1221, 1228, 1236, and 1241.

¶ **1263.** *Membership.*—The board shall be composed of the district lay leader, who shall be chairman, the associate district lay leaders, program directors elected by the district board, local-church lay leaders, the district superintendent, one or more pastors selected by the board, the district director of United Methodist Men, the district president of the Women's Society of Christian Service, and the district president of United Methodist Youth.

¶ **1264.** *Officers.*—The district lay leader shall be elected annually by the Annual Conference on nomination of the district board. The associate district lay leader for lay life and work, the associate district lay leader for stewardship and finance, the district director of United Methodist Men, other directors as authorized by the conference board, the recording secretary, and the treasurer shall be elected annually by the district board.

¶ 1265. *Tenure and Vacancies.*—All elections of board members shall be for the term of one year. Any vacancy occurring in the district board shall be filled by the board.

¶ 1266. *Executive Committee.*—There shall be an **executive committee,** consisting of the district lay leader, who shall be chairman, the associate district lay leaders, district directors of special program activities selected by the board, the district director of United Methodist Men, the district superintendent, and the elected officers.

¶ 1267. *Commissions and Committees.*—The district board may function through two commissions: the **Commission of Lay Life and Work** and the **Commission of Stewardship and Finance.** A Committee on United Methodist Men may be formed as part of the Commission of Lay Life and Work, with the district director of United Methodist Men as chairman. Other committees may be formed as the district board deems advisable. The scope of work shall be related to that described for the general divisions and conference Commissions of Lay Life and Work and Stewardship and Finance. (*See* ¶¶ 1206, 1214-15, 1221, 1236, 1241, and 1259-60.) A **Committee on Lay Speaking** may be organized for the purpose of screening and certifying lay speakers recommended by local churches. The committee, when organized, shall be composed of the district director of lay speaking, the district superintendent, and such other persons as needed.

¶ 1268. *Meetings.*—The board and/or its executive committee shall meet as often as necessary to perform its duties.

¶ 1269. *Finances.*—The board, through its duly elected officers, shall cooperate with the conference Board of the Laity to obtain from its allocated funds such sums as may be necessary to carry on its proposed program of work.

¶ 1270. *District Lay Leader and Associates.*—The work of the district lay leader and his associates is related to that of their conference counterparts, described in ¶¶ 1257-58.

¶ **1271.** *District Director of United Methodist Men.*—**The district director of United Methodist Men** is expected to keep himself informed about the potential ministries of United Methodist Men, to encourage and support men in local congregations as they seek to be on mission, and to serve as chairman of the district Committee on United Methodist Men when such committee is formed. He shall maintain liaison with the Jurisdictional and Annual Conference organizations and with the Section on United Methodist Men of the General Board of Education (¶ 1221.7).

¶ **1272.** *Local Fellowships of United Methodist Men.* See ¶¶ 159.4, 1220-25.

LAY SPEAKER

¶ **1273.** *Lay Speaker.*—A **lay speaker** is a member of a local church certified by his Charge Conference as qualified to perform the following duties, subject to the consent and direction of the pastor:

1. To serve the church in any way in which the witness of the spoken word inspires the laity to better churchmanship, to give assistance and support to the program emphases of the church, and to assist in giving better leadership to the work of the church.

2. To conduct services of worship and hold meetings for prayer and exhortation when requested by the pastor or district superintendent.

¶ **1274.** *Character.*—A candidate recommended for lay speaker shall be a person of evident Christian character, conduct, and concern; he shall have potential natural gifts and grace, a willingness to seek to improve himself in knowledge and understanding of the Bible, and a desire to grow in Christian grace.

¶ **1275.** *Requirements.*—1. To become a lay speaker the candidate shall:

a) Be recommended by the Administrative Board of his church or the Charge Conference (¶ 145.8).

b) Be certified by the district Committee on Lay Speaking, preferably on completion of the training course for lay speakers recommended by the General Board of the Laity.

2. It is recommended that a consecration service be held in the district on an appropriate occasion.

¶ **1276.** *Reporting.*—A lay speaker shall report to the Charge Conference and be subject to an annual examination by it of his character, gifts, labors, and usefulness, and a renewal of certificate, to be signed by the president thereof.

Section X. Board of Missions.

THE AIMS OF MISSIONS

¶ **1277.** God, Creator, Redeemer, and Life-Giver summons the Church to mission in the world. The aims of this mission are:

1. To witness in all the world, by word and deed, to the self-revelation of God in Jesus Christ and the acts of love by which he reconciles men to himself.

2. To evoke in men the personal response of repentance and faith through which by God's grace they may find newness of life in righteous, loving relationships with God and their fellowmen.

3. To bring men together into a Christian community for worship and fellowship and to send men into the world as servants in the struggle for justice and meaning.

4. To reveal in ministry the love of God for all who suffer.

5. To move men to live in awareness of the presence and life-giving power of God's Holy Spirit, in acknowledgment of his rule over earthly history and in confident expectation of the ultimate consummation of his purpose.

CONSTITUTION—ORGANIZATION

¶ **1278.** *Article 1. Name.*—The name of this organization shall be the **Board of Missions** of The United Methodist Church, hereinafter called the board. Its objectives are religious, philanthropic, and educational.

¶ **1279.** This board is a union of the Board of Missions of The Evangelical United Brethren Church and the Board of Missions of The Methodist Church.

¶ **1280.** *Article 2. Incorporation.*—1. The board shall be incorporated. Within the board there shall be three divisions—namely the World Division, the National Division, and the Women's Division of the Board of Missions of The United Methodist Church—which shall each also be incorporated and which shall be the corporate successors, respectively, of the World Division, the National Division, and the Woman's Division of the Board of Missions of The Methodist Church and the corporate successors of the Board of Missions of The Methodist Church and of the Board of Missions of The Evangelical United Brethren Church. The board and its divisions shall be incorporated in such state or states as the board may select.

2. The Board of Missions of The United Methodist Church shall be the successor to the following corporations: The Board of Missions of The Evangelical United Brethren Church, the Home Missions and Church Erection Society of the Church of the United Brethren in Christ, the Foreign Missionary Society of the United Brethren in Christ, the Woman's Missionary Association of the Church of the United Brethren in Christ, the Missionary Society of the Evangelical Church, and the Board of Church Extension of the Evangelical Church, and as such successor it shall be and is authorized and empowered to receive from its said predecessor corporations all trust funds and assets of every kind and character, real, personal, or mixed, held by them, and it shall and hereby is authorized to administer such trusts and funds in accordance with the conditions under which they have been previously received and administered by the said predecessor corporations.

3. It shall have control of all the work formerly controlled and administered by the following: the Board of Missions and Church Extension of The Methodist Church; the Missionary Society, the Board of Foreign Missions, the Board of Home Missions and Church Extension, the Woman's Foreign Missionary Society, the Woman's Home Missionary Society, the Wesleyan Service Guild, and the Ladies' Aid Societies of the Methodist Episcopal Church; the Board of Missions, including the Woman's Missionary Society, the Woman's Board of Foreign Missions, the Woman's Board of Home Missions, the Woman's Missionary Council, and the Board of Church Extension of the Methodist Episcopal Church, South; the Board of Missions of the

Methodist Protestant Church; and such other corporations or agencies of the General Conference as do similar work; but this list shall not be construed as exclusive.

4. Subject to the limitations hereinafter specified, each of the incorporated divisions shall be subject to the supervision and control of the General Conference of The United Methodist Church in all things not inconsistent with the Constitution and laws of the United States and of the states of incorporation.

¶ 1281. *Article 3. Board of Managers.*—The management, business, property, and all affairs of the Board of Missions of The United Methodist Church shall be governed and administered by a **Board of Managers,** which shall be composed as follows:

1. Fifteen bishops, representing all the jurisdictions, resident in the United States, and in addition representatives of overseas churches, three of whom shall be bishops from Central Conferences and two of whom may be from affiliated autonomous churches, all to be elected by the Council of Bishops (and subject to such travel regulations as are provided in the Discipline for overseas bishops).

2. Members elected quadrennially by the Jurisdictional Conferences as follows: one minister and three lay members, two of whom shall be women, from each jurisdiction for each 600,000 members or major fraction thereof in the jurisdiction; *provided* that no jurisdiction, in addition to the bishops, shall have fewer than two ministers and six lay members, four of whom shall be women and two men. In nominating and electing such members the Jurisdictional Conference shall have as a basis for choice the following: (*a*) one minister and one layman designated by each Annual Conference of the jurisdiction, on nomination of its conference Board of Missions; (*b*) six additional names nominated by the College of Bishops of the jurisdiction; (*c*) twice the necessary number of laywomen, designated by the jurisdiction Women's Society of Christian Service from three members nominated by each conference Women's Society of Christian Service of the jurisdiction. Vacancies among these members shall be filled by the bishops of the jurisdiction in which the vacancies occur ad interim, having regard to the various classifications of members.

3. Twenty-one laymen, at least three from each jurisdiction,

elected quadrennially by the board, on nomination of the Council of Bishops, to serve as members at large of the board.

4. Twenty-one women, at least three from each jurisdiction, elected quadrennially by the board, on nomination of the Women's Division, to serve as members at large of the board.

5. Six young people divided equally according to sex, three of whom shall be of high school age and nominated to the board by the national United Methodist youth organization and three nominated to the board on recommendation of the Office of Campus Ministry in consultation with the United Methodist student leaders in the University Christian Movement.

6. The general secretary and treasurer of the board and the associate general secretaries of the three divisions and the Joint Commission on Education and Cultivation, all of whom shall be without vote.

7. The term of office of all members whose election is provided for in this paragraph shall begin and the board shall organize at a meeting to be held within ninety days after the adjournment of the last meeting of the several Jurisdictional Conferences held after the adjournment of the General Conference.

¶ **1282.** *Article 4. General Executive Committee.*—There shall be a **general executive committee,** which shall exercise the powers of the board ad interim and carry into effect the actions of the board. It shall be composed of the members of the executive committees of the divisions and the Joint Commission on Education and Cultivation. The president of the board shall serve as chairman. It shall submit annually the records of its proceedings.

¶ **1283.** *Article 5. Divisions and Joint Agencies.*—The board shall conduct its activities directly and through three divisions (namely the World Division, the National Division, and the Women's Division), a Joint Commission on Education and Cultivation, and a Joint Committee on Missionary Personnel.

¶ **1284.** The divisions shall report regularly to the board and its executive committee to keep the same fully informed concerning their plans and activities.

¶ **1285.** *Article 6. World Division.*—1. The **World Division** shall be composed of board members as follows: one half the member bishops resident in the United States in addition to five bishops from overseas; one half the ministers, the laymen, the women, and the youth; the president of the Board of Missions ex officio and the president of the Women's Division ex officio; and, without vote, the general secretary and treasurer of the board and the associate general secretary of the division. The division shall meet annually at the time of the meeting of the board and at such other times as it shall deem necessary.

2. There shall be an **executive committee,** which shall exercise the powers of the division ad interim. It shall be composed of twenty-two members of the division: three bishops, four ministers, four laymen, and one student representative elected by the division; eight women elected by the Women's Division as provided in ¶ 1287.2; the president of the Board of Missions ex officio and the president of the Women's Division ex officio.

¶ 1286. *Article 7. National Division.*—1. The **National Division** shall be composed of board members as follows: one half the member bishops resident in the United States; one half the ministers, the laymen, the women, and the youth; the president of the Board of Missions ex officio and the president of the Women's Division ex officio; and, without vote, the general secretary and treasurer of the board and the associate general secretary of the division. The division shall meet annually at the time of the meeting of the board and at such other times as it shall deem necessary.

2. There shall be an **executive committee,** which shall exercise the powers of the division ad interim. It shall be composed of twenty-two members of the division: three bishops, four ministers, four laymen, and one student representative elected by the division; eight women elected by the Women's Division as provided in ¶ 1287.2; the president of the Board of Missions ex officio and the president of the Women's Division ex officio.

¶ 1287. *Article 8. Women's Division.*—1. The **Women's Division** shall be composed of board members as follows: one third of the member bishops resident in the United States, two ministers, two laymen, all the women, one half the youth, and, without vote, the general secretary and treasurer of the board and the associate general secretary of the division. The division shall meet annually at the time of the meeting of the board and at such other times as it shall deem necessary.

367

2. The Women's Division shall elect an **executive committee,** which shall exercise the powers of the division ad interim. It shall be composed of nineteen members, of whom the division shall elect eight each from those who are members of the World and National Divisions to serve also on their respective committees (¶¶ 1285.2, 1286.2) and, from each group of eight, four to serve in addition on the executive committee of the Joint Commission on Education and Cultivation (¶ 1288.2).

¶ **1288.** *Article 9. Joint Commission on Education and Cultivation.*—1. The **Joint Commission on Education and Cultivation** shall be composed of thirty-three voting board members as follows: the chairman of the Joint Committee on Missionary Personnel; three bishops, three ministers, and three laymen each, elected by the World and National Divisions; twelve women, six each from the members of the World and National Divisions, elected by the Women's Division; the president of the Board of Missions ex officio and the president of the Women's Division ex officio; and, without vote, the general secretary and treasurer of the board and the associate general secretary of the commission.

2. There shall be an **executive committee,** which shall exercise the powers of the commission ad interim. It shall be composed of the chairman of the Joint Committee on Missionary Personnel, the president of the Board of Mission ex officio and president of the Woman's Division ex officio, and eighteen other members elected by the divisions from the membership of their executive committees as follows: one bishop, two ministers and two laymen each, elected by the World and National Divisions; and eight women, elected by the Women's Division as provided in ¶ 1287.2.

¶ **1289.** *Article 10. Joint Committee on Missionary Personnel.*— The **Joint Committee on Missionary Personnel** shall be composed of eighteen board members elected by the divisions as follows: one bishop, two ministers, and three laymen elected by the World Division; one bishop, two ministers, and three laymen elected by the National Division; and six women, three each from the members of the World and National Divisions, elected by the Women's Division. The committee may also include two members at large selected for their professional competence needed in the work of the committee.

¶ **1290.** *Article 11. United Methodist Committee for Overseas Relief.*—There shall be a **United Methodist Committee for Overseas Relief.** The committee shall be composed as follows: three bishops from the General Board of Missions; one lay and one ministerial member from each jurisdiction, elected by the respective Jurisdictional Conferences; and four area secretaries from the World Division, elected by the Board of Missions. The general secretary of the Board of Missions and the associate general secretary of the World Division of the Board of Missions shall be ex officio members of the committee with the right to vote. The committee shall be empowered to co-opt not more than seven members at large whose special knowledge or experience would increase the competence of the committee.

¶ **1291.** *Article 12. Properties, Funds, and Endowments.*—1. All properties, trust funds, annuity funds, permanent funds, and endowments now held and administered by the Board of Missions of The Methodist Church, the Board of Missions of The Evangelical United Brethren Church, and their respective divisions, shall be carefully safeguarded and administered in the interest of those persons and causes for which said funds were established; such properties, trust funds, annuity funds, permanent funds, and endowments shall be transferred to the Board of Missions of The United Methodist Church or its respective divisions from merged boards and societies only when such transfers can be made in accordance with the laws of the states where the several boards and societies are chartered and on the recommendation of the respective divisions and the approval of such boards and societies. Funds of the three administrative divisions and their preceding corporations and societies which are subject to appropriation shall be appropriated only on recommendation of the respective divisions.

2. (*a*) The income of the divisions of the board, exclusive of the Women's Division (¶ 1339), shall be derived from apportionments, assessments, or askings distributed to jurisdictions, Annual Conferences, and pastoral charges by the budget-making agency of the General Conference in such manner as the General Conference may prescribe, and from church schools, gifts, donations, freewill offerings, annuities, bequests, specials, and other sources from which missionary and benevolence funds are usually derived, in harmony with the

Discipline of The United Methodist Church and actions of the General Conference. Funds for the fulfillment of the responsibilities of the Women's Division shall be derived from annual voluntary pledges, offerings, gifts, devises, bequests, annuities, or money received through special emphases and from meetings held in the interest of the division.

b) Cultivation for Advance specials shall be through channels of the Church other than the Women's Societies of Christian Service and Wesleyan Service Guilds.

c) All contributions to and income on all funds of the Board of Missions or its respective divisions should be used for current expenses and annual appropriations unless otherwise designated by the donor.

3. Askings shall be received from the fields, and budgets shall be prepared by the World and National Divisions in such manner as the board may prescribe, consistent with its constitution and charter, and this combined budget shall be presented to the budget-making agency of the General Conference.

4. In the allocation of funds to the World and National Divisions the board shall recognize the principle of making distribution on an equitable basis.

5. The board shall not appropriate for the regular maintenance of its work in any one year more money than was received by it for appropriation the previous fiscal year.

OFFICERS AND STAFF

¶ 1292. *Article 13. Board.*—1. *Corporate Officers.*—The board shall elect as its corporate officers a president, four vice-presidents (the nominees being the presidents of the three divisions and of the Joint Commission on Education and Cultivation), a treasurer, a recording secretary, and such other officers as it shall deem necessary. Vacancies shall be filled by the board or its executive committee. The board shall determine the powers and duties of its officers.

2. *Elected Staff.*—The board shall nominate and elect a general secretary, a treasurer, and such other staff as it shall deem necessary. The board shall determine the powers and duties of its elected staff.

3. *Advisory Committee.*—There shall be an **advisory committee,**

consisting of the president of the board, the presidents of the divisions and commission, and the general secretary of the board ex officio. It shall be advisory to the general secretary and shall have the responsibility for presenting to the board and its executive committee items of business which are of general concern and which may have been omitted during business procedures.

¶ 1293. *Article 14. Divisions.*—1. *Corporate Officers.*—Each division shall elect as its corporate officers a president, one or more vice-presidents, a treasurer, a recording secretary, and such other officers as it shall deem necessary. Vacancies shall be filled by the divisions or their executive committees. The divisions shall determine the powers and duties of their officers.

2. *Elected Staff.*—The board shall elect, on nomination of each division and in consultation with the general secretary of the Board of Missions, an associate general secretary of the Board of Missions, who shall have administrative responsibility for the division and shall be responsible to the general secretary of the Board of Missions. It shall also elect, on nomination of each division, one or more assistant general secretaries, who shall be responsible to the associate general secretary of the division, and such other staff as the division shall deem necessary. Due provision shall be made for the inclusion of overseas representatives on the staff of the World Division.

The board shall elect, on nomination of each division and in consultation with the general secretary of the Board of Missions, an associate treasurer of the Board of Missions, who shall have fiscal responsibility for the division. He or she shall be responsible to the treasurer of the Board of Missions for fiscal procedures and to the associate general secretary for all administrative procedures.

¶ 1294. *Article 15. Joint Commission on Education and Cultivation.*—1. *Officers.*—The Joint Commission on Education and Cultivation shall elect as its officers a president, one or more vice-presidents, and such other officers as it shall deem necessary. Vacancies shall be filled by the commission or its executive committee. The commission shall determine the powers and duties of its officers.

2. *Elected Staff.*—The board shall elect, on nomination of the commission and in consultation with the general secretary of the Board of Missions, an associate general secretary of the Board of Missions,

who shall have administrative responsibility for the commission and shall be responsible to the general secretary of the Board of Missions. It shall also elect, on nomination of the joint commission, one or more assistant general secretaries, who shall be responsible to the associate general secretary of the commission, and such other staff as the commission shall deem necessary.

¶ 1295. *Article 16. Joint Committee on Missionary Personnel.*— 1. *Officers.*—The Joint Committee on Missionary Personnel shall elect as its officers a chairman, one or more vice-chairmen, and such other officers as it shall deem necessary. Vacancies shall be filled by the committee. The committee shall determine the powers and duties of its officers.

2. *Elected Staff.*—The board shall elect, on nomination of the committee, an executive secretary and such other staff as the committee shall deem necessary.

¶ 1296. *Article 17. United Methodist Committee for Overseas Relief.*—The United Methodist Committee for Overseas Relief is authorized to elect its own officers, to appoint subcommittees as desired, to employ such staff as the committee may deem necessary, and to provide for its necessary expenses of administration and promotion out of the undesignated receipts. Its officers and staff shall be bonded.

¶ 1297. The board and its divisions shall continue to recruit, elect and/or appoint, utilize, and promote staff members without regard to race and color.

¶ 1298. *Article 18. Staff Participation of Women.*—1. Of the following five staff positions within the board, namely the general secretary and the associate general secretaries of the divisions and joint commission, a minimum of two shall be occupied by women.

2. Of the following staff positions within the World and National Divisions, namely the associate general secretaries, assistant general secretaries, and associate treasurers, a minimum of one third of the total shall be occupied by women.

3. Of the total elected staff positions of the board a minimum of 40 percent chall be occupied by women.

¶ 1299. *Article 19. Retirement.*—The retirement age for all personnel of the Board of Missions shall be age sixty voluntary and age sixty-five compulsory.

¶ **1300.** *Article 20. Board.*—The Board of Missions shall have authority to make bylaws and regulate its proceedings in harmony with the Discipline of The United Methodist Church, its own Disciplinary constitution, and its charter. Bylaws may be amended by a two-thirds vote of the members present and voting thereon at a regular or special meeting; *provided* that notice of such amendment has previously been given to the members. The board shall have the power and right to do any and all things which shall be authorized by its charter. It shall have authority to develop and carry out its functions as described in ¶ 1305; to buy, acquire, or receive by gift, devise, or bequest property, real, personal, and mixed; to hold mortgage, sell, and dispose of property; to sue and be sued; to borrow money in case of necessity; to develop and maintain ecumenical relations to carry out its responsibilities; and to administer its affairs through its respective divisions and joint agencies.

¶ **1301.** *Article 21. Divisions.*—1. The divisions shall have authority to make bylaws and to regulate their proceedings in harmony with the charter and constitution of the board and with its approval to develop and carry out the functions of the divisions as described in ¶¶ 1306-08; to buy and sell property; to solicit and accept contributions, subject to annuity under the board's regulations; and to recommend the appropriation of their funds for the work of the joint agencies of the board.

2. The Women's Division shall have authority:

a) To organize Jurisdiction Society-Guilds, conference, district, and local church Women's Societies of Christian Service and Wesleyan Service Guilds, which shall be auxiliary to the Board of Missions through the Women's Division in The United Methodist Church.

b) To recommend constitutions and make bylaws for the Women's Society of Christian Service and the Wesleyan Service Guild.

c) To appropriate funds for the work of the World and National Divisions.

d) To serve as the national official policy-making body of the Women's Society of Christian Service and the Wesleyan Service Guild with the officers of the Women's Division designated as the national officers of the society and guild.

¶ **1302.** *Article 22. Joint Commission on Education and Cultivation.*—The Joint Commission on Education and Cultivation shall have authority to make bylaws and to regulate its proceedings in harmony with the charter and constitution of the board, and with the approval of the board to develop and carry out the functions described in ¶1309, to recommend to the board through its divisions appropriations for its work, to administer such funds as are allocated to it by the board, and to solicit Advance special funds for the work of the World and National Divisions.

¶ **1303.** *Article 23. Joint Committee on Missionary Personnel.*— The Joint Committee on Missionary Personnel shall have authority to recommend bylaws to the board for its approval, to develop and carry out the functions of the committee described in ¶ 1310, to regulate its proceedings in harmony with its bylaws, to recommend to the board through its divisions appropriations for its work, and to administer such funds as are allocated to it by the board.

¶ **1304.** *Article 24. United Methodist Committee for Overseas Relief.*—The United Methodist Committee for Overseas Relief shall have the authority to incorporate, to make bylaws, and to regulate its proceedings in harmony with the charter and constitution of the Board of Missions for the purpose and functions as defined in the Discipline of The United Methodist Church. It shall be the representative of The United Methodist Church in the fields of overseas relief, of rehabilitation for victims of disaster and endemic circumstance, and of services to refugees. If at any time the Council of Bishops, the Council on World Service and Finance, and the Board of Missions decide that the specific work of the committee is no longer needed, the committee shall be discharged, and its responsibilities and assets shall be assigned to such agency as those three bodies may determine.

FUNCTIONS

¶ **1305.** *Article 25. Board.*—1. The functions of the board shall be:

a) To seek, as an agency of the Christian church, to respond to God's action in Christ and his work in the world through engaging in evangelistic, educational, social, medical, and agricultural work in every part of the world and to promote and support all phases of missionary and church-extension activity in the United States and in other countries.

b) To establish and review the objectives of the Board of Missions and the work in mission of The United Methodist Church.

c) To establish appropriate organization of board and staff to accomplish its programs and achieve established objectives, including making bylaws, electing officers, establishing committees for its work, nominating its staff, removing for cause, and filling vacancies occurring in its own body, subcommittees, or staff.

d) To determine policy and program, to establish goals and priorities, to project long-range plans, to evaluate the program and services of the Board of Missions and its divisions, to evaluate the performance of the staff and its progress in fulfilling its purpose, and through the programs of the divisions and joint agencies of the Board of Missions to seek to achieve its objectives.

e) To establish, nurture, expand, and have general oversight of the missionary and church-extension programs in home and overseas areas and to execute them through the respective divisions and joint agencies.

f) To determine, on recommendation of the divisions and joint agencies, the areas to be served and the nature of the work to be undertaken.

g) To recruit, prepare, and, upon recommendation of the divisions, commission missionaries and assign them to the appropriate divisions for service and support.

h) To secure, appropriate, and spend money to underwrite its program and achieve its objectives.

i) To build, equip, and maintain churches, hospitals, homes, schools, orphanages, parsonages, and other institutions of Christian service and to enlist, train, and support the workers for the same.

j) To receive and properly administer all properties and trust funds, permanent funds, annuity funds, and other special funds coming into the possession of the board as a board for missionary and other purposes.

k) To coordinate and harmonize the work of the various units.

l) To receive and act upon the reports of the divisions, executive

375

secretaries, and treasurers; official reports from home and overseas fields; and reports of all its committees.

m) To foster, strengthen, and promote missionary understanding, interest, and concern throughout The United Methodist Church.

n) To assist the organization and maintenance of cooperative relations with the boards, committees, and other agencies of the General Conference; with the Jurisdictional, Central, and Annual Conference boards and committees, and other agencies; and with interdenominational and other missionary agencies in the home and overseas fields.

o) To develop and maintain the ecumenical relations necessary for the full discharge of the above functions.

p) To elect, on nomination of the divisions and joint agencies, the staff of the respective divisions and joint agencies, to remove them for cause, and to fill vacancies.

q) To give direction to the Board of Missions staff and its work through the assignment of responsibilities and the delegation of authority to the executives and through general oversight of the administration.

r) To make a report of its activities during the quadrennium to the General Conference and the Jurisdictional Conferences.

2. The board and its divisions shall perform their functions in harmony with the policy of The United Methodist Church to eliminate discrimination based on race or color.

¶ 1306. *Article 26. World Division.*—The functions of the World Division shall be:

1. To develop and administer the program of the Church in areas outside the United States and its dependencies, including those programs previously administered by The Methodist Church and The Evangelical United Brethren Church, and to supervise the work of the various departments of the division.

2. To foster sound relationships with sister churches outside the United States and to encourage among them interrelationships in mission.

3. To establish goals, priorities, and long-range plans which will enable the division to achieve its objectives and those of the Board of

Missions, and to review and evaluate its program in terms of these objectives.

4. To review the proposed annual budgets from the overseas fields, including askings to the World Division for recurring and capital grants, and to recommend budgets to the Board of Missions.

5. To receive and administer the world service gifts for the general missionary activity of The United Methodist Church overseas.

6. To receive and administer the Advance special gifts for world missionary work cultivated through the Joint Commission on Education and Cultivation.

7. To receive and administer funds requested and allocated by the Women's Division, keeping in mind the special needs of women.

8. To make annual reports to the Board of Missions.

9. To accept for assignment to its various fields of service, upon recommendation of the Joint Committee on Missionary Personnel, missionaries who have been approved by the Board of Missions.

¶ 1307. *Article 27. National Division.*—The functions of the National Division shall be:

1. To develop and administer the mission and church-extension program in areas within the United States, Puerto Rico, and the Virgin Islands, including those programs previously administered by The Methodist Church and The Evangelical United Brethren Church, and to supervise the work of the division.

2. To formulate the objectives for the national mission of The United Methodist Church, to determine the fields of service and the nature of the work to be undertaken, and to establish policies governing these programs.

3. To establish goals, priorities, and long-range plans which will enable the division to achieve its objectives and those of the Board of Missions, and to review and evaluate its program in terms of these objectives.

4. To review the proposed annual budgets from national fields, including askings to the National Division for recurring and capital grants, and to recommend budgets to the Board of Missions.

5. To receive and administer the world service gifts for the general missionary activities of The United Methodist Church in home fields.

6. To receive and administer the Advance special gifts for Na-

tional Division work cultivated through the Joint Commission on Education and Cultivation.

7. To administer all donation aid, loan funds, and endowments, contributed and established for the work of church extension, except such as may be administered by the Jurisdictional and Annual Conferences.

8. To receive and administer funds requested and allocated by the Women's Division, keeping in mind the special needs of women.

9. To make annual reports to the Board of Missions.

10. To accept for assignment to its various fields of service, upon recommendation of the Joint Committee on Missionary Personnel, missionaries and deaconesses who have been approved by the Board of Missions.

¶ 1308. *Article 28. Women's Division.*—The functions of the Women's Division shall be:

1. To recommend program and policies to Women's Societies of Christian Service and Wesleyan Service Guilds.

2. To interpret the mission of Christ and his Church as stated in the purpose of the Women's Society of Christian Service and the Wesleyan Service Guild.

3. To provide resources and opportunities for women that enrich their spiritual life and increase their knowledge and understanding of the needs of the world and their responsibility in meeting those needs.

4. To secure funds through the channels of Women's Societies of Christian Service and Wesleyan Service Guilds for the support of the program of the Church through the Board of Missions, with special concern for the needs and responsibilities of women.

5. To project plans specially directed toward leadership development of women through appropriate planning with the other divisions and agencies of the board.

6. To strengthen the Church's challenge to women to enlist in church-related vocations as missionaries and deaconesses at home and abroad.

7. To enlist women in activities that have a moral and religious significance for the public welfare and that contribute to the establishment of a Christian social order around the world.

8. To plan with other agencies of the Church and community in areas of common concern and responsibility.

9. To give visible evidence of our oneness in Christ by uniting in fellowship and service with other Christians, including the World Federation of Methodist Women, Church Women United, and other similar groups, thereby strengthening the ecumenical witness and program of the Church.

¶ **1309.** *Article 29. Joint Commission on Education and Cultivation.*—1. The functions of the Joint Commission on Education and Cultivation shall be:

a) To undergird with education and cultivation the total program of the Board of Missions.

b) To initiate and develop programs through which individuals and groups may understand the biblical background and theological basis for the Christian world mission, the involvement of The United Methodist Church in the missionary enterprise, and the possibilities for personal witness, involvement in, and support of this mission.

c) To prepare, sell, and distribute publications and audio-visual and other materials for the work of the board.

d) To cooperate with the Board of Education through the Interboard Committee on Missionary Education, with other agencies of The United Methodist Church, and with interdenominational agencies in leadership development, curriculum development, the preparation and distribution of missionary materials, and other ventures.

e) To promote missionary councils, conventions, institutes, summer conferences, and other meetings throughout the Church for the purpose of developing a missionary spirit, of training leadership on all levels, of disseminating missionary information, and of acquainting the Church with the plans and policies of the board.

f) To promote an annual call to prayer and self-denial and all other special mission emphases.

g) To encourage an emphasis on missionary education in colleges, universities, and schools of theology.

h) To help foster throughout the Church an ecumenical understanding and involvement in the Christian world mission.

i) To cultivate, through channels of the Church other than Women's Societies of Christian Service and Wesleyan Service Guilds, the Advance special gifts for home and foreign missionary work administered by the World and National Divisions.

j) In consultation with the divisions of the Board of Missions and in cooperation with the Division of Interpretation of the Program Council and other appropriate agencies of the Church, to develop and coordinate the plans for cultivating missionary giving; *provided,* however, that all such plans shall be subject to and in harmony with the general financial system of The United Methodist Church as adopted by the General Conference.

2. In fulfilling these functions the commission shall seek the cooperation of Jurisdictional and Annual Conferences, district superintendents and pastors, local churches, Women's Societies of Christian Service and Wesleyan Service Guilds, men's groups and other groups within the Church.

¶ 1310. *Article 30. Joint Committee on Missionary Personnel.—* 1. The functions of the Joint Committee on Missionary Personnel shall be:

a) To recommend to the board the standards and qualifications of missionary candidates, including deaconesses, for home and foreign service.

b) To enlist, cultivate, appraise, recommend, and supervise preparation of candidates for missionary service at home and abroad and for deaconess service in the United States.

c) To cooperate in the work of the Interboard Committee on Enlistment for Church Occupations.

d) To recommend the reinstatement of missionaries and the transfer of missionaries between the divisions.

2. A person shall be constituted a missionary or deaconess when he or she has met the requirements of the committee and has been accepted and commissioned as a missionary or deaconess.

¶ 1311. *Article 31. United Methodist Committee for Overseas Relief.—*1. The functions of the United Methodist Committee for Overseas Relief shall be as follows:

a) To minister in the spirit of Jesus Christ to persons in need without regard to their religion, race, or nationality.

b) To cooperate with Church World Service, the Division of Inter-Church Aid, Refugee, and World Service of the World Council of Churches, and other interdenominational relief agencies as the committee may deem wise.

c) To supplement, when considered desirable, the work of other agencies ministering in the spirit of Jesus Christ to the relief of human suffering.

d) To give assistance for a limited period to the national workers and the people of United Methodist churches overseas who are in need because of war or other disasters. In countries where the Board of Missions is at work, it is expected that the administration of specifically United Methodist relief be through the representative of the board and the bishops in charge and, where possible, the indigenous church.

e) To transmit to the Church appeals for help and to receive and allocate funds contributed by churches, groups, or individuals for the purposes stated above; *provided* that no churchwide appeal for funds shall be made without the approval of the Council of Bishops and the Council on World Service and Finance.

f) To acknowledge gifts by its own vouchers. (*See* ¶ 867.)

2. In order to provide adequate means for the prosecution of its work, the committee, in addition to those receipts from voluntary gifts, the One Great Hour of Sharing offering (¶ 875), and the Fellowship of Suffering and Service offering (¶ 877), shall be included in any churchwide appeal to meet emergencies growing out of war, internal strife, or natural disaster. Financial promotion shall be by the Division of Interpretation of the Program Council in consultation with the executive secretary of the committee.

General Provisions for the World Division

¶ 1312. *Article 32. Liaison Committee.*—1. The Board of Missions, through its World Division, shall request each Central Conference, Annual Conference, Provisional Annual Conference, affiliated autonomous Methodist church, or united church, where applicable, to make provision for liaison functions with the board through a committee which is representative of all phases of the world mission, particularly of the needs and responsibilities of women. The World Division shall develop with sister churches such administrative and fiscal relationships as will stimulate partnership in mission and determine the particular role of each in the joint commitment.

2. The duties of the committee shall be:

a) To meet regularly at the call of the chairman or the executive committee, which shall be composed of the chairman, vice-chairman, and secretary.

b) To elect a vice-chairman, who shall be authorized to preside at meetings in the absence of the chairman, and a secretary, whose responsibility shall be to forward the minutes and the report of its recommendations promptly to the board.

c) To consult with the board on all matters of mutual concern.

d) To receive and transmit to the board reports from all the institutions and agencies of the Church which receive aid from the board.

e) To make requests for missionary personnel as desired.

f) To prepare estimates of funds requested from the board for aid to work in the conference and for aid to institutions and other projects, except the financial requirement for missionary support, which is the direct responsibility of the board.

3. There shall be a **Subcommittee on Women's Work** of the committee, which shall deal with all the concerns of women in the Church appropriate to the committee. This subcommittee shall be composed of all women members of the committee and up to three additional members co-opted as desired. It shall be chaired by the bishop or officer of the area and shall have at least two regular meetings in the year.

¶ 1313.   In a Central Conference in which there is an executive board or council of cooperation constituted, the estimates for the maintenance and development of the work, prepared by the various Liaison Committees, may be presented to the World Division after approval by such board or council. The estimates shall be presented conference by conference, and by projects within the conferences.

¶ 1314.   In a Central or Provisional Central Conference where there is no executive board or council of cooperation, the estimates shall be sent directly to the World Division from the Liaison Committee of each Annual or Provisional Annual Conference.

¶ 1315.   *Article 33. Administration of New World-Division Com-*

mitments.—Where the World Division, with the approval of the Board of Missions, plans to open work in countries beyond its present commitments, the division shall do so either through a working agreement negotiated with the church or churches already in the area or a united mission organization. Only where neither of these approaches is possible should a United Methodist mission be organized. Such a mission organization shall be structured in accordance with local conditions and administered by the World Division.

¶ **1316.** *Article 34. Missionaries.*—All missionaries who serve in fields outside the United States should relate themselves as directly as possible to the organized Church in these fields through membership in a local church or Annual Conference.

¶ **1317.** *Article 35. Missionaries Serving Other Churches.*—1. Missionaries of The United Methodist Church, on action of the Board of Missions, may be assigned to serve in affiliated autonomous churches, in independent churches, in churches resulting from the union of Methodist churches and other communions, or in other evangelical denominations.

2. Such missionaries, while retaining their membership in their home local churches or Annual Conferences and without impairing their relationship to the Board of Missions, shall, while on service in such fields, be free to accept such rights and privileges as may be offered to them by such churches.

GENERAL PROVISIONS FOR THE NATIONAL DIVISION

¶ **1318.** The associate general secretary of the National Division shall communicate to the bishops such information as may be available concerning missions and the appointment of workers in their respective areas.

¶ **1319.** *Article 36. Mission Responsibilities.*—The National Division shall give special study and promotion to mission work, including social welfare, education, and medical services in urban and rural areas, and in Missions and Annual and Provisional Annual Conferences. It shall organize such programs and conduct such activities as the development of the work may require, with special attention to the needs of people in transitional relationships. It shall assign staff members to develop these programs. They shall administer such appropriations as are committed to them. They shall cooperate with other boards and agencies as their work may affect the group involved.

¶ **1320.** *Article 37. Sections, Service Units, and Departments.*—The National Division shall consist of the following sections: the **Section of Home Fields,** the **Section of Church Extension,** and the **Section of Joint Services.** Additional sections or subunits may be established as the needs of the work require.

1. In the Section of Home Fields there shall be a **Service Unit of Parish and Community Development,** which shall include the Departments of Urban Ministries, Town and Country Ministries, and Missions and Provisional Annual Conferences, and a **Service Unit of Social Welfare, Medical, and Educational Work,** which shall include the Departments of Community Centers, Children's Homes and Residences, Educational Work, Medical Work and Retirement Homes, and Goodwill Industries.

2. In the Section of Church Extension there shall be a Department of Church Extension, a Department of Finance and Field Service, and a Department of New Church Development.

3. In the Section of Joint Services (the National Division) there shall be a Department of Research and Survey, a Department of Architecture, and a Department of Deaconess Work.

SECTION OF HOME FIELDS

¶ **1321.** *Article 38. Service Units.*—1. *Service Unit of Parish and Community Development.*—(a) The **Department of Urban Ministries,** in cooperation with conference boards or committees, shall evaluate the urban church situation and recommend to the National Division and to Annual Conferences and local leaders policies and programs for the conduct of urban ministry in cities with a population of more than ten thousand. It shall aid in the organization and development of Christian centers and city societies. It shall cooperate with other denominations and with other agencies in the development of community and of services for the enrichment of individual, family, and community life in metropolitan regions.

b) The **Department of Town and Country Ministries,** in cooperation with conference boards or committees, shall study and survey the town and country church situation and recommend to the National Division policies and programs to improve the economic, social, educational, and religious life of persons in towns with a population of less than ten thousand and in rural areas. It shall cooperate with other denominations and with other agencies in the development of community and of services for the enrichment of individual, family, and community life in town and country areas. It shall provide for the training, assigning, and supervision of professional church and community workers. There shall be consultation with advisory committees regarding personnel, programs, budgets, areas of need, and other matters.

c) The **Department of Missions and Provisional Annual Conferences** shall study and survey the church situation and recommend to the National Division policies and programs for the enrichment of church and community life in Missions and Provisional Annual Conferences. This department shall be related also to the Section of Church Extension and shall be responsible for church-extension service in Missions and Provisional Annual Conferences.

2. *Service Unit for Social Welfare, Medical, and Educational Work.*— (*a*) The **Department of Community Centers** shall provide the general supervision and administration of the community centers related to the National Division. It shall review askings and administer appropriations for community centers. There shall be opportunities for guidance and counsel relative to administration, personnel, program, budgets, and other matters needed for the effective operation of the work. Provision shall be made for field consultation services and the development of training opportunities and materials.

b) The **Department of Children's Homes and Residences** shall provide the general supervision and administration of the child-care agencies and residences for business women related to the National Division. It shall review askings and administer appropriations for such residences and child-care agencies. There shall be opportunities for guidance and counsel relative to administration, personnel, program, budgets, and other matters needed for the effective operation of the work. Provision shall be made for field consultation services and the development of training opportunities and materials. A cooperative relationship shall be maintained with the Board of Health and Welfare Ministries.

c) The **Department of Medical Work and Retirement Homes** shall provide the general supervision and administration of the hospitals, medical work, and retirement homes related to the National Division. It shall review askings and administer appropriations for medical work, hospitals, and retirement homes. There shall be opportunities for guidance and counsel relative to administration, personnel, budgets, and other matters needed for effective service. A cooperative relationship shall be maintained with the Board of Health and Welfare Ministries.

d) The **Department of Educational Work** shall make provision for the general administration and supervision of the educational work and institutions related to the National Division. It shall review askings and administer appropriations for educational work and institutions. There shall be training opportunities for guidance and counsel relative to administration, personnel, curriculum, budgets, and other matters needed for the effective operation of the work. A cooperative relationship shall be maintained with the Division of Higher Education of the Board of Education.

e) The **Department of Goodwill Industries** shall provide for the religious, educational, social, and industrial welfare of the handicapped and unfortunate. It shall promote and establish **Goodwill Industries** in various centers; shall review missionary askings and administer appropriations for Goodwill Industries; shall endorse and assist only those local Goodwill Industries which are organized and conducted according to its standards, rules, and regulations; and shall urge them to cooperate with the departments, sections, divisions, and boards of The United Methodist Church, and with other organizations serving the handicapped and unfortunate. The division may conduct national and regional institutes and such other special training activities as will help to develop the specialized leadership required for the direction of Goodwill Industries.

Section of Church Extension

¶ **1322.** *Article 39. Departments.*—1. *Department of Church Extension.*—There shall be a **Department of Church Extension,** which shall seek to revitalize and extend the mission of the Church in its local setting. It will help to develop new forms of congregational life and promote innovations of ministry. It will also lend support to pilot projects in interdenominational cooperation. It shall do this by assisting in the building of churches, parsonages, and other mission buildings where help is most needed under the following regulations:

a) Local churches seeking financial aid from the division shall submit preliminary architectural plans to the division, or such committee as it may designate, for approval before final working drawings are started. (*See* ¶ 1323.)

b) It shall appropriate money for the various types of work in the field and the conduct of the work of the office. The division and its executive committee, or such other committee as it may designate, shall determine what should be donated or loaned to each applicant.

c) All applications for aid from the division shall be made through the conference Board of Missions. Grants shall be made by the division, its executive committee, or such other committee as it may designate, on recommendation of the appropriate committee and the secretary or secretaries.

d) In granting donations to churches and parsonages it shall require from the trustees of each aided local church an obligation which shall be a lien on the property involved for the return of the amount donated in the event that the work cease or the property be alienated from The United Methodist Church; *provided* that these provisions may be waived in cases involving donations of five thousand dollars or less. Said lien may be subordinated to enable the trustees of the church involved to give a first mortgage for a loan. In case of relocation, the division's investment and lien may be transferred to the new property.

e) When a donation is granted by the division where the property involved is held in trust by the Board of Trustees of the Annual Conference or by a board of trustees elected by and responsible to the General Conference, no lien shall be required by the division; *provided* that the trustees agree, with the approval of the Annual Conference or the General Conference, that the property shall not be conveyed without protecting the claim of the division.

f) The division or its constituent corporations shall raise and administer a loan fund and a revolving loan fund which shall be held separate from funds secured for general distribution.

g) Under the provisions of the Methodist General Conference of 1960 there shall be a Methodist Investment Fund, incorporated by the division and under its administrative jurisdiction. The Evangelical United Brethren Investment Fund shall be merged, as soon as legally feasible, with the Methodist Investment Fund to form the **United Methodist Investment Fund.** The purpose of the United Methodist Investment Fund shall be to extend the mission of the Church through the granting of loans for construction and major improvement of churches, parsonages, and mission buildings.

h) It shall cooperate with the conference Boards of Missions in providing for consultations between city (metropolitan) and district missionary societies and district Boards of Church Location and Building in the development of standards and procedures for local-church building projects in the fields of site selection, study and approval of architectural plans, and financing programs.

2. *Department of Finance and Field Service.*— (*a*) There shall be a **Department of Finance and Field Service,** the functions of which shall be: (1) to raise funds for church, parsonage, and Christian educational buildings and equipment, for renovating, remodeling, and repair projects, and for other institutions and causes, such as conference pensions, schools of theology, Wesley Foundations, colleges, hospitals, homes, and community centers; (2) to raise funds for the retirement of church and other institution obligations—a nominal charge shall be made for fund-raising services; (3) to assist and guide churches in developing effective budgets and other financial plans; (4) to provide for consultation with district, conference, and missionary fund-raising personnel.

b) A fund may be set up by the division, to be secured from gifts and legacies, the income of which shall be used for the support of the above functions.

3. *Department of New Church Development.*—There shall be a **Department of New Church Development,** which shall encourage the founding of new congregations in communities not already adequately supplied. It shall render the following services:

a) Provide an organizing pastor for new congregations.

b) Supply a consulting pastor to assist and work with pastors appointed to new church situations, and provide training and assistance in program development.

c) Conduct workshops and seminars in new church development.

d) Provide field consultation on specific new church projects.

e) Conduct surveys in the fields of new congregation life and ministry.

f) Promote new forms of congregation, ministry, and service.

SECTION OF JOINT SERVICES

¶ **1323.** *Article 40. Departments.*—1. *Department of Architecture.*—The National Division shall make provision for the fulfillment of the following purposes in its architectural work:

a) To coordinate and disseminate information and recommendations on church-planning in dialogue with church agencies and other organizations.

b) To help local churches analyze their needs and prepare a written program around which the building may be designed.

c) To prepare guidance material which will assist building committees and architects in planning church buildings.

d) To evaluate and constructively criticize preliminary plans.

e) To counsel with churches and architects and, on request and as schedules permit, to counsel at the building site.

2. *Department of Research and Survey.*—The National Division shall conduct surveys and research studies in both cities and rural territories, giving attention to migrations of population, new and growing communities, changed neighborhoods, and religious conditions of racial and other groups. It shall cooperate with conference boards in making surveys. It may promote kindred activities on college and seminary campuses and within various areas of The United Methodist Church. It may produce and circulate materials designed to aid administrators and pastors in conducting community self-studies and surveys.

3. *Counseling Service for Nonprofit Housing.*—The National Division shall provide a consultative service, giving guidance and assistance in nonprofit housing for low and middle income families.

4. *Department of Deaconess Service.*— (*a*) The office of deaconess is hereby authorized in The United Methodist Church. A deaconess is a professionally competent laywoman who, in response to God's claim on her life, and who, having met the requirements of the Joint Committee on Missionary Personnel, has been duly consecrated by a bishop and commissioned and licensed for a ministry of special need. A deaconess may serve in any agency of The United Methodist Church in the United States and/or its dependencies. A deaconess may also serve in agencies or work outside The United Methodist Church; *provided* that such work is approved by the National Division.

b) The appointment of a deaconess shall be made as follows: (1) recommendation to an appointment by the Committee on Deaconess Service after consultation with the bishop of the area and (2) confirmation of the appointment by the National Division. The appointment shall be made by the bishop of the Annual Conference and will be printed in the Annual Conference journal.

c) A deaconess shall hold her church membership in a local church within the conference where her appointment is located, and she shall be a voting member of the Charge Conference of that church. A deaconess holding a staff position with a general board or a connectional agency of The United Methodist Church may hold her church membership in an Annual Conference within reasonable distance of the headquarters of the board or agency she serves.

d) A deaconess shall be seated at the sessions of the Annual Conference with the privilege of the floor but without vote, unless she is a duly elected delegate.

e) A deaconess shall be subject to the administrative authority of the agency to which she is appointed. In matters of her appointment she shall be finally subject to the authority of the National Division through the Committee on Deaconess Service and shall, therefore, enter into no contract for her service which would nullify this authority.

f) A pension plan shall be provided for deaconesses. (1) For all deaconesses commissioned on or after July 24, 1940, there shall be a contributory plan, with the employing agency and the deaconess sharing contributions as determined from time to time by actuarial studies. (2) For deaconesses commissioned or consecrated previously to July

24, 1940, former agreements are continued, and the administrations with which they were connected are responsible for the pensions. (3) A deaconess employed by a church or agency having its own pension plan shall participate in that plan during her term of service with that church or agency.

g) A deaconess shall surrender her credentials when she is no longer available for appointment by The United Methodist Church. A person may be reinstated as a deaconess on recommendation of the Committee on Deaconess Service and with the approval of the National Division.

h) All properties, trust funds, permanent funds, other special funds, and endowments now held and administered by or for the several forms of administration of deaconess work under the uniting churches shall be carefully safeguarded and administered by the several forms of the administration in the interest of those persons and causes for which said funds were established.

i) The Board of Missions shall elect an executive secretary of the Department of Deaconess Service who shall be a deaconess who shall be nominated by the National Division in consultation with the chairman of the Committee on Deaconess Service.

¶ 1324. *Article 41. Committee on Deaconess Service.*—1. There shall be a **Committee on Deaconess Service,** which shall be advisory to the National Division and shall make recommendations to it.

2. The Committee on Deaconess Service shall be composed of one bishop chosen by the Council of Bishops; two deaconesses and one minister chosen by each Jurisdiction Association for Deaconesses and Home Missionaries; the president of each Jurisdiction Society-Guild; three representatives, at least one man, chosen by the National Division; the president of the Women's Division; one representative each from the Boards of Pensions, Health and Welfare Ministries, and Education; the executive secretary of the Interboard Committee on Enlistment for Church Occupations; and one staff representative of the Joint Committee on Missionary Personnel. The committee may co-opt others as needed. The executive secretary of the Department of Deaconess Service shall be a member without vote.

3. The committee shall meet annually. Its officers shall be elected quadrennially.

4. The functions of the committee shall be:

a) To recommend new channels and fields of service for deaconesses and new approaches through which they may provide creative leadership and support as instruments of God's redemptive activity in the lives of people.

b) To study and recommend to the National Division policies and procedures, including standards, relative to the office of deaconess and its relationship to the Church and society.

c) To initiate and recommend programs of continuing education for deaconesses that will contribute to their spiritual, professional, and emotional growth.

d) To initiate, recommend, and cooperate with agencies and boards in interpreting the office of deaconess.

5. There shall be an executive committee and other committees as are necessary for carrying out the duties of the committee.

¶ **1325.** *Article 42. Jurisdiction Association for Deaconesses and Home Missionaries.*—1. In each geographical jurisdiction there shall be a **Jurisdiction Association for Deaconesses and Home Missionaries.**

2. Membership of the jurisdiction association shall include:

a) All active deaconesses and home missionaries working within the bounds of the jurisdiction.

b) The president of the Jurisdiction Society-Guild, the president of each conference Women's Society of Christian Service, the ministerial representative to the Committee on Deaconess Service, and members of the Committee on Deaconess Service living within the bounds of the jurisdiction.

c) All deaconesses and home missionaries with the retired relationship who are living within the bounds of the jurisdiction shall be honorary members without vote.

3. The functions of the association shall be:

a) To promote the deaconess and home missionary relationship as authorized by the National Division through the Committee on Deaconess Service and the Joint Committee on Missionary Personnel.

b) To provide opportunities for fellowship among deaconesses and home missionaries and other workers in the geographical jurisdiction and Annual Conferences and to fulfill other duties in harmony with the constitution, as may be set forth in the bylaws.

4. The association shall elect its officers quadrennially: a president, who shall be a deaconess, a vice-president, a secretary, and a treasurer.

5. There shall be a meeting of the association held annually or biennially.

6. There shall be an executive committee and other committees as are necessary for carrying out the duties of the association.

¶ 1326. *Article 43. Annual Conference Promotion of Deaconess Service.*—1. The interpretation of the office of deaconess and the enlistment of women to this office in the Church shall be the responsibility of the Annual Conference Commission on Enlistment for Church Occupations, to which one deaconess shall be assigned in conferences where one or more deaconesses are working, and of the Women's Society of Christian Service in cooperation with the National Division through the Committee on Deaconess Service and the Joint Committee on Missionary Personnel.

2. The National Division, through the Committee on Deaconess Service, shall work in cooperation with the conference Committees on Education and Missions and with the conference Board of Health and Welfare Ministries in initiating, exploring, and recommending new channels and fields of service for deaconesses.

¶ 1327. *Article 44. City or District Societies.*—The National Division shall promote the organization of **city (metropolitan) or district missionary societies** wherever possible and practicable. These societies shall be amenable to the Annual Conference Board of Missions.

¶ 1328. 1. Such a society may be organized under such name as it may determine wherever, in the judgment of the bishop or bishops and district superintendents concerned, it is deemed advisable. When two or more districts, conferences, episcopal areas, or jurisdictions have churches in the same city or metropolitan area, it is recommended that the society be so organized as to include all these churches. The bishops involved shall initiate the effort to develop the society. Charges in communities adjacent to a city but not attached to the city may be included in the society.

2. All bishops, district superintendents, and superintendents of

Missions or Provisional Annual Conferences having jurisdiction within the geographical territory covered by the society, and all pastors therein, shall be ex officio members of the society or its board of managers. The membership shall also include adequate representation from Women's Societies of Christian Service and governing boards of agencies related to the National Division. Each Charge Conference in the territory shall be entitled to at least one lay representative, and there shall be representatives elected by the conference Board of Missions.

3. The purpose of such a society is to promote and coordinate the work of the Church in cities and contiguous communities. The work of the society may include the organization of church schools, the organization (but not the constituting) of churches, mission aid to churches, adaptation of ministries of downtown and inner-city churches to their changed communities, formation of inner-city parishes or group ministries, development of ministries among non-English-speaking peoples, acquisition of real estate, erection of buildings, and the securing and holding of endowments for the society and for dependent churches.

¶ **1329.**　In order to receive financial assistance from the division the society shall meet the following conditions:

1. It shall be organized according to the Discipline.

2. It shall have an executive committee, meeting at least once each quarter.

3. It shall be actively at work.

4. It shall have made a report to the division including: (*a*) number of ministers, deaconesses, or missionaries supported in whole or in part, amount paid to each, and kind of work in which each is engaged; (*b*) expenses of administration; (*c*) total amount raised by the society and how expended; (*d*) such other items as the division shall require.

5. It shall endeavor to raise annually by offerings or otherwise an amount at least equal to that appropriated to it by the National Division, exclusive of appropriations made for work among foreign-speaking people, and shall report annually to the National Division.

¶ **1330.**　Each Annual Conference shall promote the work of the societies and arrange for the publication of their reports in the conference journal, providing a separate column for such in connection with the statement of the benevolence support.

¶ 1331. If the society has an executive officer giving his entire time to the work, it is recommended that he be invited into consultation with the bishop and district superintendents in the consideration of the appointments that affect missions or churches administered or aided by the society.

¶ 1332. The society, after consultation with the conference Board of Missions, shall have authority, in the territory covered by its constitution or charter, to make apportionments to the pastoral charges and to receive all moneys for its program. It shall report annually to the conference board.

¶ 1333. Each pastor whose charge lies within the territory of the society shall each year present the interests of the society to his congregation, take an offering for it or provide for the amount apportioned in the benevolence budget, and report the amount received to the Annual Conference.

¶ 1334. Any local church within its territory expecting to receive aid from the society for buildings or improvement shall be required to secure, as a condition to receiving such aid, the approval of the society with respect to location, plans, and methods of financing.

¶ 1335. In a metropolitan area the National Division may cooperate, with the approval of the bishops and the conferences, in the organization of a **Metropolitan Commission,** which may be composed of bishops and district superintendents involved and a selected group of ministers, laymen, and laywomen, representing conference Boards of Missions, Committees on Urban Ministries, conference Women's Societies of Christian Service, city missionary societies, local churches, representatives of other boards and agencies, and others who have skills and experience enabling them to fulfill creative planning and strategy functions for United Methodism in the metropolitan area.

The purpose of such a commission is to promote long-term planning and to provide a coordinating framework for United Methodism's metropolitan mission strategy. These functions may be fulfilled in cooperation with the district or city (metropolitan) society as deemed appropriate.

¶ 1336. *Article 45. Administration of a Mission.*—1. Administration of a **Mission** in the United States or its territories shall be in the National Division until requirements have been met for the organization of a Provisional or an Annual Conference.

2. The Mission shall meet annually and shall be composed of all regularly appointed missionaries, both lay and clerical, mission traveling preachers, and other lay members. The number of lay members and the method of their appointment shall be determined by the Mission.

3. The bishop in charge of a Mission may appoint a superintendent of the Mission or as many superintendents of the Mission as may be wise and for whom support has been provided. He shall determine the groups or charges over which the respective superintendents shall have supervision.

4. A bishop, or in his absence one of the superintendents chosen by ballot by the Mission, shall preside at the annual meeting. This meeting shall exercise, in a general way, the functions of a District Conference. It shall have power to license persons to preach, to pass on the character of preachers not members of an Annual Conference, to receive on trial mission traveling preachers, and to recommend to an Annual Conference proper persons for deacon's orders. The presiding officer shall, at the annual meeting, assign the missionaries and mission traveling preachers to the several charges for the ensuing year; *provided* that no missionary shall be transferred to or from a Mission without previous consultation with the National Division.

5. Examinations of lay pastors and traveling preachers shall be held by the Mission and certified to an Annual Conference. The Mission also shall make recommendations for reception on trial in an Annual Conference.

General Provisions for the Women's Division

¶ 1337. *Article 46. Responsibilities and Scope.*—1. The Women's Division shall include in its responsibilities those formerly carried by the Woman's Society of Christian Service of The Methodist Church and the Women's Society of World Service of The Evangelical United Brethren Church and those of other organizations of women of similar purposes which have operated or are operating in the charges of the uniting churches.

2. The scope of the division shall be rooted in the concerns and responsibilities of the Church in today's world, including the special needs and interests of women. It shall foster spiritual growth, missionary outreach and service, and Christian social witness through the Women's Society of Christian Service, including the Wesleyan Service Guild.

¶ **1338.** *Article 47. Sections.*—The Women's Division shall be organized into three sections, namely the Section of Program and Education for Christian Mission, the Section of Christian Social Relations, and the Section of Finance.

1. The **Section of Program and Education for Christian Mission** shall coordinate, through the Joint Committee for Program Coordination of the Joint Commission on Education and Cultivation and the Women's Division, plans and programs for Women's Societies of Christian Service and Wesleyan Service Guilds with the joint commission and such other agencies as may have channels to the local church; initiate plans and programs for the enrichment and development of leadership and service among women, after appropriate planning with other units of the board and in keeping with the division's function; promote, in cooperation with the Section of Finance, plans for securing funds through the channels of the Women's Societies of Christian Service and Wesleyan Service Guilds to support the work of the Church at home and abroad; project plans for the organization, promotion, and cultivation of Women's Societies of Christian Service and Wesleyan Service Guilds and strengthen those already established; and bring its plans and programs to the Women's Division for recommendation to Women's Societies of Christian Service and Wesleyan Service Guilds.

2. The **Section of Christian Social Relations** shall create plans, provide opportunities, communicate information, and establish relationships that challenge women to follow Jesus Christ and respond to the gospel in national and international relationships; establish and utilize liaison and service relationships with other units of the Board of Missions; unite with other agencies of the Church in the cooperation and projection of plans related to areas of common re-

sponsibility; share fully in ecumenical programs and plans that are concerned with responsibilities in the area of Christian social relations; and bring its plans and programs to the Women's Division for recommendation to Women's Societies of Christian Service and Wesleyan Service Guilds.

3. The **Section of Finance** shall recommend financial policies to the division, appraise periodically the effectiveness of such policies, and recommend changes as necessary; report regularly to the division; cooperate with the Section of Program and Education for Christian Mission in promotional plans for securing funds through the channels of the Women's Societies of Christian Service and Wesleyan Service Guilds for the support of the work of the Church at home and abroad; receive requests from sections and associated divisions and agencies; and bring recommendations to the Women's Division for appropriations in order to fulfill its responsibilities within the total amount available for the work. Such appropriations shall be recommended to the section by its Committee on Appropriations, which shall include additional Women's Division representatives named by the other two sections, the Joint Commission on Education and Cultivation, and the World and National Divisions.

¶ 1339.   *Article 48. Finances.*—The funds for the fulfillment of the responsibilities of the Women's Division shall be derived from annual voluntary pledges, offerings, gifts, devises, bequests, annuities, or money received through special emphases and from meetings held in the interest of the division. All funds, except those designated for local purposes, shall be forwarded through the channels of finance of the Women's Societies of Christian Service to the treasurer of the division. Undesignated funds received by the Women's Division shall be allocated by the division, on recommendation of its Section of Finance, to the work of the several sections of the Women's Division and to the other divisions and agencies of the board for the fulfillment of the responsibilities of the division. Funds appropriated for the work of the other divisions and agencies of the board may be given with specific designations and time limits after which unspent funds are to be returned to the division.

¶ 1340.   *Article 49. Assembly.*—There may be an assembly of United Methodist women, including a delegated body termed the

Assembly. The division shall determine the time and place of meeting and the purpose, composition, functions, and power of the Assembly. It may speak as an assembly on major issues of concern to women and may make recommendations to the Women's Division.

¶ 1341. *Constitution of the Jurisdiction Women's Society of Christian Service.*—1. *Article 1. Name.*—There shall be in each jurisdiction a **jurisdiction Women's Society of Christian Service,** auxiliary to the General Board of Missions through the Women's Division. This shall include the Wesleyan Service Guild for employed women. Hereinafter, it shall be called the Jurisdiction Society-Guild.

2. *Article 2. Authority.*—Each Jurisdiction Society-Guild shall have authority to promote its work in accordance with the program and policy of the General Board of Missions through the Women's Division. It shall also recommend to the division such plans and policies as will make the work within the jurisdiction more effective.

3. *Article 3. Membership.*—The Jurisdiction Society-Guild shall be composed of its president and planning body; six delegates from each conference Women's Society of Christian Service, including the Wesleyan Service Guild, all of whom shall be conference officers; all the women members of the jurisdictional Board of Missions and any member of the Women's Division living within the jurisdiction; a representative of the Jurisdiction Association for Deaconesses and Home Missionaries; all the bishops of the jurisdiction; and such other persons as the Jurisdiction Society-Guild may determine.

4. *Article 4. Meetings and Elections.*—There may be a meeting of the Jurisdiction Society-Guild during the last year of the quadrennium, at which time the women nominees to the General Board of Missions shall be elected according to the Discipline (¶ 1281.2c). The president and any other officers shall also be elected. There may be other meetings as needed.

5. *Article 5. Amendments.*—Proposed amendments to this constitution shall be sent to the recording secretary of the Women's Division at least forty days prior to the last annual meeting of the division in the quadrennium.

¶ 1342. *Constitution of the Conference Women's Society of Christian Service.*—1. *Article 1. Name.*—In each Annual Conference there shall be organized a **conference Women's Society of Christian**

Service, auxiliary to the Jurisdiction Society-Guild and to the General Board of Missions through the Women's Division. This shall include the Wesleyan Service Guild for employed women.

2. *Article 2. Function.*—The function of the conference society shall be to unite all the societies within the conference in an earnest effort for the promotion of the work of the conference Women's Society of Christian Service and to plan and direct the work of the society within the conference in accordance with the constitution and bylaws of the Women's Division.

The scope of the work of the conference society shall include the needs and interests of women and the concerns and responsibilities of the Church in the world. The conference society shall foster spiritual growth, missionary outreach and service, and Christian social witness through district and local societies.

3. *Article 3. Authority.*—Each conference society shall have authority to promote its work in accordance with the program and policy of the General Board of Missions through the Women's Division.

4. *Article 4. Membership.*—The conference Women's Society of Christian Service shall be composed of all members of local societies within the bounds of the conference. The resident bishop shall be a member of the conference society and of its executive committee.

5. *Article 5. Officers and Committees.*—The conference society shall elect a president, a vice-president, a secretary, a treasurer, and a Committee on Nominations. Additional officers and committees shall be elected or appointed in accordance with the plans of the Women's Division as may be set forth in the bylaws of the conference society. The conference society shall confirm the election of the conference officer of the Wesleyan Service Guild.

6. *Article 6. Meetings and Elections.*— (*a*) There shall be an annual meeting of the conference society, at which time there shall be presented a program designed to meet the needs of the conference in harmony with the purpose, plans, and responsibilities of the Board of Missions through the Women's Division and the Jurisdiction Society-Guild. Officers and the Committee on Nominations shall be elected, the necessary business transacted, and pledges made for the ensuing year.

b) The voting body of the annual meeting of the conference society shall be composed of representatives from societies in local churches as determined by the conference society, such district officers as the conference society may determine, the conference officers and chairmen of committees, and any members of the Women's Division and any officers of the Jurisdiction Society-Guild residing within the bounds of the conference.

c) At the annual meeting of the conference society prior to the quadrennial meeting of the Jurisdiction Society-Guild, six conference officers shall be elected according to provisions of ¶ 1341.3 for membership in the Jurisdiction Society-Guild.

d) At the annual meeting of the conference society prior to the quadrennial meeting of the Jurisdiction Society-Guild, the conference society shall nominate three women for membership on the General Board of Missions, the names to be sent to the Jurisdiction Society-Guild according to the instructions in ¶ 1281.2 (*c*).

7. *Article 7. Relationships.*—The president of the conference society shall be a member of the Annual Conference (as set forth in ¶ 36). Designated officers shall represent the conference society on the various boards, councils, commissions, and committees of the conference as the constitutions and bylaws of such agencies provide.

8. *Article 8. Amendments.*—Proposed amendments to this constitution shall be sent to the recording secretary of the Women's Division at least forty days before the last annual meeting of the division in the quadrennium.

¶ 1343. *Constitution of the District Women's Society of Christian Service.*—1. *Article 1. Name.*—There shall be a **district Women's Society of Christian Service** auxiliary to the conference Women's Society of Christian Service and the General Board of Missions through the Women's Division. This shall include the Wesleyan Service Guild for employed women.

2. *Article 2. Function.*—The function of the district society shall be to unite all the societies within the district in an earnest effort for the promotion of the work of the conference Women's Society of Christian Service.

The scope of the work of the district society shall include the needs and interests of women and the concerns and responsibilities of the Church in the world. The district society shall foster spiritual growth, missionary outreach and service, and Christian social witness through local societies.

3. *Article 3. Authority.*—Each district society shall have authority to promote its work in accordance with the program and policy of the General Board of Missions through the Women's Division.

4. *Article 4. Membership.*—All members of Women's Societies of Christian Service in the local churches of the district shall be considered members of the district society. The district superintendent shall be a member of the district society and of its executive committee.

5. *Article 5. Officers and Committees.*—The district society shall elect a president, a vice-president, a secretary, a treasurer, and a Committee on Nominations. Additional officers and committees shall be elected or appointed, in accordance with the plans of the Women's Division as may be set forth in the bylaws for the district society. The district society shall confirm the election of the district officer of the Wesleyan Service Guild.

6. *Article 6. Meetings and Elections.*—There shall be an annual meeting of the district society at which time there shall be presented a program designed to meet the needs of the district in harmony with the purpose, plans, and responsibilities of the Board of Missions through the Women's Division and the conference Women's Society of Christian Service. Officers and the Committee on Nominations shall be elected, the necessary business transacted, and pledges made for the ensuing year.

7. *Article 7. Relationships.*—Designated officers shall represent the district society on the various boards, councils, commissions, and committees of the district as the constitution and bylaws of such agencies provide. The district president shall be the only district representative with vote on the conference executive committee.

8. *Article 8. Amendments.*—Proposed amendments to this constitution shall be sent to the recording secretary of the Women's Division at least forty days prior to the last annual meeting of the division in the quadrennium.

¶ 1344. *Local-Church Women's Society of Christian Service.*— There shall be a Women's Society of Christian Service in the local church, auxiliary to the conference Women's Society of Christian Service, as provided in ¶ 159.3.

Councils

¶ **1345.** *Missionary Councils.*—1. There may be a **General Missionary Council,** composed of persons to be designated by the Board of Missions, on recommendation of the Joint Commission on Education and Cultivation from the elected membership and staff personnel of the General, Jurisdictional, and Annual Conference Boards of Missions and Women's Societies of Christian Service. Meetings of this council may be held at such times and places as the Joint Commission on Education and Cultivation or the council itself may determine for the consideration of any or all matters relating to missions and church extension and for the dissemination of missionary information and inspiration throughout the Church.

2. There may be a **jurisdictional Missionary Council** held within each jurisdiction at such times and places as the jurisdictional Board of Missions may determine in consultation with the Joint Commission on Education and Cultivation and in harmony with its plans.

Cooperation with Other Boards and Agencies

¶ **1346.** *Authority for Work Overseas.*—Other agencies of The United Methodist Church shall conduct work in foreign fields only with the consent of and in cooperation with the Board of Missions.

¶ **1347.** *Interboard Committee on Christian Education.*—For the purpose of more effectively promoting Christian education outside the United States there shall be an **Interboard Committee on Christian Education,** composed of twenty-two members. Ten shall be from the Board of Education: the general secretary and five other staff members of the Division of the Local Church, the general secretary and one other staff member of the Division of Curriculum Resources, and two members of the board. Ten shall be from the World Division of the Board of Missions: the associate or assistant general secretary, associate treasurer, six staff secretaries, and two board members, one of whom shall be a woman. The other two shall be the executive secretary of the Interboard Committee on Missionary Education and the staff member responsible for Youth Service Fund education.

¶ **1348.** There shall be an **executive secretary** for the committee, and such other staff as may be needed, who shall be elected by the Board of Missions on nomination of the committee. He shall be confirmed by the Board of Education. He shall carry out policy decisions of the Interboard Committee on Christian Education and shall report to it. He shall also maintain such relationship to the Board of Education through the Division of the Local Church as shall be appropriate and necessary to fulfill his responsibilities to the Interboard Committee on Christian Education.

¶ **1349.** 1. The committee shall meet annually and at such other times as it shall determine and shall report its actions to the Board of Education and the Board of Missions at their annual meetings.

2. It shall have a budget for its work provided by the two boards. The major responsibility for the budget rests on the Board of Missions, supplemented by support from the Board of Education, in which the Youth Service Fund shall have a part (¶ 1083.1).

¶ **1350.** *Interboard Committee on Missionary Education.*—For the purpose of promoting effective cooperation between the Board of Missions and the Board of Education in missionary education, there shall be an **Interboard Committee on Missionary Education,** composed of the general secretaries of the three divisions of the Board of Education and five voting members appointed by that board. There shall be, from the Board of Missions, an equal number, which shall consist of one secretary and one voting member each from the Joint Commission on Education and Cultivation and the three divisions. During the period between the General Conference and the organization of the new committee for the ensuing quadrennium, the members who have served on the committee during the last quadrennium shall continue to function. The committee shall provide for age-group subcommittees and such other subcommittees as may be needed. This committee and its subcommittees shall be advisory and creative in character. The promotion of plans and materials created by this committee shall be a responsibility of the Board of Education and the Board of Missions. The committee shall have a budget provided for its work by the two boards on such ratio as they may decide. The committee shall meet annually and at such other times as it may determine.

¶ **1351.** The duties of this committee shall be:

1. To develop a unified program of missionary education for all

age groups in the local church and in the colleges, universities, and schools of theology.

2. To cooperate with the Program-Curriculum Committee of the Board of Education in providing missionary information for church-school literature and in the planning and preparation of curriculum materials on missions.

3. To cooperate in the publication of books for missionary education in the Church.

4. To develop cooperative plans for the missionary education and missionary giving of children, youth, and adults.

5. To report annually to the Board of Missions and to the Board of Education.

¶ 1352. There shall be an **executive secretary** of the committee, who shall be elected by the Board of Education, on nomination of the committee, and shall be confirmed by the Board of Missions. He shall be the secretary for missionary education of the Board of Education with staff relationship to the Division of the Local Church. He shall also be the secretary for missionary education of the Board of Missions, having staff relationship to the Joint Commission on Education and Cultivation. The committee shall nominate annually to the Board of Education for election and to the Board of Missions for confirmation such staff as may be needed. They shall be members of the staff of the Joint Commission on Education and Cultivation of the Board of Missions and also of the staff of the Division of the Local Church of the Board of Education. Staff members shall assume their responsibilities when they have been elected and confirmed by the two boards.

¶ 1353. *Interboard Committee on Town and Country Ministries.*—1. There shall be an **Interboard Committee on Town and Country Ministries,** composed of six bishops composing a Committee on Town and Country Ministries of the Council of Bishops, whose chairman shall convene this committee early in the quadrennium, and representatives elected by agencies as follows: three from the National Division of the Board of Missions, one of whom shall be a woman; three from the Board of Education; and one each from the Board of Evangelism, the Board of the Laity, and the Division of Human Relations of the Board of Christian Social Concerns. In addition, staff members of the participating agencies whose specific function is town and country ministries shall be ex officio members. The committee may invite other persons to meet with it as consultants. Expenses of members attending meetings shall be borne by the agencies which they represent. Expenses of the consultants shall be borne by the agency extending the invitation.

2. The members shall hold office for the quadrennium and/or until their successors are chosen.

3. The functions of the committee shall be:

a) To provide a means of cooperative planning among the participating agencies for the strengthening of town and country ministries in The United Methodist Church.

b) To plan national or regional conferences on town and country ministries.

c) To ascertain the phases of rural work that the participating agencies propose to carry on and to give assistance to coordinating the programs for full service to town and country churches.

d) To prepare a clear statement on interdenominational cooperation with regard to the allocation of new fields of work and to the disposition of properties through federations, union churches, exchange of fields, withdrawals, and similar forms of cooperative work.

4. The committee shall organize by electing such officers and subcommittees as may be needed and shall determine the frequency of its meetings. It shall report annually to the participating agencies and may make suggestions concerning work in town and country churches.

¶ 1354. *Joint Committee on Architecture.*—There shall be a **Joint Committee on Architecture,** composed of staff personnel as follows: four staff members from the National Division of the Board of Missions, four staff members from the Division of the Local Church of the Board of Education, and four representatives from the Commission on Worship. It shall have authority to prepare standards for the architecture of churches, parsonages, and religious educational buildings and to recommend these standards to the cooperating boards. It shall meet annually and at such other times as its work may require.

¶ 1355. *Crusade Scholarship Committee.*—1. There shall be a program of scholarships and fellowships to provide assistance for the training of future leaders for mission, enabling persons from churches abroad and from minority groups in the United States to obtain preparation in their respective fields, for service to the Church and society.

2. There shall be a **Crusade Scholarship Committee,** composed of twenty-two members elected quadrennially as follows: twelve (five of whom shall be women) from the Board of Missions, seven of whom shall be elected by the World Division (of whom three shall be specialists in the field of international education) and five of whom shall be elected by the National Division (of whom two shall be specialists in the field of education in the United States) ; seven (of whom five shall be specialists in international education) from the Board of Education, elected by the Division of Higher Education; and three from the Division of Interpretation, elected by the division. The general secretary of the Board of Missions shall be a member ex officio of the committee, without vote. Vacancies shall be filled as early as possible by the agency in which they occur.

3. The committee shall elect its officers quadrennially.

4. The committee shall be responsible for the selection of persons for scholarships and fellowships provided by the One Great Hour of Sharing offering and by other grants received for the crusade scholarship program. Persons coming under the World Division shall be nominated by the duly established committee of the national Church where such committee exists.

5. The committee shall provide for the administration of the program, including the provision of an office and the approval of a budget for administration.

6. The committee shall elect such staff as is deemed necessary for its ongoing work. The staff shall be confirmed by the Board of Missions. The staff shall be administratively related to the general secretary of the Board of Missions for the purpose of personnel administration, including salary review, pension, office management, employment practices, and such other matters as may be agreed upon between the Crusade Scholarship Committee and the Board of Missions.

7. The committee shall hold an annual meeting and shall meet at such other times as necessary to transact its business.

8. The Crusade Scholarship Committee may recommend changes in the name of the committee to the Board of Missions, the Division of Higher Education of the Board of Education, and the Division of

Interpretation of the Program Council, and if approved by each of these bodies, the new name shall become effective immediately.

¶ **1356.** *Joint Commission on Cooperation and Counsel.*—1. In continuation of the historical relationship between The Methodist Church and the Christian Methodist Episcopal Church, there shall be a **Joint Commission on Cooperation and Counsel.** Its purpose shall be to foster cooperation at all levels and in all places between The United Methodist Church and the Christian Methodist Episcopal Church and to recommend and encourage those plans and services which may be undertaken better together than separately. It shall promote joint plans with and through established agencies of the two cooperating churches.

2. The commission shall be composed of thirty members, fifteen from each cooperating communion, appointed as provided in their respective Disciplines. Such appointments shall take account of the total life of the Church but give major emphasis to those agencies that provide a channel of common concern and cooperative endeavor. The fifteen members from The United Methodist Church shall be named by the Council of Bishops as follows: five from the Board of Missions, four from the Board of Education, and two each from the Boards of Evangelism, Christian Social Concerns, and the Laity. These agencies shall be responsible for expenses of their respective representatives.

3. The commission shall meet annually, or more often at the call of the officers.

4. The expenses involved in the commission's work shall be borne by the appropriate agency or agencies designated by each denomination.

5. The commission shall elect a chairman, a vice-chairman, and a secretary at the annual meeting immediately succeeding each General Conference.

JURISDICTIONAL BOARDS

¶ **1357.** In each jurisdiction there may be a **jurisdictional Board of Missions,** auxiliary to the general board, as the Jurisdictional Conference may determine.

ANNUAL CONFERENCE BOARDS

¶ **1358.** *Composition and Purpose.*—1. The **conference Board of Missions** shall be auxiliary to the general and jurisdictional boards, shall represent the board in all its promotional activities within the bounds of the Annual Conferences, and shall cooperate with the Annual Conference Program Council. It shall be composed of the following members, elected quadrennially: one or more lay members and an equal number of ministers from each district; five members at large, to include one young adult churchman (eighteen to thirty years of age), nominated by the conference nominating committee and elected quadrennially by the Annual Conference; a representative of the conference Board of Education; the chairman of Christian outreach and one other representative, eighteen years of age or younger, elected by the conference United Methodist Youth Fellowship; one student chosen by the state or regional student organization operating within the conference territory; and the conference and district missionary secretaries, the conference lay leader, the conference secretary of evangelism, the president and the chairman of missionary education of the conference Women's Society of Christian Service, the executive secretary and the chairman of the Commission on Town and Country Ministries, the presidents and full-time executives of city (metropolitan) and district missionary societies, the chairman of the Committee on Urban Ministries, the chairman of the Commission on Minimum Salaries, and any members of the general board residing within the bounds of the conference. The district superintendents may be members of the board at the discretion of the Annual Conference.

2. Every effort shall be exercised to make the membership of the boards and of the committees of the boards broadly inclusive.

¶ **1359.** 1. The board shall elect its own officers and two representatives to each city (metropolitan) or district missionary society organized within the bounds of the conference.

2. It shall hold its annual meeting at the call of the president or any three members, on due notice. The transactions for the year shall be reported by the president to the Annual Conference, and a detailed statement of all disbursements of missionary and church-extension aid within the conference shall be printed in the conference journal. It

shall receive reports from missionaries who have gone out from the conference.

3. It may hold a midyear meeting, at which time necessary business may be transacted and open meetings planned for a general and public discussion of all matters pertaining to home and foreign missions and church extension.

¶ **1360.** The officers and three additional members elected by the board shall constitute an executive committee, which shall exercise the powers of the board ad interim. The president of the Annual Conference Women's Society of Christian Service shall be a member of the executive committee.

¶ **1361.** The board shall make nominations in accordance with ¶ 1281.2*a* for membership on the general board.

¶ **1362.** The board shall cooperate with the general board and the Annual Conference Program Council in carrying out the policies and promoting all phases of the work of missions and church extension. It shall also represent the interests of the United Methodist Committee for Overseas Relief and shall promote its projects in the conference. It shall cooperate with the Joint Commission on Education and Cultivation in developing an effective program of education and cultivation within the conference. To expedite this program there shall be created a **Committee on Education and Cultivation,** of which the conference missionary secretary shall be chairman and all district missionary secretaries shall be members. There shall also be on the committee at least one layman and one laywoman elected by the board and one district superintendent selected by the Cabinet.

¶ **1363.** *Secretaries.*—1. The Annual Conference, on nomination of the board and in consultation with the Cabinet, may elect annually an **executive secretary** of the board, who, if he is a ministerial member of the conference, shall be appointed by the bishop. He shall be a member of the board without vote and shall perform such duties in the field of missions and church extension as may be assigned by the board. The expense of his salary and of his office shall be included in the budget of the board.

2. The Annual Conference, on nomination of the board, shall elect annually a **conference missionary secretary,** to be publicly assigned by the bishop. A vacancy in this office during the conference

year may be filled by the executive committee. This secretary shall promote the policies and plans of the board, and shall be its representative in the conference. He shall work in full cooperation with the conference program director of the Annual Conference Program Council.

¶ 1364. *Budget.*—The promotional work of the board shall be included in the conference benevolence budget.

¶ 1365. *Missions Anniversary.*—The board shall cooperate with the Annual Conference program committee in arranging for a **missions anniversary** at each conference session, in which the work of the General Board of Missions shall be presented. The president of the conference board shall have charge of such anniversary.

¶ 1366. *Home Missions and Church Extension.*—In the program of home missions and church extension within the bounds of the Annual Conference the board shall act as follows:

1. After consultation with the bishops, the district superintendents, the city (metropolitan) or district missionary societies, the Metropolitan Area Planning Commission (where organized), the Committee on Urban Ministries, and the Commission on Town and Country Ministries, the board shall develop and recommend to the Annual Conference a conference-wide plan for home missions and church extension within the bounds of the conference. It shall give due consideration to the missionary and church-extension needs of the several districts, placing special emphasis on the unchurched areas and the population and other community changes.

With the district superintendents it shall also give due consideration to the responsibilities and resources of the National Division in home missions work and support and in church-extension planning and assistance in the fields of survey, site selection, architecture, fund raising, and loans for new churches.

2. It shall coordinate and/or make such studies and surveys as are needed for the development of such a conference-wide strategy and program.

3. In order to help provide adequate financial resources for the conference-wide program of home missions and church extension, the board shall, at least quadrennially, in consultation with the Cabinet and, where advisable, with city (metropolitan) or district missionary

boards or societies, provide for a survey of the missionary and church-extension needs of the several districts, placing special emphasis on the unchurched areas and the population and other community changes with a view to determining in each what should be the overall financial objective. From this study an adequate conference-initiated financial program shall be formulated with a view to meeting these needs. A priority list of projects to be developed shall be prepared. The list and all revisions shall be filed with the National Division.

4. On recommendation of its executive committee or its Committee on Home Missions the board shall review and approve or adjust the askings of the district superintendents for the mission aid program before they are presented to the general board, keeping in mind that in making the final decision on all askings from the several conferences the National Division must take into account the comparative missionary needs of each project and its permanent value of service to the entire Church.

5. It may estimate annually the amount necessary for the support of conference missionary work and also the amount necessary for conference church extension and shall report both estimates to the Commission on World Service and Finance of the conference. The amount raised on these apportionments shall be administered by the board and applied respectively to missions and to church extension. The work of the board shall be subject to the approval of the Annual Conference. The board shall seek to cover all unoccupied territory in the conference by the establishment and support of missions, but missions shall be established only with the consent of the bishop in charge and his Cabinet and with due consideration to the board's quadrennial plan of survey and strategy.

6. The board, its executive committee, or its Section of Church Extension, composed of not less than one third of its members, shall review, approve or adjust, and certify the applications to the National Division for loans and donations. Through such committee or section it shall administer such funds as come into its possession for church extension within the conference; *provided* that it may turn over all its church-extension funds to the National Division, which shall expend them within the bounds of the conference under the direction of the conference board. It shall provide for consultation between

city (metropolitan) and district missionary societies, district Boards of Church Location and Building, and the National Division in the development of standards and procedures for local-church building projects in the fields of site selection, study and approval of architectural plans, and financial programs.

7. In the administration of such funds as come into its possession for church-extension purposes within the conference, it shall have authority to lend or donate any part thereof, whichever in its judgment will better accomplish the desired end. When funds lent or donated are returned, it shall administer them as a portion of the total church-extension funds at its disposal. The foregoing shall not apply to conference board loan funds administered prior to the General Conference of 1948 by the Section of Church Extension of the former Division of National Missions of The Methodist Church. If, however, an Annual Conference so elects, funds lent may become a part of the conference board loan fund, to be administered by the National Division on the same terms, conditions, and policies used by the division.

¶ 1367. *Committee on Research and Survey.*—The board may appoint a **Committee on Research and Survey,** which shall conduct surveys and make research studies within the bounds of the conference and shall cooperate with the National Division in its work of research and survey.

¶ 1368. *Church and Community Committee.*—1. The board may form, in consultation with the Cabinet and the chairmen of other boards to be represented, a **Church and Community Committee.** The committee shall be composed of such members as the conference Board of Missions may determine. The bishops and district superintendents are ex officio members of the committee.

2. The Church and Community Committee shall work with appropriate representatives of community agencies, other denominations and interdenominational and interfaith bodies, and other boards and agencies of The United Methodist Church in the execution of the following responsibilities:

a) The regular performance of research studies and community surveys essential for planning and decision-making on the church and community concerns of the conference.

b) The development and utilization of long-term planning and strategy resources for the home mission and extension work of the conference Board of Missions across both rural and urban areas in cooperation with the Cabinet and appropriate council boards and agencies. This assumes a regularized appraisal and definition of needs, resources, objectives, programs, and evaluation processes.

c) The development of church and community programs which will improve the effectiveness of urban and town and country ministries, including joint endeavors with other denominations and with social agencies similarly involved in community planning and problems.

d) The facilitation of communication and joint action on community concerns with the National Division and local or district societies, commissions, or committees.

3. The committee may elect such officers and appoint such subcommittees as deemed necessary for the conduct of its responsibilities. The committee, which provides an integrating church and community alternative to the Committee on Urban Ministries and the Committee on Town and Country Ministries, may have subcommittees on specific rural or urban concerns.

¶ 1369. *Urban and Town and Country Ministries.*—A separate Committee on Urban Ministries and a separate Committee on Town and Country Ministries may be established as an alternate to the Church and Community Committee.

1. *Committee on Urban Ministries.*— (*a*) The board may appoint, in consultation with the Cabinet, a **Committee on Urban Ministries** to function as a subcommittee of the Board of Missions. The committee shall be composed of clergy and laity experienced in the fields of city church work, urban planning and renewal, health, welfare, recreation, education, industry, and labor, and representatives of such church agencies as church-extension and research committees, city (metropolitan) and district missionary societies, Boards of Laity, Women's Societies of Christian Service, and Commissions on Town and Country Ministries.

b) The committee may work with lay and clergy leaders on the conference, district, and local-church level to: (1) help initiate and participate in urban coalitions and other associations with leaders in business, finance, industry, labor, education, and welfare in cities all across the nation; (2) help develop effective community organizations of residents in inner-city communities and the suburbs to the end that people may share in the decision-making processes on matters which vitally affect them and will open and use more channels of communication between all people in the metropolitan areas; (3) participate in new creative forms of planning, living, working, and worshiping under new concepts which can be made possible through the development of federal, state, and local efforts such as the Model Cities program; (4) develop the special ministries and new structures, including recruitment, training, and use of laymen and clergy, appropriate to new metropolitan needs; (5) encourage provision on the Annual Conference, district, and local-church levels for substantial new funds with which the above-mentioned and other desired measures may be undertaken; and (6) cooperate with representatives of other churches and faiths in developing and implementing plans, programs, and funding for these new efforts.

2. *Committee on Town and Country Ministries.*— (a) The board may appoint, in consultation with the Cabinet, a **Committee on Town and Country Ministries** to function as a subcommittee of the Board of Missions. The committee shall be composed of such members as the conference Board of Missions may determine. All church and community workers and other special workers in the conference employed by The United Methodist Church in rural communities shall be members of the committee.

b) The functions of the committee shall be to work with the conference and its agencies in program areas of town and country responsibility. It shall conduct surveys and research studies of town and country areas within the bounds of the conference; develop cooperative procedures between the Church and social and governmental agencies, and with the town and country departments of state councils of churches, and with the churches of other denominations in local communities; work to improve the effectiveness of town and country churches and pastors; recommend a program to coordinate the work of the participating boards and agencies in this program area; and outline a program of town and country ministries to be presented to the participating agencies and to the conference. In program areas of town and country ministries the conference shall consult with the committee or its executive committee.

3. *Commission on Town and Country Ministries.*—As a further alternative, each Annual Conference may set up quadrennially a **Commission on Town and Country Ministries,** composed of such members as the conference may determine. The commission shall be amenable to the Annual Conference Board of Missions.

¶ **1370.** *Committee on Parish and Community Development.*—The board may appoint, in consultation with the Cabinet, a **Committee on Parish and Community Development** in place of a Committee on Urban Ministries and a Commission on Town and Country Ministries. It shall have the combined responsibilities and representative composition as set forth in ¶¶1368-69.

DISTRICT ORGANIZATION

¶ **1371.** *District Missionary Secretary.*—There shall be a **district missionary secretary** in each district, appointed by the district superintendent after consultation with the conference missionary secretary and publicly assigned by the bishop. A vacancy in this office during the conference year may be filled by appointment by the district superintendent. This secretary shall work in cooperation with the district superintendent and conference missionary secretary.

¶ **1372.** *District Missionary Institute.*—There shall be held annually in each district a training program which may be a **district missionary institute,** workshop, missionary festival, or rally. It shall be for the purpose of informing, training, and motivating the pastors, and members of Commissions on Missions and other laymen of local churches within the whole district. The board, through its Committee on Education and Cultivation, shall project conference-wide plans for education and cultivation. The district superintendents and district missionary secretaries shall promote and conduct the program in their respective districts. They shall consult with the chairman of missionary education of the district Women's Society of Christian Service and the district lay leader. The Joint Commission on Education and Cultivation shall cooperate with them in furnishing recommendations and resources for the program, including current study books, literature, audio-visual aids, speakers, and methods. Plans should include adequate time and number of meetings to reach all churches effectively.

¶ **1373.** *District Secretary of Town and Country Ministries.*—A **district secretary of town and country ministries** may be elected for each district by the conference Commission on Town and Country Ministries, on nomination by the district superintendent after consultation with the executive secretary of the commission. He shall work in close cooperation with the executive secretary of the commission in all phases of the town and country program. His chief functions shall be to expedite all program aspects in his district, to assist the district superintendent in implementing the program, and to serve as liaison between the district and conference programs. (*See* ¶ 1369.)

Note: For other district agencies in the field of missions see ¶¶ 1327-35, city or district missionary societies, and ¶ 1343, district Women's Society of Christian Service.

For a description of the organization and duties of the Commission on Missions in the local church see ¶ 158.3.

Section XI.   Board of Pensions.

GENERAL ADMINISTRATION

¶ **1374.** *Name, Corporations, and Locations of Offices.*—1. There shall be a **General Board of Pensions** of The United Methodist Church, hereinafter called the board or the general board, with its principal office and place of business in Evanston, Illinois, having the general supervision and administration of the support, relief, and assistance and pensioning of ministers and their families, other church workers, and lay employees of The United Methodist Church, hereinafter referred to as beneficiaries, in succession to the Board of Pensions of The Evangelical United Brethren Church and in succession to the General Board of Pensions of The Methodist Church. The Board of Pensions of The Evangelical United Brethren Church, which is incorporated under the laws of the State of Ohio in that name, and the Board of Pensions of The Methodist Church, which is incorporated under the laws of the State of Illinois in that name, and the Board of

417

Pensions of The Methodist Church, which is incorporated under the laws of the State of Maryland in that name, and the Board of Pensions of The Methodist Church, which is incorporated under the laws of the State of Missouri in that name, shall be continued, subject to the direction, supervision, and control of the General Board of Pensions of The United Methodist Church, but with their corporate names changed to and to be known as The Board of Pensions of The United Methodist Church, Incorporated in Ohio, and The Board of Pensions of The United Methodist Church, Incorporated in Illinois, and The Board of Pensions of The United Methodist Church, Incorporated in Maryland, and The Board of Pensions of The United Methodist Church, Incorporated in Missouri, respectively.

2. The general supervision and administration of the pension and benefit funds, plans, and programs of The United Methodist Church, subject to the direction, supervision, and control of the board, shall be conducted by and through the office of the board in Evanston, Illinois.

3. The board shall have authority to establish, maintain, and discontinue from time to time such auxiliary offices as it shall deem proper and advisable.

¶ **1375.** 1. *Membership.*— (a) The board shall be composed of one bishop, elected by the Council of Bishops; one minister and one layman from each jurisdiction, elected by the respective Jurisdictional Conferences; four ministers and four laymen, not more than two from the same jurisdiction, elected by the General Conference on nomination of the Council of Bishops; and eight members at large, not more than two from the same jurisdiction, nominated and elected by the board in such manner as it shall provide in its bylaws.

b) The ministerial membership of the board shall be limited to ministerial members of an Annual Conference in full connection and in the effective relation.

c) The general secretary of the board shall be an ex officio member thereof, without vote.

d) The terms of all members so elected shall be four years, to take effect at the annual meeting of the board following the General Conference. Members shall serve during the terms for which they are elected and until their successors shall have been elected and qualified.

e) A vacancy in the membership shall be filled for the unexpired term by the board.

f) The members of the board shall constitute the membership of the respective Boards of Directors of the aforesaid four constituent corporations. The general secretary shall be an ex officio member of each, without vote.

2. *Meetings.*—The annual meetings of the board and of the Boards of Directors of the constituent corporations shall be held at the same date and place, at which time the board shall review and consider responsibilities committed to its care and take such action as it deems advisable in the furtherance of the best interest of the funds, plans, and programs administered by the board. Special meetings of the board may be called by any two of the officers hereinafter named in ¶ 1376.

3. *Quorum.*—A majority of the members of the board shall constitute a quorum.

¶ **1376.** 1. *Officers.*—The board shall elect at its annual meeting next following the General Conference a president, a vice-president, and a recording secretary, all of whom shall be members of the board, and shall also elect a general secretary and a treasurer, all for four-year terms. The officers so elected shall serve during the terms for which they were elected and until their successors shall have been elected and qualified. The officers of the board shall also be elected by, and serve as the officers of, each of the four constituent corporations of the board. A vacancy in any of these offices may be filled by the board for the remainder of the unexpired term. Other offices that are deemed desirable and to the best interest of the board for carrying out its purposes may be created by the board, and persons may be elected or appointed to fill such offices.

2. *Executive Committee.*—An **executive committee** shall be elected by the board. The same committee shall also respectively be elected by, and serve as the executive committee of, each of the four constituent corporations unless otherwise required by applicable laws of the respective states of incorporations, in which case the board shall recognize such laws, and the board and the corporations shall have power to comply therewith.

3. *Committee on Rules and Regulations.*—The board shall elect quadrennially from its membership a **Committee on Rules and Regu-**

lations, which shall consist of the bishop, one minister, and one layman from each jurisdiction and two ministers and two laymen from the membership of the board at large, whose responsibility it shall be to study the operation of the several pension and benefit funds, plans, and programs administered by the board, to present its recommendations for revision of the rules and regulations of the said pension and benefit funds, plans, and programs for consideration and action by the board, under authority granted to the board by the General Conference, and to present to the General Conference such proposed revisions of the Discipline as may be recommended by the board.

¶ 1377. *General Authorizations.*—1. The General Board of Pensions is authorized to adopt and further any and all plans, to undertake any and all activities, and to create, obtain, accept, receive, manage, and administer any and all assets or property, absolute or in trust for specified purposes, for the purpose of increasing the revenues and of providing for, aiding in, and contributing to the support, relief, and assistance and pensioning of ministers and their families and other church workers and lay employees in The United Methodist Church and its constituent boards, organizations, and institutions; to do any and all acts and things deemed by the board to be necessary and convenient in connection therewith or incident thereto; and to perform any and all other duties and functions from time to time imposed, authorized, or directed by the General Conference of The United Methodist Church. No proposal shall be made to the General Conference which changes a benefit presently in effect without first securing through the General Board of Pensions an actuarial opinion concerning the cost and other related aspects of the proposed change.

2. The board is authorized to manage, administer, revise, continue, discontinue, create, and consolidate pension and benefit funds, plans, and programs in such manner as may be deemed by the board to be reasonably necessary to achieve an efficient, equitable, and adequate operation; and to receive, hold, manage, and disburse the moneys related thereto in accordance with the provisions of the respective funds, plans, and programs.

3. The board is authorized to receive, hold, manage, merge, consolidate, administer, and invest and reinvest, by and through its constituent corporations, all connectional pension and benefit funds, sub-

ject to the other provisions of the Discipline, and with due regard to any and all special contracts, agreements, and laws applicable thereto.

4. The board is authorized to receive, hold, manage, administer, and invest and reinvest, by and through its constituent corporations, endowment funds belonging to Annual Conferences or other funds for pension and benefit purposes to be administered for such Annual Conferences; *provided,* however, that at no time shall any part of the principal of the endowment funds be appropriated by the board for any other purpose. The net income of such funds shall be accounted for annually by the board and paid over to the Annual Conferences concerned.

5. The board is authorized, on request of an Annual Conference or conference organization or a board or agency of The United Methodist Church, to receive therefrom distributable and reserve pension funds and to make the periodic pension payments to the beneficiaries of such Annual Conference, conference organization, board, or agency, in accordance with a schedule of distribution which shall be provided for the guidance of the board in making such payments. The board shall report annually the details of transactions under this provision. The board shall be entitled to recover the cost of performing such services.

6. The board, by and through its constituent corporations, is authorized and empowered to receive any gift, devise, or bequest made or intended for beneficiaries of The United Methodist Church, being the legal successor to and vested with the legal title to any and all such gifts, devises, and bequests. If the language or terms of any gift, devise, or bequest are inexact or ambiguous, the board shall dispose of or administer the same in the manner deemed most equitable according to the apparent intent of the donor as determined by the board after careful inquiry into the circumstances in connection with the making of such gift, devise, or bequest, and after granting full opportunity to all interested parties to be heard, after due and timely written notice of the time and place of hearing. Such notice shall be mailed to each and all interested parties through their respectively known representatives, at their last known addresses.

7. The four constituent corporations shall, until otherwise determined by the board, continue to collect, receive, and administer

such gifts, devises, and bequests and other funds as may be specifically designated to them by donors, subject to the rules, regulations, and policies of the board with respect thereto. All undesignated gifts, devises, bequests, and donations shall be collected, received, and administered under the direction of the board.

8. The board shall share in the funds raised for the world service budget of The United Methodist Church as provided for in ¶¶ 862-63 of the Discipline and in enabling acts.

9. The appropriations from the net earnings of the publishing interests which are contributed to the pension programs of The United Methodist Church, and of the several Annual Conferences, shall be distributed on the basis determined by the board.

10. The board shall compile and maintain complete service records of ministerial members in full connection, associate members, and probationary members of the Annual Conferences of The United Methodist Church and of lay pastors whose service may be related to potential annuity claims. Such service records shall be based on answers to the Disciplinary questions as published in the journals of the several Annual Conferences and in the General Minutes of The United Methodist Church, or in comparable publications of either or both of the uniting churches, and from information provided by Annual Conference Boards of Pensions.

11. The board shall administer a clearinghouse for the allocation of pension responsibility among the several Annual Conferences, in accordance with the principle of divided annuity responsibility, and for the collection and distribution of pension funds related to such responsibility.

a) For each beneficiary involved in the operation of the clearinghouse the board shall determine the division of responsibility on account of approved service rendered.

b) The board shall have authority to determine the pension responsibility of each Annual Conference, in accordance with the principle of divided annuity responsibility, and to collect from each Annual Conference, as determined on the basis of their respective pension programs, the amount required by the clearinghouse to provide the pension benefits related thereto. Each Annual Conference shall provide funds to meet its annuity responsibility to beneficiaries of other

Annual Conferences on the same basis as it provides pension payments for beneficiaries related directly to itself.

c) The board is authorized and empowered to make all the rules concerning details that may be necessary to the operation of the clearinghouse.

12. The board is authorized and empowered to continue the operation, management, and administration of the following pension and benefit funds, plans, and programs for such time and in such manner as may be deemed by the board to be reasonably necessary to fulfill the purposes thereof; to merge, combine, or consolidate two or more such pension or benefit funds, plans, and programs as are under its jurisdiction, and to make rules and regulations necessary thereto if such action is deemed by the board to be consistent with and in furtherance of the purposes of the said funds, plans, and programs; these to include but not to be restricted to: The Senior Plan; Ministers Reserve Pension Fund; The Minister's Reserve Pension Plan; The Current Income Distribution Pension Plan; Joint Contributory Annuity Fund; Staff Pension Fund; The Pension Plan for Lay Employees; Lay Employees Pension Fund; Hospitalization and Medical Expense Program; Death Benefit Program; Bishops Reserve Pension and Benefit Fund, in consultation with the Council on World Service and Finance; The Printing Establishment of The United Brethren in Christ Fund; The Home Office Pension Fund of the Board of Missions, in consultation with the Board of Missions; Chaplains Pension Fund, in consultation with the Commission on Chaplains and Related Ministries; Retirement Allowance for Bishops, General Church Officers, and Staff Personnel Plan of the former Evangelical United Brethren Church, with funds to be provided by the Council on World Service and Finance; Temporary General Aid Fund, in consultation with the Commission on Interjurisdictional Relations, or its successor, as determined by the General Conference, with funds to be provided by the Council on World Service and Finance.

13. The board is authorized to prepare and publish a pension manual related to the funds, plans, and programs administered by the General Board of Pensions, and such other materials not inconsistent with the Discipline as may be deemed reasonably necessary by the board to its efficient operation.

14. In all matters not specifically covered by General Conference legislation or by reasonable implication, the board shall have authority to adopt rules, regulations, and policies for the administration of the support of beneficiaries of The United Methodist Church.

¶ **1378.** *Permanent Funds.*—1. The **Chartered Fund** shall be administered by the General Board of Pensions for the benefit of all the Annual and Provisional Annual Conferences in The United Methodist Church, the boundaries of which are within the United States, its territorial and insular possessions, and Cuba, unless the General Conference shall order otherwise. Once a year the net earnings of the fund, after provision for depreciation, shall be divided equally among such Annual and Provisional Annual Conferences in accordance with the restrictive rule contained in ¶ 20.

2. The General Board of Pensions shall order and direct that the income from the **General Endowment Fund for Conference Claimants** (formerly known as the General Endowment Fund for Superannuates of The Methodist Episcopal Church, South) held by The Board of Pensions of The United Methodist Church, Incorporated in Missouri, shall be distributed on account of service of conference claimants rendered in an Annual Conference of The United Methodist Church; *provided,* however, that such distribution shall be restricted to Annual Conferences which, directly or through their predecessor Annual Conferences, participated in raising this fund, in proportion to the number of approved years of annuity responsibility of each Annual Conference as shall be determined by the General Board of Pensions.

Annual Conference Administration

¶ **1379.** *Powers, Duties, and Responsibilities.*—1. The Annual Conference, on recommendation of the conference Board of Pensions, shall determine the admissibility and validity of service approved for pension credit and the payments, disallowances, and deductions thereunder, subject to the provisions of the Discipline and the rules and regulations of the pension funds, plans, and programs of The United Methodist Church.

2. Service rendered by a minister, in either or both of the uniting churches, prior to church union shall be approved for pension credit

in accordance with provisions of the pension funds, plans, and programs of the respective churches pertaining thereto.

3. The following years of approved service in an Annual Conference of The United Methodist Church are eligible to be counted for pension credit:

a) By a minister who is a probationary member or who is in the effective relation as an associate member or a member in full connection in the Annual Conference: (1) as pastor, associate or assistant pastor, or other minister in a pastoral charge; (2) as district superintendent, presiding elder, conference president, conference superintendent, or other full-time salaried official of the conference; (3) under special appointment to an institution, organization, or agency which in the judgment of the Annual Conference rendered to it some form of service, direct or indirect, sufficient to warrant pension credit, or to a community church, or as an evangelist; *provided,* however, that such institution, organization, agency, community church, or evangelist accepts and pays such apportionments as the conference may require, with the recommendation that this apportionment shall be equal to twelve times the annuity rate of the conference, and *provided* further, that pension related to such service may be arranged through one of the pension funds or plans administered by the General Board of Pensions; (4) as a student appointed to attend school, not to exceed three years; *provided,* however, that all years for which annuity credit was given under previous legislation on account of appointment to attend school are eligible to be counted for determining the annuity claim thereon, and *provided* further, that if a conference member who shall have served under appointment six consecutive years in full membership with annuity credit shall desire to return to school, he may be granted up to three additional years. This additional credit shall be valid only if he returns to his conference and serves under appointment therein for three consecutive years; (5) as a minister on sabbatical leave; and (6) as a minister on disability leave subsequent to the 1968 Uniting Conference, not to exceed fifteen years.

b) By an approved supply pastor prior to church union: as pastor or assistant pastor of a pastoral charge in full-time service under appointment, for which the cash support per annum from all church sources is not less than the minimum salary established by the conference for full-time approved supply pastors; *provided,* however, that in order to qualify for a pension an approved supply pastor must have rendered not less than four consecutive years of full-time service with pension credit in one Annual Conference and must be recognized by the Annual Conference as a retired lay pastor.

c) By a person classified by the Board of the Ministry as eligible to be appointed as a full-time lay pastor: as pastor or assistant pastor of a pastoral charge in full-time service under appointment; *provided,* however, that such credit shall be conditional and subject to provisions hereinafter stated in this paragraph.

4. The following provisions shall apply in determining approval for pension credit, eligibility for pension, and allocation of responsibility:

a) Full-time service of a ministerial member or a lay pastor shall be required as a normal condition for pension credit; *provided,* however, that such credit may be granted for part-time service by a three-fourths vote of those present and voting in the Annual Conference, on recommendation of the conference Board of Pensions.

b) Full-time service shall mean that full time is devoted to the work of a pastor by one who has not attained the age of mandatory retirement for a conference member, who is not attending school as a regular student, who is not substantially employed in nonpastoral work, and whose cash support per annum from all church sources is not less than the minimum salary established by the conference for those in his classification.

c) Service as a chaplain on full-time duty prior to December 31, 1946, which previous legislation includes as eligible to be counted in determining the annuity claim on an Annual Conference, shall be so recognized.

d) A year of service rendered concurrently by a minister and his wife, whether on the same pastoral charge or otherwise, as members of an Annual Conference or as lay pastors therein, shall be counted only as one year.

e) Pension responsibility on account of appointment to attend school by a probationary member or a minister in full connection shall be allocated to the Annual Conference in which he shall thereafter first serve a full year with pension credit under appointment other than to

426

attend school; *provided,* however, that if no such service is rendered, the responsibility shall be allocated to the Annual Conference in which membership was held at the time of appointment to attend school.

f) Service of a lay pastor may be approved for pension credit only by vote of the Annual Conference, on recommendation of the conference Board of Pensions, after consultation with the district superintendents. Such approval of service rendered in the year next preceding the session of the conference shall be recorded under the following Disciplinary question, which shall be included in the business of the conference: "What lay pastors are granted pension credit on account of approved full-time service during the past year?" If at any session the conference does not grant credit for such service, it may do so later under the Disciplinary question, "What other personal notation should be made?"

g) Upon recommendation of the conference Board of Pensions and by a three-fourths vote of those present and voting in the Annual Conference, pension credit may be granted to a ministerial member of the conference on account of full-time service previously rendered as an approved lay pastor or approved supply pastor to an institution, organization, or agency, which in the judgment of the Annual Conference rendered to it some form of service sufficient to warrant pension credit; *provided,* however, that such institution, organization, or agency shall accept and pay such apportionment as the conference may require.

h) A pension shall be payable on account of pension credit for a full-time lay pastor only on condition that the lay pastor shall have been admitted as a ministerial associate member or member in full connection in an Annual Conference and has subsequently been placed in the retired relation by the conference; *provided,* however, that on recommendation of the conference Board of Pensions and approval by the Annual Conference, a pension based on such service may be granted to a retired lay pastor who attained age forty-five prior to July 1, 1968, and who on that date was either serving as a full-time approved lay pastor or had completed four consecutive years of approved supply service with pension credit.

5. On recommendation of the conference Board of Pensions and

approval by the Annual Conference, special appointments shall be listed in the conference journal as follows: (*a*) with pension credit by the Annual Conference or (*b*) with pension responsibility on the institution or agency served. If at any session the conference fails to make such listing, it may be done subsequently, whenever desirable, under the Disciplinary question, "What other personal notation should be made?"

6. The Annual Conference, on recommendation of the conference Board of Pensions, shall have the power to revise, correct, or adjust a minister's record of pension credit as set forth in his service record. Prior to the revision of such record, the General Board of Pensions may be requested to review relevant data and report its findings thereon. Such revisions, corrections, and adjustments shall be published in the journal of the Annual Conference in answer to Disciplinary questions and shall be reported to the General Board of Pensions by the conference Board of Pensions.

7. The annuity rate for approved service of conference members shall be determined each year by the Annual Conference without restriction, but it is recommended that such rate be not less than 1 percent of the average salary of the conference as computed by the General Board of Pensions. The annuity rate for approved service of lay pastors and (former) approved supply pastors shall also be determined by the conference each year and may be the same as the rate for service of conference members, but it shall be no less than 75 percent of that rate.

8. The Commission on Chaplains and Related Ministries may provide a pension through the Chaplains Pension Fund, if not otherwise provided, on account of service rendered by a chaplain on full-time duty with the armed forces of the United States or to an institution, organization, or agency, in accordance with rules and regulations determined jointly by the General Board of Pensions and the Commission on Chaplains and Related Ministries.

9. The responsibility for pension for service approved for pension credit shall rest with the Annual Conference in which the service was rendered or its legal successor.

10. Pension for service approved for pension credit by an Annual Conference shall be provided by the Annual Conference under one

of the pension funds, plans, or programs administered by the General Board of Pensions of The United Methodist Church.

11. An Annual Conference may not make any arrangement with a life insurance company for the purchase of annuities for the benefit of individual effective or retired ministers or take any steps to nullify, in whole or in part, the pension plans and programs of The United Methodist Church by making contracts with outside parties.

12. The Annual Conference shall be responsible for annually providing moneys in the amount necessary to meet the requirements of the pension and benefit funds, plans, and programs of the conference.

13. At the time of retirement a beneficiary shall receive benefits in accordance with the provisions of the pension or benefit fund, plan, or program in effect at the time retirement takes place. If retirement takes place prior to the age of voluntary retirement, payments of grants, in the form of relief or other assistance, for the period from the time of retirement until such beneficiary qualifies for benefits provided by the fund, plan, or program in which he participated prior to the time of retirement, may be approved on the recommendation of the conference Board of Pensions by a three-fourths vote of those present and voting in the Annual Conference.

14. The responsibility for providing pension on account of service rendered in a Mission or Provisional Annual Conference within the United States, which has been approved for pension credit, shall rest jointly with (a) the Mission or Provisional Annual Conference concerned, (b) the General Board of Pensions, and (c) the National Division of the Board of Missions. The revenue for pension purposes covering such service shall be provided by the aforesaid parties in accordance with such plan or plans as may be mutually agreed to by them.

¶ 1380. *Conference Board of Pensions.*—1. *Authorization.*— There shall be organized in each Annual Conference a conference board, auxiliary to the General Board of Pensions, to be known as the **conference Board of Pensions,** hereinafter called the board, which shall have charge of the interests and work of providing for and contributing to the support, relief, assistance, and pensioning of ministers and their families, other church workers, and lay employees of The

United Methodist Church, its institutions, organizations, and agencies within the Annual Conference, except as otherwise provided for by the general board.

2. *Membership.*— (a) The board shall be composed of not less than twelve members not indebted to pension and benefit funds, plans, and programs or receiving pensions therefrom; ministers in the effective relation and laymen in equal number, elected for a term of eight years and so arranged in two equal classes that one half shall be elected quadrennially; and in addition thereto, any ministerial member of the conference or lay member of a church within the conference who is a member of the General Board of Pensions. A vacancy in the membership of the board may be filled by the board for the remainder of the conference year in which the vacancy occurs, subject to the same qualifications before provided, and at its next session the conference shall fill the vacancy for the remainder of the unexpired term.

b) The members shall assume their duties at the adjournment of the conference session at which they were elected.

3. *Organization.*—The board shall organize by electing a chairman, vice-chairman, secretary, and treasurer, who shall serve during the ensuing quadrennium or until their successors shall have been elected and qualified. These officers shall constitute an **executive committee**; *provided,* however, that three members may be added thereto by the board. The duty of the executive committee shall be to administer the work of the board during the conference year in the interim between regular or special meetings of the board. The office of secretary may be combined with that of treasurer. The treasurer may be a person who is not a member of the board, in which case he shall be an ex officio member of the executive committee, without vote. Calls for special meetings of the board shall be issued by the secretary on request of the chairman, or the vice-chairman when the chairman is unable to act.

4. *Financing Pension and Benefit Programs.*— (a) The board shall compute the amount to be apportioned annually to meet the requirements of the pension and benefit programs of the conference.

b) The conference Commission on World Service and Finance shall include in its recommendations to the Annual Conference the amounts computed by the board which are required to meet the needs of the pension, benefit, and relief programs of the conference.

c) Distributable pension funds from all sources, unless otherwise ordered by the Annual Conference or otherwise restricted by specific provisions or limitations, shall be disbursed by, or under the direction of, the conference Board of Pensions.

d) The board may accumulate a fund from the income for pension purposes, in order to stabilize the pension program of the conference.

5. *Reports to the Annual Conference and the General Board.*— (*a*) The board shall report to the Annual Conference and to the General Board of Pensions the names, addresses, and years of service approved for pension credit of the annuitants of the conference, the names of those who have died during the year, and the names of dependent children of deceased ministerial members of the conference, and shall show separately the amount paid to each beneficiary by the conference from the annuity and necessitous funds.

b) The board shall report to the General Board of Pensions immediately following the session of the conference, on forms provided for that purpose by the general board, and shall report also the names and addresses of ministers who are members of funds, plans, or programs administered by the general board.

6. *Proportional Payment.*—The board shall compare the records of the amounts paid by each pastoral charge for the support of pastors and for pension benefit purposes, computing the proportional distribution thereof and keeping a permanent record of defaults of the ministers of the conference who have failed to observe the following provisions pertaining to proportional payment, and shall render annually to each minister who is in default a statement of the amounts in default for that and preceding years.

a) When the apportionment to the pastoral charges for the pension and benefit program of the Annual Conference has been determined, payments made thereon by each pastoral charge shall be exactly proportionate to payments made on the salary or salaries of the minister or ministers serving it.

b) The treasurer of the pastoral charge shall be primarily responsible for the application of proportional payment, but in the event of his failure to apply it, the pastor shall adjust his cash salary and the payment according to the proper ratio, as provided above, before he enters the respective amounts in his statistical report to the Annual Conference.

c) The conference statistical tables shall provide separate columns for reporting the amount apportioned to each pastoral charge for pension and benefit purposes and the amount paid thereon.

d) On retirement, the amount that a pastor is in default shall be subject to deduction from his pension, in accordance with rules and regulations of the specific program or programs under which his pension is provided.

e) If a retired minister, while serving as a supply pastor, fails to observe the provisions of this paragraph pertaining to proportional payment in any conference year, the amount of such default shall be deducted from his pension the ensuing conference year.

f) It shall not be permissible for a pastor to receive a bonus of other supplementary compensation tending to defeat proportional payment. The board may recommend to the conference that the pastor's pension credit be disallowed for the year during which such bonus or supplementary compensation was so received.

7. *Depositories and Bonding.*— (*a*) The conference Board of Pensions shall designate a bank or banks or other depository or depositories for deposit of the funds held by the board and may require a depository bond from such depository or depositories.

b) The board, through the conference Commission on World Service and Finance, shall provide a fidelity bond in suitable amount for all persons handling its funds.

¶ 1381. *Other Annual Conference Organizations.*—1. Annual Conferences, hereafter in this section called conferences, are authorized to establish, incorporate, and maintain investment funds, preachers aid societies, and organizations and funds of similar character, under such names, plans, rules, and regulations as they may determine, the directors of which shall be elected or otherwise designated by the conference, where permissible under the laws of the state of incorporation, and the income from which shall be applied to the support of the pension program through the conference Board of Pensions.

2. Distributable pension funds from all sources, unless otherwise

ordered by the Annual Conference, shall be disbursed by or under the direction of the conference Board of Pensions, excepting only such funds as are otherwise restricted by specific provisions or limitations in gifts, devises, bequests, trusts, pledges, deeds, or other similar instruments, which restrictions and limitations shall be observed.

3. It shall not be permissible for any conference or permanent fund organization thereof to deprive its beneficiaries who are beneficiaries in other conferences of the privilege of sharing in the distribution of the earned income of such funds through the clearinghouse administered by the General Board of Pensions.

4. A conference subject to the laws of the state in which it is incorporated shall have power to require from its ministerial members and lay pastors who are serving with pension credit from the conference an annual contribution to either its permanent or reserve fund or for current distribution or to a preachers aid society for the benefit of its beneficiaries, subject to the following provisions:

a) The annual payment may be made in installments as provided by the conference.

b) The making of such payment shall not be used as the ground of contractual obligations upon the part of the conference or as the ground of any special or additional annuity claim of a member against the conference; neither shall it prevent disallowance of his annuity claim by conference action.

c) The conference may fix a financial penalty for failure of the member to pay.

d) In case his membership in the conference is terminated under the provisions of the Discipline, the conference may refund the amount so paid, in whole or in part, after hearing has been given to him, in case such hearing is requested.

e) Ministers entering a conference shall not be charged an initial entry fee by any organization mentioned in § 1 above; furthermore, the annual contribution required from a ministerial member of the conference or a lay pastor shall not exceed an amount equal to 3 percent of his support.

f) If a minister is required to make a contribution to one of the pension funds, plans, or programs administered by the General Board of Pensions, he shall not be required by the conference or by any organization thereof related to the support of beneficiaries to make any other contribution for pension purposes.

5. Each conference, on recommendation of its conference Board of Pensions or one of the organizations mentioned in § 1 above, shall select a Sunday in each year to be observed in the churches as **Retired Ministers Day,** in honor of the retired ministers, their wives, and the widows of ministers and in recognition of the Church's responsibility for their support. The bishop shall request each conference in his area to insert a Retired Ministers Day in its calendar, and he shall diligently promote the observance of it.

¶ **1382.** *Financial Policy.*—The following rules shall apply to the financial administration of Annual Conference pension and pension-related funds:

1. A member of the board connected or interested in any way with the securities, real estate, or other forms of investment sold to or purchased from such funds, or with an insurance program or a contract under consideration by the board, shall be ineligible to participate in the deliberation of the investment committee or of the board or to vote in connection therewith.

2. No officer or member of a conference agency handling such funds shall receive a personal commission, bonus, or remuneration, direct or indirect, in connection with the purchase or sale of any property, the loan of any money, the letting of any annuity or insurance contract, the making or acceptance of any assignment, pledge, or mortgage to secure the payment of any loan, or for the purchase or sale of any securities or other properties from or to that agency, or be eligible to obtain a loan in any amount from funds committed to the care of that agency. No investment shall be purchased from or sold to any member of the board or any member of the family of a member of the board.

3. To prevent development of any conflict of interest or preferential treatment and to preserve good will and confidence throughout the Church, no local church, church-related institution, or organization thereof shall be eligible to obtain a loan in any amount from such funds.

4. The principle of diversification of investments shall be ob-

served with primary consideration given to the soundness and safety of such investments.

5. Real property may hereafter be accepted as consideration for gift annuity agreements only with the stipulation that the annuity shall not exceed the net income from the property until such property shall have been liquidated. Upon liquidation, the annuity shall be paid upon the net proceeds at the established annuity rate.

6. An Annual Conference agency handling such funds shall not offer higher rates of annuity than those listed in the annuity schedule approved by the Council on World Service and Finance.

7. On order of the Annual Conference, there shall be printed in the journal a list of the investments held by each agency handling such funds directly or indirectly under the control of the Annual Conference, or such list may be distributed directly to the members of the Annual Conference at their request. A copy of all such lists of investments shall be filed annually with the General Goard of Pensions.

8. The borrowing of money in any conference year by a conference corporation or organization to enable the conference Board of Pensions to meet the requirements of the pension and benefit programs shall be done only on authority of the conference granted by three-fourths vote of the members present and voting.

¶ 1383. *Joint Distributing Committees.*—1. *Authorizations.*— Whenever two or more Annual or Provisional Annual Conferences are to be merged, in whole or in part, there shall be elected by each conference affected a Distributing Committee of three members and three alternates, which shall act jointly with similar committees from the other conference or conferences. The **Joint Distributing Committee** thus formed shall have power and authority: (*a*) to allocate the pension responsibility involved; (*b*) to distribute equitably the permanent funds and other pension assets of the conference or conferences affected, taking into consideration the pension responsibility involved; (*c*) to the extent not otherwise previously provided for by the conference or conferences involved, to apportion or distribute equitably any other assets or property and any other liabilities or obligations. It shall be governed by the legal restrictions or limitations of any contract, trust agreement, pledge, deed, will, or other legal instrument.

2. *Organization.*—The committee shall be convened by the general secretary of the General Board of Pensions, or by some other officer of that board designated by him in writing, and shall elect from its membership a chairman, a vice-chairman, and a secretary.

3. *Powers, Duties, and Responsibilities.*—(*a*) The committee shall determine the number of years of service approved for pension credit rendered in the conferences which will lose their identity in the merging of conference territories, and the findings of the committee shall be final unless substantial evidence to the contrary is presented, and the annuity payments by the continuing conference or conferences shall be made accordingly. The determination of pension benefits in The United Methodist Church shall recognize all pension rights to which ministers are entitled under the pension plans in existence at the time of church union and shall recognize all approved service which has been rendered in The Evangelical United Brethren Church and The Methodist Church prior to the date of church union.

b) The committee shall keep complete minutes of its transactions, and a copy thereof shall be filed with the secretary of each Annual Conference involved and with the General Board of Pensions.

c) Until the committee's work shall have been completed, the corporate organization of each conference in the process of merger shall be maintained. After the committee shall have completed its work, the officers of such corporation, subject to the completion of its business, shall dissolve or merge it, in accordance with the laws governing the incorporation thereof, after being authorized to do so by the conference involved.

d) The committee, having completed its work in connection with the merger or mergers for which it was organized and having filed copies of its findings and actions with the secretaries of the conferences involved for publication in the respective conference journals, and with the General Board of Pensions, shall be dissolved; subject, however, to recall by the general secretary of the General Board of Pensions in the event of the discovery and presentation to the general board of data substantially at variance with those previously submitted, for the purpose of reviewing such data and possible revision of its previous actions.

Section XII.   Standing Commissions.

COMMISSION ON WORSHIP

¶ 1384.   1. There shall be a **Commission on Worship,** composed of the book editor ex officio and two bishops, one minister and one lay person from each jurisdiction, and three members from the Church at large, elected by the General Conference on nomination of the Council of Bishops. Vacancies during the quadrennium shall be filled by the Council of Bishops.

2. The officers of the commission shall be a chairman, a vice-chairman, an **executive secretary,** and a treasurer, elected quadrennially in such manner as it may determine.

3. The commission shall meet at least once a year and at such other times as the commission and its officers shall determine.

4. The expense of the commission shall be borne by the General Administration Fund. The commission shall present a proposed budget to the Council on World Service and Finance for its consideration and action.

¶ 1385.   The functions of the commission shall be:

1. To cultivate beauty, dignity, and meaning in the worship experience of the Church.

2. To encourage by means of manuals and other publications, and by seminars, workshops, and other media, good taste and practice in the conduct of worship, church music, church architecture, and the use of the arts in the Church.

3. When need arises, to prepare forms of worship and to revise existing orders of worship for recommendation to the General Conference.

4. To supervise future editions of *The Book of Worship for Church and Home,* as may be authorized by the General Conference.

5. To make recommendations to the General Conference concerning future editions of the United Methodist hymnal.

6. To advise with any of the general agencies of the Church in

the publication and circulation of any orders of service and other liturgical materials bearing the imprint of The United Methodist Church.

7. To advise with official publications of the Church concerning material offered in the fields of worship and liturgical arts.

8. To consult with the Television, Radio, and Film Commission on matters of joint concern.

9. To encourage in our schools of theology and pastors' schools the best possible instruction in the meaning and conduct of worship.

10. To advise with those responsible for planning the program of the General Conference and other general assemblies of the Church regarding the worship services on these occasions.

11. To offer suggestions and direction to the Commissions on Worship of the various conferences and of the local churches. (*See* ¶¶ 158.6, 1387.)

12. To relate The United Methodist Church to the Department of Worship and the Arts of the National Council of Churches and to the Interdenominational Bureau of Architecture.

¶ **1386.** It shall be the purpose of the commission to enrich, and not to govern, the devotional life of the Church, recalling our dual heritage of liturgical and free worship and that "it is not necessary that rites and ceremonies should in all places be the same" (¶ 91, Article XXII, Articles of Religion).

¶ **1387.** 1. Each Annual Conference may constitute a **conference Commission on Worship,** which shall be auxiliary to the general and jurisdictional commissions, to report each year to the conference in such manner as the conference may direct. It shall be composed of at least one ministerial and one lay member from each district. Any member of the general commission within the conference shall be an ex officio member.

2. The commission shall meet at least once before each regular conference session. It shall organize with a chairman, vice-chairman, and secretary.

3. The duties of the commission shall be to act in cooperation with the general commission and the Annual Conference Program Council:

a) To promote the interests of worship within the bounds of the conference.

b) To foster the use of the best resources for worship at conference meetings and in all the churches of the conference.

c) To promote the use of *The Book of Worship for Church and Home* and *The Methodist Hymnal* in all the churches of the conference.

d) To plan and promote seminars and demonstrations on ways of worship and the use of hymns, within the bounds of the conference.

e) To provide exhibits at the conference sessions in such fields as architecture, church appointments, etc.

f) To cooperate with the Board of Education and the National Fellowship of Methodist Musicians of The United Methodist Church (*see* ¶ 1066.3, note 10) in promoting seminars and all other conferences on church music.

¶ **1388.** The hymnals of The United Methodist Church are the hymnals of The Evangelical United Brethren Church and *The Methodist Hymnal;* the Ritual of the Church is that contained in the *Book of Ritual* of The Evangelical United Brethren Church, 1959, and *The Book of Worship for Church and Home* of The Methodist Church.

COMMISSION ON CHAPLAINS AND RELATED MINISTRIES

¶ **1389.** 1. There shall be a Commission on Chaplains and Related Ministries, which shall represent The United Methodist Church:

a) In the recruitment, endorsement, and general oversight of all United Methodist ministers serving as chaplains in the Armed Forces and federal agencies; in industry; in state and local, public and private institutions; and of directors of Christian education at military bases. Chaplains serving in similar institutions of The United Methodist Church may be included in the program at their request when they have met the qualifications required by the commission. The commission shall render such other services to those chaplains and their constituencies as may be referred to it by the Council of Bishops.

b) In planning and implementing the ministry of the Church to its lay people who are in the military service and in institutions. It shall work in cooperation with the General Board of Evangelism and with the various agencies of the Church in preparing materials, planning programs, and otherwise providing a continuing ministry to these persons. It shall work with the local church in helping it to fulfill its responsibility of keeping in touch with its people who are away from home. It shall continue the responsibilities formerly delegated to the Commission on Camp Activities of The Methodist Church and the Committee on Defense Communities of The Evangelical United Brethren Church.

2. The commission shall be composed of six bishops, one from each jurisdiction and one at large, and five ministers and five laymen, elected by the General Conference on nomination of the Council of Bishops. Vacancies shall be filled by the Council of Bishops. The commission shall elect not more than five representative chaplains as members for a two-year term. A member bishop shall serve as chairman.

3. The commission is authorized to receive and distribute such share of the Fellowship of Suffering and Service offering as may be determined by the General Conference, and such other funds and special gifts as are or have been specifically given to the Commission on Chaplains.

Commission on Ecumenical Affairs

¶ **1390.** 1. There shall be a **Commission on Ecumenical Affairs,** composed of fifty-six members of The United Methodist Church elected by the General Conference on nomination of the Council of Bishops. These shall include two each from the Boards of Missions and of Education, the Commission on Worship, the General Board of the National Council of Churches, and the Assembly of the World Council of Churches; three from the Executive Committee of the World Methodist Council and two from its affiliate World Federation of Methodist Women; and three youth representatives (at least one a student) ; *provided* that among the foregoing there shall be not less than four bishops, three laymen, and three laywomen. In addition there shall be fourteen representatives from United Methodist schools of theology, two from Central Conferences, and from each jurisdiction, a bishop, a minister, a layman, and a laywoman.

2. The commission shall:

a) Proclaim and work for the unity of the Church.

b) Recommend to the Council of Bishops qualified members of The United Methodist Church for ecumenical councils, agencies, and meetings.

c) Analyze the relationship of The United Methodist Church to the resolutions, pronouncements, and actions of the ecumenical councils and agencies and publicize the same, and channel materials coming from the ecumenical councils and agencies to the proper agencies of the Church and materials coming from the Church and its agencies to the proper agencies of the ecumenical councils.

d) Explore, receive, study, and recommend action on proposals for union of The United Methodist Church with other denominations.

e) Interpret The United Methodist Church in the light of the New Testament definitions of the Church, in the light of church history, and in its relationships to the ecumenical councils, agencies, and movements.

f) Report periodically to the Church, to the General Conference, and to the Council of Bishops on the participation of The United Methodist Church in the various phases of the ecumenical movement.

3. In carrying out its work the commission shall give attention to ecumenical studies; to the relationship of The United Methodist Church to ecumenical organizations, including the World Methodist Council; to church union; and to such additional concerns as relate to ecumenical interests and responsibilities of the Church.

4. When responsible conversations are initiated with other Christian churches concerning church union, the commission shall create a committee for such purpose, whose chairman shall be a member of the Commission on Ecumenical Affairs, with the provision that one half its membership shall derive from the commission and one half shall be named from the Church at large on the basis of special competence for the negotiations in view. Provision shall be made for the *ad hoc* committee in the course of its work to advise and consult with the commission.

5. The commission shall elect its president from among the bishops who constitute its membership at the beginning of each quadrennium. It shall elect vice-presidents from among its membership to preside over the business of subcommittees needful for the work of the commission, and such other officers as are necessary. It shall elect a general secretary and engage such other personnel as are necessary for the discharge of its responsibilities.

6. The commission shall divide its work into at least the following three subcommittees: (*a*) **Committee for Liaison, Consultation, and Church Union,** (*b*) **Committee for Promotion and Interpretation,** and (*c*) **Committee for Studies.** The commission may create additional committees as needed.

7. The Council on World Service and Finance shall make provision for the support of the work of the commission, including provision for a general secretary and associated staff and an office for the commission.

8. Vacancies in membership due to death or resignation in the interim shall be filled by the Council of Bishops.

¶ **1391.** 1. Each Annual Conference may create a **conference Commission on Ecumenical Affairs,** which shall be coordinate to the general commission, to report each year to the conference in such manner as the conference may direct. It may be composed of at least one ministerial and one lay member from each district, but others may be added as the conference directs. Any member of the general commission residing within the conference bounds shall be an ex officio member.

2. The commission shall meet at least twice between conference annual sessions. It shall organize with a chairman, vice-chairman, and secretary. The chairman shall be a member of the Annual Conference Program Council.

3. The duties of the commission shall be to act in cooperation with the Annual Conference Program Council and with the general commission as outlined in ¶ 1390 and as the general commission may suggest, to take initiative on ecumenical concerns, and to serve such specific tasks within the conference as the conference directs or as are allowed by conference rules, for example:

a) To guide the conference in developing understanding of the nature of the ecumenical movement and its implications for United Methodists.

b) To relate the conference to the work of councils of churches and to nominate for conference election the delegates to state councils of churches.

c) To relate the conference to judicatories of other denominations and to nominate for conference election fraternal delegates to local (state) and/or judicatory (conference, diocese, or convention) sessions of denominations which are participating in union consultations involving The United Methodist Church.

d) To stimulate participation of the conference and districts and congregations in local councils, conferences, or federations of churches and in studies sponsored by interchurch agencies or the general commission.

e) To stimulate participation in programs of ecumenical action, such as short-term voluntary service, ecumenical work camps, student travel seminars, and mission projects.

f) To cooperate in providing for specific ecumenical endeavors, such as Pentecost Sunday, Week of Prayer for Christian Unity, Consultation on Church Union emphases, Reformation Sunday, and interdenominational study forums and groups.

g) To stimulate understanding and conversations with members of other Protestant churches and of Orthodox and Roman Catholic churches.

h) To fulfill other functions as may be assigned by the Annual Conference and to respond to such requests as may be made by its leadership.

COMMISSION ON PUBLIC RELATIONS AND METHODIST INFORMATION

¶ 1392. There shall be a **Commission on Public Relations and Methodist Information,** which shall gather news of public interest concerning United Methodist activities and opinion and disseminate it through the secular press, the religious press, radio, television, and other legitimate media of public information; *provided* that in its relations with the media it serves and with the public generally, the commission may use such abbreviation of its name as it may deem appropriate.[12] It shall be composed of twelve persons, one of whom shall be a bishop who shall act as chairman. The three members shall have been elected by the General Conference of the Evangelical United Brethren Church on nomination of the Board of Bishops, and nine members shall have been elected by the General Conference of The Methodist Church on nomination of the Council of Bishops. Care shall be taken to nominate persons whose experience in public relations, journalism, advertising, radio and television, business, or the Church particularly qualifies them for this service. Vacancies occurring between sessions of the General Conference shall be filled by the commission. Members shall hold office until the next session of the General Conference or until their successors are elected.

¶ 1393.　The commission is authorized to employ a general secretary, who may be known as director, and such other persons as may be necessary to give effect to its purpose.

¶ 1394.　The expense of the commission shall be borne by the General Administration Fund. The commission shall present a proposed budget to the Council on World Service and Finance for its consideration and action.

¶ 1395.　1. The commission shall be the official general news gathering and distributing agency for The United Methodist Church and its general agencies. It may arrange with other general agencies for some persons in those organizations to represent the commission in direct release of United Methodist news items to the religious and/or secular press.

2. The commission shall have general supervision over planning public relations and procedures for making releases throughout the Church in the United States. It may encourage and work with area and conference directors of public relations, may assist in pastors' schools and conduct seminars in public relations, and may prepare instruction materials for local-church use concerning public relations.

3. The commission shall maintain a cooperative relationship with

---

[12] In keeping with the provision of this statement regarding abbreviation, the Commission on Public Relations and Methodist Information is commonly referred to as United Methodist Information.

the editors of all boards and other agencies and with the editors of area and conference periodicals.

¶ **1396.** There may be **area, conference, and district Commissions or Committees on Public Relations and Methodist Information,** to be constituted and organized as the respective governing bodies may determine. Such commissions or committees shall be related to the general commission.

¶ **1397.** There may be a local-church **Committee on Public Relations,** which shall be elected annually by the Administrative Board. This committee shall elect its own chairman and secretary. It shall provide a program of information for the public with which it deals, including the community and the members and friends of the Church, using every possible medium of communication available. It shall also serve the several program agencies of the local church in public information and promotion. (*See* ¶ 161.4.)

Commission on Archives and History

¶ **1398.** *Name.*—The name of the official historical agency of The United Methodist Church shall be the **Commission on Archives and History.**

¶ **1399.** *Incorporation.*—The Commission on Archives and History shall be incorporated under the laws of whatever state the commission may determine, and as such it shall be the successor of the Association of Methodist Historical Societies, Lake Junaluska, North Carolina, and The Historical Society of The Evangelical United Brethren Church, Dayton, Ohio. The commission shall take note that the historical materials, relics, and equipment in the World Methodist Building, Lake Junaluska, are owned jointly by the Association of Methodist Historical Societies and the World Methodist Council, and at the time of incorporation the commission shall confer with the American Section of the World Methodist Council and shall decide whether it is feasible to continue the joint ownership in The United Methodist Church. The instrument of incorporation shall provide for the commission to own real property and to receive gifts and bequests. The process of incorporation shall be consummated as soon as feasible after the two churches have officially united.

¶ 1400. *Purpose.*—1. The purpose of the commission shall be to gather, preserve, hold title to, and disseminate materials on the history of The United Methodist Church and its antecedents. It shall cooperate with other bodies, especially the International Methodist Historical Society and the World Methodist Council. It shall do any and all things necessary to promote and care for the historical interest of The United Methodist Church. It shall maintain archives and libraries in which shall be preserved historical records and materials of every kind relating to The United Methodist Church. It shall provide guidance for the creation and preservation of archives at all levels of The United Methodist Church.

2. The commission shall have responsibility for and supervision of the archives and the libraries at Dayton, Ohio, and Lake Junaluska, North Carolina, and other depositories of similar character, if any, established by The United Methodist Church.

¶ 1401. *Membership of the Commission.*—1. The commission shall be constituted quadrennially, and its members and all officers elected by it shall hold office until their successors have been chosen.

2. The commission shall be composed of thirty members. Initially, four members shall be nominated by The Historical Society of the former Evangelical United Brethren Church and elected by the Uniting Conference; *provided* that one of the four shall be a seminary or college professor of history. Ten members shall be nominated by the Association of Methodist Historical Societies of the former Methodist Church and elected by the Uniting Conference. In addition the following shall be members: the secretary of the Council of Bishops; two other bishops appointed by the Council of Bishops; the secretary of the General Conference; a member of the Methodist Librarians' Fellowship, designated by it; the presidents of the jurisdictional Commissions on Archives and History; the president, executive secretary, and treasurer of the American Section of the World Methodist Council; the editorial director of the general church periodicals; the book editor; and the manager of Abingdon Press. After the 1968-72 quadrennium the fourteen members at large shall be nominated by the Commission on Archives and History of The United Methodist Church and elected by the General Conference. The commission may

fill interim vacancies among the fourteen elected members during the quadrennium.

¶ **1402.** *Meetings.*—The commission shall meet annually at such time and place as it may determine, subject to the provisions of the act of incorporation. The commission may hold special meetings on the call of the president. A majority of the members of the commission shall constitute a quorum.

¶ **1403.** *Officers.*—The commission shall elect from its membership a president, vice-president, secretary, treasurer, and such other officers as may be needed. The president shall be a bishop. The officers shall perform the duties usually incident to their positions.

¶ **1404.** *Staff.*—The commission shall elect an **executive secretary** and such other staff officers as may be needed. The executive secretary shall be the executive and administrative officer and shall carry on the work of the commission, keep the records and minutes, serve as editor of official publications of the commission, supervise the depositories, make an annual report to the commission, and furnish such reports as are required to the General Conference and General Conference agencies. He shall attend all meetings of the commission and the executive committee and have the privilege of the floor without vote. Archivists, curators, and librarians employed by the commission shall be responsible to the executive secretary. They shall attend meetings of the commission and the executive committee when it is deemed necessary by the executive secretary. When in attendance, they shall have the privilege of the floor without vote.

¶ **1405.** *Executive Committee.*—There shall be an **executive committee,** composed of the president, vice-president, secretary, treasurer, and two other members of the commission elected by it. The executive committee shall perform the duties and exercise the authority of the commission between meetings. Its minutes shall be submitted to the commission for approval. The executive committee and the commission may vote on any matter by mail. Mail polls shall be directed by the executive secretary, who shall state clearly the propositions to be voted on and announce the results to all the members.

¶ **1406.** *Finances.*—The commission shall be financed by appropriations of the General Conference, the sale of literature and historical materials, subscriptions to the commission's official publications, dues from associate members, and gifts and bequests of interested individuals and organizations.

¶ **1407.** *Historical Society.*—1. The commission may organize a **Historical Society** of The United Methodist Church and encourage individuals to become members of it for the purpose of promoting interest in the study and preservation of the history of The United Methodist Church and its antecedents. They shall be encouraged to cooperate with the Annual Conference, Jurisdictional Conference, and General Commissions on Archives and History in the promotion of the historical interests of the Church. The officers of the commission shall be the officers of the Historical Society.

2. Individuals may become members of the Historical Society by paying such dues as the commission may direct, in return for which they shall receive the official publications and the publicity materials issued by the commission.

3. Once each quadrennium the commission may hold a **Historical Convocation,** to which may be invited members of the Historical Society, members of Jurisdictional and Annual Conference historical organizations, heads of departments of history in the universities, colleges, and seminaries of The United Methodist Church, and such other persons as may be interested.

¶ **1408.** *Archives.*—1. *Definition.*—Archives, as distinguished from libraries, house not primarily books but documentary materials such as records, minutes, journals, diaries, reports, pamphlets, letters, papers, manuscripts, maps, photographs, audio-visuals, recordings, and any other items, regardless of physical form or characteristic, which pertain to the current activities and the history of The United Methodist Church.

2. *Procedures.*— (*a*) The commission shall establish a central archives of The United Methodist Church and such regional archives as in its judgment may be needed.

b) The bishops, General Conference officers, general boards, commissions, committees, and agencies of The United Methodist Church shall deposit official minutes or journals, or copies of the same, in the archives quadrennially and shall transfer correspondence, records, papers, and other archival materials described above from their offices to the archives when they no longer have operational usefulness.

c) The general boards, commissions, committees, and agencies of The United Methodist Church shall place two copies of all their publications, of whatever kind, as they are issued in the archives or in lieu thereof shall file a statement with the archivist affirming that they are preserving copies of all such items in their own libraries or depositories.

d) Official documents, or copies thereof, such as articles of incorporation, constitutions, bylaws, and other official papers of the boards and agencies of The United Methodist Church shall be deposited in the archives.

e) The records and official papers of temporary and special church committees which are general, jurisdictional, interconference, or area-wide in scope, and the records and official papers, and a copy or copies thereof, of institutions, organizations, and conferences of The United Methodist Church and its antecedents, which are dissolved or merged, shall be deposited in the archives.

f) The bishops, General Conference officers, and the general boards, commissions, committees, and agencies of The United Methodist Church are urged to counsel with the central archivist concerning the preservation of all materials.

g) Jurisdictional and Annual Conference secretaries shall deposit two copies of their respective conference journals quadrennially or annually, as the case may be, in the central archives and in the appropriate regional archives.

h) Secretaries of Jurisdictional and Annual Conference boards, commissions, committees, and agencies shall deposit annually, or as often as they meet, copies of their minutes (as distinguished from reports which are printed separately or in the Jurisdictional and Annual Conference journals) in the central archives and in the appropriate regional archives.

i) Ministers and laymen in positions of leadership and influence at any level of the Church possessing personal or official papers important for church history shall be encouraged to deposit or bequeath such papers to the archives.

j) Organizations and individuals may negotiate appropriate restrictions on the use of materials which they deposit in the archives.

k) Upon recommendation of its executive committee, the commission may authorize the transfer of materials to an organization, agency, or family.

l) All materials in the archives shall be available for research and exhibition, subject to such restrictions as may be placed on them.

¶ **1409.** *Historical Shrines, Landmarks, and Sites.*—1. All nominations for the designation of buildings and locations as United Methodist historical shrines or landmarks shall be referred to the Commission on Archives and History. Through its Committee on Historical Shrines and Landmarks the commission shall consider the merits of each nomination and shall make such recommendations as it deems appropriate to the ensuing General Conference for its action and determination. The commission shall not recommend any building or location for designation as a United Methodist historical shrine or landmark unless it has been designated and registered as a historical site by an Annual or Jurisdictional Conference and has met the requirements established by the commission.

2. *Historical Shrines.*—To qualify for designation as a **historical shrine** of The United Methodist Church, a building or a location must have been linked with significant events and outstanding personalities in the origin and development of The United Methodist Church or its antecedents so as to have distinctive historical interest and value for the denomination as a whole, as contrasted with local or regional historical significance, and it must have features that invite and justify pilgrimages.

3. *Landmarks.*—Buildings and locations which have little remaining in the way of structure or monuments to invite pilgrimages but which otherwise qualify as historical shrines may be designated as **historical landmarks.**

4. *Sites.*—Jurisdictional and Annual Conferences may designate as **historical sites** buildings and locations within their regions which have been related to significant events and important personalities in the origin and development of The United Methodist Church or its antecedents. The president of the Commission on Archives and History of the conference making such a designation shall advise the general commission, which shall in turn keep a register of all historical sites.

5. *Present Shrines.*—The historical shrines of the two churches at the time of union shall be the historical shrines of The United Meth-

odist Church: Acuff's Chapel, Highway 11W between Blountville and Kingsport, Tenn.; Albright Memorial Chapel, Kleinfeltersville, Pa.; Barratt's Chapel, near Frederica, Del.; Edward Cox House, Bluff City, Tenn.; Green Hill House, Louisburg, N. C.; John Street Church, New York City; Old McKendree Chapel, Jackson, Mo.; Otterbein Church, Baltimore, Md.; Rehobeth Church, near Union, W. Va.; St. George's Church, Philadelphia; St. Simon's Island, Brunswick, Ga.; Cemetery and Site of Old Stone Church, Leesburg, Va.; Robert Strawbridge's Log House, near New Windsor, Md.; and Wyandot Indian Mission, Upper Sandusky, Ohio.

¶ 1410. *Jurisdictional Commission.*—There may be a **jurisdictional Commission on Archives and History** in each jurisdiction, auxiliary to the general commission, as the Jurisdictional Conference may determine.

¶ 1411. *Annual Conference Commission.*—1. In each Annual Conference there shall be an **Annual Conference Commission on Archives and History.** The commission shall be elected by the Annual Conference upon the nomination of its nominating committee. The number of members of the commission and their term of office shall be as the conference may determine. It shall be the duty of the commission to cooperate with and report, when requested, to the General and jurisdictional Commissions on Archives and History, to preserve the records of the Annual Conference, to collect and preserve data relating to the organization and history of the conference, to maintain a historical and archival depository and to see that all current items which obviously will have value for future history are preserved therein, to provide for the ownership of real property and to receive gifts and bequests, to assist the bishop or the conference program committee in planning for the historical hour at Annual Conference sessions, and to encourage and assist the local churches in preserving their records and compiling their histories.

2. The commission may organize an Annual Conference Historical Society and encourage individuals to become members of it for the purpose of promoting interest in the study and preservation of the history of the conference and its antecedents. The officers of the Annual Conference Commission on Archives and History shall be the officers of the Annual Conference Historical Society. Individuals may

become members of the Historical Society by paying dues as the society may direct, and in return they shall receive official publications and publicity materials issued by the commission and the society.

¶ **1412.** *Committee on Records and History.*—1. There may be a **Committee on Records and History** in each local church, elected by the Charge Conference, which shall be responsible for assisting the pastor to see that all church and Charge Conference records are kept on the official record blanks provided for that purpose. The committee shall examine the records at the end of each conference year and shall report the results of its examination to the Charge Conference in the ensuing year. The committee, with the pastor, shall be responsible for preparing, where it does not already exist, a history of the local church or churches from the time of organization, shall provide for preserving the same in permanent form, and shall bring the history up to date at the close of each year. The committee shall see that any and all minutes and record books no longer in current use are deposited with the church historian and shall cooperate with him in providing a permanent place for the safekeeping of these records and historical materials. The committee shall cooperate with the Annual Conference Commission on Archives and History and the Annual Conference Historical Society, if any, by sharing historical information and materials pertaining to the local church.

2. The Charge Conference shall elect a **church historian,** who shall be the secretary of the Committee on Records and History.

Section XIII.　Council of Secretaries.

¶ **1413.** 1. There shall be a **Council of Secretaries,** whose membership shall consist of the full-time chief executives, whether they be general secretaries or executive secretaries, plus the associate general secretaries, where authorized by the Discipline, for the following: Board of Missions, Board of Education, Board of Evangelism, Board of Christian Social Concerns, Board of the Laity, Board of Pensions, Board of Health and Welfare Ministries, General Program Council, The Methodist Publishing House, Commission on Chaplains and Related Ministries, Commission on Ecumenical Affairs, Commission on Public Relations and Methodist Information, Commission on Religion and Race, Council on World Service and Finance, United Methodist

Committee for Overseas Relief, Commission on Archives and History, the American Section of the World Methodist Council, American Bible Society, Interboard Committee on Missionary Education, Interboard Committee on Enlistment for Church Occupations, and the editorial director of general church periodicals.

2. The council shall meet at least seminannually to consider matters of common interest and cooperation among the several general agencies of the Church. It shall consider, in cooperation with the General Program Council, existing and emerging conditions and needs where the cooperative services of two or more agencies are needed and shall devise ways and means of meeting those needs when they fall within the Disciplinary functions of two or more general agencies. It shall seek to further cooperation between existing agencies in their regular work and in carrying out such additional responsibilities as the General Conference and Program Council may place on them. It shall report annually to the Council of Bishops and to the Council on World Service and Finance and quadrennially to the General Conference.

Section XIV.   Interdenominational Agencies.

¶ 1414.   1. The United Methodist Church is a member of the **World Methodist Council,** its predecessor Methodist and Evangelical United Brethren churches having been charter members of such body. The members of the section representing The United Methodist Church shall be nominated by the Council of Bishops, due regard being given to geographical representation. Financial support of the World Methodist Council shall be channeled through the Central Treasury, as shall be directed by the Council on World Service and Finance.

2. Each affiliated autonomous church and each affiliated united church which is a member of the World Methodist Council shall be entitled to send delegates as proposed in ¶¶ 642 and 645, respectively, to the World Methodist Council and to receive from the General Administration Fund the expense of travel and per diem allowances; *provided* that they shall elect to receive travel and per diem allowances for the meetings of the World Methodist Council instead of the General Conference of The United Methodist Church. No affiliated au-

tonomous church or affiliated united church shall be entitled to send delegations at the expense of the General Administration Fund to both the World Methodist Council and the General Conference.

¶ **1415.** 1. The United Methodist Church is a member of the **National Council of the Churches of Christ in the United States of America,** its predecessor Methodist and Evangelical United Brethren churches having been charter members of such body. It has borne its proportionate share of financial support and through the Interdenominational Cooperation Fund is authorized and directed to continue its support. (*See* ¶ 892.)

2. The representatives of The United Methodist Church to the Assembly, the General Board, and other agencies of the National Council of Churches shall be nominated by the Council of Bishops and elected by the General Conference, due regard being given to geographical representation. When representatives must be chosen or vacancies must be filled between sessions of the General Conference, the Council of Bishops is authorized and instructed to do so.

3. United Methodist support of the National Council of Churches shall be channeled through the Central Treasury, as shall be directed by the Council on World Service and Finance, which shall give due credit for United Methodist gifts and contributions to this cause and shall include them in its annual financial report to the Church. The sources of income shall include: (*a*) the National Council of Churches' share of the Interdenominational Cooperation Fund, as determined by the General Conference and (*b*) such payments by the general agencies of the Church as each agency may deem its responsibility and proportionate share in the cooperative program of the council. Personal, group, or local-church gifts shall be included as a part of the ratio distribution of the Interdenominational Cooperation Fund.

¶ **1416.** 1. The United Methodist Church is a member of the **World Council of Churches,** its predecessor Methodist and Evangelical United Brethren churches having been charter members of such body. It should bear its proportionate share of financial support and through the Interdenominational Cooperation Fund is authorized and directed to continue its support.

2. The representatives of The United Methodist Church to the Assembly and other agencies of the World Council of Churches shall

be nominated by the Council of Bishops and elected by the General Conference, due regard being given to geographical representation. When representatives must be chosen or vacancies must be filled between sessions of the General Conference, the Council of Bishops is authorized and instructed to do so.

3. United Methodist support of the World Council of Churches shall be channeled through the Central Treasury, as shall be directed by the Council on World Service and Finance, which shall give due credit for United Methodist gifts and contributions received by the World Council of Churches and shall include them in its annual financial report to the Church.

¶ 1417.   To encourage the wider circulation of the Holy Scriptures throughout the world and to provide for the translation, printing, and distribution essential thereto, the **American Bible Society** shall be recognized as one of the general missionary agencies of The United Methodist Church, and the Council on World Service and Finance shall make appropriate provisions for participating in its support.

¶ 1418.   **Religion in American Life, Incorporated,** is recognized as an interdenominational and interfaith agency through which The United Methodist Church may work to direct attention to church attendance and loyalty to the Christian faith. In endorsing this program the Council of Bishops shall nominate to its Board of Directors five members, to be elected by the General Conference. Further, the Council on World Service and Finance shall recommend to the General Conference for its action and determination the amount to be included in the General Administration Fund as the United Methodist share in this participation.

Section XV.   Quadrennial Commissions and Study Committees.

¶ 1419.   *Theological Study Commission on Doctrine and Doctrinal Standards.*—1. There shall be appointed a **Theological Study Commission on Doctrine and Doctrinal Standards,** authorized to study Part II of the Plan of Union and other pertinent references in the Discipline and in the history of doctrine in the Methodist and Evangelical United Brethren churches, and to bring to the General Conference of 1972 a progress report concerning "Doctrine and Doctrinal

Standards in The United Methodist Church." If the commission deems it advisable, it may undertake the preparation of a contemporary formulation of doctrine and belief, in supplementation to all antecedent formulations. In its work this commission shall collaborate with the Social Principles Study Commission (¶ 1420) and in all its formulations shall give due attention to the integrity of theological and ethical concerns in the Wesleyan tradition.

2. The Theological Study Commission on Doctrine and Doctrinal Standards shall be composed of thirty-one members elected by the Uniting Conference upon nomination of the Council of Bishops, the membership to include: (*a*) seven selected from the faculties of the theological schools related to The United Methodist Church; (*b*) four from each of the five jurisdictions, which four shall include in each case two clergy, one of whom shall be a parish minister, and two laymen; (*c*) four from the Central Conferences, which four shall include two clergy and two laymen; and (*d*) of the total thirty-one members, at least three women.

3. The Council of Bishops shall designate a date and place for the first organizational meeting of the commission and shall appoint a convener.

¶ **1420.** *Social Principles Study Commission.*—1. There shall be a **Social Principles Study Commission,** appointed with authorization to study Part III of the Plan of Union and to bring to the General Conference of 1972 a recommendation concerning The United Methodist Church's statement of social principles.

2. The Social Principles Study Commission shall be composed of twenty-seven members elected by the Uniting Conference upon nomination of the Council of Bishops, the membership to include: (*a*) seven selected from a panel of not less than fifteen submitted jointly by the officers of the Commissions on Social Concerns of the two denominations; (*b*) four from each of the five jurisdictions, which four shall include in each case two clergy and two laymen; and (*c*) of the total twenty-seven members, at least three women.

3. The Council of Bishops shall designate a date and place for the first organizational meeting of the study commission and shall appoint a convener.

¶ **1421.** *Structure Study Commission.*—1. There shall be a **Structure Study Commission,** appointed with authorization to study thoroughly the board and agency organizational structure of The United Methodist Church and to bring to the General Conference its recommendation for the structuring of the boards and agencies of the Church.

2. The study commission is authorized, at its discretion, to hold hearings in various places in an effort to ascertain the needs of the local churches and how the witness and mission of the local church may become more relevant and effective.

3. The study commission is directed to work in consultation with the Council of Secretaries and the responsible officers of the various boards and agencies of the Church.

4. The study commission shall be composed of twenty-two members elected by the Uniting Conference upon nomination of the Council of Bishops, the membership to include: (*a*) fifteen selected from a panel of not less than thirty persons not employed by any board or agency of either denomination, submitted jointly by the Councils of Secretaries of the two denominations; (*b*) seven selected for nomination by the Council of Bishops, and (*c*) of the twenty-two members, not less than three women.

5. In its report to the General Conference the commission shall make recommendations for the continuing study of organizational structure.

6. The Council of Bishops shall designate a date and place for the first organizational meeting of the study commission and shall appoint a convener.

¶ **1422.** *Commission on the Structure of Methodism Overseas.*— 1. There shall be a **Commission on the Structure of Methodism Overseas** for the quadrennium 1968-72. Recognizing the difference in conditions that exist in various fields of the world and the changes taking place in those fields, this commission shall continue to study the structure and supervision of The United Methodist Church in its work outside the United States and its territories and its relationship to other church bodies, and in particular shall review the historical development, structure, and operation of Central Conferences and the legislation pertaining thereto, and shall prepare such recommendations as it considers necessary for presentation to the General Conference of 1972 or of any special session held prior thereto. All resolutions and petitions related to Central Conferences presented to the General Conference shall be referred to this commission for consideration, action, and report to the General Conference.

2. The commission shall be constituted as follows: four bishops administering in Jurisdictional Conferences, four bishops administering in Central Conferences, one minister and one layman from each Jurisdictional Conference, and one person from each Central Conference; *provided* that a Central Conference having a church membership of 200,000 or more shall have two representatives. All these shall be nominated by the Council of Bishops and approved by the General Conference. There shall be added to the commission by the Board of Missions four persons, two men and two women. Bishops having supervision of work outside the United States and its territories and bishops of affiliated autonomous churches (¶¶ 640-47) shall be considered consultative members of the commission and shall be called in, when available, at the time of meeting of the commission. When a representative of a Central Conference cannot be present to represent his field, the bishop or bishops of that field shall designate someone to represent it. Those members of the commission representing Central Conferences who are not delegates to the General Conference or who are not in the United States at the time the commission meets shall be replaced by persons who are in the United States, on nomination of the bishops of the Central Conferences they represent.

3. The commission shall meet immediately following election for organization, annually at a time and place to be established by the commission or its chairman, and immediately before each session of the General Conference.

4. In its report to the General Conference the commission shall make recommendations for the continuing study of the structure of United Methodism outside the United States of America.

5. The expenses of this commission shall be paid from the General Conference Expense Fund.

¶ **1423.** *Commission on Religion and Race.*—There shall be a **Commission on Religion and Race** for the quadrennium 1968-72. This commission shall be composed of two bishops appointed by the Council of Bishops, five persons from each jurisdiction elected by the Jurisdictional Conference, and seven members at large to be elected by the commission. It is recommended that at least two of the five persons elected by each Jurisdictional Conference be Negroes and that at least one be of another racial or ethnic minority group. It is also recommended that at least three of the seven members at large elected by the commission be Negroes and that at least one be of another racial or ethnic minority group.

Section XVI. Miscellany.

¶ **1424.** In the event of a vacancy in any of the general church offices constituted by the General Conference, the board under which such general church officer serves shall fill the vacancy.

¶ **1425.** If a member of any general board or agency who was chosen to represent a certain jurisdiction shall remove his residence permanently from such jurisdiction, his place shall automatically become vacant.

¶ **1426.** If any member of a jurisdictional board or agency who was chosen to represent a certain Annual Conference shall remove his residence permanently from such Annual Conference, his place shall automatically become vacant.

¶ **1427.** Unless otherwise specified in the Discipline for a specific purpose, the term "quadrennium" shall be deemed to be the period from the adjournment of a General Conference to the adjournment of the next regular quadrennial session of a General Conference. (*See also* ¶ 817 for fiscal quadrennium.)

¶ **1428.** All boards, commissions, and committees established by a General, Jurisdictional, Central, Annual, or other Conference shall meet and organize as promptly as feasible following the conference in question. Unless otherwise specified in the Discipline, every board, commission, and committee shall continue in responsibility until its successor board, commission, or committee is organized.

Chapter Six
CHURCH PROPERTY

Section I. All Titles—in Trust.

¶ **1501.** The United Methodist Church is organized as a **connectional structure,** and titles to all properties held at General, Jurisdictional, Annual, or District Conference levels, or by a local church or charge, or by an agency or institution of the Church, shall be held in trust for The United Methodist Church and subject to the provisions of its Discipline.

¶ **1502.** The word "Methodist" is not by our approval or consent to be used as, or as a part of, a trade name or trademark or as a part of the name of any business firm or organization, except by corporations or other business units created for the administration of work undertaken directly by The United Methodist Church.

¶ **1503.** *Trust Clauses in Deeds.*—1. Except in conveyances which require that the real property so conveyed shall revert to the grantor if and when its use as a place of divine worship has been terminated, all written instruments of conveyance by which premises are held or hereafter acquired for use as a place of divine worship for members of The United Methodist Church or for other church activities shall contain the following trust clause:

In trust, that said premises shall be used, kept, and maintained as a place of divine worship of the United Methodist ministry and members of The United Methodist Church; subject to the Discipline, usage, and ministerial appointments of said church as from time to time authorized and declared by the General Conference and by the Annual Conference within whose bounds the said premises are situated. This provision is solely for the benefit of the grantee, and the grantor reserves no right or interest in said premises.

2. All written instruments by which premises are held or hereafter acquired as a parsonage for the use and occupancy of the ministers of The United Methodist Church shall contain the following trust clause:

In trust, that such premises shall be held, kept, and maintained as a place of residence for the use and occupancy of the ministers of

The United Methodist Church who may from time to time be entitled to occupy the same by appointment; subject to the Discipline and usage of said church, as from time to time authorized and declared by the General Conference and by the Annual Conference within whose bounds the said premises are situated. This provision is solely for the benefit of the grantee, and the grantor reserves no right or interest in said premises.

3. In case the property so acquired is to be used for both a house of worship and a parsonage, the provisions of both trust clauses specified in §§ 1 and 2 above shall be inserted in the conveyance.

4. In case the property so acquired is not to be used exclusively for a place of worship, or a parsonage, or both, all written instruments by which such premises are held or hereafter acquired shall contain the following trust clause:

In trust, that said premises shall be kept, maintained, and disposed of for the benefit of The United Methodist Church and subject to the usages and the Discipline of The United Methodist Church. This provision is solely for the benefit of the grantee, and the grantor reserves no right or interest in said premises.

5. However, the absence of a trust clause stipulated in §§ 1, 2, 3, or 4 above in deeds and conveyances previously executed shall in no way exclude a local church or church agency from or relieve it of its connectional responsibilities to The United Methodist Church. Nor shall it absolve a local congregation or church agency or Board of Trustees of its responsibility and accountability to The United Methodist Church; *provided* that the intent and desires of the founders and/or the later congregations or Boards of Trustees are shown by any or all of the following indications: (*a*) the conveyance of the property to the trustees of a local church or agency of any predecessor to The United Methodist Church; (*b*) the use of the name, customs, and polity of any predecessor to The United Methodist Church in such a way as to be thus known to the community as a part of such denomination; (*c*) the acceptance of the pastorate of ministers appointed by a bishop or employed by the superintendent of the District or Annual Conference of any predecessor to The United Methodist Church.

¶ 1504. Nothing in the Plan of Union at any time after the

union is to be construed so as to require any existing local church of any predecessor denomination to The United Methodist Church to alienate or in any way to change the title to property contained in its deed or deeds at the time of union, and lapse of time or usage shall not affect said title or control. Title to all property of a local church, or charge, or agency of the Church shall be held subject to the provisions of the Discipline, whether title to the same is taken in the name of the local church trustees, or charge trustees, or in the name of a corporation organized for the purpose, or otherwise.

¶ **1505.** Subject to and in accordance with the laws of the state, province, or country, the governing body of any church unit or agency owning land in trust for The United Methodist Church as provided in this Discipline may lease said land for the production of oil, gas, coal, and other minerals, upon such terms as it may deem best; *provided,* however, that such production shall not interfere with the purpose for which said land is held. The moneys received from such leases as rentals, royalties, or otherwise, shall be used so far as practicable for the benefit of the church unit and for the promotion of the interests of The United Methodist Church. The lessee shall have no control over or responsibility for the payments made under such lease.

Section II. Compliance with Law.

¶ **1506.** All provisions of the Discipline relating to property, both real and personal, and relating to the formation and operation of any corporation, and relating to mergers, are conditioned upon their being in conformity with the local laws, and in the event of conflict therewith the local laws shall prevail; *provided,* however, that this requirement shall not be construed to give the consent of The United Methodist Church to deprivation of its property without due process of law or to the regulation of its affairs by state statute where such regulation violates the constitutional guarantee of freedom of religion and separation of Church and state or violates the right of the Church to maintain connectional structure; and *provided* further, that the services of worship of every local church of The United Methodist Church shall be open to all persons without regard to race, color, or national origin. "Local laws" shall be construed to mean the laws of the country, state, or other like political unit within the geographical bounds of which the church property is located.

¶ 1507. In order to secure the right of property, with the appurtenances thereof, of the churches and parsonages of The United Methodist Church, care shall be taken that all conveyances and deeds be drawn and executed in due conformity to the laws of the respective states, provinces, and countries in which the property is situated and also in due conformity to the laws of The United Methodist Church. Deeds shall be registered or recorded directly upon their execution.

Section III. Audits and Bonding of Church Officers.

¶ 1508. All persons holding trust funds, securities, or moneys of any kind belonging to the General, Jurisdictional, Annual, or Provisional Annual Conferences or to organizations under the control of the General, Jurisdictional, Annual, or Provisional Annual Conferences shall be bonded by a reliable company in such good and sufficient sum as the conference may direct. The accounts of such persons shall be audited at least annually by a recognized public or certified public accountant. A report to an Annual Conference containing a financial statement which the Discipline requires to be audited shall not be approved until the audit is made and the financial statement is shown to be correct. Other parts of the report may be approved pending such audit.

Section IV. General Conference Property.

¶ 1509. There shall be a Board of Trustees of thirteen members incorporated under the name of **The Board of Trustees of The United Methodist Church.** This board shall be composed of six ministers and seven lay persons, all of whom shall be members of The United Methodist Church and at least twenty-one years of age. They shall be nominated, without reference to jurisdictional membership, by the Council of Bishops and be elected by the General Conference for a term of eight years; except as to the first such board, of which three clerical and four lay members shall be elected for a term of four years, and three clerical and three lay members shall be elected for a term of eight years, and they shall serve until their successors have been elected and qualified. Between General Conferences the Council of Bishops is designated to act on resignations and to fill vacancies in the membership of this board until the next session of the General Conference. Vacancies on the board may be filled by the Council of Bishops for the unexpired term.

¶ **1510.** This corporation shall receive and administer new trusts and funds, and so far as may be legal be the successor in trust of: The Board of Trustees of The Evangelical United Brethren Church, incorporated under the laws of Ohio; The Board of Trustees of The Church of the United Brethren in Christ, incorporated under the laws of Ohio; the Board of Trustees of The Evangelical Church, an unincorporated body; The Board of Trustees of The Methodist Church, incorporated under the laws of Ohio; The Trustees of The Methodist Episcopal Church, incorporated under the laws of Ohio; The Board of Trustees of The Methodist Episcopal Church, South, incorporated under the laws of Tennessee; and the Board of Trustees of The Methodist Protestant Church, incorporated under the laws of Maryland; and so far as may be legal, as such successor in trust, it is authorized to receive from any of its said predecessor corporations all trust funds and assets of every kind and character, real, personal, or mixed, held by them or any one of them, or to merge into itself any one or more of its said predecessor corporations. Any such trusts and funds coming to it as successor corporation, either by transfer or by merger, shall be administered in accordance with the conditions under which they have been previously received and administered by said predecessor corporations or unincorporated body.

¶ **1511.** Nothing herein contained shall be construed to require the dissolution of any of said predecessor corporations, and they shall continue to administer such funds as may not be legally transferred to the new corporation.

¶ **1512.** The object and duty of this board shall be to receive, collect, and hold in trust for the benefit of The United Methodist Church any and all donations, bequests, and devises of any kind or character, real or personal, that may be given, devised, bequeathed, or conveyed unto said board or to The United Methodist Church as such for any benevolent, charitable, or religious purpose, and to administer the same and the income therefrom in accordance with the directions of the donor, trustor, or testator, and in the interests of the church, society, institution, or agency contemplated by such donors, trustors, or testators under the direction of the General Conference. The board shall have power, at its discretion and on the advice of competent investment counsel, to invest, reinvest, buy, sell, transfer, and convey any and all funds and properties which it may hold in trust, subject always to the terms of the legacy, devise, or donation. It shall have authority to determine the intent of the donor, trustor, or testator with respect to the use and disposition both of the corpus and of the income of each separate gift, bequest, or acquisition which it may receive; and if the terms of the gift, bequest, or other instrument involved are vague, uncertain, or impossible of literal fulfillment, it shall have authority within its sound discretion to determine the use or uses of each such fund which shall conform with the general purposes of the donor, trustor, or testator; *provided* that such purposes can reasonably be determined from the terms of the gift, bequest, or other applicable instrument. If the specific or general purposes of the donor, trustor, or testator cannot be reasonably determined by the board with respect to any particular fund, such fund shall be held by the board as an undirected fund.

¶ 1513. The board may intervene and take all necessary legal steps to safeguard and protect the interests and rights of The United Methodist Church anywhere, in all matters relating to property and rights to property—whether arising by gift, devise, or otherwise, or where held in trust or established for the benefit of The United Methodist Church or its membership—or to abandoned church property, where Annual Conference trustees neglect to take necessary steps to protect the interests of the members of The United Methodist Church in such property.

¶ 1514. It shall be the duty of the pastor within the bounds of whose charge any such gift, bequest, or devise is made to give prompt notice thereof to said board, which shall proceed to take such steps as are necessary and proper to conserve, protect, and administer the same. But the board may decline to receive or administer any such gift, devise, or bequest for any reason satisfactory to the board.

¶ 1515. The Board of Trustees of The United Methodist Church is amenable to the General Conference and shall make to each

465

General Conference a full, true, and faithful report of its doings, of all funds, moneys, securities, and property held in trust by it, and of its receipts and disbursements during the quadrennium. The beneficiary of a fund held in trust by the board shall be entitled to a report at least annually on the condition of such fund and on the transactions affecting it. The amount of income accruing during a quadrennium from any undirected fund or funds held by the board shall be reported to the Council on World Service and Finance at least sixty days prior to the General Conference, for its recommendation.

¶ **1516.** The Board of Trustees of The United Methodist Church shall meet annually at such time and place as it may determine, or as shall be designated by its president and secretary. A majority of the members shall constitute a quorum.

¶ **1517.** There shall be a fund known as **The Permanent Fund** to be held and administered by the board, the principal of which shall be kept intact forever, and the interest accumulating from said fund shall be used by the board as the General Conference shall direct.

¶ **1518.** 1. There shall be a charitable corporation which shall hold title to certain property of The United Methodist Church located in Washington, D. C., at Ward Circle at the intersection of Nebraska and Massachusetts Avenues. The objectives to be carried on and promoted by **The Methodist Corporation** shall be and are exclusively for religious, charitable, scientific, literary, and educational purposes, including religious education and Christian social concerns. No part of the net earnings of the corporation shall inure to the benefit of any private shareholder or individual. The **Board of Directors** of this corporation shall be elected for a four-year term by the General Conference and shall consist of (*a*) one bishop, one minister, and one layman from each jurisdiction, nominated by the Council of Bishops, and (*b*) three representatives each from the Council of Bishops, Council on World Service and Finance, General Program Council, and Board of Christian Social Concerns, nominated by these respective bodies. The bishop resident in Washington, D. C., shall be ex officio chairman. Interim vacancies may be filled by the Board of Directors.

2. The corporation shall have complete authority to develop a program for the utilization of the property and to implement it by the sale or lease of all or any part thereof to any agency of The United

Methodist Church, subject to compliance with the terms of this Discipline, on such terms as the Board of Directors may deem appropriate to overall utilization of the property in the best interest of The United Methodist Church and its program. The corporation is also authorized to liquidate the project in whole or in part if and when it concludes that it is not in the best interest of The United Methodist Church to undertake a development or a further holding of the property. The corporation is authorized to receive and expend gifts and bequests for the development of this property. In the event of the dissolution of the corporation, its remaining assets and funds, after the payment and satisfaction of all debts, shall be conveyed, assigned, and transferred by the Board of Directors to such religious, charitable, scientific, literary, or educational organization or organizations as the General Conference of The United Methodist Church shall direct. No funds or property shall be distributed among or inure to the benefit of any private shareholder or individual.

3. The carrying charges of the property shall be paid from the General Administration Fund. The corporation shall not have authority to commit the General Conference to any other financial obligation without approval of the General Conference. However, if circumstances make it appropriate to proceed with any phase of property development between sessions of the General Conference, the Council on World Service and Finance is authorized to empower the corporation to solicit funds during such quadrennium under such conditions and restrictions as the said council may deem appropriate.

4. The corporation shall report to each succeeding General Conference as long as The United Methodist Church holds an interest in the property.

Section V. Annual Conference Property.

¶ 1519. 1. Each Annual Conference shall have a **Board of Trustees**, which shall be incorporated unless the conference is incorporated in its own name. In either case the board shall consist of twelve persons, who must be at least thirty years of age and of whom six shall be ministers in the effective relation in the conference and six shall be lay members in good standing of local churches within the bounds of the conference, and such persons shall be the directors of the corporation. They shall be elected by the conference for a term of three years, except as to the first board, one third of whom shall be elected for a term of one year, one third for a term of two years, and one third for a term of three years, and shall serve until their successors have been elected and qualified; *provided,* however, that existing incorporated trustees of any Annual Conference may continue unaffected by this subsection unless and until such charter is amended.

2. The said corporation shall receive, collect, and hold in trust for the benefit of the Annual Conference any and all donations, bequests, and devises of any kind or character, real or personal, that may be given, devised, bequeathed, or conveyed to the said board or to the Annual Conference as such for any benevolent, charitable, or religious purpose, and shall administer the same and the income therefrom in accordance with the directions of the donor, trustor, or testator, and in the interest of the church, society, institution, or agency contemplated by such donor, trustor, or testator, under the direction of the Annual Conference. The board shall have the power to invest, reinvest, buy, sell, transfer, and convey any and all funds and properties which it may hold in trust, subject always to the terms of the legacy, devise, or donation; *provided,* however, that the foregoing shall not apply to churches, colleges, camps, conference grounds, orphanages, or incorporated boards. When the use to be made of any such donation, bequest, or devise is not otherwise designated, the same shall be used as directed by the Annual Conference. Funds committed to this board may be invested by it only in collateral that is amply secured and after such investments have been approved by the said board or its agency or committee charged with such investment, unless otherwise directed by the Annual Conference.

3. The board may intervene and take all necessary legal steps to safeguard and protect the interests and rights of the Annual Conference anywhere and in all matters relating to property and rights to property whether arising by gift, devise, or otherwise, or where held in trust or established for the benefit of the Annual Conference or its membership.

4. It shall be the duty of the pastor within the bounds of whose charge any such gift, bequest, or devise is made to give prompt notice

thereof to said board, which shall proceed to take such steps as are necessary and proper to conserve, protect, and administer the same; *provided,* however, that the board may decline to receive or administer any such gift, devise, or bequest for any reason satisfactory to the board. It shall also be the duty of the pastor to report annually to the Board of Trustees of his Annual Conference a list of all property, including real, personal, or mixed, within his charge belonging to or which should be under the control or jurisdiction of the said board.

5. The board shall make to each session of the Annual Conference a full, true, and faithful report of its doings, of all funds, moneys, securities, and property held in trust by it, and of its receipts and disbursements during the conference year. The beneficiary of a fund held in trust by the board shall also be entitled to a report at least annually on the condition of such fund and on the transactions affecting it.

¶ 1520. When authorized by two thirds of the Annual Conferences comprising an episcopal area, an **episcopal residence** for the resident bishop may be acquired, which shall be under the management and control of, and the title to which shall be held in trust by, the trustees of the Annual Conference within which the residence is located; and the purchase price and maintenance cost thereof shall be equitably distributed by the trustees among the several conferences in the area. Any such property so acquired and held shall not be sold or disposed of except with the consent of a majority of the conferences that participate in the ownership. Should an Annual Conference contribute to the purchase of an episcopal residence and later be transferred to an area not owning one, if it shall ask payment for its equity, such claim shall not be denied.

¶ 1521. The Board of Trustees shall meet at least annually and organize by electing a president, vice-president, secretary, and treasurer, whose duties shall be those usually pertaining to such offices. They shall be amenable to the Annual Conference. Vacancies shall be filled by the Annual Conference for the unexpired term.

Section VI. District Property.

¶ 1522. 1. A **district parsonage** for the district superintendent may be acquired, when authorized by the Charge Conferences of two thirds of the charges in the district or when authorized by a two-thirds vote of the District Conference, subject to the advice and approval of the district Board of Church Location and Building as provided in ¶¶ 1523-27.

2. The title of district property may be held in trust by a **district Board of Trustees,** of not fewer than three nor more than nine members having the same qualifications provided for trustees of local churches (¶ 1528), who shall be nominated by the district superintendent and elected by the District Conference. Where there is no District Conference, they may be elected by the district Board of Stewards or by the Annual Conference on nomination of the district superintendent. They shall be elected for a term of one year and serve until their successors shall have been elected, and shall report annually to the District Conference or Annual Conference. If the title to the district parsonage is not held by a district Board of Trustees, the same shall be held in trust by the trustees of the Annual Conference of which such district is a part, and such trustees shall report annually to the Annual Conference. Except as the laws of the state, territory, or country prescribe otherwise, district property held in trust by a district Board of Trustees may be mortgaged or sold and conveyed by them only by authority of the District Conference or Annual Conference, or if such property is held in trust by the trustees of the Annual Conference, it may be mortgaged or sold and conveyed by such trustees only by authority of the Annual Conference. The purchase price and maintenance cost of a district parsonage shall be equitably distributed among the charges of the district by the district Board of Stewards.

3. When district boundaries are changed by division, rearrangement, or consolidation so that a district parsonage purchased, owned, and maintained by one district is included within the bounds of another district, each such district shall be entitled to receive its just share of the then reasonable value of the parsonage in which it has invested funds; and the amount of such value and just share shall be determined by a committee of three persons, appointed by the bishop of the area, who shall not be residents of any of the said districts. The committee shall hear claims of each district regarding its interest therein before making decision. From any such determination there is reserved unto each of the interested districts the right of appeal to the

next succeeding Annual Conference. Any sum received as or from such share shall be used for no other purpose than purchase or building of a parsonage in the district. The same procedure shall be followed in determining equities of a district in any other property which may be included in another district by changes in district boundaries.

¶ **1523.** There shall be in each district of an Annual Conference a **district Board of Church Location and Building,** consisting of the district superintendent, three ministers, and three laymen nominated by the district superintendent and elected annually by the Annual Conference; *provided* that in a district of great geographical extent an additional board may be so elected. The board shall file a report of any actions taken with the Charge Conference of each local church involved, and the report so filed shall become a part of the minutes of the said conference or conferences. The board shall also make a written report to the District Conference (or if there is no District Conference, to the district superintendent), and this report shall become a part of the records of that conference.

¶ **1524.** 1. The Board of Church Location and Building shall investigate all proposed local-church building sites, ascertaining that such sites are properly located for the community to be served and adequate in size to provide space for future expansion and parking facilities. (*See* ¶¶ 142.1, 1545.2.)

2. If there is a Metropolitan Commission (¶ 1335) in the district, the board shall consider its recommendations in planning a strategy for continuing the service of The United Methodist Church in changing neighborhoods. If not, the board shall study the duties assigned to such a commission and seek ways to provide continuity of service in parishes where there is a change in the racial or cultural character of the residents, to the end that the resolutions of the General Conference involving such neighborhoods be given careful consideration.

¶ **1525.** 1. The board shall require any local church in its district, before beginning or contracting for construction or purchase of a new church or educational building or a parsonage, or remodeling of such a building if the cost will exceed 10 percent of its value, to submit for consideration and approval a statement of the need for the proposed facilities, preliminary architectural plans, an estimate of the cost, and a financial plan for defraying such costs, as provided in ¶ 1545.4-.5. Before finally approving the architectural plans it shall ascertain whether the preliminary plans have been reviewed as provided in ¶¶ 1066.5, 1323.1.

2. When the local church has secured final architectural plans and specifications and a reliable and detailed estimate of the cost of the proposed undertaking as provided in ¶ 1545.7, the board shall require their submission for consideration and approval. The board shall study carefully the feasibility and financial soundness of the undertaking and ascertain whether the financial plan will provide funds necessary to assure prompt payment of all proposed contractual obligations, and it shall report its conclusions to the church in writing.

¶ **1526.** A decision of the board disapproving such purchase, building, or remodeling shall be final unless overruled by the Annual Conference, to which there is reserved unto the local church the right of appeal.

¶ **1527.** The above provisions shall apply to the acquisition of a district parsonage.

Section VII. Local-Church Property.

¶ **1528.** In each pastoral charge consisting of one local church there shall be a **Board of Trustees,** consisting of not fewer than three nor more than nine persons, each of whom shall be not less than twenty-one years of age and at least two thirds of whom shall be members of The United Methodist Church. By action of the Charge Conference the local church may limit the age of trustees to a maximum of seventy-two years of age.

¶ **1529.** The members of the Board of Trustees shall be divided into three classes, and each class shall as nearly as possible consist of an equal number of members. At the Charge Conference, on nomination by the Committee on Nominations, of which the pastor shall be chairman (or if the committee fails to nominate, on nomination of the pastor), or from the floor, it shall elect, to take office at the beginning of the ensuing conference year, to serve for a term of three years or until their successors have been duly elected and qualified, the required number of trustees to succeed those of the class whose terms then expire; *provided,* however, that nothing herein shall be construed to prevent the election of a trustee to succeed himself. The Charge Conference may assign the responsibility for electing trustees to a Congregational Meeting.

¶ **1530.** 1. In a pastoral charge consisting of two or more local churches, a **Church Local Conference,** constituted and organized under the Discipline of The United Methodist Church in each local church therein, shall be vested with authority and power in matters relating to the real and personal property of the local church concerned. Such Church Local Conference shall elect the Board of Trustees of such local church in number and manner described in ¶ 1529, and the duties of such trustees, duly elected, shall be the same as and identical with the duties described in ¶ 1532. The duties, authority, and power vested in the Church Local Conference, in so far as they relate to the property, real and personal, of the local church concerned, are the same as and identical with the authority and power vested in the Charge Conference of a pastoral charge of one local church (¶ 1532) ; and the authority, power, and limitations therein set forth shall be applicable to the Church Local Conference as fully and to the same extent as if incorporated herein. The effect of the provisions for a Church Local Conference is to give to each local church in a charge of two or more churches, rather than to the pastoral Charge Conference, supervision over and control of its own property, subject to the limitations prescribed in the Discipline with regard to local-church property.

2. Whenever required under the Discipline of The United Methodist Church for matters relating to real or personal property of the local church or to mergers of churches, a local church in a pastoral charge consisting of two or more local churches shall organize a Church Local Conference. The membership of the Church Local Conference shall consist of the persons specified for membership of the Charge Conference (¶ 144.2) so far as the officers and relationships exist within the local church, except that the pastor shall be a member of each Church Local Conference. The provisions of ¶ 144.2-.8 relating to membership qualification and procedures of a Charge Conference shall be applicable to membership qualifications and procedures of a Church Local Conference.

¶ 1531. 1. A pastoral charge composed of two or more churches, each having a local Board of Trustees, may have in addition a **Board of Trustees for the charge as a whole.** This board shall hold title to and manage the property belonging to the entire charge, such as parsonage, campground, burial ground, and such other property as may be committed to it. It shall receive and administer funds for the charge in conformity with the laws of the state, province, or country in which the property is located. This board shall consist of not less than three persons, at least two thirds of whom shall be members of The United Methodist Church and at least twenty-one years of age. These trustees shall be elected by the Charge Conference for three years or until their successors are elected. By action of the Charge Conference the local church may limit the age of trustees to a maximum of seventy-two.

2. The Board of Trustees of a charge shall provide for the security of its funds, keep an accurate record of its proceedings, and report to the Charge Conference to which it is amenable.

3. The Board of Trustees of a charge shall cause an appraisal to be made and recommend the value of parsonage rent at least once during the quadrennium, the same to be included by the minister in the local-church statistical report to the Annual Conference.

4. When two or more local churches compose a single pastoral charge having a parsonage and one or more thereof is separated from such charge and established as a pastoral charge or united with another pastoral charge which does not own a parsonage, each such local church shall be entitled to receive its just share of the then reasonable value of the parsonage in which it has invested funds, and the amount of such value and just share shall be determined by a committee of three persons, appointed by the district superintendent, who shall be members of The United Methodist Church but not of any of the interested local churches. Such committee shall hear all interested parties and shall take into account the investment of any church in any such property before arriving at a final determination. From any such determination there is reserved to each of the interested churches the right of appeal to the next succeeding Annual Conference, the decision of which shall be final and binding. Any sum received as or from such share shall not be applied to current expense or current budget.

¶ **1532.** In a pastoral charge consisting of one local church, the Charge Conference, constituted as set forth in this Discipline, shall be vested with power and authority as hereinafter set forth in connection with the property, both real and personal, of the said local church, namely:

1. If it so elects, to direct the Board of Trustees to incorporate the local church, expressly subject, however, to the Discipline of The United Methodist Church and in accordance with the pertinent local laws and in such manner as will fully protect and exempt from any and all legal liability the individual officials and members, jointly and severally, of the local church, and the Charge, Annual, Jurisdictional, and General Conferences of The United Methodist Church, and each of them, for and on account of the debts and other obligations of every kind and description, of the local church.

2. To direct the Board of Trustees with respect to the purchase, sale, mortgage, incumbrance, construction, repairing, remodeling, and maintenance of any and all property of the local church.

3. To direct the Board of Trustees with respect to the acceptance or rejection of any and all conveyances, grants, gifts, donations, legacies, bequests, or devises, absolute or in trust, for the use and benefit of the local church, and to require the administration of any such trust in accordance with the terms and provisions thereof and of the local laws appertaining thereto. (*See* ¶ 1536.)

4. To do any and all things necessary to exercise such other powers and duties relating to the property, real and personal, of the local church concerned as may be committed to it by the Discipline.

¶ **1533.** The Board of Trustees shall organize as follows:

1. Within thirty days after the beginning of the ensuing conference year each Board of Trustees shall convene at a time and place designated by the chairman, or by the vice-chairman in the event that the president is not reelected a trustee or because of his absence or disability is unable to act, for the purpose of electing officers of the said board for the ensuing year and transacting any other business properly brought before it.

2. The Board of Trustees shall elect from the membership thereof, to hold office for a term of one year or until their successors shall be elected, a chairman, vice-chairman, secretary, and if need requires,

475

treasurer; *provided,* however, that the chairman and vice-chairman shall not be members of the same class; and *provided* further that the offices of secretary and treasurer may be held by the same person; and *provided* further that the chairman shall be a member of the local church. The duties of each officer shall be the same as generally connected with the office held and which are usually and commonly discharged by the holder thereof. The Church Local Conference may, if it is necessary to conform to the local laws, substitute the designations "president" and "vice-president" for and in place of "chairman" and "vice-chairman."

3. Where necessity requires, as a result of the incorporation of a local church the corporation directors, in addition to electing officers as provided in § 2 above, shall ratify and confirm, by appropriate action, and if necessary elect, as officers of the corporation the treasurer or treasurers, as the case may be, elected by the Charge Conference in accordance with the provisions of the Discipline, whose duties and responsibilities shall be as therein set forth. If more than one account is maintained in the name of the corporation in any financial institution or institutions, each such account and the treasurer thereof shall be appropriately designated.

4. "Trustee," "trustees," and "Board of Trustees," as used herein or elsewhere in the Discipline, shall be construed to be synonymous with "director," "directors," and "Board of Directors" applied to corporations.

¶ **1534.** 1. Should a trustee withdraw from the membership of The United Methodist Church or be excluded therefrom, his trusteeship therein shall automatically cease from the date of such withdrawal or exclusion.

2. Should a trustee of a local church or a director of an incorporated local church refuse to execute properly a legal instrument relating to any property of the church when directed so to do by the Charge Conference and when all legal requirements have been satisfied with reference to such execution, the said Charge Conference may by majority vote declare his membership on the Board of Trustees or Board of Directors vacated.

3. Vacancies occurring in a Board of Trustees shall be filled by

election for the unexpired term. Such election shall be held in the same manner as for trustees.

¶ **1535.** The Board of Trustees shall meet at the call of the pastor or of its president at least annually at such times and places as shall be designated in a notice to each trustee at a reasonable time prior to the appointed time of the meeting. Waiver of notice may be used as a means to validate meetings legally where the usual notice is impracticable. A majority of the members of the Board of Trustees shall constitute a quorum.

¶ **1536.** Subject to the direction of the Charge Conference as hereinbefore provided, the Board of Trustees shall receive and administer all bequests made to the local church; shall receive and administer all trusts; shall invest all trust funds of the local church in conformity with laws of the country, state, or like political unit in which the local church is located; and shall have the supervision, oversight, and care of all real property owned by the local church and of all property and equipment acquired directly by the local church or by any society, board, class, commission, or similar organization connected therewith; *provided* that the Board of Trustees shall not violate the rights of any local-church organization elsewhere granted in the Discipline; *provided* further, that the Board of Trustees shall not prevent or interfere with the pastor in the use of any of the said property for religious services or other proper meetings or purposes recognized by the law, usages, and customs of The United Methodist Church, or permit the use of said property for religious or other meetings without the consent of the pastor, or in his absence the consent of the district superintendent; and *provided* further, that pews in the United Methodist Church shall always be free; and *provided* further, that the Church Local Conference may assign certain of these duties to a building committee as set forth in ¶ 1545.

¶ **1537.** If the local laws do not prescribe that title to property, both real and personal, shall be otherwise taken and held, in which event the provisions thereof shall take precedence and shall be observed and the provisions hereof subordinated thereto, the title to all real property now owned or hereafter acquired by an **unincorporated local church,** and any organization, board, commission, society, or similar body connected therewith, shall be held by and/or conveyed and transferred to its duly elected trustees, who shall be named in the written instrument conveying or transferring title, and their successors in office and their assigns, as the Board of Trustees of such local church (naming it and the individual trustees), in trust, nevertheless, for the use and benefit of such local church and of The United Methodist Church. Every instrument of conveyance of real estate shall contain the appropriate trust clause as set forth in the Discipline (¶ 1503).

¶ **1538.** Prior to the purchase by an unincorporated local church of any real estate, a resolution authorizing such action shall be passed at a meeting of the Charge Conference by a majority vote of its members present and voting at a regular meeting or a special meeting of the Charge Conference called for that purpose; *provided,* however, that not less than ten days' notice of such meeting and the proposed action shall have been given from the pulpit or in the weekly bulletin of the church; and *provided* further, that written consent to such action shall be given by the pastor and the district superintendent. (*See* ¶ 1545.)

¶ **1539.** If the local laws do not prescribe that title to real property of an **incorporated local church** shall be otherwise taken and held, in which event the provisions thereof shall take precedence and shall be observed and the provisions hereof subordinated thereto, the title to all property, both real and personal, now owned or hereafter acquired by an incorporated local church, and any organization, board, commission, society, or similar body connected therewith, shall be held by and/or conveyed to the corporate body in its corporate name, in trust, nevertheless, for the use and benefit of such local church and of The United Methodist Church. Every instrument of conveyance of real estate shall contain the appropriate trust clause as set forth in the Discipline (¶ 1503).

¶ **1540.** Prior to the purchase by a local-church corporation of any real estate, a resolution authorizing such action shall be passed by the Charge Conference in corporate session, or such other corporate body as the local laws may require, with the members thereof acting in their capacity as members of the corporate body, by a majority vote of those present and voting at any regular or special meeting called for that purpose; *provided* that not less than ten days' notice of such meeting and the proposed action shall have been given from the pulpit or in the weekly bulletin of the local church; and *provided* further, that written consent to such action shall be given by the pastor and the district superintendent; and *provided* further, that all such transactions shall have the approval of the Charge Conference.

¶ 1541. Any real property owned by, or in which an unincorporated local church has any interest, may be sold, transferred, or mortgaged subject to the following procedure and conditions:

1. Notice of the proposed action and the date and time of the regular or special meeting of the Charge Conference at which it is to be considered shall be given at least ten days prior thereto (except as local laws may otherwise provide) from the pulpit of the church or in its weekly bulletin.

2. A resolution authorizing the proposed action shall be passed by a majority vote of the Charge Conference members present and voting and by a majority vote of the members of said church present and voting at a special meeting called to consider such action.

3. The written consent of the pastor of the local church and the district superintendent to the proposed action shall be necessary and shall be affixed to the instrument of sale, transfer, or mortgage.

4. The resolution authorizing such proposed action shall direct that any contract, deed, bill of sale, mortgage, or other necessary written instrument be executed by and on behalf of the local church by any two of the officers of its Board of Trustees, who thereupon shall be duly authorized to carry out the direction of the Charge Conference; and any written instrument so executed shall be binding and effective as the action of the local church.

¶ 1542. Any real property owned by, or in which an incorporated local church has any interest, may be sold, transferred, or mortgaged subject to the following procedure and conditions:

1. Notice of the proposed action and the date and time of the regular or special meeting of the members of the corporate body, i.e., members of the Charge Conference at which it is to be considered, shall be given at least ten days prior thereto (except as local laws may otherwise provide) from the pulpit of the church or in its weekly bulletin.

2. A resolution authorizing the proposed action shall be passed by a majority vote of the members of the corporate body present and voting at any regular or special meeting thereof called to consider such action and by a majority vote of the members of said church present and voting at a special meeting called to consider such action; *provided* that for the sale of property which was conveyed to the church to be sold and its proceeds used for a specific purpose a vote of the members of said church shall not be required.

3. The written consent of the pastor of the local church and the district superintendent to the proposed action shall be necessary and shall be affixed to the instrument of sale, conveyance, transfer, or mortgage.

4. The resolution authorizing such proposed action shall direct and authorize the corporation's Board of Directors to take all necessary steps to carry out the action so authorized and to cause to be executed, as hereinafter provided, any necessary contract, deed, bill of sale, mortgage, or other written instrument.

5. The Board of Directors at any regular or special meeting shall take such action and adopt such resolutions as may be necessary or required by the local laws.

6. Any required contract, deed, bill of sale, mortgage, or other written instrument necessary to carry out the action so authorized shall be executed in the name of the corporation by any two of its officers, and any written instrument so executed shall be binding and effective as the action of the corporation.

¶ **1543.** Real property acquired by a conveyance containing trust clauses may be sold in conformity with the provisions of the Discipline of The United Methodist Church when its use as a church building or parsonage, as the case may be, has been, or is intented to be, terminated; and when such real estate is sold or mortgaged in accordance with the provisions of the Discipline of The United Methodist Church, the written acknowledged consent of the proper district superintendent representing The United Methodist Church to the action taken shall constitute a release and discharge of the real property so sold and conveyed from the trust clause or clauses; or in the event of the execution of a mortgage, such consent of the district superintendent shall constitute a formal recognition of the priority of such mortgage lien and the subordination of the foregoing trust provisions thereof; and no bona fide purchaser or mortgagee relying upon the foregoing record shall be charged with any responsibility with respect to the disposition by such local church of the proceeds of any such sale or mortgage; but the Board of Trustees receiving such proceeds shall manage, control, disburse, and expend the same in conformity to the order and direction of the Church Local Conference, subject to the provisions of the Discipline of The United Methodist Church with respect thereto.

¶ 1544. 1. No real property on which a church building or parsonage is located shall be mortgaged to provide for the current (or budget) expense of a local church, nor shall the principal proceeds of a sale of any such property be so used. This provision shall apply alike to unincorporated and incorporated local churches.

2. A local church, whether or not incorporated, on complying with the provisions of the Discipline, may mortgage its unencumbered real property as security for a loan to be made to a conference Board of Missions or a city or district missionary society; *provided* that the proceeds of such loan shall be used only for aiding in the construction of a new church.

¶ 1545. Any local church planning to build or purchase a new church or educational building or a parsonage, or to remodel such a building if the cost will exceed 10 percent of its value, shall take the following steps:

1. It shall secure the written consent of the pastor and the district superintendent.

2. It shall secure approval of the proposed site by the district Board of Church Location and Building as provided in the Discipline.

3. Its Charge Conference shall authorize the project at a regular or called meeting, not less than ten days' notice (except as local laws may otherwise provide) of such meeting and the proposed action having been given from the pulpit or in the weekly bulletin, and shall appoint a **building committee** of not fewer than three members of the local church to serve in the development of the project as hereinafter set forth; *provided* that the Charge Conference may commit to its Board of Trustees the duties of a building committee as here described.

4. The building committee shall:

a) Estimate carefully the building facilities needed to house the church's program of worship, education, and fellowship and/or to provide a residence for present and future pastors and their families.

b) Ascertain the cost of property to be purchased.

c) Develop preliminary architectural plans, complying with local building and fire codes, which shall clearly outline the location on the site of all proposed present and future construction. In all new church building plans and in all major remodeling plans, adequate provisions should be made to facilitate entrance, seating, exit, parking, and the use of facilities for persons with physical disabilities.

d) Secure an estimate of the cost of the proposed construction.

e) Develop a financial plan for defraying the total cost, including an estimate of the amount the membership can contribute in cash and pledges and the amount the local church can borrow if necessary.

5. The building committee shall submit to the district Board of Church Location and Building, for its consideration and approval, a statement of the need for the proposed facilities, and the architectural plans and financial estimates and plans.

6. The pastor, with the written consent of the district superintendent, shall call a Church Conference, giving not less than ten days' notice (except as local laws may otherwise provide) of the meeting and the proposed action from the pulpit or in the weekly bulletin. At this conference the building committee shall submit, for approval by the membership, its recommendations for the proposed building project, including the data specified herein.

7. After approval of the preliminary plans and estimates the building committee shall develop detailed plans and specifications and secure a reliable and detailed estimate of cost and shall present these for approval to the Charge Conference and to the district Board of Church Location and Building, which shall study the data and report its conclusions.

8. The local church shall acquire a fee simple title to the lot or lots on which the building is to be erected, by deed of conveyance, executed as provided in this chapter, and shall pay the purchase price thereof in full before beginning construction.

9. If a loan is needed, the local church shall comply with the provisions of ¶¶ 1541-42.

10. The local church shall not enter into a building contract or, if using a plan for volunteer labor, incur obligations for materials until it has cash on hand, pledges payable during the construction period, and (if needed) a loan or written commitment therefor which will assure prompt payment of all contractual obligations and other accounts when due.

11. Trustees or other members of a local church shall not be required to guarantee personally any loan made to the church by any board created by or under the authority of the General Conference.

¶ 1546. On acquisition or completion of any church building, parsonage, or other church unit, a service of consecration may be held. Before any church building, parsonage, or other church unit is formally dedicated, all indebtedness against the same shall be discharged.

¶ 1547. Two or more local churches may merge and become a single church by pursuing the following procedure:

1. The merger must be proposed by the Charge Conference of each of the merging churches by a resolution stating the terms and conditions of the proposed merger.

2. The plan of the merger as proposed by the Charge Conference of each of the merging churches must in addition, if a Charge Conference includes two or more local churches, be approved by the Church Local Conference of each local church in accordance with the requirements of ¶ 1530.

3. The merger must be approved by the superintendent or superintendents of the district or districts in which the merging churches are located.

4. The requirements of any and all laws of the state or states in which the merging churches are located affecting or relating to the merger of such churches must be complied with, and in any case where there is a conflict between such laws and the procedure outlined in the Discipline, said laws shall prevail and the procedure outlined in the Discipline shall be modified to the extent necessary to eliminate such conflict.

¶ 1548. When two or more local churches are united, merged, or consolidated, the Charge Conferences of the constituent churches shall respectively take action to consummate legally the same and shall direct the respective Boards of Trustees with respect to the transfer or disposition of the property, real and personal, as the local laws and the Discipline may require.

¶ **1549.** 1. With the consent of the presiding bishop and of a majority of the district superintendents and of the district Board of Church Location and Building, and at the request of the Charge Conference or of a meeting of the membership of the church, where required by local law, and in accordance with the said law, the Annual Conference may instruct and direct the Board of Trustees of a local church to deed church property to a federated church.

2. With the consent of the presiding bishop and of a majority of the district superintendents and of the district Board of Church Location and Building and at the request of the Charge Conference or of a local meeting of the membership of the church, where required by local law, and in accordance with said law, the Annual Conference may instruct and direct the Board of Trustees of a local church to deed church property to another evangelical denomination under an allocation, exchange of property, or comity agreement; *provided* that such agreement shall have been committed to writing and signed and approved by the duly qualified and authorized representatives of both parties concerned.

¶ **1550.** 1. With the consent of the presiding bishop and of a majority of the district superintendents and of the district Board of Church Location and Building of the district in which the action is contemplated, the Annual Conference may declare any local church within its bounds discontinued or abandoned. It shall be the duty of its Board of Trustees to make such disposition of the property thereof as the Annual Conference shall direct; and if no such lawful trustees remain or if for any reason said trustees fail to make such disposition, then it shall be the duty of the trustees of the Annual Conference to sell or dispose of said property in accordance with the direction of the Annual Conference; and it shall be the duty of the trustees thus effecting sale to remove, in so far as reasonably possible, all Christian and church insignia and symbols from such property. In the event of loss, damage to, or destruction of such local-church property, the trustees of the Annual Conference are authorized to collect and receipt for any insurance payable on account thereof, as the duly and legally authorized representative of such local church.

2. All the deeds, records, and other official and legal papers of a church that is so declared to be abandoned or otherwise discontinued shall be collected by the district superintendent in whose district said church was located and shall be deposited for permanent safekeeping with the secretary of the Annual Conference. The conference may subsequently authorize that such records be deposited for safekeeping with its Historical Society.

3. Any gift, legacy, devise, annuity, or other benefit to a pastoral charge or local church that accrues or becomes available after said charge or church has been discontinued or abandoned shall become the property of the trustees of the Annual Conference within whose jurisdiction the said discontinued or abandoned church was located.

4. When a church property has been abandoned by its membership and no abandonment action has been taken by the Annual Conference and circumstances make immediate action necessary, the Annual Conference trustees may take control of the property, with the consent of the presiding bishop and the district Board of Church Location and Building of the district in which the property is located. And in the event of the sale or lease of said property the trustees of the Annual Conference shall recommend to the Annual Conference at its next session the disposition of the proceeds derived from such sale or lease.

¶ **1551.** The Board of Trustees shall annually make a written report to the Charge Conference, in which shall be included the following:

1. The legal description and the reasonable valuation of each parcel of real estate owned by the church.

2. The specific name of the grantee in each deed of conveyance of real estate to the local church.

3. An inventory and the reasonable valuation of all personal property owned by the local church.

4. The amount of income received from any income-producing property and a detailed list of expenditures in connection therewith.

5. The amount received during the year for building, rebuilding,

remodeling, and improving real estate, and an itemized statement of expenditures.

6. Outstanding capital debts and how contracted.

7. A detailed statement of the insurance carried on each parcel of real estate, indicating whether restricted by co-insurance or other limiting conditions and whether adequate insurance is carried.

8. The name of the custodian of all legal papers of the local church, and where they are kept.

9. A detailed list of all trusts in which the local church is the beneficiary, specifying where and how the funds are invested and in what manner the income therefrom is expended or applied.

¶ 1552. In static and declining population areas, churches of fifty members or less shall study, under the leadership of the district superintendent, the district Advisory Committee, if any, and the conference Commission on Town and Country Ministries, their potential in the area to determine whether or not they shall continue to develop programs as organized churches or give special attention to relocation or merger with other congregations.

¶ 1553. The provisions herein written concerning the organization and administration of the local church, including the procedure for acquiring, holding, and transferring real property, shall not be mandatory in Central Conferences, Provisional Central Conferences, Provisional Annual Conferences, or Missions; and in such instances the legislation in ¶¶ 629-59 shall apply.

Section VIII. Requirements—Trustees of Church Institutions.

¶ 1554. Trustees of schools, colleges, universities, hospitals, homes, orphanages, institutes, and other institutions owned or controlled by The United Methodist Church shall be at least twenty-one years of age. At all times not less than three fifths of them shall be members of The United Methodist Church, and all must be nominated, confirmed, or elected by some governing body of the church or by some body or officer thereof to which or to whom this power has been delegated by the governing body of the church; *provided* that the number of trustees of any such institution owned or controlled by any Annual Conference or Conferences required to be members of

The United Methodist Church may be reduced to not less than the majority by a three-fourths vote of such Annual Conference or Conferences; and *provided* further, that when an institution is owned and operated jointly with some other denomination or organization, said requirement that three fifths of the trustees shall be members of The United Methodist Church shall apply only to the portion of the trustees representing The United Methodist Church.

Chapter Seven
JUDICIAL ADMINISTRATION

Section I. The Judicial Council.

¶ 1701. *Members.*—The **Judicial Council** shall be composed of nine members, five of whom shall be ministers other than bishops and four of whom shall be laymen. They shall be at least forty years of age and members of The United Methodist Church. Elections shall be held at each session of the General Conference for only the number of members whose terms expire at such session. A member's term of office shall be eight years; *provided*, however, that a member of the council whose seventieth birthday precedes the first day of the regular session of a General Conference shall be released at the close of that General Conference from membership or responsibility in the council, regardless of the date of expiration of office.

Members of the council shall be nominated and elected in the manner following: At each quadrennial session of the General Conference the Council of Bishops shall nominate by majority vote three times the number of ministers and laymen to be elected at such session of the General Conference. The number to be elected shall correspond to the number of members whose terms expire at the conclusion of such session. Each of the jurisdictions and the overseas churches as a group shall be represented by at least one nominee, but it shall not be a requirement that each of the jurisdictions or the overseas churches be represented by an elected member. At the same daily session at which the above nominations are announced, nominations of both ministers and laymen may be made from the floor, but at no other time. The names of all nominees, identified with the conference to which each belongs and a biographical sketch which does not exceed one hundred words, shall be published in the *Daily Christian Advocate* immediately prior to the day of election, which shall be set by action of the General Conference at the session at which the nominations are made; and from these nominations the General Conference shall elect without discussion, by ballot and by majority vote, the necessary number of ministerial and lay members.

¶ **1702.** *Alternates.*—There shall be six alternates for the ministerial members and six alternates for the lay members, and their qualifications shall be the same as for membership on the Judicial Council. The term of the alternates shall be for eight years; *provided,* however, that an alternate whose seventieth birthday precedes the first day of the regular session of a General Conference shall be released at the close of that General Conference from membership or responsibility in the council regardless of the date of expiration of his term of office.

The alternates shall be elected in the manner following: from the ministerial and lay nominees remaining on the ballot after the election of the necessary number of members of the Judicial Council to be elected at sessions of the General Conference, the General Conference shall by separate ballot, without discussion and by majority vote, elect the number of ministerial and lay alternates to be chosen at such session of the General Conference. An election shall be held at each session of the General Conference for only the number of ministerial and lay alternates whose terms expire at such session of the General Conference, or to fill vacancies.

¶ **1703.** *Vacancies.*—1. If a vacancy in the membership of the Judicial Council occurs at the conclusion of a General Conference because of a required retirement of a member because of age, such vacancy shall be filled by General Conference election of a minister to fill a ministerial vacancy and a layman to fill a lay vacancy, such election to be held in the manner hereinbefore provided in this section, and the person so elected shall hold office during the unexpired term of the member whom he succeeds.

2. If a vacancy in the membership of the council occurs during the interim between sessions of the General Conference, a ministerial vacancy shall be filled by the first-elected ministerial alternate and a

lay vacancy by the first-elected lay alternate. The alternate filling such vacancy shall hold office as a member of the Judicial Council for the unexpired term of the member whom he succeeds. In the event of any vacancy, it shall be the duty of the president and secretary of the council to notify the alternate entitled to fill it.

3. In the event of the enforced absence of one or more members of the council at or during a session of the General Conference, such temporary vacancy may be filled for that session of the General Conference or the remainder thereof, as provided above in this paragraph; *provided,* however, that nothing in this provision shall affect the validity of any action of the council so long as a quorum is present.

4. Any permanent vacancy among the alternates shall be filled by election at the next quadrennial session of the General Conference of a minister to fill a ministerial vacancy and a layman to fill a lay vacancy, and the person or persons so elected shall hold office during the unexpired term of the alternate whom each respectively succeeds.

5. If vacancies in the membership of the Judicial Council occur after exhaustion of the list of alternates, the council is authorized to fill such vacancies for the remainder of the quadrennium.

¶ 1704. The term of office of the members of the council and of the alternates shall expire upon the adjournment of the General Conference at which their successors are elected.

¶ 1705. Members of the council shall be ineligible for membership in the General Conference or Jurisdictional Conference or in any general or jurisdictional board or for administrative service in any connectional office.

¶ 1706. The Judicial Council shall provide its own method of organization and procedure, both with respect to hearings on appeals and petitions for declaratory decisions. All parties shall have the privilege of filing briefs and arguments and presenting evidence, under such rules as the council may adopt from time to time. The council shall meet at the time and place of the meeting of the General Conference and shall continue in session until the adjournment of that body, and at least one other time in each calendar year and at such other times as it may deem appropriate, at such places as it may select from time to time. Seven members shall constitute a quorum. An affirmative vote of at least six members of the council shall be necessary to declare any act of the General Conference unconstitutional. On other matters a majority vote of the entire council shall be sufficient. The council may decline to entertain an appeal or a petition for a declaratory decision in any instance in which it determines that it does not have jurisdiction to decide the matter.

¶ 1707. 1. The Judicial Council shall determine the constitutionality of any act of the General Conference upon an appeal by a majority of the Council of Bishops or one fifth of the members of the General Conference.

2. The Judicial Council shall have jurisdiction to determine the constitutionality of any proposed legislation when such declaratory decision is requested by the General Conference or by the Council of Bishops.

¶ 1708. The Judicial Council shall determine the constitutionality of any act of a Jurisdictional or a Central Conference upon an appeal by a majority of the bishops of that Jurisdictional or Central Conference or upon an appeal by one fifth of the members of that Jurisdictional or Central Conference.

¶ 1709. The Judicial Council shall hear and determine the legality of any action taken by any General Conference board or body, or Jurisdictional or Central Conference board or body, upon appeal by one third of the members thereof, or upon request of the Council of Bishops or a majority of the bishops of the Jurisdictional or Central Conference wherein the action was taken.

¶ 1710. The Judicial Council shall hear and determine the legality of any action taken by a General Conference board or body, or Jurisdictional or Central Conference board or body, on a matter affecting an Annual or a Provisional Annual Conference, upon appeal by two thirds of the members of the Annual or Provisional Annual Conference present and voting.

¶ 1711. The Judicial Council shall hear and determine any appeal from a bishop's decision on a question of law made in a Central, District, Annual, or Jurisdictional Conference when said appeal has been made by one fifth of that conference present and voting.

¶ 1712. The Judicial Council shall pass upon and affirm, modify, or reverse the decisions of law made by bishops in Central, District, Annual, or Jurisdictional Conferences upon questions of law submitted to them in writing in the regular business of a session; and in order to facilitate such review, each bishop shall report annually in writing to the Judicial Council, on forms provided by the council, all his decisions of law, with a syllabus of the same. No such episcopal decision shall be authoritative, except in the case pending, until it has been passed upon by the Judicial Council, but thereafter it shall become the law of the Church to the extent that it is affirmed by the council.

¶ 1713. The Judicial Council shall hear and determine an appeal of a bishop when taken from the decision of the Trial Court in his case.

¶ 1714. The Judicial Council shall have power to review an opinion or decision of a Committee on Appeals of a Jurisdictional Conference if it should appear that such opinion or decision is at variance with an opinion or decision of a Committee on Appeals of another Jurisdictional Conference on a question of law. Under such circumstances:

1. Any person, conference, or organization interested therein may appeal the case to the Judicial Council on the ground of such conflict of decisions; or

2. The Committee on Appeals rendering the last of such opinions or decisions may certify the case to, and file it with, the Judicial Council on the ground of such conflict of decisions; or

3. The attention of the president of the Judicial Council being directed to such conflict or alleged conflict of decisions, he may issue an order in the nature of a writ of certiorari, directing the secretaries of the Committees on Appeals involved to certify a copy of a sufficient portion of the record to disclose the nature of the case and the entire opinion and decision of the Committee on Appeals in each case to the Judicial Council for its consideration at its next meeting.

The Judicial Council shall hear and determine the question of law involved but shall not pass upon the facts in either case further than is necessary to decide the question of law involved. After deciding the question of law, the Judicial Council shall cause its decision to be certified to each of the Committees on Appeals involved, and such Committees on Appeals shall take such action, if any, as may be necessary under the law as determined by the Judicial Council.

¶ 1715. *Declaratory Decisions.*—1. The Judicial Council, on petition as hereinafter provided, shall have jurisdiction to make a ruling in the nature of a **declaratory decision** as to the constitutionality, meaning, application, or effect of the Discipline or any portion thereof or of any act or legislation of a General Conference; and the decision of the Judicial Council thereon shall be as binding and effectual as a decision made by it on appeal under the law relating to appeals to the Judicial Council.

2. The following bodies in The United Methodist Church are hereby authorized to make such petitions to the Judicial Council for declaratory decisions: (*a*) the General Conference; (*b*) the Council of Bishops; (*c*) any General Conference board or body, on matters relating to or affecting the work of such board or body; (*d*) a majority of the bishops assigned to any jurisdiction, on matters relating to or affecting jurisdictions or the work therein; (*e*) any Jurisdictional Conference, on matters relating to or affecting jurisdictions or Jurisdictional Conferences or the work therein; (*f*) any Jurisdictional Conference board or body, on matters relating to or affecting the work of such board or body; (*g*) any Central Conference, on matters relating to or affecting Central Conferences, or the work therein; (*h*) any Central Conference board or body, on matters relating to or affecting the work of such board or body; and (*i*) any Annual Conference, on matters relating to Annual Conferences or the work therein.

3. When a declaratory decision is sought, all persons or bodies who have or claim any interest which would be affected by the declaration shall be parties to the proceeding, and the petition shall name such parties. If the president of the council determines that other parties not named by the petition would be affected by such a decision, such additional parties shall also be added, and the petitioner or petitioners, upon direction of the secretary of the Judicial Council, shall then be required to serve all parties so joined with a copy of the petition within fifteen days after such direction by the secretary of the Judicial Council. In like manner any interested party may, on his or its own motion, intervene and answer, plead, or interplead.

¶ 1716. The decisions of the Judicial Council of The Methodist Church, heretofore issued, shall have the same authority in The United Methodist Church as they had in The Methodist Church, persuasive as precedents except where their basis has been changed by the terms of the Plan of Union or other revisions of church law.

¶ 1717. The Judicial Council shall have such other duties and powers as may be conferred upon it by the General Conference.

¶ 1718. All decisions of the Judicial Council shall be final. However, when the Judicial Council shall declare any act of the General Conference unconstitutional, that decision shall be reported back to that General Conference immediately.

¶ 1719. The decisions of the Judicial Council on questions of law, with a summary of the facts and of the opinion, shall be filed with the secretary of the General Conference and shall be published in the following manner:

1. Following each session of the Judicial Council the official publications of the Church shall publish an official summary, prepared by the secretary of the council, of the decisions arrived at during that session.

2. The decisions of the Judicial Council rendered during each year shall be published in the General Minutes.

Section II. Trials.

¶ 1720. Church trials are to be regarded as an expedient of last resort. Only after every reasonable effort has been made to correct any wrong and adjust any existing difficulty should steps be taken to institute a trial.

All trials should be conducted in a consistent Christian manner by a properly constituted court, after due investigation. The administration of oaths shall not be required.

¶ 1721. *Offenses.*—1. A bishop, ministerial member of an Annual Conference,[13] or lay pastor (ordained or unordained) [14] shall be liable to accusation and trial upon any one or more of the following charges:

a) Immorality, crime, or other imprudent and unchristian con-

---

[13] A ministerial member of an Annual Conference may be an associate or a probationary member, an ordained deacon, or a member in full connection ordained elder.

[14] A lay pastor is a person who is licensed to preach, whether under appointment or not, including the person formerly ordained local deacon or local elder, who retains his ordination credentials. (*See also* ¶ 307.3, note 6.)

duct.

b) Habitual neglect of duties as a member or officer in the Church.

c) Disobedience to the order and discipline of The United Methodist Church.

d) Disseminating doctrines contrary to the established standards of doctrine of the Church.

e) Unministerial conduct or maladministration in office.

2. A lay member of the Church shall be liable to accusations and trial upon any one or more of the charges set forth in §§ *a, b, c,* and *d* above.

¶ **1722.** *Limitations.*—No charge shall be entertained for any alleged offense which shall not have been committed within two years immediately preceding the filing of the complaint except where there is a conviction in a criminal court, and in such cases the charges shall not be entertained unless they are filed within one year after the entry of final judgment in that case.

¶ **1723.** *Charges.*—1. A charge shall not allege more than one offense; several charges against the same person, however, with the specifications under each of them, may be presented at one and the same time and may be tried together. When several charges are tried at the same time, a vote on each specification and charge must be separately taken.

2. Amendments may be made to a bill of charges at the discretion of the presiding officer; *provided* that they relate to the form of statement only and do not change the nature of the alleged offense and do not introduce new matter of which the accused has not had due notice.

3. Charges and specifications for all trials shall define the offense by its generic term as set forth in ¶ 1721 and shall state in substance the facts upon which said charges are based.

¶ **1724.** *Counsel.*—1. In all cases an accused person shall be entitled to appear and be represented by counsel of his own selection, a ministerial member of The United Methodist Church if the accused is a bishop or an elder and either a lay or ministerial member of the said Church if the accused is a lay member. An accused person shall be entitled to have his counsel heard in oral or written argument or both.

2. In all cases of trial where counsel has not been provided, such

counsel shall be appointed by the presiding officer. The counsel for the Church and for the accused each shall be entitled to one assistant counsel of his own choosing.

¶ **1725.** *Notice.*—1. All notices required or provided for in this chapter shall be in writing, signed by or on behalf of the person or body giving or required to give such notice, and shall be addressed to the person or body to whom it is required to be given. Such notices shall be served at least seven days in advance by delivering a copy thereof to the party or chief officer of the body to whom it is addressed in person or by registered mail addressed to the last-known residence or address of such party. The fact of the giving of the notice shall affirmatively appear over the signature of the party required to give such notice and become a part of the record of the case.

2. In all cases wherein it is provided that notice shall be given to a bishop or district superintendent and the charges or complaints are against that particular person, then such notice (in addition to being given to the accused) shall be given, in the case of a bishop, to another bishop within the same jurisdiction and, in the case of a district superintendent, to the bishop in charge.

¶ **1726.** *Trials.*—1. In all cases of investigation or trial, notice to appear shall be given to such witnesses as either party may name and shall be issued in the name of the Church and be signed by the presiding officer of the Trial Court.

2. It shall be the duty of a minister or a member of the Church to appear and testify when summoned.

3. As soon as the court has convened, the accused shall be called upon by the presiding officer to plead to the charge, and his pleas shall be recorded. If he pleads "guilty" to the charges preferred against him, no trial shall be necessary, but evidence may be taken with respect to the appropriate penalty, which shall thereupon be imposed. If he pleads "not guilty" or if he should neglect or refuse to plead, the plea of "not guilty" shall be entered for him, and the trial shall proceed. The court may adjourn from time to time as convenience or necessity may require. The accused shall, at all times during the trial except as hereinafter mentioned, have the right to produce his testimony and that of his witnesses and to make his defense.

4. If in any case the accused person, after due notice (seven days)

has been given him, shall refuse or neglect to appear at the time and place set forth for the hearing, the investigation or trial may proceed in his absence. In all cases sufficient time shall be allowed for the person to appear at the given place and time and for the accused to prepare for the investigation or trial. The president of the tribunal to investigate or try the case shall decide what constitutes "sufficient time."

5. The court shall be a continuing body until the final disposition of the charge. If any member of the court shall be unable to attend all of the sessions, he shall not vote upon the final determination of the case, but the rest of the court may proceed to judgment. It shall require a vote of at least two thirds of the original membership of the court to sustain the charges.

6. All objections to the regularity of the proceedings and the form and substance of charges and specifications shall be made at the first session of the trial. The presiding officer, upon the filing of such objections, shall, or on his own motion may, determine all such preliminary objections and may dismiss the case or in furtherance of truth and justice permit amendments to the specifications or charges not changing the general nature of the same.

7. Objections of any party to the proceedings shall be entered on the record.

8. No witness afterward to be examined shall be present during the examination of another witness if the opposing party objects. Witnesses shall be examined first by the party producing them, then cross-examined by the opposite party, after which any member of the court or either party may put additional questions. The presiding officer of the court shall determine all questions of relevancy and competency of evidence.

9. In case of investigation, trial, or appeal, the presiding officer shall not deliver a charge reviewing or explaining the evidence or setting forth the merits of the case. He shall express no opinion on the law or the facts while the court is deliberating unless the parties in interest be present. He shall remain and preside until the decision is rendered and the findings are completed, which he shall thereupon sign and certify.

¶ 1727.   *Testimony.*—1. The testimony shall be taken by a stenographer, if convenient, and reduced to writing and certified by the presiding officer and secretary. The record, including all exhibits, papers, and evidence in the case, shall be the basis of any appeal which may be taken.

2. A witness may not be disqualified because he is not a member of The United Methodist Church.

3. The presiding officer of any court before which a case may be pending or the bishop in charge of an Annual Conference shall have power, whenever the necessity of the parties or of witnesses shall require, to appoint, on the application of either party, a commissioner or commissioners, either a minister or layman or both, to examine the witnesses; *provided* that three days' notice of the time and place of taking such testimony shall have been given to the adverse party. Counsel for both parties shall be permitted to examine and cross-examine the witness or witnesses whose testimony is thus taken. The commissioners so appointed shall take such testimony in writing as may be offered by either party. The testimony properly certified by the signature of the commissioner or commissioners shall be transmitted to the presiding officer of the court before which the case is pending.

¶ 1728. *Records.*—1. In all investigations and trials the records shall be accurate and full; they shall include the proceedings in detail and all the evidence, taken stenographically if possible, the documents admitted, together with the charges, specifications, and findings, and shall be approved and attested by the presiding officer and secretary. In all the investigations and trials the presiding officer shall appoint a secretary to keep a record of the proceedings and documents, of which records, when properly attested, the said presiding officer shall be the custodian. If no appeal is taken, the custodian shall deliver the entire record to the secretary of the conference concerned for record in its journal of the final disposition of the case.

2. If appeal is taken, the custodian shall deliver the entire record to the president of the proper appellate court, and after it has been used in the court, it shall be returned to the secretary of the conference concerned for notation in its journal of the final disposition of the case.

3. The secretaries of Charge, District, Annual, and Jurisdictional Conferences shall be the custodians of the records of all trials occurring in their bodies respectively, and in case of appeal they shall deliver

said records to the president or secretary of the proper appellate court. After the said appeal has been heard, the records shall be returned to the conference from which they came.

¶ 1729.   *Appeals.*—1. In all cases of appeal the appellant shall within thirty days give notice of appeal and at the same time shall furnish to the officer receiving such notice, and to the counsel for the Church, a written statement of the grounds of his appeal, and the hearing in the appellate court shall be limited to the grounds set forth in such statement.

2. When any appellate court shall reverse, in whole or in part, the findings of a Trial Court, or remand the case for a new trial, or change the penalty imposed by that court, it shall return to the Annual Conference or to the secretary of the Trial Court a statement of the grounds of its action.

3. An appeal shall not be allowed in any case in which the accused has failed or refused to be present in person or by counsel at his trial. Appeals, regularly taken, shall be heard by the proper appellate court, unless it shall appear to the said court that the appellant has forfeited his right to appeal by misconduct, such as refusal to abide by the findings of the Committee of Investigation or of the Trial Court; or by withdrawal from the Church; or by failure to appear in person or by counsel to prosecute the appeal; or prior to the final decision on appeal from his conviction, by resorting to suit in the civil courts against the complainant or any of the parties connected with the ecclesiastical court in which he was tried.

4. The right of appeal, when once forfeited by neglect or otherwise, cannot be revived by any subsequent appellate court.

5. The right to take and to prosecute an appeal shall not be affected by the death of the person entitled to such right. His heirs or legal representatives may prosecute such appeal as he would be entitled to do if he were living.

6. The records and documents of the trial, including the evidence, and these only, shall be used in the hearing of any appeal.

7. In no case shall an appeal operate as suspension of sentence. The findings of the Trial Court must stand until they are modified or reversed by the proper appellate court.

8. In all cases where an appeal is made and admitted by the

appellate court, after the charges, findings, and evidence have been read and the arguments concluded, the parties shall withdraw, and the appellate court shall consider and decide the case. It may reverse, in whole or in part, the findings of the Trial Court, or it may remand the case for a new trial. It may determine what penalty, not higher than that affixed at the trial, may be imposed. If it neither reverses, in whole or in part, the judgment of the Trial Court, nor remands the case for a new trial, nor modifies the penalty, that judgment shall stand. The appellate court shall not reverse the judgment nor remand the case for a new trial on account of errors plainly not affecting the result.

9. In all cases the right to present evidence shall be exhausted when the case has been heard once on its merits in the proper court, but questions of law may be carried on appeal, step by step, to the Judicial Council.

10. The order of appeals on questions of law shall be as follows: from the decision of the district superintendent presiding in the Charge or District Conference to the bishop presiding in the Annual Conference, and from the decision of the bishop presiding in the Annual Conference to the Judicial Council, and from a Central Conference to the Judicial Council.

11. When an appeal is taken on a question of law, written notice of the same shall be served on the secretary of the body in which the decision has been rendered. It shall be his duty to see that an exact statement of the question submitted and the ruling of the chair thereon shall be entered on the journal. He shall then make and certify a copy of the question and ruling and transmit the same to the secretary of the body to which the appeal is taken. The secretary who thus receives said certified copy shall present the same in open conference and as soon as practicable lay it before the presiding officer for his ruling thereon, which ruling must be rendered before the final adjournment of that body, that said ruling together with the original question and ruling may be entered on the journal of that conference. The same course shall be followed in all subsequent appeals.

12. Errors or defects in judicial proceedings shall be duly considered when presented on appeal.

a) In regard to cases where there is an investigation under

¶ 1740.2-.4 but no trial is held as a result thereof, errors of law or administration committed by a district superintendent are to be corrected by the presiding officer of the next Annual Conference on request in open session, and in such event the conference may also order just and suitable remedies if injury resulted from such errors.

b) Errors of law or defects in judicial proceedings which are discovered on appeal are to be corrected by the presiding officer of the next Annual Conference upon request in open session, and in such event the conference may also order just and suitable remedies if injury has resulted from such errors.

¶ **1730.** *Appeal of a Bishop.*—1. A bishop shall have the right of appeal to the Judicial Council in case of an adverse decision by the Trial Court; *provided* that within thirty days after his conviction he notify the secretary of the Jurisdictional Conference in writing of his intention to appeal, unless such decision shall be rendered within thirty days prior to the meeting of such conference, in which case notice shall be given within ten days after his conviction.

2. A bishop elected by a Central Conference shall have the right of appeal to the Judicial Council in case of an adverse decision by the Central Conference; *provided* that within thirty days after the decision of the Central Conference he shall notify the secretary of the Central Conference in writing of his intention to appeal, unless such decision shall be rendered within thirty days prior to the meeting of such conference, in which case notice shall be given within ten days after his conviction.

3. It shall be the duty of the secretary of the Jurisdictional or the Central Conference, on receiving notice of such appeal, to notify the secretary of the Judicial Council, and the council shall fix the time and place for the hearing of the appeal and shall give due notice of the same to the appellant and to the secretary of the Jurisdictional or Central Conference, who in turn shall notify the counsel for the Church.

¶ **1731.** *Appeal of a Ministerial Member of an Annual Conference.*—1. Each Jurisdictional Conference, upon nomination of the College of Bishops, shall elect a **Court of Appeals,** composed of nine itinerant elders, who have been at least six years successively members of The United Methodist Church or of one of the churches forming the union, and an equal number of alternates. This court shall serve until its successors have been confirmed. This court shall have full power to hear and determine appeals of ministerial members taken from any Annual Conference within the jurisdiction. The court shall elect its own president and secretary and shall adopt its own rules of procedure, and its decisions shall be final, except that an appeal may be taken to the Judicial Council upon questions of law. (*See* ¶ 1729.9.)

2. In case of conviction in a Trial Court a ministerial member shall have the right of appeal to the jurisdictional Court of Appeals as above constituted; *provided* that within thirty days after his conviction he shall notify the president of the conference in writing of his intention to appeal.

3. When notice of an appeal has been given to the president of the Trial Court, he shall give notice of the same to the secretary of the Court of Appeals of the Jurisdictional Conference and submit the documents in the case. The Jurisdictional Conference Court of Appeals shall give notice to the president of the conference from which the appeal is taken and to the appellant of the time and place where the appeal will be heard. Both the Annual Conference and the appellant may be represented by counsel. The president of the conference shall appoint counsel for the Church.

4. The Court of Appeals of the Jurisdictional Conference when acting as a Court of Appeals shall determine two questions only:

a) Does the weight of the evidence sustain the charge or charges?

b) Were there such errors of law as to vitiate the verdict?

These questions shall be determined by the records of the trial and the argument of counsel for the Church and for the accused. The court shall in no case hear witnesses.

5. All necessary traveling and sustenance expense incurred by the Court of Appeals, the counsel for the Church, and the counsel for the defendant, in the hearing of an appeal case coming from an Annual Conference and appearing before any jurisdictional Court of Appeals, shall be paid out of the administration fund of the Jurisdictional Conference in which the proceedings arise.

¶ 1732. *Appeal of a Lay Pastor.*—1. In case of conviction a lay pastor (*see* ¶ 1721, note 14) shall be allowed to appeal to the Annual Conference; *provided* that within thirty days after his conviction he shall signify in writing to the superintendent of the district his determination to appeal.

2. An appeal by a lay pastor from a Charge Conference within the jurisdiction of a Mission shall be to the annual meeting of the said Mission.

¶ 1733. *Appeal of a Church Member.*—1. The Charge Conference of each charge shall elect from among the members of the Church a person of sound judgment and experience in the affairs of the Church as a **trier of appeals** for members.

2. Any member of the Church against whom judgment shall have been rendered by a Trial Court may appeal to the Court of Appeals, as hereinafter constituted, by giving written notice of his desire to the district superintendent within thirty days after judgment is rendered.

3. When thirty days' notice of appeal shall have been given, or sooner if agreed upon, the superintendent, having due regard for the wishes and rights of the appellant, shall convene a Court of Appeals. It shall be constituted of not fewer than seven nor more than nine triers of appeals in his district, but the trier of appeals of the charge to which the accused member belongs shall not be summoned. The district superintendent shall give not less than ten nor more than thirty days' notice to all persons concerned of the time and place at which the Court of Appeals shall assemble. The appellant shall have the right of challenge for cause of disqualification by reason of personal interest or other grounds deemed sufficient by the presiding officer, and he shall have the right of peremptory challenge of three of the panel summoned. The members of the court present and ready to proceed with the hearing shall not fall below seven, which number shall constitute a quorum. The district superintendent shall preside. The court may order a new trial or acquit the accused or impose any penalty prescribed in ¶ 1755.

4. The findings of the Court of Appeals shall be certified by the district superintendent to the pastor of the church of which the accused is a member for consistent proceedings.

5. If the district superintendent shall find the convening of such a court to be impracticable or seriously inconvenient to the parties involved, he shall have the appeal heard by a Charge Conference within

his district other than that of the local church. The proceedings shall be the same as provided in the foregoing subparagraphs.

¶ **1734.** *Status of a Bishop or Ministerial Member Deposed or Expelled.*—1. In case a bishop or ministerial member shall have been deposed from the ministry without being expelled from the Church, he shall be given a **certificate of membership** in the Church signed by the president and secretary of the conference.

2. In case a bishop or a ministerial member shall have been deposed from the ministry or expelled from the Church for teaching publicly or privately doctrines contrary to the established standards of doctrine of the Church, he shall not again be licensed to preach until, if a ministerial member, he shall have satisfied the Annual Conference from which he was deposed or expelled or if a bishop, he shall have satisfied the Annual Conference from which he was elected bishop and shall have promised in writing to desist wholly from disseminating such doctrine.

3. When a ministerial member is deprived of his credentials of ordination, by expulsion or otherwise, they shall be filed with the papers of his Annual Conference.

¶ **1735.** When a ministerial member desires to surrender his credentials and retain his membership in The United Methodist Church, he shall be permitted to do so and to designate the local church in which he will hold membership. The secretary of the conference to which he surrenders his credentials shall issue to him a **certificate of membership** in the Church; *provided* that no minister shall be permitted to take such action when charges involving his character have been made and sustained or are pending. When his character is involved in cases where the law permits final adjustment by the surrender of credentials, this shall be also the surrender of membership in the Church.

¶ **1736.** The Annual Conference to which credentials were surrendered as provided in ¶¶ 1734.3, 1735 may restore the same at its discretion if no charges or complaints against the minister were pending at the time of his surrendering the said credentials and if at the time of his request for the restoration of the said credentials he is a member in good standing of The United Methodist Church and shall present from his Charge Conference a certificate of his character and a recommendation for the restoration of his credentials. In cases of surrender of credentials under situations involving the character of the minister, the said credentials may be restored only after the lapse of a period of at least two years and upon the following conditions:

1. That the conference holding the credentials shall be assured that there has been a complete amendment of life upon the part of the former holder of the credentials.

2. That he shall have been readmitted as a probationary member into the Annual Conference from which he withdrew or admitted to another Annual Conference as a probationary member or licensed as a lay pastor by some District or Charge Conference.

3. That the Annual Conference which has admitted him on trial (if another than the one from which he withdrew) or the District or Charge Conference which licensed him shall present to the Annual Conference holding his credentials a certificate of his good character and a recommendation that his credentials be restored.

¶ **1737.** When a lay pastor (*see* ¶ 1721, note 14) is deprived of his credentials of ordination by expulsion or otherwise, the district superintendent shall require them of him and shall file them with the Annual Conference in the bounds of which the lay pastor resides.

¶ **1738.** Should a lay pastor later produce to the Annual Conference a recommendation from the District or Charge Conference for the restoration of his credentials, signed by its president and secretary, they may be restored to him.

¶ **1739.** *Investigation and Trial of a Bishop.*—1. A bishop is amenable for his conduct to the Jurisdictional or Central Conference in which he has residential or presidential supervision, or to the Jurisdictional or Central Conference to which he is related.

2. If a bishop shall be accused in writing of any of the offenses hereinbefore mentioned (¶ 1721) in the interval between sessions of the Jurisdictional Conference, the district superintendent within whose district the offense is said to have been committed shall call the Committee of Investigation of that Annual Conference, who shall carefully inquire into the case, and if in the judgment of the majority of them there is reasonable ground for such accusation, they shall prepare and sign the proper charges and specifications and send a copy of the same to the accused and to the president of the College of Bishops of the

jurisdiction in which the offense took place. The said president shall call together at some convenient place, in not less than ten nor more than fifteen days from the time he receives the charges, nine ministers in full connection of the said jurisdiction and also the witnesses by whom the accusation is expected to be proved. The said president or some other bishop of the jurisdiction appointed by him shall preside at the investigation. If possible, the accused shall have the right to make a statement in his own behalf and to interrogate witnesses, but shall not himself present any. If six or more of these ministers in full connection determine that a trial is justified, they shall order one, and the College of Bishops may suspend the bishop pending trial as hereinafter provided.

3. In case a trial is ordered, the president of the College of Bishops of the said jurisdiction shall within seven days from the date on which a trial is ordered fix the time and place of it, which shall be in not less than thirty or more than sixty days from the date of such order. The **Trial Court** shall be constituted as follows:

a) The bishop shall arrange for a meeting of the accused and his counsel and the counsel for the Church as early as practicable after the trial is ordered to select the members of the Trial Court.

b) The bishop shall nominate as proposed members of the Trial Court thirteen ministerial members in full connection from a list made up of the Committees of Investigation of not fewer than four Annual Conferences within the jurisdiction.

c) The Church and the accused each shall have the right of peremptory challenge to the number of four and of unlimited challenge for cause.

d) For each name stricken from this list of thirteen through the exercise of the right of challenge, the bishop shall add another from the eligible group until the required number of thirteen is thus selected. If necessary to complete the panel, nominations may be made from other ministerial members in full connection in the jurisdiction.

e) By a continuation of this same process, four alternates shall be chosen, who shall be called in the order of their election to serve.

f) Should the accused be the president of the College of Bishops of the jurisdiction, then a copy of such charges and specifications shall be sent to the secretary of the College of Bishops of that jurisdiction, who shall perform the duties hereinabove prescribed for the president or designate another bishop of the same jurisdiction.

4. The court as thus constituted shall have full power to try the accused and by a vote of nine or more to suspend him from the exercise of the functions of his office, to depose him from his office or the ministry or both, to expel him from the Church, or in case of minor offenses to fix a lesser penalty. Its findings shall be final, subject to appeal to the Judicial Council as hereinafter provided, and shall be reported to the Jurisdictional Conference for entry on its journal. The records of the trial, including the testimony, shall be assigned by the president and secretary of the Trial Court and shall be placed in the custody of the secretary of the Jurisdictional Conference, together with all the documents in the case, for preservation with the papers of the Jurisdictional Conference, and shall be the basis of any appeal which may be taken.

5. An accusation preferred during the session of a Jurisdictional Conference shall be made directly to the Committee on Episcopacy, which shall investigate the charge and if it considers a trial necessary, shall report to the Jurisdictional Conference. If the Committee on Episcopacy should decide a trial necessary, it shall formulate charges and specifications, conforming them to the grade of offense involved in the accusation, and it shall appoint one or more of its members to prosecute the case. The bill of charges and specifications shall be a part of the report of the committee to the Jurisdictional Conference.

6. Every case to be tried under the process stated in § 5 above shall be referred to a Trial Court, which shall consist of thirteen ministerial members in full connection and a presiding officer, all of whom shall be appointed by the president in the chair or in such manner as the conference may determine. The Church and the accused each shall have, in addition to the right of unlimited challenge for cause, the right of peremptory challenge to the number of four. The court as thus constituted shall have full power to try the accused and by a two-thirds vote to suspend him from his office, to depose him from his office or the ministry or both, to expel him from the Church, or in the case of minor offenses to fix a lesser penalty. Its findings shall be final, subject to appeal to the Judicial Council as hereinafter provided.

7. A bishop suspended or deposed shall have no claim upon the Episcopal Fund for salary, dwelling, or any other expenses from the date of such suspension or deposition, but in case he is thereafter found not guilty of the charge or charges for which he was suspended or deposed, his claim upon the Episcopal Fund for the period during which he was deprived of the functions of his office shall be paid to him.

8. If an alleged offense has been committed beyond the bounds of any district, the district superintendent within the bounds of whose district the bishop resides shall proceed as hereinbefore provided.

9. The several Central Conferences shall make suitable rules for the investigation and trial of charges against bishops elected by them. In the absence of such rules, the same procedure shall be followed as is provided for the investigation and trial of bishops in Jurisdictional Conferences; *provided,* however, that an appeal may be taken to the Judicial Council. If an accused bishop is the only bishop in his Central Conference, the Council of Bishops shall designate one of their number to conduct the trial.

¶ 1740. *Trial of a Ministerial Member of an Annual Conference.*—1. Each Annual Conference at each session, upon nomination of the presiding bishop, shall elect five itinerant elders, men of experience and sound judgment in the affairs of the Church, who shall be known as the **Committee of Investigation,** and five reserves chosen in like manner to serve in the absence or disqualification of the principals.

2. If a ministerial member of an Annual Conference, whether on probation or in full connection, in the interval between sessions of his conference, shall be accused of any of the offenses enumerated in ¶ 1721, his district superintendent (or the district superintendent of the district within the bounds of which such acts are alleged to have taken place) shall call the Committee of Investigation to inquire into the same and, if possible, bring the accused and accuser face to face. The accused shall have the right to make a statement in his own behalf but shall not present any witnesses before the Committee of Investigation. The district superintendent of the accused (or such other district superintendent as shall be appointed) shall preside throughout the proceedings and shall certify the judgment of the committee to the Annual Conference.

3. If the accused is a district superintendent, the bishop in charge shall call in the superintendent of any other district who shall summon the Committee of Investigation of the Annual Conference of which the accused is a member to investigate the case, and he shall preside at the investigation.

4. If in the judgment of a majority of the Committee of Investigation there is reasonable ground for such accusation, they shall prepare and sign the proper charges and specifications and send a copy to the accused, to the bishop in charge, to the district superintendent duly appointed by the bishop in charge, and to the secretary of the Annual Conference. On recommendation of the Committee of Investigation, the bishop may suspend the accused from all ministerial services pending the trial.

5. The bishop in charge, or the district superintendent duly appointed by the bishop in charge, within ten days after receipt of a copy of such charges, shall appoint counsel for the Church and notify the accused in writing to appear at a fixed time and place no less than seven days after service of such notice and within a reasonable time thereafter to select the members of the Trial Court. At the appointed time, in the presence of the accused and his counsel, if requested, and counsel for the Church, thirteen elders in full connection shall be selected as a **Trial Court**. They shall be selected from a panel of twenty-one elders in full connection of the Annual Conference of which the accused is a member, who have been nominated by the majority of the district superintendents of that conference. The counsel for the Church and the accused shall each have peremptory challenges to the number of four and challenges for cause without limit. If by reason of challenges for cause being sustained the number is reduced below thirteen, additional elders shall be nominated, in like manner as was the original panel, to take the places of the numbers challenged, who likewise shall be subject to challenge for cause. This method of procedure shall be followed until a Trial Court of thirteen members has been selected. The presiding officer in charge shall also fix the time and place for the trial, notice of which shall be given in writing to the accused by the counsel for the Church seven days in advance of the time fixed; *provided* that with the consent of the accused the time of the trial may be fixed at an earlier date. The bishop in charge, or an-

other bishop invited by him, or a district superintendent appointed by him, shall preside at the trial. The presiding officer shall appoint a secretary, who shall keep a record of the proceedings and of the testimony. The court thus constituted shall have full power to try the accused and upon his conviction by a vote of nine or more thereof shall have power to suspend him from the exercise of the functions of his office, to depose him from his office or the ministry or both, to expel him from the Church, or in case of conviction of minor offenses to fix a lesser penalty. Its findings shall be final, subject to appeal to the Committee on Appeals of the Jurisdictional Conference or the Central Conference, as the case may be. It shall make a faithful report in writing of all its proceedings, signed by the president and secretary of the committee, to the secretary of the Annual Conference for permanent record, and deliver to him therewith the bill of charges, the evidence taken, and the decision rendered, together with all documents brought into the trial.

6. When accusation against a ministerial member is preferred during the session of an Annual Conference, it shall be referred to the Annual Conference Committee of Investigation, which committee shall report to the conference whether or not a trial is deemed necessary. The Committee of Investigation, when reporting a case for trial, shall formulate a bill of charges and specifications. The presiding bishop shall appoint some elder in full connection with the conference as counsel for the Church.

7. The conference may constitute a Trial Court of thirteen elders in full connection to try the accused in the same manner as in § 5 above. The Trial Court, in the presence of a bishop or of a chairman whom the president of the conference shall have appointed, and one of the secretaries of the conference, shall try the case. The Trial Court thus constituted shall have full power, upon conviction of the accused by two-thirds vote thereof, to expel him from the ministry and membership of the Church, to depose him from the ministry of the Church, to suspend him from his office in the ministry, or in connection with a minor offense to fix a lesser penalty. Its findings shall be final, subject to appeal to the Committee on Appeals of the Jurisdictional Conference. It shall make a faithful report in writing of all its proceedings, duly signed by the president and secretary of the Trial Court, to the

secretary of the Annual Conference for entry in its journal, and deliver to him therewith the bill of charges and specifications, the evidence taken, and the decision rendered, with all documents brought into the trial.

8. Any ministerial member residing beyond the bounds of his own conference shall be subject to the investigation prescribed in §§ 1-5 above under the authority of the superintendent of the district within which he resides or within which he is employed. The Committee of Investigation shall consist of the Committee of Investigation of that conference. If he resides or is employed within the bounds of a Mission, he shall be subject to investigation under the authority of the superintendent of the district within which he holds his Charge Conference membership or of the superintendent of the Mission and the Committee of Investigation of the same. If he is the superintendent of the Mission, the bishop in charge shall appoint an elder in full connection to act in the case.

9. An Annual Conference may entertain and try charges against its ministerial members though no investigation of them has been held or though the investigation has not resulted in suspension.

10. In all the foregoing cases the papers, including the record, charges, evidence, and findings, shall be transmitted to the ensuing session of the Annual Conference of which the accused is a member; on which papers, and on such other evidence as may be admitted, and also upon such other charges or specifications as may be presented, due notice of the same having been given to the accused, the case shall be determined.

11. Any ministerial member who shall hold a religious service within the bounds of a pastoral charge not his own when requested by the preacher in charge or the district superintendent not to hold such service shall be deemed guilty of disobedience to the order and discipline of the Church, and if he shall not refrain from such conduct, he shall be liable to investigation and trial.

12. If a ministerial member is charged with disseminating publicly or privately doctrines which are contrary to the established standards of doctrine of the Church, and the minister so offending shall solemnly promise the Committee of Investigation not to disseminate such erroneous doctrines in public or private, it may waive suspension in

order that the case may be laid before the next Annual Conference, which shall determine the matter.

¶ 1741. *Withdrawal Under Complaints or Charges.*—When a bishop or a ministerial member is accused of an offense under ¶ 1721 and desires to withdraw from the Church, the Jurisdictional or Central Conference in the case of a bishop, or the Annual Conference in the case of a ministerial member, may permit him to withdraw; in which case the record shall be "Withdrawn under complaints." If formal charges have been presented, he may be permitted to withdraw; in which case the record shall be "Withdrawn under charges." In either case his status shall be the same as if he had been expelled.

¶ 1742. In all matters of judicial administration the rights, duties, and responsibilities of ministerial members of Missions and Provisional Annual Conferences are the same as those in Annual Conferences, and the procedure is the same.

¶ 1743. *Investigation and Trial of a Lay Pastor.*—Each District Conference at each session, upon nomination of its president, shall elect three lay pastors (*see* ¶ 1721, note 14) and two reserves, of experience and sound judgment in the affairs of the Church, who shall be known as the **Committee of Investigation.** The reserves shall serve in the absence or disqualification of the principals. Where no District Conference exists, the Annual Conference Committee of Investigation shall act.

¶ 1744. When a lay pastor, ordained or unordained, whether or not under appointment, is accused of any of the offenses enumerated in ¶ 1721, the district superintendent shall call the Committee of Investigation to meet, before which it shall be the duty of the accused to appear. If in the judgment of a majority of the Committee of Investigation there is reasonable ground for such accusation, they shall prepare and sign the proper charges and send a copy to the accused and to the district superintendent; and the accused may be suspended from all ministerial services pending trial. In all such cases at least seven days' notice shall be given the accused by the district superintendent. Such notice shall contain a full statement of the charges.

¶ 1745. The district superintendent, within ten days after giving notice of the charges, shall select a **Trial Court** of nine members and seven reserves, of experience and sound judgment in the affairs of the Church, who shall be lay pastors or, when necessary, members of the Church. The reserves shall serve in the absence or disqualification of the principals. The Church and the accused shall have three peremptory challenges and unlimited challenges for cause. The committee, in the presence of the district superintendent or the elder in full connection appointed by him and a secretary appointed by the committee, shall have full power to consider and determine the case and by a two-thirds vote to convict the accused. They may suspend him from the functions of his office, depose him from his office or the ministry or both, expel him from the Church, or for a minor offense impose a lesser penalty. The secretary shall make a correct report in writing of all proceedings, evidence, and findings to the secretary of the District Conference and shall deliver to him all the papers in the case. Where there is no District Conference, the Charge Conference of which the accused is a member shall act.

¶ **1746.** In case of unchristian temper, words, or actions, the lay pastor so offending shall be admonished by his district superintendent. Should a second transgression take place, one or two members of the Church are to be taken as witnesses.

¶ **1747.** If on due trial a lay pastor is found neglectful of his duties or unacceptable in his ministry, he may be deprived of his ministerial office; in which case, if he is ordained, the district superintendent shall require him to surrender his credentials that they may be returned to the Annual Conference.

¶ **1748.** If a lay pastor shall disseminate, publicly or privately, doctrines contrary to the established doctrinal standards of the Church, the same procedure shall be observed as prescribed in ¶¶ 1744-45.

¶ **1749.** A lay pastor who shall hold religious services within the bounds of a pastoral charge not his own when requested not to do so by the pastor in charge or district superintendent shall be deemed guilty of disobedience to the order and discipline of the Church and shall be brought to investigation or trial.

¶ **1750.** When a lay pastor has given evidence of being so unacceptable or inefficient as to be no longer useful in his work and the District or Charge Conference for that reason refuses to pass his character, the District or Charge Conference shall investigate the case;

and if it appears that the complaint is well founded and if he fails to give the conference satisfactory assurance that he will amend or voluntarily surrender his credentials, the conference may depose him from the ministry. He may defend himself before the conference, in person or by representative. The president of the District or Charge Conference shall in this case comply with the requirements of ¶ 1747.

¶ 1751. In Provisional Annual Conferences or Missions in the United States, its territories, and insular possessions, the power to try lay pastors shall remain with the respective District or Charge Conference, but lay pastors so tried and convicted shall have the right of appeal to the annual session of the Provisional Annual Conference or the Mission.

¶ 1752. *Withdrawal Under Complaints or Charges.*—When a lay pastor is accused of an offense under ¶ 1721 and desires to withdraw from the Church, the District Conference or, where there is no District Conference, the Charge Conference may permit him to withdraw; in which case the record shall be "Withdrawn under complaints." If formal charges have been presented, he may be permitted to withdraw; in which case the record shall be "Withdrawn under charges." In either case the status of the person withdrawn shall be the same as if expelled.

¶ 1753. When a deaconess is accused of an offense and desires to withdraw from the Church, the Annual Conference Committee on the Lay Worker may recommend to the Committee on Deaconess Service that she be permitted to withdraw; in which case the record shall be "Withdrawn under complaints." If formal charges have been presented, such deaconess may be permitted to withdraw; in which case the record shall be "Withdrawn under charges." In either case the status shall be the same as if the deaconess had been expelled.

¶ 1754. *Investigation and Trial of a Church Member.*—If a member is alleged to be guilty of any of the offenses listed in ¶ 1721, he shall first be interviewed and, if appropriate, reproved by the pastor or church lay leader. If he shall persist in the offense complained of, he shall be brought to trial through the procedures herein set forth.

¶ 1755. *Investigation.*—If charges are made in writing to the pastor in charge against a member of the church, the pastor in charge shall call a **Committee of Investigation,** composed of seven members of the church in good standing, and shall preside at the investigation. The accused and the accuser shall be brought face to face if possible, and the accused shall have right of making a statement in his own behalf and of interrogating witnesses, but shall not have the right of presenting witnesses. If the Committee of Investigation determines that a trial is justified, it shall formulate the charges and specifications and order a trial.

¶ **1756.** If a member is brought to trial, it shall be before a **Trial Court** composed of not fewer than seven nor more than twelve members. They shall be chosen by the Charge Conference by ballot. The accused member and the person conducting the prosecution may each challenge anyone so chosen for cause of disqualification by reason of personal interest or having formed and expressed an opinion concerning the matter, and shall also have three peremptory challenges. If the pastor deems it advisable for obtaining a fair trial, the Charge Conference shall call a committee of like members from any part of the district. The same right of challenge shall be recognized. The district superintendent or an elder in full connection appointed by him shall preside at the trial.

¶ **1757.** If the accused shall be found guilty by the decision of at least two thirds of the Trial Court, they shall so declare, and the president of the Trial Court shall at once pronounce the member to be expelled from the Church; *provided,* however, that the Trial Court may impose a lesser penalty because of mitigating circumstances or other grounds.

¶ **1758.** If within sixty days after his conviction under the foregoing provisions the accused shall make application in writing to the district superintendent for a new trial on the ground of newly discovered evidence, and shall submit therewith a written statement of the same, and if it shall appear that such evidence is material to the issue involved, the district superintendent shall grant a new trial. In no case shall a new trial be granted upon newly discovered evidence which could have been obtained for the trial by the exercise of due diligence or which is merely cumulative in its effect.

¶ **1759.** An expelled member shall have no privileges of the society or of the Sacraments of the Church without repentance, contrition, and satisfactory reformation according to the determination of the Charge Conference. In such case that body may restore the member into full membership.

¶ **1760.** *Withdrawal Under Complaints or Charges.*—When a member of the Church is accused of an offense and desires to withdraw from the Church, the Charge Conference may permit such member to withdraw; in which case the record shall be "Withdrawn under complaints." If formal charges have been presented, such member may be permitted to withdraw; in which case the record shall be "Withdrawn under charges." In either case the status shall be the same as if the member had been expelled.

APPENDIX

ENABLING LEGISLATION

¶ **1901.** 1. The term "the Plan of Union" shall include:
Enabling Legislation
The Proposed Discipline for 1968
The latter includes:
Historical Statement
Part I—The Constitution
Part II—Doctrinal Statements and The General Rules
Part III—Social Principles
Part IV—Organization and Administration

2. The Plan of Union shall be acted upon by The Evangelical United Brethren Church in accordance with the procedures required by its Discipline (1967), namely:

It shall require for adoption a two-thirds affirmative vote of the members of the General Conference present and voting thereon (¶ 178), but the "Enabling Legislation" and "Part I—The Constitution" shall require for adoption a three-fourths affirmative vote of the members of the General Conference present and voting thereon and a two-thirds affirmative vote of the aggregate number of members of all the Annual Conferences in North America, present and voting thereon (¶ 177). Favorable action by the General Conference and the Annual Conferences shall be deemed in compliance with the Church's Constitutional Law and authority to remove from its Constitutional Law all material not covered by the new Constitution and to include to the extent appropriate such material elsewhere in the Discipline.

3. The Plan of Union shall be acted upon by The Methodist Church in accordance with the procedures required by its Discipline (1964), namely:

It shall require for adoption a majority affirmative vote of the members of the General Conference present and voting thereon, but the "Enabling Legis-

519

lation" and "Part I—The Constitution" shall require for adoption a two-thirds majority of the General Conference present and voting and a two-thirds majority of all members of the several Annual Conferences present and voting (¶ 10.2)—unless the Judicial Council shall rule that a three-quarters majority is required. Favorable action by the General Conference and the Annual Conferences shall be deemed in compliance with the Church's Constitution and authority to remove from its Constitution all material not covered by the new Constitution and to include to the extent appropriate such material elsewhere in the Discipline.

4. If the Plan of Union is adopted by the two 1966 General Conferences:

a) The Evangelical United Brethren Church and The Methodist Church shall forthwith send to their respective Annual Conferences for action in 1967 the "Enabling Legislation" and "Part I—The Constitution."

b) The Evangelical United Brethren Church shall make provision for the calling of a special session of its General Conference to meet in 1968 at the time and place of The Methodist Church General Conference of 1968.

c) The two General Conferences shall make provision for appropriate commissions to continue the study and perfection of "Part IV—Organization and Administration" of the Plan of Union.

5. The Plan of Union having been adopted by the requisite votes of the respective Annual Conferences, in 1968 the two General Conferences shall meet separately for the transaction of any necessary business. Neither such General Conference, acting separately, shall have the right to alter or amend any part of the Plan of Union as adopted by the General Conferences of 1966.

6. Having completed their respective necessary business, the two General Conferences of 1968 shall unite for a Uniting Conference, all voting members of both General Conferences being voting members of the Uniting Conference; *provided* that by vote of the Uniting Conference it may at any time and from time to time suspend its business in order to permit the two General Conferences to meet separately for the preparation of nominations for the boards and agencies of The United Methodist Church or other necessary business. The two

churches shall establish a joint agency or commission charged with the duty of preparing an appropriate celebration of unification.

7. The Plan of Union shall become effective when, in the course of the Uniting Conference's service of unification, the president of the Board of Bishops of The Evangelical United Brethren Church and the president of the Council of Bishops of The Methodist Church shall announce, respectively, that the Plan of Union has been adopted by the requisite votes of their respective churches.

8. The Plan of Union contemplates that the administrative agencies of the Church shall be unified and start functioning immediately upon the Plan of Union becoming effective, where necessary or advisable retaining separate units acting under the agency board. In unifying the work of the agencies there shall be, as between the two churches, an equitable distribution of administrative posts, and no person presently employed shall be expected to serve at less than such person's compensation immediately prior to union. If as a result of unification of agencies personnel are required to change residence, the agency responsible will be expected to make reasonable provision for the costs involved.

9. The objective toward which the new Church moves is an inclusive Church with no overlapping of Annual Conference boundaries. The Plan of Union contemplates that unification of church structure shall take place in steps as follows:

Step One

a) Upon the Plan of Union becoming effective, all Annual Conferences of both uniting churches will automatically become part of a Jurisdiction or a Central Conference or a Provisional Central Conference of the united Church, in each case as shown on the attached schedule.

Step Two

b) Wherever in a Jurisdiction or in a Central Conference or in a Provisional Central Conference, Annual Conference boundaries overlap, the Annual Conferences involved shall designate committees or agencies to study the possibility of, and bring about as soon as practicable and mutually agreeable, the uniting or rearranging of Annual Conferences and Annual Conference boundaries to the end that there shall be no overlapping of Annual Conference boundaries. Whenever in the uniting or rearranging of Annual Conferences an itinerant preacher in full connection with a particular Annual Conference shall be transferred to another Annual Conference, he shall automatically be in full connection with such other Annual Conference irrespective of any tests which such Annual Conference may have regarding the admission of new members.

c) Annual Conferences shall not, for a period of twelve years following union, have their names or boundaries changed without their consent (¶ 41). This shall not prevent voluntary action by Annual Conferences, and it is anticipated that most, and perhaps all, such Annual Conferences will have taken steps necessary to eliminate overlapping with other Annual Conferences substantially prior to the expiration of the specified time. At the end of the twelve years, if any such Annual Conferences still remain, authority to eliminate overlapping by the redefining of Annual Conference boundaries will vest in the jurisdiction (¶ 26.4) or in the Central Conference (¶ 30.4), as the case may be; but nothing herein contained shall be construed as preventing the elimination of Annual Conferences based on race.

d) So far as the Annual Conferences formerly of the Methodist Central Jurisdiction are concerned, efforts shall be made to carry out the "Plan of Action for the Elimination of the Central Jurisdiction" as adopted by the Methodist General Conference of 1964. This Plan of Action outlines and urges a procedure designed to bring about the elimination of the Central Jurisdiction by September 1, 1967. The carrying out of the Plan of Action was entrusted by the General Conference to a quadrennial Commission on Interjurisdictional Relations consisting of twenty-four (24) members, four (4) from each jurisdiction, the four members in each case constituting a jurisdictional commission. The General Conference Commission of twenty-four is specifically charged:

If by September 1, 1967, for any reason the Central Jurisdiction shall not have been dissolved by the procedures of Amendment IX (¶ 47ix), the commission shall draft a plan for its termination to report to the General Conference of 1968.

The 1966 session of the Methodist General Conference unmistakably expressed its determination to bring about not only the elimination of the Central Jurisdiction but also the merger of the separate Negro Annual Conferences formerly part of that jurisdiction with the conferences of the Regional Jurisdictions and the elimination of any structural organization based on race. The resolution adopted by the General Conference and submitted by it to the other bodies named therein reads in part:

By the adoption of this resolution each Annual Conference, each Jurisdictional Conference, the General Conference, each College of Bishops, and the Council of Bishops express their determination to do everything possible to bring about the elimination of any structural organization in The Methodist Church based on race at the earliest possible date and not later than the close of the Jurisdictional Conferences of 1972. They further express their earnest determination to do everything possible to develop greater understanding and brotherhood in Methodism as well as in the world.

Both denominations desire and intend that union shall in no way delay or impede, but rather facilitate, strengthen, encourage, and hasten such elimination of any racial structure or distinction.

Step Three

e) The uniting of congregations will be encouraged wherever and whenever a single church can better serve the needs of the community.

10. The Uniting Conference, by majority vote unless otherwise specified, shall have the following authorities:

a) To adopt rules of order and make provision for presiding officers.

b) To amend or alter any part of "Part IV—Organization and Administration" of the Discipline, which had been adopted in principle by the 1966 General Conferences, provided that if, upon a call, by motion of any delegate, seconded by another delegate from the same former denomination and supported by one third of the members of that denomination voting, the members of the two former denominations shall vote separately, and in case of such vote by denominations no such amendment or alteration shall be effective unless adopted by vote of a majority of the delegates coming from The Evangelical United Brethren Church and a majority of the delegates coming from The Methodist Church, in each case at the time present and voting.

c) To approve the use of a name or names for the Church outside the United States and the translation of the name of the Church into languages other than English (*see* ¶ 2).

d) To recommend to the Annual Conferences of the Church proposals for constitutional amendments so that, the requisite votes having been taken in the Annual Conferences (¶ 64), such constitutional amendments can become effective upon the General Conference of 1972 (or of a special session of the General Conference called for an earlier date) having taken the requisite vote (¶ 64). The Constitution, Division Five, Article II, specifically provides that amendments to the Constitution may originate in either the General Conference or the Annual Conferences (¶ 65).

e) To elect members to the General Conference agencies of the Church for the quadrennium beginning in 1968 in accordance with the provisions of the Discipline, ¶ 815.1, which provides for the relative representation in such agencies, upon nominations made as follows: for those members which are to come from The Evangelical United Brethren Church membership, upon nomination by that Church arrived at by such procedures as that Church may determine and for those members which are to come from The Methodist Church membership, upon nomination by that Church arrived at by such procedures as that Church may determine.

f) To establish for The United Methodist Church (1) a fiscal year and (2) the date to be used as the date of its founding.

g) Anything in the Constitutional Law of The Evangelical United Brethren Church, the Constitution of The Methodist Church, or the Constitution of The United Methodist Church (*see* ¶ 54) to the contrary, notwithstanding to assign bishops originally elected by the Central Jurisdiction and not already assigned to a regional jurisdiction, and originally elected by The Evangelical United Brethren

Church, who will be on the active list and eligible for assignment at the close of the Jurisdictional Conferences of 1968, to the five jurisdictions on the following basis: (1) there shall be assigned to each of the five jurisdictions at least one bishop originally elected by The Evangelical United Brethren Church; (2) the bishops originally elected by the Central Jurisdiction of The Methodist Church and not already assigned shall be assigned so that there shall be one bishop in the Southeastern Jurisdiction and one bishop in the South Central Jurisdiction and one bishop in the Western Jurisdiction; and (3) there shall be assigned to the Northeastern Jurisdiction and the North Central Jurisdiction, in each instance, an additional bishop originally elected by The Evangelical United Brethren Church. The bishops originally elected by the Central Jurisdiction shall be assigned as recommended by the Methodist Council of Bishops, and the bishops originally elected by The Evangelical United Brethren Church shall be assigned as recommended by that Church's Board of Bishops. These assignments shall become effective upon the opening of the Jurisdictional Conferences of 1968.

This contemplates that there will come to the Union twenty-nine (29) active bishops originally elected by the regional jurisdictions, five (5) active bishops originally elected by the Central Jurisdiction, and seven (7) active bishops originally elected by The Evangelical United Brethren Church, a total of forty-one (41). If before the Uniting Conference of 1968 there shall be a vacancy in the Board of Bishops of The Evangelical United Brethren Church, the Evangelical United Brethren Church shall be entitled in accordance with its procedures to elect to fill the vacancy. If before the Uniting Conference of 1968 there shall be one or more vacancies in the College of Bishops of the Central Jurisdiction of The Methodist Church, upon the Plan of Union being adopted by the requisite vote in the Annual Conferences of The Evangelical United Brethren Church and of The Methodist Church, the Central Jurisdiction shall be entitled at a special session to elect to fill the vacancy or vacancies. On the basis of the Plan of Union and within the formula based on current membership, each regional jurisdiction in its 1968 Jurisdictional Conference may, if it so desires, elect at least one new bishop.

During the interim between the opening of the Uniting Conference of 1968 and the close of the Jurisdictional Conferences of 1968, all bishops shall continue episcopal supervision of the Annual Conferences under their supervision at the time of the opening of the Uniting Conference.

At the Jurisdictional Conferences of 1968 each jurisdiction shall be entitled, but shall not be required, to elect additional bishops up to the number allowed. The number allowed shall be the number provided in the formula stated in the Discipline of The United Methodist Church (*see* ¶ 397) plus a temporary increase for the 1968-72 quadrennium of one (1) (because of the assignment of a bishop originally elected by the Central Jurisdiction), but the prescribed quota otherwise provided for in the Discipline shall remain in force and in the Jurisdictional Conferences of 1972, and thereafter new elections shall be made up to the limit of such quota.

h) To appoint special study commissions or *ad hoc* committees for the purpose of studying and making recommendations concerning creedal statements, statements of social principles, the structure and duties of boards and agencies, or any other matters.

---

* Footnote for information:
Bishops available for assignment in 1968 under the Plan of Union, elected by:

	Regional Jurisdiction	Central Jurisdiction	EUB	Total
Northeastern	5	1	2	8
North Central	6	1	2	9
Southeastern	8	1	1	10
South Central	7	1	1	9
Western	3	1	1	5
	29	5	7	41

Now serving in:
Northeastern: Mathews, Booth, Taylor (elected by Central Juris.), Wicke, Ward, Lord (to retire 1968—Corson, Halloway; Middleton died).
North Central: Pryor, Webb, Thomas (elected by Central Juris.), Loder, Kearns, Ensley, Alton (to retire 1968—Garrison, Raines, Nall).
Southeastern: Smith, Goodson, Hunt, Hardin, Henley, Pendergrass, Short, Finger (to retire 1968—Garber, Gum).
South Central: Galloway, Pope, Stowe, Walton, Frank, Copeland, Slater (to retire 1968—Martin, Smith).
Western: Stuart, Kennedy, Palmer (to retire 1968—Grant, Tippett).
Central: Golden, Moore (Harris died).
EUB: Kaebnick, Howard, Herrick, Mueller, Heininger, Milhouse, Sparks.

SCHEDULE FOR ENABLING LEGISLATION

Jurisdictions and Annual Conferences

North Central Jurisdiction

Canada
Central Illinois
Dakota
Detroit
East Wisconsin
Iowa
Illinois
Indiana
Indiana North
Indiana South
Michigan (E)
Michigan (NC)
Minnesota (E)
Minnesota (NC)
North Dakota

North Indiana
North Iowa
Northeast Ohio
Northwest Indiana
Ohio
Ohio East
Ohio Miami
Ohio Sandusky
Ohio Southeast
Rock River
South Dakota
South Iowa
Southern Illinois
West Wisconsin
Wisconsin

Northeastern Jurisdiction

Baltimore
Central New York
Central Pennsylvania
Eastern
Erie
Maine
New England
New England Southern
New Hampshire
New York (E)
New York (NE)
Northern New Jersey
Northern New York

Peninsula
Philadelphia
Puerto Rico Provisional
Southern New Jersey
Susquehanna
Troy
Western New York
Western Pennsylvania (E)
Western Pennsylvania (NE)
West Virginia (E)
West Virginia (NE)
Wyoming

South Central Jurisdiction

Central Kansas
Central Texas

Nebraska (SC)
New Mexico

(Central West)
Indian Mission
Kansas (E)
Kansas (SC)
Little Rock
Louisiana (C)
Louisiana (SC)
Missouri
Missouri East
Missouri West
Nebraska (E)

North Arkansas
North Texas
Northwest Texas
Oklahoma
Oklahoma-Texas
Rio Grande
Southwest
Southwest Texas
Texas (C)
Texas (SC)
West Texas

Southeastern Jurisdiction

Alabama-W. Florida
Central Alabama
Cuba
Florida (E)
Florida (C)
Florida (SE)
Georgia
Holston
Kentucky (E)
Kentucky (SE)
Louisville
Memphis
Mississippi (C)
Mississippi (SE)
North Alabama

North Carolina
North Carolina-Virginia
North Georgia
North Mississippi
South Carolina (C)
South Carolina (SE)
South Georgia
Tennessee (E)
Tennessee (SE)
Tennessee-Kentucky
Upper Mississippi
Virginia (E)
Virginia (SE)
Western North Carolina

Western Jurisdiction

Alaska Mission
California
California-Nevada
Idaho
Montana (E)
Montana (W)
Northwest Canada

Oregon
Pacific Northwest (E)
Pacific Northwest (W)
Rocky Mountain (E)
Rocky Mountain (W)
Southern California-Arizona

Central Conferences and Annual Conferences

Africa Central Conference

Angola
Central Congo
Rhodesia

Southeast Africa
Southern Congo

Central and Southern Europe

Austria Provisional
Belgium
Bulgaria Provisional
Czechoslovakia
Hungary Provisional

North Africa Provisional
Poland
Switzerland (M)
Switzerland (E)
Yugoslavia Mission

China Central Conference

Germany Central Conference

Central Germany (M)
Eastern Germany (E)
Northeast Germany (M)
Northwest Germany (M)

South Germany (M)
South Germany (E)
Southwest Germany (M)
West Germany (E)

Latin America Central Conference

Argentina
Bolivia
Chile
Costa Rica Provisional

Panama Provisional
Patagonia Provisional
Peru Provisional
Uruguay

Liberian Central Conference

Northern Europe Central Conference

Baltic and Slavic Provisional
Denmark
Finland Provisional

Finland-Swedish Provisional
Norway
Sweden

Pakistan Provisional Central Conference

Indus River
Karachi Provisional

Philippines Central Conference

Middle Philippines   Philippines
Northern Philippines   Mindanao
Northwest Philippines

Sierra Leone Provisional Central Conference

Sierra Leone

Southeastern Asia Central Conference

Malaya   Sarawak
Malaysia Chinese   Sarawak Iban Provisional

Southern Asia Central Conference

Agra   Lucknow
Bengal   Madhya Pradesh
Bombay   Moradabad
Delhi   North India
Gujarat   South India
Hyderabad   Nepal Mission

Episcopal Visitation

Hong Kong and Taiwan (M)
Puerto Rico (E)

Note: (E) stands for Evangelical United Brethren, (M) Methodist, (C) Central Jurisdiction, (NC) North Central Jurisdiction, (NE) Northeastern Jurisdiction, (SC) South Central Jurisdiction, (SE) Southeastern Jurisdiction, (W) Western Jurisdiction.

At the time of union some Annual Conferences as above listed may overlap jurisdictional boundaries, but pending realignment, this shall not be deemed a violation of the Constitution, Division Two, Section VIII, Article I (¶ 42).

INDEX

The numbers refer to paragraphs (¶¶) and to subparagraphs. Subparagraphs are indicated by the figures following decimal points. The paragraphs are arranged according to the following plan:

Numbers in **bold-faced** type indicate main references or definitions.

Administrative Board, *cont'd:*
For obligations of church, 151
.5
Secretary of, 146.2
Secretary of enlistment, 149, 152
.2
Special meetings, 148.2
Staff, salaries for, 151.3*d*
State of the church, review of,
151.3*c*
Study activities, coordinator of,
152.3
Superintendent of study program
of the church (church school
superintendent) , 149, 152.3
Tenure, 151.2
Treasurer, church
Duties of, 152.5
Member of, 149
Remittance to conference
treasurer, 152.5
See also Treasurer, local
church
Trustees, 149, 151.1
United Methodist Men, 149
Vice-chairman, 150
Voting, 149
Women's Society of Christian
Service, 149
Work area chairmen, 149
World service, support of, 151.4-
.5
Young adults, members at large,
146.3
Youth members, 149

**Administrative Committee on the
Youth Service Fund,** 1083.2

Adult
Council. *See* Council on Minis-
tries
Ministry, 1117, 1123.1
Work, 666.1, 670.1

Advance, 871-78
Administration of, 873.4, 876
Committee on Specials, 873.2

Advance, *cont'd:*
Communications between donor
and recipient, 873.2, .5
Conference Advance specials, 874
District promotion of Advance
specials, 874.4
Expenses of promotion, 876.3
Fellowship of Suffering and Ser-
vice, 877
General Advance Committee, 872
General Advance special, 873
One Great Hour of Sharing, 875
Promotion of, 876
Receipts for, 873 ？
Remittance of, 873.3, 911
Report forms, 874.5
Reports to Advance Committee,
873.4
Special committees, 878
Special funds, solicitation of,
1302
Special gifts, administration of,
1306.6, 1307.6, 1309.1*i*
Special object, 873.2
Specials, 833, 842.1
Treasurer of, 876.2
Undesignated special, assuming
responsibility for, 873.2

Advisory Committee on Planning,
832.3*d-e*

Affiliated autonomous churches,
640-47
Autonomous church, becomes af-
filiated, 647.7
Bishop, 1281.1, 1422.2
Board of Missions, liaison with,
640-41, 1312
Contractural agreements, 642
Definition of, 640
Episcopal visitation to, 644
Missionaries serving in, 1317.1
Overseas conferences, procedures
for becoming, 647
Transfer of ministers of, 646
World Methodist Council, dele-
gates to, 1414.2

Board of Education, *cont'd:*
sion of the Local Church
Divisions, financing of, 1021
Divisions report work, budget to
board, 1025.3
Educational program in the local
church, 1087
Employees of the board, 1018
Executive committee, 1013
General and associate general
secretaries members of Council
of Secretaries, 1413.1
General secretaries of divisions,
1016, 1025.3
Incorporation, 1010.2
Interboard Committee on Christian Education, 1074.2
Interboard Committee on Enlistment for Church Occupations,
1084
Interboard Committee on Missionary Education, 1075
Interboard Committee on Town
and Country Ministries, 1074.1
Joint Commission on Education
and Cultivation, cooperation
with, 1309.1*d*
Jurisdictional boards, 1103
Division of Curriculum Resources, cooperation with,
1094
Division of the Local Church,
cooperation with, 1069.1,
1072
Recommendations to, 1029.4
Reports to, 1121
Joint Commission on Cooperation and Counsel, 1074.4
Joint Committee on Architecture,
1074.3, 1079
Meetings, 1010.3
Members ineligible to be salaried
officers, 1017
Membership, 1011
Nominating committee, 1012
Officers, 1014
Organization, 1010
Powers, 1019-25
President, nominated by nomi-

Board of Education, *cont'd:*
nating committee, 1012.2*b*
Program Council representative,
832.1*d*
Program-Curriculum Committee,
158.1, 1086
Publications, manufactured, published and distributed through
Publishing House, 971
Purpose, 1007
Quorum, 1010.3
Race Relations Sunday, promotion of, 1023. *See also* Special
days
Recommendations to, 1086.1*b*,
1112
Recording secretary, 1012.2
Reports to, 1078.1, 1083.2
Secretarial Council, **1025.6**, 1086
.1*b*
Section on United Methodist
Men, 1271
Successor corporations, 1022
Supervision of Christian education, 1008
Treasurer of, 1015
University Senate, elects members
to, 1056.1
Vacancies, 1011.4
Youth ministry, 1080

Board of Evangelism, 1125-61
Aim of evangelism, 1125
Amenable to General Conference, 1142
Annual Conference board, 1146-
55
Amenable to Annual Conference, 1153
Bylaws, 1154
Chairman, 1149
Commission on Enlistment for
Church Occupations, representation on, 666.1
Committee on Family Life,
representation on, 1117
Committees on Evangelism receive guidance from, 1136,
1146

Board of Lay Activities, 1184

Board of the Ministry, 665.4a
Amenability, 665.15-.16
Commission on Enlistment for
Church Occupations, member
on, 666.1
Department of the Ministry
Cooperation with, 665.4e, .5e,
1043.4
Relationships with, 1045
Disability leave, recommendation
for, 357.1-.2
District Committee on the Minis-
try, representative on, 665.4d
Duties, 665.5
Joint Committee on Disability,
members on, 665.24
License to preach
Examination for, 319
Issuance of, 318
Renewal of, 320
Meetings, 665.4c
Membership, 665.4e
Ministerial conduct, inquiry into,
663.5
Officers, 665.4b
Prior effective relation in Annual
Conference, determination of,
376
Purpose, 665.4c
Recommendations of, 347, 353,
358-60, 363.1-.2, 367-69, 375.2,
.4-.5, 665.5j
Recommendations to, 145.5, 665
.19, .24d
Registrar, 665.12-.14
Reports by, 665.5g, .8-.10, .13
Reports to, 353, 390.7, 665.5c
Seminary loan fund, 665.7

Board of Missions, 1277-1373
Advance specials, 874, 876.5,
1291.2b
Advisory committee, 1292.3
Affiliated autonomous church,
640
Agreements for, 647.8
Aims of missions, 1277

Board of Missions, *cont'd:*
Annual Conference board, 1358-
70
Budget, 1364
Church and Community Com-
mittee, 1368
Commission on Enlistment for
Church Occupations, repre-
sentative to, 666.1
Commission on Missions, guid-
ance of, 158.3
Committee on Parish and Com-
munity Development, 1370
Committee on Research and
Survey, 1367
Executive committee, 1360
Executive secretary, 1363.1
Home Missions and Church
Extension, 1366
Meetings, 1359.2-.3
Membership, 1358
Missionary secretary, 1363.2
Missions anniversary, 1365
New local church, 142.1
In Provisional Annual Confer-
ence, 654
Purpose, 1362
Urban and town and country
ministries, 1369
Assistant and associate general
secretary, 1293.2, 1294.2
Associate treasurer, 1293.2
Authority of, 1300
Board of Christian Social Con-
cerns, liaison members on, 983
Board of Managers, 1281
Bylaws, 1300
Central Conferences, financial ob-
ligations in, 631.31
Commission on Ecumenical Af-
fairs, members on, 1390.1
Commission on the Structure of
Methodism Overseas, members
on, 1422.2
Commission on Town and Coun-
try Ministries, 1369.3
Committee on Town and Coun-
try Ministries, 1369.2

547

Central Conference, *cont'd:*
Investigation and trial of members, 631.17. *See also* Trials
Journals, 630.7, 631.14
Local governments, recognition of, 631.23-.24, .27
Maintenance of work, estimates for, 1313-14
Meetings, 630.2-.3
Membership, 629.2
Missionary Conferences amenable to, 631.1, .11, .14
Missions amenable to, 631.1, .11, .14
Number of bishops, prohibited from determining, 631.8
Powers and duties, 631
Presiding officer, 630.3, .5
Property, 631.27-.31
Proportionate representation, rule of, 630.9
Questions of law, decisions on, 1711-12
Reports to, 631.4, 664.1
Rights of appeal of members, 631.17
Ritual, adaptation of to local situation, 631.18-.19
Secretary reports to General Conference secretary, 631.7
Theological Study Commission on Doctrine and Doctrinal Standards, members of, 1419.2
Women's unit, 631.16
World Federation of Methodist Women, member of, 631.15

Certificate
Of baptism, 120
Of location, 366
Of organization, 662.10
Of transfer, 138-39

Certification Council, 1169.3

Chancellor, 661.7

Chaplain
Of institution, military unit, cam-

Chaplain, *cont'd:*
pus pastor, 116
Military personnel, reception of, 117
Pension credit, 1379.4c
Reports by, 117
See also Commission on Chaplains and Related Ministries

Charge Administrative Board, 145.11

Charge Conference, 11, 48-49, 144-47
Administrative Board
Amenable to, 148
Commitment of duties to, 151.6
Executive agency, 151
Implementation of proposals, 145.2
Members at large, 145.3b, 146.3
Supervision of, 145.1
Age-level coordinators elected by, 145.3a, 155.1
Amenability, 145.14
Annual Church Conference, 147
Annual Conference
Lay members elected by Charge Conference, 145.3a
Lay pastor ineligible, 146.1
Appointed staff (local church), salary set by, 145.9
Basic salary plan, ratification of, 925.1
Benevolences, 145.10
Board of Trustees, annual report from, 1551
Chairman elected by Charge Conference
Committee on Finance, 145.3d
Committee on Pastor-Parish Relations, 145.3c
Council on Ministries, 145.3a, 154
Charge Administrative Board, 145.11
Church historian, election of, 1412.2

Commission on Worship, *cont'd:*
Meetings, 1384.3
Membership, 1384.1
Officers, 1384.2
Program Council, representative
to, 832.1*d*
Purpose, 1386
Television, Radio, and Film
Commission, consultation with,
1385.8

Commissions on Church Union,
page 16

Commissions, standing, 1384-1412

Committee/Commission on Christian Higher Education and
Campus Ministry
Area/regional, 1114.3-.4
Department of the Ministry, relations with, 1036.1, 1048
Recommendations by, 1112

Committee for Liaison, Consultation, and Church Union, 1390.6

Committee for Overseas Relief
Fund, 856.5

Committee for Promotion and Interpretation, 1390.6

Committee for Studies, 1390.6

Committee of Administrators of
United Ministries in Higher
Education, 1036.2

Committee of Investigation
Bishop, investigation of, 1739.2
District Conference, 1743
Local-church committee, 1755

Committee on Appeals, 1714

Committee on Deaconess Service,
1324, 1753

Committee on Camps and Conferences
Annual Conference committee,
1111.2-.3, 1124.2
District committee, 1111.2, 1124

Committee on Campus Religious
Life, 1037.2

Committee on Christian Higher
Education and Campus Ministry, 1114.1

Committee on Confirmation Resources, 1078

Committee on Episcopacy, 55, 621.2,
624
Bishop, accusations against made
to, 1739.5
Bishop's assignment to churchwide responsibility, renewal of,
385
Bishop's sabbatical leave, approval of, 386

Committee on Evangelism, district,
662.9, **1156-58.** *For details see*
Board of Evangelism, district
Committee on Evangelism

Committee on Family Life, 1077
Annual Conference committee,
1117
Division of Curriculum Resources, cooperation with, 1095
Expenses of, 879

Committee on Finance, 145.3*d*,
151.1, 158.5, **161.3**
Administration of, 151.1
Administrative Board, consultation with, 151.3*d*
Chairman elected by Charge Conference, 145.3*d*
Chairman member of Administrative Board, 149
Election of, 145.3*d*

Council of Bishops, *cont'd:*
cies on, 1389.2
Commission on Ecumenical Affairs, 1390.1, .8
Commission on Religion and Race, appointment of bishops to, 1423
Commission on Structure of Methodism Overseas, nomination of, 1422.2
Commission on Worship, fills vacancies on, 1384.1
Committee on Family Life, election of members to, 1077.2
Committee on Official Forms and Records, election of bishop to, 855
Conference overseas desiring to be autonomous, participation in committee on, 647.3
Conference of United Methodist Bishops called by, 389
Council on World Service and Finance, nominations to, 850
Declaratory decision, petition for, 1715.2
Division of Interpretation, consultation with, 833.6-.7
Episcopal Fund, notification to treasurer of retired bishop called back into active service, 890
Episcopal visitation in mission fields not in Central or Provisional Central Conferences, 639
Evangelistic activities of Church, promotion of, 387
Fellowship of Suffering and Service, vote to discontinue, 877
General Conference secretary, nomination of, 606
Interboard Committee on Enlistment for Church Occupations, bishops named to, 1084.2
Judicial Council, nomination of members to, 1701
Methodist Corporation, The, representatives to, 1518.1
National Council of Churches,

Council of Bishops, *cont'd:*
representatives to, 1415.2
Proclamation of autonomy for overseas conference, president's signature, 647.4
Program Council
Designation of convener, 827.2
Election of members to, 827.1
Recommendations to, 1390.2b
Religion in American Life, Inc., nomination of members to Board of Directors, 1418
Reports to, 831.12, 836.7, 1131.1, 1390.2f, 1413.2
Sabbatical leave, approval of, 386
Schedule of members elected to agencies, 815.1e
Secretary of, 836.7
Social Principles Study Commission, 1420.2-.3
Special days and appeals referred to Division of Interpretation, 878
Structure Study Commission, 1421.4, .6
Theological Study Commission on Doctrine and Doctrinal Standards, 1419.2-.3
United Methodist Committee for Overseas Relief, discharge of, 1304
University Senate, appointment of members to, 1056.1
World Council of Churches, 1416.2
World Methodist Council, nomination of delegates to, 1414.1

Council of Secretaries, 1413
Program Council, members of, 827.1
Structure Study Commission, consultation with, 1421.3

Council on Local Church Program, 1009

Council on Ministries, 153-60, 845-47

Courses of study, *cont'd:*
Correspondence work, 1046.5
Department of the Ministry, 1043.3, 1046
Pastors' schools, 1046.3

Court of Appeals
Charge Conference, 1733.3-.5
Jurisdictional, 1731

Crime, 96 IIIC.2

Crusade Scholarship
Committee, 875.3, 1355
Fund, 875.3

Curriculum, 1085-86
Educational program of Church, 1085
Program-Curriculum Committee, 1086
See also Division of Curriculum Resources

D

Daily Christian Advocate, 1701

Deacon, 307
Appeal of, 1731
Eligibility for order of elder, 314
Mission, 374
Offenses, 1721.1
Ordination, 390.9
Status of expelled, 1734
Trial, 1740
Withdrawal under complaint, 1741

Deaconess
Administrative Board, 149
Annual Conference, member of, 660.2
Appointment of, 1323.4
Commission on Enlistment for Church Occupations, 666.1
District Conference, member of, 670.1
Pension plan, 1323.4
Surrender of credentials, 1323.4g
Withdrawal under complaint or charges, 1753

Deeds, trust clauses, 1503

Department of Campus Ministry, 1035-41. *For details see* Division of Higher Education, Department of Campus Ministry

Department of Christian Stewardship, Evangelical United Brethren, 1184

Department of Higher Education, National Council of Churches, 1036.2

Department of the Ministry, 1042-51
Adjudicator of conflicts, 308.5
Board of the Ministry, cooperation with, 665.4e, .5e
Committee on Confirmation Resources, director member of, 1078.2
License to preach, course of study for, 318
Reports to, 665.9
Schools of theology, consultation with, 1053
See also Division of Higher Education, Department of the Ministry

Department of Records, 854.3a, c, 879

Department of Statistics, 854.3b-c, 879

Department of Worship and the Arts, National Council of Churches, 1385.12

Depositories, 913-14

Director
Of adult ministry
Conference, 1111.2
District, 1123.1
Of camps and conferences, 1111.2

Director, *cont'd:*
Of children's ministry
Conference, 1111.2
District, 1123.1
Of Christian education, 1115
Of Christian social concerns,
1004.1, 1005
Of Christian stewardship, EUB,
1190
Of education, 1114.2, 1118, 1122
Of family ministry, 1123.1
Of health and welfare ministries,
1174
Of the ministry, 1044.1
Of music, 1115
Of youth ministry
Conference, 1111.2, 1122
District, 1123.1

Disability leave, 357

Discrimination, 96 IIID.1

District Advisory Committee, 1552

District boards. *For district boards
see individual board listings*

District Committees. *For district
committees see individual committee listings*

District Conference, 47, **669-70**
Advance specials, promotion of,
874.4
Business, order of, 670.2
Call to meet, 669
Church-school superintendent
member of, 670.1
Committee on Camps and Con-
ferences, district, 1124
Directors or deans, confirmation
of nominations, 1124.2
Lay pastor
Investigation of, 1750
Withdrawal under complaint
or charges, 1752
Licenses to preach, 670.3
Membership, 670

District Conference, *cont'd:*
Minister from other church, re-
ception of, 375.1
Questions of law, decisions on,
1711-12
Reports by, 670.2
Reports to, 665.21, 670.3
Secretary of publishing interests,
979
Trial records, secretary custodian
of, 1728.3

District missionary society, 142.1,
1327-35

District Program Council, 844

District property, 1522-27
Board of Church Location and
Building, 1522.1, **1523-26**
Board of Trustees, 1522.2
Parsonage, 1522

**District secretary on enlistment for
church occupations,** 666.1, .4

District steward, 145.3*a*, 670.1, 904

District superintendent, 58, 354
Annual Church Conference, au-
thorization of, 147
Apportionments for support, 920
Benevolences, 145.10
Board of Church Location and
Building, district, member of,
1523
Board of Stewards, district, mem-
ber of, 904
Board of Trustees, district, nom-
ination of, 1522.2
Certificate of transfer, 138
Charge Conference
Consultation with, 145.9
Meetings, 144.3
Minutes, copy of, 146.2
President of, 144.4
Special session, call for, 144.6
Church services, consent required
for discontinuance of, 351.2

Division of Curriculum Resources,
cont'd:
sources published by, 1101
Program-Curriculum Committee
Financing, 1086.4
General secretary member of,
1086.2
Participation in, 1089
Representation on, 1086.2c
Publisher sitting with, 1102
Purpose, 1088

Division of General Welfare, 997

Division of Higher Education,
1026-64
Advisory committee, 1025.2
Annual Conference, cooperation
with, 1027.2
Auxiliary societies, 1034
Board of Christian Social Concerns, liaison member on, 983
Campus-Church Relations Committee, 1037.3
Commission on Standards for
Campus Ministry, 1039
Committee/Commission on Christian Higher Education and
Campus Ministry, cooperation
with, 1114.4a
Committee on Campus Religious
Life, 1037.2
Committees, 1026.6
Cooperation with other agencies,
1031
Department of Campus Ministry,
1035-41
Administrative responsibility,
1035
Annual Conference, cooperation with, 1041.3
Board of Education, nomination of students to, 1011.3
Campus Christian movement,
1035, 1040
Ecumenical approach, 1037
Interboard Committee on Enlistment for Church Occupations, 1084.2

Division of Higher Education,
cont'd:
Recommendations to, 1039.1
Reports by, 1039.1
Representation on agencies,
1036.2
Responsibilities, 1036
Student representative, nomination of, 1130.1
University Christian Movement, 1041.1-.2
Wesley Foundations, Boards of
Directors, 1037.1
World Student Christian Federation, 1041.1-.2
Young Adult Ministry, relationship with, 1035
Department of Educational Institutions, 1028
Department of Educational
Work, cooperative relationship
with, 1321.2d
Department of the Ministry,
1042-51
Board of the Ministry, cooperation with, 1043.4, 1045
Certification of course offerings, 1047
Continuing study of the ministry, 1049
Correspondence work, 1046.5
Courses of study, 1046
Department of the Ministry,
National Council of
Churches, relationship with,
1045
Four-year course of study,
1046.1
Functions, 1043
Interboard Committee on Enlistment for Church Occupations, 1045, 1084.2
Pastors' schools, 1046.3
Program of selective enlistment, 1048
Relationships with other agencies, 1050
Reports by, 1049
Responsibilities of, 1042, 1045

567

H

Health and Welfare Ministries Week, 1177

Health and welfare representative, 145.3*b*, 146.4

Honorary members of Charge Conference, 146.7

Historical Convocation, 1407.3

Historical shrines, landmarks, sites, 1409

Historical Society, 1407

Human relations, rights, 96 IIID, 97

Hymnals, 1388
Promotion of, 1387.3*c*
Recommendations on, 1385.5

I

Insignia of The United Methodist Church, 833.8

Institutions, educational
Adequate endowment for, 1064.3
Classifications of, 1062
Committee on Christian Higher Education and Campus Ministry, conference, responsibility for, 1114.1
Discontinuance of, 1064.1
Financial needs reported, 1112
Investigation of, 1060
Merger of, 1064.1
Minimum goals for support, 1114 .4*d*
New institutions, 1064.1
Number of, 1064.2
Status information, 1063
University Senate, approval of required, 1064.4

Institutions, trustees of, 1554

Insurance plans, 821.13

Interagency Committee on Research, 832.2*e-f*
Committee on Official Forms and Records, representation on, 855

Interagency Staff Committee on Research, 832.2*d*

Interboard Commission on the Local Church, 824

Interboard Committee on Christian Education, 1347-49
Board of Education, cooperation with, 1074.2
Division of Curriculum Resources, cooperation with, 1093, 1095

Interboard Committee on Enlistment for Church Occupations, 1084
Board of Health and Welfare Ministries, cooperation with, 1169.5*c*
Commission on Enlistment for Church Occupations, relationship to, 666.2
Council of Secretaries, executive secretary member of council, 1413.1
Department of the Ministry, cooperation with, 1045, 1048
Division of Curriculum Resources, cooperation with, 1095
Division of the Local Church, cooperation with, 1068.3
Joint Committee on Missionary Personnel, cooperation with, 1310.1*c*
Program-Curriculum Committee, executive secretary member of, 1086.2*c*

Interboard Committee on Missionary Education, 1350-52
Administrative Committee on the

Joint Committee on Disability, 357.4, 665.24

Joint Committee on Missionary Personnel
Authority of, 1303
Cooperation with other agencies, 1311.16c
Deaconess, 1310.2
Elected staff, 1295.2
Functions, 1310
Funds for, 1311.2
Interboard Committee on Enlistment for Church Occupations, cooperation with, 1310.1c
Joint Commission on Education and Cultivation, chairman member of, 1288
Membership, 1289
Missionary, 1310.2
Officers, 1295.1
Vouchers, 1311.1f

Joint Distributing Committee, 1383

Journal
Conference
Agency secretaries' expenses, 918
Roster, directors of Christian education, music, etc., 1115.2
Treasurer's annual statement, 897
Program, 833.3

Judicial Administration, 1701-60

Judicial Council, 56, 60-62, 1701-19
Absence from sessions of, 1703.3
Alternates, 1702
Appeal of, 630.5
Annual Conference presiding bishop, 1729.10
Bishop's decision, 1711
Central Conference, 1729.10
Decline of appeal, 1706
Authority of, 1716
Bishop, appeal of, 1713, 1730
Committee on Appeals, reviews

Judicial Council, cont'd:
decisions of, 1714
Decisions of, 1718-19
Declaratory decisions, 1715
Determinations of, 1707-10
Expenses of, 879
Functions, 1706-17
Ineligibility of members for membership on other agencies, 1705
Meetings, 1706
Membership, 1701
Organization, 1706
Overseas conference desiring to be autonomous, 647.3
Procedure, 1706
Questions of law carried to, 1729.9
Quorum, 1706
Retirement, 1701-2
Right of appeal to, 623
Term of office, 1704
Vacancies, 1703
Vote required, 1706
Writ of certiorari, 1714.3

Jurisdiction, vacancies in boards or agencies, 1424-25

Jurisdiction Society-Guild, 1341

Jurisdictional Conference, 8, 22-26, 51, 612-28
Annual Conference journals, authority over, 627
Appeal of legality of actions of boards and agencies, 1709
Apportionments, distribution of, 902
Bishop
Amenable to, 1739.1
Presides over, 390.2
Board of Christian Social Concerns, conference elects members, 983
Board of Education, conference elects members, 1011.1
Board of Evangelism, conference elects members, 1130.1
Board of Health and Welfare

Methodist Publishing House, The,
cont'd:
President of, 944, 956, 959-60
1413.1
Printing for church agencies, 855,
976
Program-Curriculum Committee,
969, **1086.1-.2**
Publisher and printer for The
United Methodist Church, 929
Publisher of resources of Division
of Curriculum Resources, 1101
Real estate and buildings, 977-78
Special rules, 931

Methodist Social Creed, the, 96

Military
Chaplain, 116-17
Reception into church member-
ship, 117
Service, 96 IIE.2

Minimum Salary Fund
Apportionments for support of,
920
Payments to, for ministerial support, 921

Minister
Age-level and family councils,
member of, 156.4
Amenable to Annual Conference,
315
Annual appointments of, 316
Annual Conference, relationship
to, 315-49
Approval of, 306
Of Christian education, certifica-
tion, 1115
Continuing education of, 355
Council on Ministries, member
of, 154
Disability leave, 357
Of evangelism, 1160
Examination of conduct, 663.5
Guidance of work area chairmen
157
Leaves of absence for study, 355

Minister, *cont'd:*
License of, 305
Marriage of, 91 Art. XXI
Moral and social responsibility,
318.7 note 7, 326.3e
Of music, certification, 1115
From other churches, 375-80
Certificate of ordination from
other church, 379
Certificate of recognition from
bishop, 378
Reception into United Meth-
odist ministry, 375
Transfer from other Methodist
churches, 380
Pension. *See* Board of Pensions
Pension credit, 1379
Reports by, 928
Right to trial and appeal, 63
Sabbatical leave, 356
Service record of, 1377.10
Special appointments, 352
Statement of remuneration, 928
Transfer to other Methodist
churches, 380
Work area commissions, member
of, 158

Ministerial student, 308.4

Ministerial support, 919-28
Apportionments for basic salary
fund, 925.3-.5
Appropriations for, determina-
tion of, 920
Basic Salary Plan, 925
Church's obligation for, 919
Commission on Minimum Sal-
aries, 924
Included claims, 919
Minimum Salary Fund, 920-21,
924.4
Pastor's expenses, report of, 927
Pastor's salary, determined by
Charge Conference, 922
Payments to claimants, 921
Schedule of minimum salaries,
924